The Lay o' Last Minstrel

Sir Walter Scott and the Border Minstrel Tradition

Rupert Ferguson

www.capallbann.co.uk

The Lay of the Last Minstrel

Sir Walter Scott and the Border Minstrel Tradition

©2001 Rupert Ferguson

ISBN 186163 118 9

Cover design by Paul Mason
Cover and internal illustrations supplied by Rupert Ferguson

Published by:

Capall Bann Publishing
Freshfields
Chieveley
Berks
RG20 8TF

"The last of all the Bards was he,
Who sung of Border Chivalry;
For, well-a-day! Their date was fled,
His tuneful brethren all were dead;......"

To the memory of the late Mrs. Patricia Maxwell-Scott, whose entire life was spent in the dilligent promotion of the great literary legacy bequeathed to her by her most illustrious ancestor, Sir Walter Scott Bart., this book is most respectfully dedicated.

Acknowledgements

I would like to extend my thanks and gratitude, first of all, to the late Mrs. Patricia Maxwell-Scott, the oldest living representative of the most senior branch of the illustrious line which Sir Walter was to found, for her kindness and encouragement; not to mention the tea and sandwiches which sustained me during my rambles across the ancient landscape through which Scott himself was to travel in the company of the American writer Washington Irving. Also of considerable assistance and help were the tour guides and other assorted staff of Abbotsford Hall; her own renowned ancestor's residence in the Borders; so rightly described by Dame Jean Maxwell-Scott, Mrs. Patricia's sister, as a "romance in stone" in a recently screened B.B.C. documentary.

Thanks is also due to Mrs. Fairgreave, of the Butterfly Gift Shop in Melrose High Street, who, in addition to drawing my attention to the ancient cemetary at Lindean, pointed me in the general direction of the King's Arms Hotel, Melrose, and Frankie Preston, the local plumber and fireman; who, as is well known to all those who have been fortunate enough to have met him, must be one of the funniest men in the Borders. Frankie's assistance led me to the door of the late Adam Crawford, then universally acknowledged as Melrose's most senior citizen. Thanks to him for drawing my attention to the lyrics of the traditional Melrose Song, and the links between the ancient town where he himself was to reside for some eighty years and St. Dunstan. Long may the local traditions that once lived on in his old grey head survive for the benefit of future generations of Melrosians!

Others who made my stay and travels in the Borders memorable ones were Mrs. Thorburn of the Black Bull Inn, Earlston, and various of her regulars with whom I had much to talk about in connection with Thomas the Rhymer's Thorn; Mr. Gordon Richardson, President of the Galashiels Rugby Club; his wife Janice, whose Maplehurst Guest House in Gala's Abbotsford Road is one of the most comfortable in the neighbourhood; Liz Taylor of the Talisman bookshop in Melrose's Market Square; Dougie the barman and the patrons of the Auld Mill Inn, Gala, a traditional working class pub where the humour and jocularity of the local people, as it is described in the letters and writings of Sir Walter himself , still manifests in abundance; Sir David and Lady Steel for the tour around the newly restored and refurbished Aikwood (or Oakwood) Tower, one time residence of Sir Walter's ancestors, the Scotts of Harden; and the staff and customers of the Cross Keys in Selkirk; who entertained me whilst I was waiting for the bus back to Gala.

A big thank you too to the venerable Dr. Cripps of the Borders General Hospital, who allowed me a glance of the interior of J.G. Lockhart's summer retreat at Chiefswood; Mr. Graham of Dunfermline House, Melrose, for the use of a 'phone and much other useful information besides; and the owners of the White Horse at Berwick-on-Tweed, who, together with their brood of children, kept me entertained whilst awaiting trains to and from Gala and London. Last but not least, thanks is also due to the countless employees of the dozens of libraries that I have visited, from Gala to Glastonbury, from Melrose to Maidstone, and without whose assistance and co-operation this book would not have been written. May all those listed get as much pleasure from what I have written as I have from having written it!

About the author

The author, Rupert Ferguson, is descended from Captain Robert Ferguson (1719-1797), brother of the famous Scottish philosopher Adam Ferguson (1723-1816); the friend of Hume, Gibbon and Adam Smith. It was under Adam Ferguson's roof that the young Sir Walter Scott was to have a memorable encounter with the poet Burns in his youth: An encounter about which he himself was to write; and which was to take place as a direct result of his life long association with Ferguson's son, and namesake, Sir Adam Ferguson.

It was as a further consequence of the above association that the author's ancestor, Robert Ferguson M.D. (1799-1865), was to visit Abbotsford in his youth; an experience which he too was to write about in turn; later on in his own eventful life. This book also contains short extracts from these as yet largely unpublished writings, which shed still further light on the degree to which Scott had been able, in the course of a generation, to bring his beloved Border Ballads out of relative obscurity and into the mainstream of public consciousness.

Continuing in his family's long literary tradition, Rupert currently works as a writer, journalist, film maker and folk singer on both sides of the Border.

Contents

Introduction

Sir Walter Scott (1771-1832), the celebrated Laird of Abbotsford, novelist, scholar, poet, lawyer, historian and man of letters, still ranks today as probably the greatest single figure in Scottish literature; just as he did during his own lifetime. One of his greatest literary achievements was his creation of the romantic image of the Gaelic speaking Highlander: Wild, untamed, untameable and uncompromising. A man to whom honour and ties of Clan and kinship come before money, materialism or even respect for the written "law". And, just as Scott's own novels are still going through many reprints, as they surely did when he was alive, this image is still with us.

When the Hollywood film actor Mel Gibson directed and starred in his blockbuster epic *Braveheart*, he was doubtless unaware, on account of the vast number of historical misconceptions that prevail in our modern society, that the image he was using had nothing whatsoever to do with the actual historical character of William Wallace, who, as a Lowlander and being ultimately of Welsh descent, his ancestors having migrated northwards in the van of the Anglo-Norman lords who accompanied St. Margaret to Scotland on her marriage to King Malcolm III, never would have worn plaid or ridden into battle like some Ancient British Chieftain. Indeed, the image that Gibson utilized came not from the pages of Mediaeval history, but from the pen of a nineteenth century novelist, Allan Massie's *Ragged Lion*; good Sir Walter himself.

One of the finest artistic representations of the image that Scott created adorns the cover of the 1985 Penguin Classics edition of *Waverley*; the first novel that Scott ever published and the book which passed its title on by giving its name to the famous Edinburgh railway station. This picture, *Disbanded*, by the great admirer of Rembrandt, John Pettie (1839-1893), could have been painted by Scott himself, if Scott had been an artist, for the image that is conjured up comes straight from what is probably the best of all of Scott's Highland novels, *Rob Roy*.

The historical character of Rob Roy, like the real life character of William Wallace, has himself received a great deal of recent Hollywood attention; and although the adventure film *Rob Roy*, starring Liam Neeson in the title role, was by no means an adaptation of Scott's novel of the same title, the image that the writer and director of the film ultimately presented to the mass audience that turned out in their droves to see it, was, once again, taken, lock, stock and barrel, from the works of the Laird of Abbotsford; who had himself been fortunate enough to make the acquaintance of some who had actually known the famous outlaw chieftain; whilst travelling in the Highlands as a young man.

The second great literary creation for which Scott is most famous is the character of the Mediaeval Saxon knight Ivanhoe. Unlike Rob Roy however, who Scott imbued with many of his own real life character traits, gleaned from the anecdotes preserved amongst the Highland people who he was to meet during the course of his extensive travels in the wilder parts of Scotland, Ivanhoe, as an "historical" character, is almost entirely imaginary. Like Gibson's William Wallace, astride his charger, face daubed with woad like some ancient warrior who has ridden straight out of the pages of Caesar or Tacitus, Ivanhoe is essentially a completely fictitious entity conjured up specifically to capture the popular imagination.

In order to understand first and foremost what Scott had created in *Ivanhoe*, however, one must turn back to what he was able to achieve in Scotland: North of the Border Scott's novels re-established once and for all the lost pride and feeling of national identity which had been taken away by the Act of Union and the brutal suppression of the last great Highland uprising- the 1745 Rebellion. With *Ivanhoe*, on the other hand, he gave to the English something that had been lost to them for several centuries, some might say since their conversion to Christianity with the coming of St. Augustine: An heroic epic to rival the ancient poem of *Beowulf*, but in a Mediaeval context which the nineteenth century reader could both understand and identify with. The result was that his popularity amongst the English readership that he had attracted to his writings, with the creation of young English heros in novels such as *Waverley*, was for all time assured. Ivanhoe first galloped onto the literary scene in 1819, the year before King George IV's Coronation. The recent tv adaptation of Scott's novel was just one of a whole host of film and television versions of this mighty yarn.

As for Scott himself, on page 1322 of the 1898 edition of Burke's *Landed Gentry*, we find an entry under the title "Constable-Maxwell-Scott (Mary Monica) of Abbotsford, Co. Roxburgh," who, the above quoted commentary informs us, was "great-great-grand. dau. and representative of Sir Walter Scott, Bart." We are then given details of Mrs. Maxwell-Scott's marriage, on

2

21st July 1874, to Hon. Joseph Constable Maxwell, J.P. and D.L. Co. Roxburgh, formerly Lieut. Rifle Brigade, born 16 Jan. 1847, 3rd son of William, Lord Herries. There then follows a list of their eight children, and the additional information that "Mr. Constable Maxwell assumed, in consequence of his marriage, the additional surname of Scott........", before the compilers give us details of the genealogical origin of the first Laird of Abbotsford; the Ragged Lion.

"This is a branch of Scott of Harden, now Lord Polwarth, and descends from Walter Scott, Laird of Raeburn (called Wat Wadspurs or "Hotspurs"), 3rd son of William Scott, 5th Laird of Harden temp. James I......."

Elsewhere, in the authorized biography of Scott by his son-in-law, John Gibson Lockhart, who married the author's daughter Sophia in 1820, the origin of the family of Scott of Harden is traced "back to the middle of the fourteenth century, when they branched off from the great blood of Buccleuch.....The antique splendour of the ducal house itself has been dignified to all Europe by the pen of its remote descendant....." Lockhart continues, "but it may be doubted whether his genius could have been adequately developed, had he not attracted, at an early critical period, the kindly recognition and support of the Buccleuchs....."

So how was it that a member of the Border Gentry, a descendant of one of the foremost Ducal Houses of the Lowlands, became the writer with whom we associate, more than any other, even Robert Louis Stevenson, whose *Kidnapped* could be said to rival *Waverley* and *Rob Roy* in certain definite respects, the romantic image of the Scottish Highlander? One of the principal reasons as to why Scott should have so excelled in this way was his own family's involvement in the Stuart Cause; as the following extract from a letter written by him to Robert Surtees of Mainsforth, author of *A History of Durham*, and like the Laird of Abbotsford a scholar in his own right, shows:

"17th Dec. 1806.

I was much flattered and interested by your long and curious letter. You flatter me very much by pointing out to my attention the feuds of 1715 and '45. The truth is that the subject has often and deeply interested me since my earliest youth. My great-grandfather was "out", as the 'phrase goes, In Dundee's wars and in 1715, and had nearly the honour to be hanged for his pains, had it not been for the interest of Duchess Anne of Buccleuch and

Monmouth, to whom I have attempted "longo intervallo", to pay a debt of grattitude.

But besides this, my Father, although a Borderer, transacted business for many Highland Lairds, and particularly for one old man called Stuart of Invernahyle, who had been out both in 1715 and '45, and whose tales were the absolute delight of my childhood. I believe there never was a man who united the ardour of soldier and tale-teller- a man of "talk" as they call it in Gaelic- in such an excellent degree, and he was as fond of telling as I was of hearing. I became a valliant Jacobite at the age of ten years, and ever since reason and reading came to my assistance I have never quite got rid of the impression which the gallantry of Prince Charles made on my imagination.

Certainly I will not renounce the idea of doing something to preserve these stories, and the memory of times and manners which, though existing as it were yesterday, have so strangely vanished from our eyes. Whether this will be best done by collecting the old tales, or by modernizing them as subjects of legendary poetry, I have never very seriously considered, but your kind encouragement confirms me in the resolution that something I must do, and that speedily......." [1] [See notes below and notes to chapters following].

Besides his creation of *Ivanhoe* and the authorship of the other novels, and in addition to his work as a poet, Scott is unique, in that he can also be accredited with another great literary achievement of which the vast majority of his readers, who are familiar with his work as a novelist, are almost entirely unaware; and which even his biographers, Lockhart, Buchan, Wilson, and of course Allan Massie, whose novel, written in the style of a lost autobiographical manuscript and entitled *Ragged Lion*, reads as if it could have been the work of the long dead Laird of Abbotsford himself, have only really touched on: The achievement of which I speak is Scott's work as a collector of Border Ballads; an achievement to which this book is itself entirely and wholeheartedly dedicated. For, it is this achievement, more than any other, which accords Scott with the status of being the last of the true bards. The only other individual, besides the Author of Waverley, who can justly be awarded the right to such laurels, is the Great War poet Robert Graves; whose magnum opus, *The White Goddess*, did for Ancient Welsh Poetry, in our own century, what Scott did for Border Balladry more than a hundred years before; something which will be looked at in full in Chapter Twelve of this book.

In order to understand Scott, his poetry and his novels, one has first to understand the ancient literary tradition in which they are rooted. And, in order to understand that literary tradition, one must first understand the historical tradition in which it is rooted; a tradition that can be traced right the way back through the Mediaeval Period, into the Dark Ages and beyond. Indeed, amongst the ballads that Scott and his friends collected can be found the remains of a lost oral literary tradition of undoubted Pictish provenance.

Amongst Scott's own introductory notes to several of the ballads in the collection that he published, there is evidence to suggest that, had the particular field of scholarship in which he was at that time working been as advanced as it has become in our own era, he would undoubtedly have reached a similar conclusion. He was aware of the fact that several of the ballads that he had recovered seemed to have evolved out of the Metrical Romances of the High Middle Ages. And, in view of the fact that we now know for certain that these same Metrical Romances evolved out of the most ancient literary traditions indiginous to these islands, it is far easier for us to draw conclusions that he would have been less able, and indeed less qualified, to set down in writing. Essentially, this book is an attempt to bring Scott's work up to date in the light of advances in modern scholarship which have taken place since the era in which he wrote. For, just as technology has advanced considerably since the opening decades of the nineteenth century, so too has research, not only into ballad origins, but also into the historical and mythological traditions with which they are connected.

Amongst the ballads of the rural peasantry can be found the lost language of pagan tradition that the church was unable to suppress. Like the ancient folk traditions of the British Isles, celebrations such as Padstow's May Day in Cornwall, the Castleton Garland Ceremony in Derbyshire, and Queensferry's Burry Man in Scotland, the ballads preserve the remnants of what are, to all intents and purposes, the most ancient manifestations of folk culture indiginous to Britain. It is therefore appropriate, in view of this, that Scott's collection of ballads should be examined fully with this fact in mind; as well as in the light of the advances in scholarship made not only by Graves in the field of Bardic and Druidic tradition, but also those made by historians such as the late John Morris and William Forbes Skene; not to mention ballad researchers such as Williams and Lloyd and the incomparable Lowry Charles Wimberley.

As well as examining Scott's work as a collector and collator of ballads then, it is the purpose of this book to examine both the ballads themselves, and the contexts in which they were collected; as a means of demonstrating their most ancient provenance. It is also hoped that by so doing, the author will give his readership some insight into the hidden language of bardic lore contained in Scott's collection: An aspect of this great literary tradition which has yet to be properly assessed by writers working in this particular field of scholarship.

During the course of this book I intend to take the reader on a journey across the ancient Border landscape through which Scott himself travelled whilst collecting his beloved ballads from the very mouths of the peasants, who had, for generations, preserved them as their principal source of domestic amusement. As well as taking us to the Borders themselves, this same journey will take the reader both north, to the more remote parts of Highland Scotland, where in many places such oral traditions are still a living part of peasant culture, even in our own century; and south; to the Welsh Marches; where some of the most noted Border Families are alleged to have had their origins. In doing this, I hope, as I have already said, to be able to trace the true sources of the ballad traditions which Scott collected; for the very first time; thus placing his achievement in his collection and publication of his ballads into proper anthropological perspective.

In addition to this I hope to provide the reader with a wealth of biographical, literary and genealogical anecdotes, which not only relate to the origins of the ballads, but also to Scott's own origins; as well as the extent to which his entire literary output, not to mention his domestic and social life, was affected by his obsession with ballads and minstrelsy. For those readers who have not been fortunate enough to have read Scott's *Minstrelsy of the Scottish Border*, the text of its three volumes consists, in essence, of an introductory essay, followed by a series of ballads, historical and romantic, ancient and modern; to each of which is attached its own section of introductory and textual notes. This volume, itself by no means as bulky as the *Minstrelsy*, is arranged somewhat differently to Scott's collection; in that many additional versions of the same ballads that Scott collected are either referred to or are included in it; together with much other material; as a means of achieving a proper historical examination of the original materials gathered by Scott and those who were to assist him in his endeavours.

I have also made numerous references to versions of Scott's ballads that are currently available on record and c.d. as a means of providing enhanced accessibility, wherever possible, to the ballads referred to in both Scott's, as well as my own, written text.

Throughout the chapters that follow we will not only be encountering the Scotts of Buccleuch, the Kerrs, the Elliots, the Johnstones and the Armstrongs, together with a whole host of other Border Clans, but also their Dark Age and early Mediaeval predecessors: individuals like Merlin and Arthur; all of whom are connected with the vast body of ancient bardic literature from which the ballads of later times were ultimately descended. And, in so doing, we shall be tracing not only the origins of the ballads, but, as has already been mentioned, the origins of Sir Walter hmself.

Amongst the pages of this book I have also taken the liberty of including extracts from the writings of one of my own ancestors, Robert Ferguson M.D., Physician to Queen Victoria; and himself a visitor to Abbotsford: A short essay by one of Robert Ferguson's own sons, Robert Norman Ronald Ferguson, the father of the famous Sufferagette author and playwrite Rachel Ferguson (1893-1957), some of whose works are still available through Virago, and in which my Grandfather's Grandfather's writings were themselves extensively quoted, appeared in *The Records of the Clan and Name of Fergusson, Ferguson and Fergus* (edited by James Ferguson and John Menzies Fergusson; for the benefit of the Clan Ferguson Society) published back in 1895 by David Douglas, Edinburgh; but no work or works in which this material is either referred to or quoted from has appeared in print since. It is therefore hoped that, by publishing the various extracts from the above that are quoted herein, the author might be able to provide Scott scholars and fanatics everywhere with a unique insight into some of those long past events that took place under the roof of Abbotsford all those years ago.

Contemporary accounts describe the young Robert Ferguson as "strikingly handsome, gifted as a linguist", and "able to sing well and accompany himself on almost any stringed instrument" [2] (see notes). In view of the fact that many of my own contemporaries would have me believe that I have at least inherited my ancestor's ability as a singer, it is perhaps appropriate that I am at present writing this book whilst at the same time preparing arrangements of some of the songs that feature in it for performance on what remains of the old Free Festival Circuit here in Britain.

Perhaps it is also appropriate, in view of the attacks that have recently been made upon Scott's scholastic integrity, on the ballad collecting front, in the televisual media, that a descendant of Robert Ferguson M.D. should be writing what is in many ways a defence of that integrity; in view of the latter's own familiarity with these ballads: A familiarity, which, as we shall see shortly, is attested to in my ancestor's own writings. Perhaps there are others better qualified to conduct such a defence. James Reed, author of *The Border Ballads* (1973), *Sir Walter Scott: Landscape and Locality* and *The Border Ballads: A Selection* (1980 and 1991), is just one individual whose name springs to mind. My qualification for this task however is rooted in my distant kinship with Sir Walter's lifelong friend, Sir Adam Ferguson, coupled with a sincere desire to see the oldest living member of the most senior branch of the Sept of Clan Scott that he himself was to found, Dame Jean Maxwell-Scott, live out the remainder of her twilight years secure in the knowledge that her ancestor's reputation has been restored.

The only thing that now remains for me to say, before winding up this short introduction, is that whatever the individual reader's opinion as regards Sir Walter's scholastic integrity at the commencement of reading this book, the author himself believes that he or she will be left in no doubts whatsoever on that score by the time the concluding essay in this text has been read and properly digested; and that they will pass judgement in favour of Scott himself, as opposed to his somewhat vociferous modern day critics.

Rupert Ferguson, August 15th 1999.

Notes to Introduction

1) Anne, Duchess of Buccleuch and Monmouth, had, as will be seen shortly, featured in Scott's *Lay of the Last Minstrel*, which had been published the previous year. Similarly, Invernahyle's encounter with Colonel Charles Whitefoord on the field of Preston Pans eventually "supplied the groundwork of the chivalrous contest between Edward Waverley and Colonel Talbot in the forty-seventh and following chapters of *Waverley*. (See Scott's revised preface to the 1829 edition of that novel). As for Surtees, he himself is probably the most controversial character connected with Scott's researches into Border traditions. For, although he was to provide Scott with much useful anecdotal material of an historical nature, as the previously quoted extract from one of Scott's letters to him shows, he also succeeded in palming the Laird of Abbotsford off with some forged ballads of his own;

most notably *The Death of Featherstonehaugh*, which, as will be seen in the following chapter, was used by Scott as the model for some of his own poetical composition. Appendix One gives a full appraisal of Surtees's relationship with both Scott, and another member of his circle, James Hogg, the celebrated "Ettrick Shepherd"; with respect to the Border Minstrel Tradition.

2) See *The Records of the Clan and Name of Fergusson, Ferguson and Fergus,* edited by James Ferguson and John Menzies Fergusson; publ. David Douglas, Edinburgh, 1895; pp.194.

Illustration 1): "The Laird of Abbotsford as Border Minstrel." Nineteenth century line engraving by Horsburgh after the portrait by Sir Henry Raeburn.

Chapter One

The Bridal of Triermain

"King Arthur has ridden from Merry Carlisle
When Pentecost was o'er;
He journeyed like errant-knight the while,
And sweetly the Summer Sun did smile
On mountain, moss, and moor......"

The Bridal of Triermain; Canto I, vv. X.

During the years 1812 and 1813, in which Byron's *Childe Harold* made its appearance, and the Laird of Abbotsford met the young man who was to eclipse him as the greatest contemporary poet in the English language, Scott published two narrative poems of his own: The first of these, *Rokeby*, is set in the Civil War, in the self same era in which he was to set his novel *Woodstock* in years to come. In the *Advertisement to.....* the first edition, the author describes the scene of the poem as being "laid at Rokeby, near Greta Bridge, in Yorkshire....." "The date of the supposed events", he then continues, "is immediately subsequent to the great battle of Marston Moor, 3rd July 1644......" Despite the Civil War setting however, at the beginning of Canto IV, we get a foretaste of what is to follow:

"When Denmark's Raven soared on high,
Triumphant through Northumbrian sky,
Till, hovering near, her fatal croak
Bade Rheged's Britons dread the yoke....."

For those readers who are ignorant of the history of the Dark Ages, the ancient Kingdom of Rheged was one of several independent principalities that sprang up in Britain after the departure of the Romans. Amongst the ancient line of Kings that ruled over this territory, which straddled the area that lies roughly between Carlisle in the north, and Merseyside in the south, was Urien of Rheged; himself the real life character upon whom the legendary Sir Uriens of Mallory's *Morte d'Arthur* was ultimately based. All the land west of the Pennines was formerly under Rheged's sway, and the ancient Welsh speaking inhabitants of this principality have passed their legacy on to our own era in the naming of the modern region of Cumbria, meaning, literally, "the land of the Cymry", or Welsh.

The second of the epic poems that Scott was to publish at this time was *The Bridal of Triermain;* which is set in the old fief of Triermain; part of the ancient Barony of Gilsland; in Cumberland. In the first canto the Baron himself is heard to summon forth his page, and bid him "ride to Lyulph's Tower", and to "greet well that sage of power....", for, "He is sprung from Druid sires....."

"*.....And British bards that tuned their lyres*
To Arthur and Pendragon's praise,
And his who sleeps at Dunmailraise..."

In writing these lines Sir Walter is speaking as much of himself as he is of the fictitious poet Lyulph. To understand fully to exactly what extent this is true, I now propose to refer the reader to the writings of Captain Walter Scott of Satchells (c.1614-1694), who was himself the son of Robert Scott of Satchells; the grandson of Walter Scott of Sinton by his second marriage; to Margaret, daughter of James Riddel of that ilk.

In addition to fathering a son by his first marriage to the daughter of William Cockburn of Henderland, who the compilers of *Burke's Landed Gentry* refer to as coming from "an ancient family in the Co. of Peebles", Scott of Sinton also sired the brother of Walter Scott of Satchells's own grandfather; in the person of Robert Scott of Sinton; whose younger son founded the branch of Harden; from whom Sir Walter Scott himself descended. Thus, the Laird of Abbotsford could claim distant kinship with this former soldier of fortune; who had run away at the age of sixteen to join the regiment which the Chief of Buccleuch, Walter the First Earl, had raised and taken to fight in the Netherlands in the year 1629.

Years later, on his return from the Continental Wars, Scott of Satchells set about writing a poetical "History of Several Honourable Families of the Right Honourable Name of Scot, in the Shires of Roxburgh, Selkirk and others adjacent, gathered out of the ancient chronicles, histories and traditions of our fathers". On the title page of this work, Scott of Satchells describes himself as:

".....An old souldier and no scholler,
And one who could write nane,
But just the letters of his name....."

The verse history, which was published in 1688, was, it is said, dictated by its author to young schoolboys, who he hired to write down the lyrics that he himself had composed, in a similar manner to the way in which the ancient Welsh poets of the Dark Ages are said to have recited many of their own bardic verses, to the "educated" scribes whose writings were to preserve these ancient compositions for the benefit of future generations. Scott is known to have read Satchells's history in his youth, and there is evidence to suggest that its author, in addition to inducing in Sir Walter his life long interest in genealogy, an interest which, as we shall see shortly, finds expression throughout his own writings, is the original model for the *Last Minstrel* around whom Scott's own first major poetical work, *The Lay of the Last Minstrel*, is itself entirely centred; a fact which will be dealt with in full later; in Chapter 21.

In the introduction to the "Lay" Sir Walter sets the scene; first by telling his readers of how his poetical composition has been "put into the mouth of an ancient Minstrel, the last of his race, who, as he is supposed to have survived the Revolution, might have caught somewhat of the refinement of modern poetry, without losing the simplicity of his original model........": The original model in question being none other than the "old Ballad or Metrical Romance......"

This passage in Scott's introduction provides us with the key to the latter's entire career as a writer. For, as those with any more than a passing familiarity with his more famous works are fully aware, his early successes in the literary fields in which he was to excell were poetical in nature; and were all essentially modelled upon the traditional ballads of his native Scottish Borderlands; as well as the Metrical Romances of the High Middle Ages.

To understand the reason why this should have been so, one has first to comprehend the exact extent to which Scott could claim a connection with the Borders, and the ballad traditions which had prevailed there for centuries. And, as has already been hinted at in the opening paragraphs of this chapter, the key to these ancient and longstanding connections can be found amongst the pages of Scott of Satchells's poetical Clan History; in which we are told something of the ancient origins of the name of Scott; when the poet tells us of how he.......

"......*came to understand,*
How the Scotts of Buckleugh gain'd both name and land:"

The original source of this knowledge, Satchells relates, was a book given to him by a fellow kinsman, one Lancelot Scott, which, he says, was....

"......*call'd Mr. Michael's creed,*
But never a word at that time could I read,
What he read to me, I have it not forgot:
It was th'original of our south country Scots.
He said, that book which he gave me,
Was Mr. Michael Scot's historie,
Which history was never yet read through,
Nor ever will for no man dare it do;
Young scholars have pick'd out some thing,
From the contents, that dare not read within."

Mr. Michael and his "historie" will feature again in our story, further on in this same chapter. In the meantime, however, let us return once again to Scott of Satchells's poetical history.

Further on our poet continues on the same subject, as he relates how Lancelot Scott had informed him of how the original progenitor of the family name had been banished from Galloway in the time of Kenneth III; who ascended the throne in 969, and ruled some twenty-five years until 994. This man, we are told, now made his way, in the company of another individual who had been banished with him, into a region bordering what is now Ettrick Forest, "which was then called Rankleburn". Scott of Satchells then reveals how, one day, whilst King Kenneth was out hunting, with "all the nobles of his court...." who had "hither" come "to see the sport", he chanced to meet with our exile from Galloway; and having "....saw him a pretty man....."

"......*asked his name, from whence he came,-*
If't please your Grace my name is John.
The deer being curried in that place,
At his Majesty's demand,
Then John of Galloway ran apace,

And fetch'd water to his hands.
The King did wash into a dish,
And Galloway John he wot,
He said thy name now after this,
Shall e'er be called John Scot.
The Forest and the deer therein,
We commit to thy hand,
For thou shalt sure the ranger be,
If thou obey command;....."

As we shall see below, many of the themes explored in Satchells's poetry likewise feature in Sir Walter's own poetical writings. In view of this then it comes as no surprise that, in the preface to the first edition of his *Bridal of Triermain*, the Laird of Abbotsford informs his readership of how, in times past, "The original purpose of poetry" was "either religious or historical, or, as must frequently happen, a mixture of both...."

Elsewhere, he continues by pointing out how "Poets, under various denominations of Bards, Scalds, Chroniclers, and so forth, are the first historians of all nations. Their intention is to relate the events they have witnessed, or....." (as Scott points out, masterfully), ".....the traditions that have reached them; and they clothe the relation in rhyme, merely as the means of rendering it more solemn to the narrative, or more easily committed to memory. But, as the poetical historian improves in the art of conveying information, the authenticity of his narrative unavoidably declines. He is tempted to dilate and dwell upon the events that are interesting to his imagination, and, conscious how indifferent his audience is to the naked truth of his poem, his history gradually becomes a romance."

In many respects Sir Walter could be said to be describing, or at least defining, whether consciously or unconsciously, the fundamental differences between Scott of Satchells's poetry and his own. Whilst Satchells concentrates exclusively upon history and genealogy, Scott's own tendency is to take his readers, as far as possible, into the realm of romance. Both poets have clearly drunk from the same cauldron of inspiration however, for both incorporate various elements derived directly from the ancient ballads into their own poetical narratives. Similarly, both poets make continual reference to the geography and landscape of the Borders. Satchells does this in his role of poetical historian, whilst Sir Walter, as one would expect, indulges his inclination towards poetical romanticization.

A classic example of the poetical romance to which Scott refers, in the above quoted from preface, is the late fifteenth century Scottish poem "*The Romans of Lancelot of the Laik*", which, as we shall see further on, may have provided a model for "*Lyulph's Tale*" in Canto I of "*The Bridal of Triermain*"; or at least inspired it: Set in the reign of King Arthur, who, as we know from the ancient Welsh histories, was a real historical character, the "Romans" possesses in every respect all of the characteristics of the romantic poetical narrative, as it is defined by Scott. And, just like the fictitious Lyulph, in the poem written by Sir Walter, the original authors who compiled the poems upon which this Mediaeval composition was based, could claim a similarly ancient pedigree.

Of further interest is the fact that the action around which the "Romans" is centred, like that with which the "Bridal" is concerned, occurs in the vicinity of Carlisle; which is located in the area bordering the Kingdom of Rheged; and what was at one time a province occupied by the Southern Picts; which formerly straddled the region between Rheged and the old North British Kingdom of Alclud on the Clyde; during the Post-Roman Era. This geographical location is of great significance, in that Carlisle likewise features in Scott of Satchells's poetical history; in connection with Sir Walter's ancestors' original domicile.

Close to Carlisle is the old Roman fort of Bowness-on-Solway. And, in Satchells's poem, we are informed of how Lancelot Scott, who, Satchells claims, provided him with much of the genealogical information recounted in his "History", "shew'd" the Captain "his ancestors' haill"; which stood "To the English side" of the Border; at a location known as "Burgh-under-Bowness", in the neighbourhood of this ancient Roman fortification. According to Lancelot Scott's testimony, as it is recounted by his kinsman, their mutual forbears

"*Did live into that spot;*
Since Carlisle walls were re-built,
By David King of Scots;....."

Elsewhere in the poem we are also told of how the original progenitor of the name of Scott, and the companion who accompanied him to the Border territory where they eventually settled, originally came from a region that was "call'd Brigants that's now called Galloway"; the two men being referred to at this point in the narrative as "Two valiant lads of those Brigants....." The fact that Satchells uses this turn of phrase when speaking of the most ancient origins of his Clan is significant for a variety of reasons. The first and most important of these is that in so doing he traces the Clan's roots, not, as we would expect, to a Scoto-Irish source, as most Clan histories relating to Highland Clans invariably do, but to an ancient North British one; thus linking Sir Walter genealogically with the very same ethnic group with which the poet identifies his own fictitious poet, Lyulph; in *The Bridal of Triermain.*

Scott himself would have known this, as his interest in Arthuriana and Dark Age heroic poetry was extensive; as shall be seen during the course of the chapters that follow. And, it is for this reason that, in retrospect, it is possible for us to conjecture that his description of Lyulph in the poem is derived entirely from this knowledge; a knowledge that was in all probability acquired as a direct result of the influence that Scott of Satchells's poem exerted upon his young and impressionable mind. Thus, it is true to say that it is impossible to understand Scott without first understanding Satchells; a fact which will be clear to anyone who has been fortunate enough to have visited Abbotsford; where Sir Walter's personal copy of Satchells's poetical history still takes pride of place amongst this long dead author's vast library.

In fact, if the truth be known, the origin of the name "Brigants" comes not from Galloway, but from the area south of the Solway Firth; which in ancient time was home to the Pre-Roman tribe known as the Brigantes; whilst what was later to become Galloway was, in that far off age, occupied by another tribe; referred to in classical sources as the Novantae. It does seem more than likely, however, that, during the ceaseless wars that raged in the area immediately after the departure of the Roman Eagles from British soil, many of the inhabitants of what had once been the old tribal "civitas" of Brigantia crossed over into Galloway. For, what sources there are remaining in the ancient Welsh and Latin tongues seem to point to this being the case.

And so, on the face of this evidence, and in view of the fact that the original ancestor of Scott's line was one of "Two valiant lads of these Brigants.....", as seen above, it is safe to conclude that he came from somewhere in the ancient Kingdom of Rheged; in the vicinity of Carlisle- the very area around which the narrative of Scott's "Bridal" is centred. And, that like his poet Lyulph, he himself could likewise claim descent from the same "Druid sires" as the fictitious bard of his poem, whose....

".....mystic tale, by bard and sage,
is handed down from Merlin's age."

In spite of this, it is indeed unfortunate that since Scott of Satchells first committed his poetical compositions to paper, the original pedigree that he claims to have been read by his kinsman, Lancelot, has disappeared altogether. The earliest traceable ancestor of the Family of Scott, by the current reckoning, is one "Uchtredus filius Scott", who is said to have been living c.1130; and of whom the anonymous editor of the 1786 edition of his poetical history writes as follows:

"The Uchtred, whom Douglas, in his Peerage of Scotland, mentions as the progenitor of all the Scots in Scotland, seems evidently to have been a descendant of the first Scot of Buccleuch. His designing himself filius Scot is proof of this. To imagine he designed himself filius Scot to signify his being the son of a Scotsman is rather absurd. Might not almost every person in the nation, with equal propriety, have designed himself the son of a Scotsman? It is more rational to suppose that filius Scot was the son of some person who was then known by the name of Scot. It behoved to be some time before the descendants of John of Buckcleuch became numerous, or so great as to be attendants at court, which seems to be the reason why Douglas cannot find them amongst the nobility till the reign of Alexander I, who succeeded to the crown in 1107....."

These last mentioned facts are important for a variety of reasons, most notably on account of the fact that we are here presented with a rational argument as to why Scott of Satchells's account of the origins of his Clan should be believed. This argument is backed up by what we know of Douglas's method of working, in that almost all of the most ancient references used in his assessments of the origins of the Scottish noble families are taken exclusively from charters. Unfortunately, for the most part, this is a most unsatisfactory working method, for, as one nineteenth century commentator is swift to point out, in connection with the situation prevalent in Scotland at this time [1] (see notes to chapters): "By the ancient Celtic laws no chief recognized a Crown charter as necessary to holding his lands, and in fact was not allowed to possess written title deeds, it being a point of honour with the Clan to love and support the chief as the Father of his people."

Indeed, when Sir Walter himself first came into this world this system had only very recently come to be stamped out in the remoter parts of the

Highlands. In the case of Clan Gregor for example, the most famous of whom was doubtless Scott's own literary hero, Rob Roy, "While the strong arm constituted the sole title to property, the MacGregors held their own, being able and willing to make their hands keep their lands. But when territorial possessions were legally secured by written tenures, they imprudently continued to trust in the right of the sword, and thus paved the way for their future misfortunes. While they pursued their simple and retired life, the great barons in the vicinity used their court influence to obtain charters over the old MacGregor possessions, and followed up the acquisition of such documentary rights by driving out the true proprieters....." [2] (see notes to chapters).

As we saw in the introduction, Scott himself was in constant contact with representatives of this ancient Highland culture, which, just a generation or so before his birth, had still preserved the last cultural remnants of this ancient oral system of legislature. Under this system the right to govern was determined not by written documents, but by the orally transmitted Clan genealogies preserved by the ancient bards. And this, more than anything, was why Sir Walter himself was always conscious of the fact that it was the bard's original purpose to "write the early history of his country....", a history that would often be "combined with traditionary and genealogical anecdotes interesting to those who were to listen to him, and this he adorned by the exertions of his genius....."

And this, as we shall see, was not only the tradition about which Sir Walter himself was to write, but also the tradition that he was to continue throughout his own extensive poetical writings; as the true successor of his kinsman and namesake, Captain Walter Scott of Satchells.

Despite the loss of records pertaining to the exact, generation by generation, descent from John Scot to Uchtred, one person to whom Satchells refers is attested to in a vast number of ancient records; that individual being none other than the "Mr. Michael Scot"; in whose possession Lancelot Scott's book had originally been. The sixth generation descendant of Uchtred, Sir Michael was, in addition to being the ancestor of the present Scots of Logie-Montrose and Usan, none other than Michael Scot the Wizard (1175-1234); the mathematician, physician, scholar and scientist, who, after entering into the service of Don Philip, clerk register to the court of Emperor Frederick II of Hohenstauffen in Sicily, rose to become one of the greatest thinkers of the Middle Ages.

Whilst studying at the University of Toledo, his knowledge of the Arabic language became sufficient for him to be able to make translations of the works of Aristotle; and his reputation as an Astrologer is proven, by his designation as Astrologer Royal to Frederick II; in the Bodleian m.s. of his work on Astronomy. In the Scottish Borders, however, Sir Michael has a very different reputation; and he has been portrayed as a black magician in the folklore of Selkirkshire; where he is said to have resided for a time at Oakwood or Aikwood Tower; now the newly restored home of Lord and Lady Steel; which lies just outside of Selkirk itself; and just a stone's throw from where Sir Walter Scott sat in judgement as Sheriff in the local courts.

Appropriately, the traditions that associate Sir Michael with necromancy and black magic are alluded to once again in Sir Walter's own writings, where, in Canto II of the "Lay", we find the following reference to this Mediaeval alchemist:

"In these far climes, it was my lot
To meet the wondrous Michael Scott;
A wizard of such dreaded fame,
That when, in Salamanca's cave,
He listed his magic wand to wave,
The bells would ring in Notre Dame!
Some of his skills he taught to me;
And warrior, I could say to thee
The words that cleft Eildon Hills in three,
And bridled the Tweed with a curb of stone;
But to speak them were a deadly sin;
And for having but thought them my heart within,
A treble penance must be done.

"When Michael lay on his dying bed,
His conscience was awakened;
He bethought him of his sinful deed,
And he gave me a sign to come with speed......

"I swore to bury his Mighty Book
that never mortal might therein look;
And never to tell where it was hid,
Save at his Chief of Branksome's need;

And when that need was past and o'er,
Again the volume to restore ...."

So, here we find the very book that Lancelot Scott read extracts from to Scott of Satchells; and which the latter poet claims no man would dare read from cover to cover. Thus, in the above extracts from the first of Sir Walter's great narrative poems, we encounter direct references to specific elements taken directly from Satchells's poetical history; combined with other legendary and mythological ingredients taken from amongst the very oral traditions still prevalent in the Laird of Abbotsford's ancestral Borderlands at the very time in which he himself was writing.

Amongst these local myths and legends was the persistent tradition that it was Michael Scott who had used his magical powers in the creation of the three great peaks that tower above the very landscape, where, in later years, Sir Walter was to construct his own beloved Abbotsford; and known collectively as the Eildon Hills. In this way Scott demonstrates, through the medium of his own poetical narrative, the original purpose of the ancient bard; as he himself defines it throughout the introductory essay attached to his own poem.

As for "Mr. Michael" of ballad fame, another of the arts that the Wizard of Aikwood is said to have mastered was the science of building; and legend has it that he was the architect of the mysterious "Castel del Monte". Built for the Emperor Frederick, with an octagonal keep and eight octagonal turrets, it has been suggested that this ornately ornamental castle was never constructed for any defensive purpose, but had some kind of occult significance which is still a mystery.

According to Robin Williamson, author of *The Craneskin Bag* (publ. Canongate, 1995), Sir Michael was "born at Balwearie in Fife, in an old square tower whose ruins are by the road between Kircaldy and Auchertool". His father's marriage, to the daughter and sole heir of Sir Richard Balwearie, led to Michael's acquisition of his maternal grandfather's estates; and with them the ancient castle of Balwearie; the sinister place of his birth.

Balwearie Castle has an evil reputation all of its own, and features in an old Scottish ballad, published by the great Scottish ballad collector Robert Jamieson; who will feature in a later chapter in connection with Thomas the

Rhymer. The ballad itself is entitled "Lamkin", and concerns the revenge of a malevolent mason, who, having built a castle for a Scottish Lord, exacts his revenge when payment is not forthcoming:

"It's Lamkin was a Mason gude
as ever built wi stane;
He built Lord Wearie's Castle
but payment he got nane.

'O pay me, Lord Wearie,
come, pay me my fee:'
I canna pay ye, Lamkin,
for I mau go o'er the sea'.

'O pay me now, Lord Wearie,
come pay me out O' hand:
'I canna pay you, Lamkin,
unless I sell my land.'

'O gin ye winna pay me,
I here sall make a vow,
Before that ye come hame again,
Ye sall hae cause to rue......"

Needless to say, when Lord Wearie eventually returns home from his voyage overseas, he finds Lamkin has killed his wife and murdered his young child. This ballad is highly significant, not in the least because a version of it was collected for Scott by James Hogg; although Scott was never to incorporate it into the *Minstrelsy*. And, in Hogg's version of *Lamkin*, we hear of how

"Lamkin was as good a Mason
As ever liftit stane;
He built to the laird o Lariston
But payment gat he nane......"

Thus, these same legends become linked with another lordly family, residing even closer to the Border region upon which the ballads and legends recounted in the *Minstrelsy* are themselves for the most part centred.

Elsewhere, James Reed quotes M.A. Richardson in connection with a fragment referred to as having been "......taken down from the recitation of an old woman of Ovington, Co. Northumberland,.....The scene of the occurrence it describes is a ruined tower seated on the corner of an extensive embankment, and surrounded by a moat, on the western side of Whittle Dene, near Ovingham. From the evidence of popular tradition (for the ballad is so imperfect as to be of itself hardly explanatory enough) it appears to relate the circumstances of a murder committed by a freebooter named Long Lonkin, through the treachery of a servant maid. A deep pool in the Dene which runs hard by is called "Long Lonkin's hole, and is stated to have been the death place of the freebooter".

Further on, Reed notes that: "Another tale associates the crime with Nafferton Castle, between Ovingham and Whittle Dene, the site of a tower known as "Lonkin's Hall" which was left uncompleted as it was being built without a license to crenellate. Hugill recalls a story in which Lonkin, a freebooter, murdered the wife and child of the Lord of Welton, in Welton Hall, and threw the bodies into a pool in the burn nearby which became known as "Lang Lonkin's Hole". Lonkin eventually hanged himself on a tree near Nafferton Castle "and for long afterwards his skull lay within the ruined walls". In yet another version of the story, Lonkin is a gentleman who kills the lady and her child because the Lord of Nafferton had been preferred to him....."

Interestingly enough, a version of this ballad appears in the pages of the late Ewan MacColl's celebrated autobiography, *Journeyman* (publ. Sidgewick and Jackson, 1990), in connection with the latter's own obsession with ancient ballads. MacColl is likewise a key figure in our story, owing to the fact that it was he who was primarily responsible for starting off the modern traditonal folk revival; itself in many ways the forerunner of Peter Gabriel's *World Music Movement;* which went mainstream in the 1980s and was largely at the root of much of the current interest in traditional forms of music.

MacColl, whose songs were to be covered by the likes of Elvis Presley and "The Pogues", was to achieve international star status as a result of his work as an original song writer; "The First Time I Ever Saw Your Face" and "Dirty Old Town" being two of his best known compositions. His rise to prominence was to commence following the opening of his world famous folk club at the Princess Louise Tavern in High Holborn during the 1950s, at a time when Trad. Jazz was the primary musical influence at the heart of the Counter Culture Mainstream in post-rationing Swinging London.

Amongst the bands and musicians directly influenced by the movement that MacColl and his wife Peggy Seeger were to found were the likes of Bert Jansch, Sandy Denny, Martin Carthy, Ashley Hutchings, Fairport Convention, Pentangle, Steeleye Span and the Druids.

An interesting coincidence then that the original venue where many of the initial performances of the music that this veritable drove of musicians were to revive, during the 'sixties and 'seventies, in the footsteps of their great mentor, MacColl, took place, was the Princess Louise. For, in a neighbouring street known as Southampton Row, stands the former residence of Bob Ferguson, cousin of Scott's lifelong friend Adam Ferguson, and the father of Robert Ferguson M.D.; whose biographical anecdotes relating to Sir Walter and his circle appear elsewhere in this volume; as has previously been noted in the introductory essay.

This coincidence is made all the more interesting by the fact that, strange as it may seem, many of the ballads lately revived by the musicians listed above were themselves collected by the Laird of Abbotsford during the course of his completion of what is perhaps his greatest literary achievement: The collection, editing and publication of his celebrated *Minstrelsy of the Scottish Border*; which made its first appearance in 1802; two full years before the penning of *The Lay*.

To understand fully exactly what Scott achieved in his compilation of this collection, we must turn to an account of his methods of working, recorded by J.E. Shortreed in his *Conversations with my father on the subject of his tours with Sir Walter Scott in Liddesdale*, which first saw the light of day in the year 1824. And, once again, the modern reader is very much indebted to James Reed with regard to this essay, in that it is quoted from extensively by the latter author in his magnum opus *The Border Ballads*. According to Reed, "Their first expedition was made in the Autumn of 1792, when Scott was 21, and the excursions continued annually for seven years".

On one of these expeditions, which took place in Spring and in weather conditions described by Shortreed snr. as "blirting" snow storms, they set out "with the express purpose o' hearing the air o' the Fray o' Suport, frae auld Jonathan Graham, the lang quaker as he was called. We went to

Newlands...." Shortreed continues, "...where Dr. Elliot was then living....." (Elliot was to be of invaluable assistance in Scott's compilation of the "Minstrelsy") "....and a man and a horse were sent ance errand for Jonathan, who came accordingly. He was a man upwards of eighty years auld I dare say. I'll never forget his appearance, tall, and sae thin as to be mair like a walking skeleton than a living being. Indeed, ye wadna hae said, to have lookit at him, that he was a living creature, until he began to recite and then he fired up and got prodigiously animated. He spoke, or rather scraughed, in a loud stentorian voice, which formed the oddest contrast imaginable wi' his worn and emaciated figure. He had a great repository of ballads and traditions in his day, but his memory and other faculties war nearly gane by the time we saw him. He could eat little or nane, poor creature, but he drank weel, and the Dr. And Sir Wr. filled him exceedingly fou o' brandy- o he was ill! Faith I thoct he wad die i' our hands ance athegither, for he fainted clean away- but we got him carried out into the fresh air, and threw water onto his auld wizened face, and rubbit him, and wrought on till he came about again, and nae sooner was he better than he set to roaring the outlandish lilt again. He made the awfuest and uncooest howling sound I ever heard. It was a mixture o' a sort o' horrible and eldritch cries, and to hae lookt at him ye wad hae thocht it impossible they could come out o' that dead trunk. He wad sune hae been as ill as ever again wi' liquor, if we had let him, but we got him to his bed. He gaed his ways hame the neist mornin', as he had come, after getting a gratuity from Sir Walter. He had gotten a sair fleg wi' the quaker's swarfin' the night before, and was in an unco taking about him till he came round again."

On another occasion, when Sir Walter had made one of his sketches of Hermitage Castle, taken "from the side o' Earnton Fell", he "stood all the time he took it to his knees in snow. But nothing...." Shortreed adds, "then did him any harm". Thus we find Scott, journeying out into the remotest areas of the Border countryside in all weathers, just to hear the traditional tunes of the ballads that he so meticulously collected.

Some modern commentators might like to compare Scott's endeavours in this field to those of the West London bluesmen of the nineteen sixties: People like John Mayall and Alexis Corner; whose own researches into the sounds of the Mississippi Delta were to influence home grown bands such as the Yardbirds and the Rolling Stones; and turn the likes of John Lee Hooker and Muddy Waters into household names.

However, in view of the absence of technology in Scott's time- recording equipment has made exotic forms of music ever more accessible in our own century, and the complete lack of a proper integrated transport system in the era in which he was working, the Laird of Abbotsford's unique achievement has to be seen for what it is: A pioneering work of uncomparable proportions. For, in the simplest terms, comparing Sir Walter's forays into these isolated village communities to a train ride across the Metropolis in search of imported record discs, is like comparing the Voyage of Columbus to a latter day flight to New York on Virgin Airways.

As for the *Minstrelsy*, which was to be gradually expanded into some three volumes over the next two years, it provides the hidden key to Scott's entire literary career. For, in his poetry, the central historical and mythological themes that he was to encounter during the course of gathering the songs that he later published in this vast collection, are worked upon and expanded, in Scott's own unique way. In the poem *"Marmion"*, for example, in Canto I, we hear of how.....

"The whiles a Northern Harper rude
Chanted a rhyme of deadly feud,
"how the fierce Thirwalls, and Ridleys all,
Stout Willimondswick,
And Hard-riding Dick,
And Hughie of Hawdon, and Will o' the Wall,
Have set on Sir Albany Featherstonehaugh,
And taken his life at the Deadman's-shaw."

This section of Scott's classic poetical tale of Flodden Field, which is centred upon the disastrous Battle of Flodden in 1513, is in fact none other than his own re-telling of one of the ballads which can be found amongst the pages of the*"Border Minstrelsy"*; under the heading *"The Death of Featherstonehaugh"*:

"Hoot awa' lads, hoot awa'
Ha' ye heard how the Ridleys and Thirlwalls, and a'
Ha' set upon Albany Featherstonehaugh,
And taken his life at the Deadmanshaugh:
There was Willimoteswick,
And Hardriding Dick,
And Hughie of Hawdon, and Will of the Wa'

I canno' tell a', I canno' tell a',
And mony a mair that the deil may knaw."

Of this ballad, which Scott describes as being of Northumbrian origin in his introductory notes, the author has the following to say: "This curious though rude rhyme....." he writes, "was taken down from the recitation of a woman eighty years of age, Mother of one of the miners in Alston Moor, by the agent of the lead mines there, who communicated it to my friend and correspondent, R. Surtees esq., of Mainsforth. She had not, she said, heard it for many years; but when she was a girl it used to be sung at merry-makings, "till the roof rung again". "......The ludicrous turn given to the slaughter, marks that wild and disorderly state of society in which a murder was not merely a casual circumstance but, in some cases, an exceedingly good jest. The structure of the ballad resembles "*The Fray of Suport*", having the same irregular stanza and wild chorus......"

As we shall see, from the following extract taken from "*The Fray of Suport*", described by Scott as "by far the most uncouth and savage" of "all the Border ditties" which had fallen into his hands; and which he says was "usually chaunted in a sort of wild recitative, except the burden, which swells into a long and varied howl, not unlike to a view hollo....",the two ballads do bear certain distinct structural similarities; most notably "The words, and the very great irregularity of the stanza......."

"Rise, ye carle coopers, frae making o' kirns and tubs,
In the Nicol forest woods.
Your craft has na left the value of an oak rod,
But if you had had ony fear o' God,
Last night ye had na slept sae sound,
And let my gear be a' ta'en.
Fy lads! Shout a' a' a' a' a',
My gear's a' ta'en.

Ah! Lads, we'll fang them a' in a net!
For I hae a' the fords o' Liddel set;
The Dunkin, and the Dour-loup,
The Willie-ford, and the Water-slack,
The Black-rack and the Trout-dub of Liddel;
There stands John Forster wi' five men at his back,
Wi' buft coat and cap of steil:

Boo! Ca' at them e'en Jock;
That ford's sicker, I wat weil.
Fy lads! Shout a' a' a' a' a',
My gear's a' ta'en.

Hoo! Hoo! Gar raise the Red Souter and Ringan's Wat,
Wi a broad elshin and a wicker;
I wat weill they'll make a ford sicker
Sae whether they be Elliots or Armstrangs,
Or rough riding Scots, or rude Johnstones,
Or whether they be frae the Tarras or Ewsdale,
They maun turn and fight, or try the deeps O' Liddel.
Fy lads! Shout a' a' a' a' a'
My gear's a' ta'en.

As the reader will note, the lists of individuals, locations (the second of the above quoted verses abounds with the names of fords along the Liddel, places ideal for watching out for marauders), and war-like Border Clans, are comparable to those found in *"The Death of Featherstonehaugh"*. Similarly, the ballad itself, which is concerned with the plight of an Englishwoman, who, "residing in Suport, near the foot of the Kershope," as is noted by Reed, "having been plundered in the night by a band of the Scottish moss-troopers, is supposed to convoke her servants and friends for the pursuit, or "Hot Trod", also has its counterpart in yet another ballad; referred to below in the following quotation from Scott's *Journal*; taken once again from the pages of Reed's *Border Ballads:*

"The Duke (of Northumberland) tells me his people in Keeldar were all quite wild the first time his father went up to shoot there. The women had no other dress than a bedgown and petticoat. The men were savage and could hardly be brought to rise from the heath either from sulleness or fear. They sung a wild tune, the burden of which was "Ourina Ourina Ourina". The females sung, the men danced round and at a certain point of the tune Ourina they drew their dirks which they always wore."

In view of this, it is easy to see how it was that, in the case of *"The Death of Featherstonehaugh"*, Scott's friend and correspondent, Surtees, had successfully palmed him off with a forged ballad of his own composition. In recent times, certain of Scott's most vociferous critics have taken it upon themselves to censure his work as a ballad collector and folklorist, despite the fact that they themselves have little or no grounding in the subjects it is necessary to study in order to pass comment upon so controversial a subject matter.

Amongst the allegations that have been circulated, in the televisual media in particular, are accusations of him being duped by local ballad singers and tale tellers, who strung him along by palming him off with bogus traditions which they had "boned up" on, in anticipation of his arrival in their communities; as a means of exacting money from him.

This gives the impression to an unsuspecting, and indeed ignorant, public, that Scott was an outsider in the Borderlands which he was wont to frequent; and was therefore in some way ignorant of the ballads and traditions which he was seeking out. In fact, nothing could be further from the truth, as Shortreed himself makes clear when he attests to how they "rade about visiting the scenes o' remarkable occurences, and roved away amang the fouk haill days at a time, for Sir Walter was very fond o' mixing with them, and by that means he became perfectly familiar wi' their character and the manners o' the country......"

And, during the course of his acquisition of this familiarity, Scott was able, as shall be seen later on in this book, to discern exactly which of the ballads that he was hearing were of ancient, or modern, provenance; the only exception to this golden rule being the remarkable "*Flowers of the Forest*"; which will itself feature in a later chapter. In the case of "*The Death of Featherstonehaugh*", which, together with "*Barthram's Dirge*" and "*Lord Ewrie*", was one of three forged ballads composed by Surtees which appear in the pages of the "*Minstrelsy*", it was not a malevolent Border peasant who palmed the Laird of Abbotsford off with these fakes, but a gentleman and a scholar; a fact which is in itself explanatory of Surtees's success.

Scott was in constant correspondence with a whole host of collectors and researchers in the field in which he was working at the time of his compilation of the *Border Minstrelsy*; many of whom are referred to by name amongst the pages of its three volumes. And, in the case of Surtees, it transpires that he was clearly dealing with someone of sufficient knowledge and poetical skill to be able to pull the wool over his eyes.

In order to understand as to why Surtees would want to do this it is important to understand that, in the world of eighteenth century literature, it was an extremely popular pastime for a poet to attempt to pass his own compositions off as genuine reliques of ancient poetry. One of the most famous examples of this can be found amongst the works of the Bristol poet, Thomas Chatterton (1752-1770); whose *"Mynstrelles Songe"* would not seem out of place in the antiquarian collections of Bishop Percy; were it not an eighteenth century "forgery":

"O! Synge untoe mie roundelaie
O! Droppe the brynie teare with mee,
Dance ne moe atte haille daie,
Lycke a reynynge ryver bee;
Mie love ys dedde,
Gon to hys death-bedde,
Al under the wyllowe tree".

Once this is understood, Surtees's actions are easily explained. As for how he was able to do this, a study of the textual notes to both *"Barthram's Dirge"* and *"Lord Ewrie"* should now be attempted. Of *"Barthram's Dirge"*, Scott informs us that the hero "of the ditty.....was shot to death by nine brothers, whose sister he had seduced, but was afterwards buried at her request, near their usual place of meeting; which may account for his being laid not in holy ground, but beside the burn. The name of Barthram, or Bertram, would argue a Northumbrian origin, and there is, or was, a Headless Cross, among the many so named, near Elsdon in Northumberland. But the mention of the Nine-Stane Burn, and the Nine-Stane Rig, seem to refer to those places in the vicinity of Hermitage Castle, which is countenanced by the mentioning of Our Lady's Chapel. Perhaps the hero may have been an Englishman, and the lady a native of Scotland; which renders the catastrophe even more probable.....They certainly did bury in former days near the Nine-Stane Burn; for the editor remembers finding a small monumental cross, with initials, lying among the heather........"

Surtees's familiarity with the locations that Scott himself was wont to frequent in search of ballad traditions- we have already examined Shortreed's testimony as to his visits to Hermitage Castle, thus enabled him to succeed in his deception. Elsewhere, in the notes to *"Lord Ewrie"*, we are told that the song in question "was written down by my obliging friend, Robert Surtees, Esq., of Mainsforth, from the recitation of Rose Smith, of Bishop Middleham, a woman aged upwards of ninety-one, whose husband's father and two brothers were killed in the affair of 1715".

In my introduction to this work I have transcribed extracts from one of Scott's letters to Surtees, in which our Ragged Lion refers to how he has been flattered "very much" by Surtees "pointing out to" his attention "the feuds of 1715 and 1745...." And, in view of the flattering nature of Surtees's correspondence with Scott on these matters, it is by no means inconceivable that Surtees's manufacture of an artificial provenance for the ballads that he forged was carried out in such a way as to hoodwink the Laird of Abbotsford by means of such flattery: Indeed, this is exactly what Scott's modern day critics have alleged happened in the case of the Border Peasants who they claim indulged in similar deceptions, in order to obtain money. These allegations are serious, for, by making them, those that do so do not just malign and libel Sir Walter, but the entire community from which he collected the songs and traditions that he later published in the "*Minstrelsy*".

An added twist in this affair revolves around the fact that Robert Surtees esq. was, like Sir Walter, a gentleman. And, in view of his gentlemanly background, the source from which these forged ballads and artificial traditions emanated was not the quarter from whence the Laird of Abbotsford would have expected to have been palmed off with deliberately faked materials. It is this element of surprise, in effect, that may explain Surtees's ability to hoodwink the editor of the "*Minstrelsy*". For, in view of the fact that, as the editors of the Dictionary of National Biography make clear, Scott had already begun to collect ballads by the time he was seven years old, an extant bound collection at Abbotsford at that time being dateable to 1783, he had been collecting and studying material of this nature for more than twenty years when the "*Minstrelsy*" rolled off the press. Bearing this in mind then, it makes it extremely unlikely that he could have been deceived, except in unusual circumstances, such as those under which the abovementioned deceptions took place.

Turning now to Scott's later achievements, as a novelist, it is interesting to note that, throughout the novels, the ballads are not only quoted extensively, but the historical characters who feature in them discussed as part of the living bardic tradition in which they are immortalized. At the head of chapter XXVI of "*Guy Mannering*" for example, we find the following quotation from "*The Ballad of Johnnie Armstrong*"; which is likewise to be found amongst the pages of the *Minstrelsy*:

"*The Elliots and Armstrongs did convene,*
They were a gallant company!"

And then, in the text below, we find Captain Brown accompanying "....his jolly landlord and the rest of his friends into the large and smoking kitchen, where the savoury mess reeked on an open table, massy enough to have dined Johnny Armstrong and his merry men....." The Armstrong in question, who will feature again during the course of this book, was a Border outlaw viewed by many of the populace as the sixteenth century equivalent of Robin Hood: Hence the reference to his "Merry Men". To understand fully what Scott set out to do, and what he was able to achieve, through his publication of the *Minstrelsy,* I would refer the reader to Allan Massie's masterful biographical novel, *Ragged Lion,* which I have previously mentioned elsewhere in this text; and in which the poet's own words are themselves re-interpreted by a twentieth century novelist:

"The ballads inflamed me. I conceived- how or just when I cannot recall- the ambition of making a collection of them, and I believed that this might prove a fit offering to lay on the altar of my country, once proud and independent, now in danger of losing its memory of itself, and so its consciousness, in the benevolent embrace of a large polity......"

Although essentially a piece of fiction, this extract consists of Massie's re-writing of an oft-quoted passage from Scott's introduction to the *Minstrelsy,* in which the author sums up as follows:

"And, trivial as may appear such an offering to the Manes of a Kingdom, once independent, I hang it upon her altar with a mixture of feelings that I shall not attempt to describe."

As we shall see, later on in our story, one of the principal works which was to influence Scott in his authorship of his *Minstrelsy of the Scottish Border,* was Bishop Percy's *Reliques of Ancient English Poetry.* Percy's *Reliques* is in many ways the forerunner of Scott's *Minstrelsy,* and its publication is described by Reed as "an event of considerable significance in social as well as literary history. On both sides of the Border" he goes on to say, "for a century or more, men had collected the songs of the people, but it was the publication in London of Percy's work that exercised such a compelling influence on an age in which Dr. Johnson could say that "*Chevy Chase*" pleased the vulgar, but did not satisfy the learned; it did not fill a mind capable of thinking strongly." Percy had rescued a folio manuscript of ballads which were being used as firelighters in the house of Humphrey Pitt of Shifnal, and used it as the basis of the "*Reliques*"......."

Elsewhere, Reed notes that, despite the fact that Percy's collection was an "uneven" work, it "made a strong impression upon the mind of the 13-year-old" Walter Scott; as this autobiographical fragment, quoted by his son-in-law, Lockhart, attests:

"I forgot the hour of dinner, was sought for with anxiety, and was still found entranced in my intellectual banquet. To read and to remember was in this instance the same thing, and henceforth I overwhelmed my schoolfellows, and all who would hearken to me, with tragic recitations from the ballads of Bishop Percy. The first time, too, I could scrape a few shillings together, which were not common occurences with me, I bought unto myself a copy of these beloved volumes; nor do I believe I ever read a book half so frequently, or with half the enthusiasm."

This, however, was not the first occasion upon which the young Sir Walter was to come into contact with the ballads of old. We shall touch upon Scott's earliest contact with Border Balladry in a little while. In the meantime, it is sufficient at this stage to demonstrate the parallels between what he himself was to do in his lifetime, and the manner in which the Welsh Bards of the early Middle Ages, to whom I shall compare the Ragged Lion over and over again throughout this book, dictated the oral traditions, that they and their predecessors had preserved for centuries, to the scribes whose manuscript writings were to ensure their survival into our own present time.

At the time when Scott and his friends set about putting together the collection of lyrics that he was to set down in the *Minstrelsy*, Britain was fast moving into the era known to historians as the Industrial Revolution. The introduction of new methods of agriculture, which would result in the gradual disappearance of large numbers of workers, who had previously tilled the soil, from the countryside, was in turn to lead to a mass migration to the new urban centres which were to spring up around the manufacturing industries that were simultaneously replacing the old cottage workshops of yesteryear. As a result, the rural communities which had preserved their own unique songs, dances and traditional customs for centuries, were gradually being broken up and their populations dispersed; a fact which would have had the effect of destroying forever the ancient poetry and song peculiar to these now vanishing village societies.

Similarly, hundreds of years before, when the English of Deira and Bernicia-the two early Saxon Kingdoms that were to become known to later generations as Northumbria, drove the North British dynasts, who had formerly ruled the region which now constitutes the Anglo-Scottish Borders, out of their original native homeland and into Wales, the bardic poems that their court poets carried with them as they retreated were written down by Christian monks for the benefit of future ages. In Scott's own poetry the Last Minstrel is himself the "modern" equivalent of these ancient bards, whose poetic traditions he saw as his duty to preserve.

Thus, it can be said, without any reasonable doubt, that Scott himself was the personification of the heroic poetic ideal that he sought to create through the image of the Last Minstrel. For, had he not been a poet, he would have been a soldier, and it is through the character of a moss trooper, William of Deloraine, who features, once again, in *The Lay of the Last Minstrel*, that the parallels between Scott's own poems, and those of the North British Bards of the Dark Ages, can at once be clearly observed:

"Sir William of Deloraine, good at need,
Mount thee on the wightest steed;
Spare not to spur, nor stint to ride,
Until thou come to fair Tweedside....."

In a poem attributed to Llywarch Hen, a bard to the court of Rheged, the very area from which, as we have already seen, Scott's own ancestors can be shown to have migrated, we find a similar description of a Dark Age British Warrior:

"Under the thigh of Geraint were swift racers,
Long their legs, grain was given them,
Ruddy ones, with the assault of black eagles......"

Further on in the "Lay" we find references to Border warfare, which, like so many of the battles fought by the Dark Age British Princes immortalized by Llywarch and his fellow poets, often involved feuds with rival clans from one's own side of the frontier, when we are told of how.....

".....Bowden Moor the marchman won,
And sternly shook his plumed head,
As glanced his eye o'er Halidon;
For on his soul the slaughter red
Of that unhallowed morn arose,

When first the Scott and Carr were foes;
When royal James beheld the fray,
Prize to the victor of the day;
When Home and Douglas in the van,
Bore down Buccleuch's retiring clan,
Till gallant Cessford's heart-blood dear
Reeked on dark Elliot's Border spear......"

In another poem attributed to Lywarch, entitled *"The Head of Urien"*, we hear of how Urien of Rheged, after leading a confederation of British allies to victory against the English, was assassinated, in the words of a Dark Age chronicler, "from jealousy, because his military skill and generalship surpassed that of all the other Kings:"

"Eurdyl will be joyless this night,
And multitudes besides:
In Aber Lleu has Urien been slain.

Eurdyl will be sorrowful from the tribulation of this night,
And from the fate that is to me befallen;
That her brother should be slain at Aber Lleu.

On Friday I saw great anxiety
Among the hosts of baptism,
Like a swarm without a hive, bold in despair.

Were there not given to me by Run, fond of war,
A hundred swarms and a hundred shields?
But one swarm was better far than all.

Were there not given to me by Run, the famous chief,
A cantrev and a hundred oxen?
But one gift was better far than those......

Decapitated is my lord, his opponents are powerful:
Warriors will not love his enemies:
Many sovereigns he has consumed.

The ardent disposition of Urien! It is sadness to me......"

In the above quoted excerpts from this mighty Dark Age epic, we hear of how Urien's sister, Eurdyl, laments for her brother, previously slain, much like the unfortunate Duchess of Buccleuch in Scott's "Lay", whose husband's own death was to occur, likewise, as a direct result of a princely rivalry. Then, we are told of the men and arms sent to the Lords of Rheged by Run, who, the late John Morris in his *Age of Arthur* (publ. Weidenfeld and Nicolson, London, 1973), appropriately, assigned to the overlordship of Selkirk and Peebles; after having first heard of how this mighty British chieftain has met his death at Aber Lleu- the estuary of the Low; which enters the sea opposite the island of Lindisfarne.

The territory into which we are transported by this poem is the very territory through which Scott's own ancestors rode and fought in later times, and the very region that inspired his own poetical works: Aber Leu is just a few miles south east, along the coast, from where Scott's sacred River Tweed empties into the North Sea. Just to the west of Abeu Lleu, on the other side of the ancient Roman road south known as "The Devil's Causeway", is Norham Castle, over which, in 1314, Sir William de Riddell, ancestor of the Riddells of Felton Park and Swinburne Castle, was himself made governor:

"Unchallenged, thence passed Deloraine
To ancient Riddell's fair domain....."

In Scott's notes to *The Lay of the Last Minstrel*, in which the above given quotation appears, we are taken, through the medium of his own meticulous researches, back into the realms of Dark Age Border history, when we are told of how "The Riddells took their name from Ryedale. Tradition carries them", the Author of Waverley then continues, "back to 727 and 936, the dates of some stone coffins there." Close by Synton and nearby Satchells, where Sir Walter and the Captain's own ancestors were wont to reside, is the village of Riddell, and it is therefore no coincidence that both of them are descended from the marriage of Walter Scot of Synton, who flourished in the reign of James IV, to a daughter of James Riddel or Riddell of that ilk.

Thus, both Scott himself, and the kinsman who inspired him, can be shown to be tied by descent to the very same landscape which is itself a central feature in the heroic poetry of the Dark Ages. And this, more than anything, is what makes Scott truly entitled to the accolade "Last of the True Bards". In the current era it is fashionable to award the great artist and visionary poet William Blake this title. Although Blake was beyond question a master genius, he was not linked to the Bardic Tradition at source, in that his concepts of what the bards truly represented was derived at second hand from the writings of, among others, William Stukeley, the great eighteenth century antiquarian; and James Macpherson, translator from the Gaelic of the ancient poems of "Ossian".

Blake was a city boy, born and bred, whereas Sir Walter Scott was fortunate enough to be introduced to an oral culture, with bardic roots, in very early childhood; whilst convalescing at his Grandparents' farm in the Borders: The illness, contracted in infancy, that was to leave the Laird of Abbotsford lame for life led to him being sent to the Border countryside, where the ballads and folklore of his ancestral homeland were to leave him with a lifelong obsession with songs and minstrelsy. Then, whilst visiting the English health resort of Bath, he was to encounter John Home, who had been instrumental in bringing about the publication of Macpherson's translations; thus tapping him in at source to a culture that Blake could only read of in books.

Scott's vast knowledge of Border genealogy is yet another reason why he can justly be accredited with being the true successor to the Ancient Bards of the North British Dark Age. For, in addition to the composition of poetry, it was also the task of the Cymric bards and their Irish counterparts to preserve the genealogies of the dynasts whom they served. And this, essentially, is why we find lengthy genealogical tracts preserved amongst the same manuscript sources as those in which we find the ancient poems of Llywarch Hen and his contemporaries: Llywarch's own pedigree is given in an ancient manuscript known in Welsh as *Bonedd Gwyr y Goggledd* or *The Pedigrees of the Men of the North* (ie. North Britain). In it he is cited as being the descendant of Urien of Rheged's own grandfather.

In a similar way, the antiquarian Border pedigrees in which Scott was to immerse himself hundreds of years later, were to show the Laird of Abbotsford to be a distant relative of the Earls of Buccleuch; ancestors of the then and present Dukes. It is therefore appropriate then, that, in the front of the *Minstrelsy* we find the following dedication:

"To His Grace, Henry Duke of Buccleuch, These Tales, which in elder times have celebrated and cheered the halls of his gallant ancestors are respectfully inscribed by His Grace's much obliged and most humble servant Walter Scott."

Thus, it is also appropriate, in view of the fact that Scott is here establishing himself as the "Clan Bard" of the House of Buccleuch, just as Llywarch was, in former times, the Royal Bard to the Kings of Rheged, that, in the introduction to the *Minstrelsy,* we find him making the following assertions:

"From the remote period when the Roman province was contracted by the ramparts of Severus until the union of the kingdoms, the Borders of Scotland formed the stage upon which were presented the most memorable conflicts of two gallant nations. The inhabitants at the commencement of this era formed the first wave of the torrent which assaulted, and finally overwhelmed, the barriers of the Roman power in Britain......If we may trust the Welsh Bards in their account of the wars betwixt the Saxons and Danes of Deira and the Cumraig (570), imagination can hardly form any idea of conflicts more desperate than were maintained on the Borders between the Ancient British and their Teutonic invaders. Thus the Gododdin describes the waste and devastation of mutual havoc in colours so glowing as strongly to recall the words of Tacitus: "Et ubi solitutidimen faciunt, pacem appellant".

He then, in a note to the above, quotes "the spirited translation of this poem by Jones", adding that "the following verses are highly descriptive of the exhausted state of the victor army:"

"At Madoc's tent the clarion sounds,
With rapid clangour hurried far:
Each echoing dell the note resounds-
But when return the sons of war!
Thou born of stern necessity,
Dull peace! The desert yields to thee,
And owns their melancholy sway."

This ancient poem is primarily concerned with recounting a disastrous cavalry raid, led out of Edinburgh by the British chief Mynyddog, ruler of the Manau Gododdin- the name of the ancient North British province that formerly occupied what is now Lothian and the Borders, and into Yorkshire at the end of the sixth century. The Battle of Catraeth, which took place at Catterick near Scotch Corner and which is at the centre of this epic poem, was the Dark Age equivalent of the Battle of Flodden in the sixteenth century. It is therefore relevant that in the *Border Minstrelsy* Scott also printed the lyrics of another composition, "in imitation of the ancient ballad", which had been penned by one of his own near relatives; and which, like his own poem "*Marmion*", has the Battle of Flodden as its principal theme. For, both battles were to change the course of history.

At Flodden, the flower of Scottish chivalry perished on the field. Similarly, at Catraeth, the Northern British of Caer Eidyn- Edinburgh, and their allies, were so resoundingly crushed that never again were they able to field a sufficiently large army to be of any consequential threat to the Saxons. Again, a descendant of Llywarch and Urien's own line, Ceneu ap Llywarch (Constantine ap Llywarch), features in "*The Gododdin*"; where he is described variously as "the valour of the North" and "the lord who was bountiful by his nature....."

As we shall see, amongst the pages of the chapters that follow, a version of the abovementioned song from the "*Minstrelsy*" to which I refer was to be immortalized by the folk rock musicians of the 'sixties. It is therefore strange, in view of this, that Scott himself has never really truly received the full credit for what he did in this direction. As an example of what I mean, I now propose to refer the reader to the sleeve notes of one of the greatest electric folk albums ever produced. The record in question is the 1968 L.P. by "Steeleye Span" entitled "*Hark the Village Wait*". Amongst the musicians who appear in the line up of the band on this particular record is Terry Woods, who, like Kirstie MacColl, Ewan's daughter, has worked with the infamous "Pogues", and Ashley Hutchings, himself famous, primarily, for being a founder member of "Fairport Convention"; a band which still hosts its own annual music festival at Cropredy; which is itself one of the most important events of the British musical calendar.

Amongst the classic folk songs recorded on this album is an old Border Ballad called "*The Twa' Corbies*". This song, we are informed, by the editor of the sleeve notes previously mentioned, is "...otherwise known as the "*Two Ravens*". First printed in Motherwell's *Minstrelsy of the Scottish Border in 1803*, he adds, "it is one of the most popular of the Scottish ballads".

As it happens, the man who has here been given the credit for having first published this song, William Motherwell, did not publish his *Minstrelsy Ancient and Modern* until 1827; and at the time that the "Twa' Corbies" first appeared in print, he was a mere six years old! In fact, the only true statement in the above extract from the above quoted sleeve notes is that the song was first published in 1803, when it appeared in the pages of Scott's *Minstrelsy!* And this, in essence, is why this book had to be written. During the course of his own lifetime, Scott was to take many of the ballads that he was to publish out of almost total obscurity and etch them permanently into the consciousness of the Scottish people. However, owing to the fact that he was to become famous, first of all, as a poet, and then as a novelist, his role in doing this has been largely overlooked in more recent times.

In Scott's notes to the version of the ballad given in his *Minstrelsy*, he informs his readership of how "This poem was communicated to me by Charles Kirkpatrick Sharpe esq., jun. of Hoddom, as written down from tradition by a lady. It is a singular circumstance that it should coincide so very nearly with the ancient dirge called "*The Three Ravens*", published by Mr. Ritson....."

Like Scott, Ritson and Kirkpatrick Sharpe were also to be instrumental in taking many of these ancient songs out of relative obscurity and into the mainstream of public consciousness; something which will also be looked at further on. In addition to fixing the ballads of his ancestral Borderland permanently into the minds of the Scottish People, Scott was also able to create a place in the popular imagination for his beloved Border Minstrel, and the environment in which he had once flourished; through the narrative in his novels: as the following extract from *Guy Mannering*, in which he describes the skills of horsemanship common to the people of the Border Hill Country, shows:

"There is an odd prejudice in these hills in favour of riding. Every farmer rides well, and rides the whole day. Probably the extent of their large pasture farms, and the necessity of surveying them rapidly, first introduced this custom; or a very zealous antiquary might derive it from the times of the Lay of the Last Minstrel, when twenty thousand horsemen assembled at the light of the beacon fires....."

Despite the fact that the era to which Scott here aludes, that of the "times of the Lay of the Last Minstrel", was a pure fiction that he himself had made up, the real Border Minstrelsy having died out gradually following the introduction of the printing press, the assembly of "Moss Troopers" around the Border beacons is something that not only occurred, but which also had its origins in the time of Llywarch and the warriors of the "Gododdin"; when:

"Three hundred men hastened forth,
Wearing gold torques,

defending the land-
and there was slaughter.
Though they were slain
they slew,
And they shall be honoured till the end of the world;
and all of us kinsmen who went,
alas,
but for one man none escaped........"

The sole survivor of this great military disaster is none other than Aneirin, the poet, who, elsewhere in the text, is praised by the bard who in past times was to preserve this, the original composition that he himself had composed:

"Gododdin, I make my claim boldly on your behalf
in the presence of the throng in the court,
With the lay of the son of Dywai of high courage-
may it be manifest in the one place that it vanquishes.
Since the courteous one,
the rampart of battle,
was slain
since the earth covered Aneirin,
poetry and the men of Gododdin are now parted......."

In Scott's time gatherings such as this truly were a thing of the past, as were the minstrels who had taken centre stage at them. However, fragments of what the ancient bards had once sung had filtered down into the ballads that were by then an integral part of the culture of the Scottish peasantry of Sir Walter's ancestral borderlands; and it was the collection and preservation of these ballads which was, and is, as we shall see, perhaps the Laird of Abbotsford's greatest literary achievement.

As an example of what I mean, I now refer the reader to the ballad of "*Kempion*", which appears in the section of the *Minstrelsy* primarily concerned with a category of lyrics which Scott places under the collective title of *Romantic Ballads*. In his introductory notes to *Kempion*, Scott informs his readers that "from the names of the personages and the nature of the adventure" with which it is primarily concerned, the ballad can be seen "to have been an old metrical romance, degraded into a ballad by the lapse of time and the corruption of reciters...."

The story of *Kempion* involves the slaying of a great snake or worm, much like the legendary *Mankeeper*, concerning which, Sir Walter observes, there "are numerous traditions amongst the Borders." The opening verses of the ballad place the location of the action at the centre of the story as having occurred in the vicinity of "Estmere Crags"; which Sir Walter tells us are none other than "the rocky cliffs of Northumberland, in opposition to Westmoreland.....near Bamborough." Thus, he tells us, we can almost certainly identify the tale of *Kempion* with that of *The Laidley Worm of Spindleton*; another ballad "to which it bears a strong resemblance". In verse six of Scott's ballad, the hero, upon hearing of the existence of this mighty dragon, utters forth the following exclamation:

"Now by my sooth,......
This fiery beast, I'll gang and see."

To which his knightly companion, Segramour, responds as follows:

"And by my sooth,........
My ae brother, I'll gang wi' thee".

This verse, as we shall now see, shows a direct link between the ballad traditions that Scott collected and the Dark Age and Arthurian literature to which I have already compared the Laird of Abbotsford's poetry. Proof of this is provided by the fact that Kempion's brother, Segramour, is none other than the Arthurian knight Sir Sagramour; who features in the writings of Sir Thomas Malory. And, interestingly enough, Sir Sagramour is allegedly buried at St. Dogmaels, near Whitland, in Cardiganshire; South Wales. This in itself provides proof of a direct link between Wales and the Borders, a link to which Scott himself was to refer amongst the pages of his own voluminous writings, in the form of the ancient memorial stone, inscribed both in Latin and Celtic Ogham characters, that formerly stood at the resting place of this Dark Age British hero.

As has already been noted, there is a ballad "somewhat resembling *Kempion*, called *The Laidley Worm of Spendleston-haugh,* which, in Scott's time, was "very popular upon the Borders". Sir Walter's reasoning for excluding it from the *Minstrelsy* and printing *Kempion* instead, he justifies by saying that it has been "often published"; and its insertion is therefore unecessary. Unlike *Kempion* however, "the most common version was either entirely composed, or rewritten, by the Revd. Mr. Lamb of Norham".

Thus, in the case of this one ballad, we not only see a fine example of Scott's dedication to scholarship in his passing over of a popular, but inauthentic, ballad, in favour of a less well known, but original, one, but also how it was he who was principally responsible for preserving the continuous chain of bardic tradition for future generations. This is one of several ballads which we will be encountering during the course of our story, which prove, beyond questionable doubt, how the Border Minstrel Tradition gradually evolved out of the earlier Bardic traditions of the Dark Ages. We shall also see in the chapters that now follow, that, if it had not been for Sir Walter and his friends who assisted him in the fulfillment of these endeavours, some, if not all, of these traditions might have died out altogether.

In Scott's introduction to *Lord Soulis*, composed by his friend, and assistant in his editorship of the *Minstrelsy*, John Leyden, a renowned scholar and intellectual heavywieght, "in imitation of the Ancient Ballad", he tells us of how "the fame of Arthur and the Knights of the Round Table, always more illustrious among the Scottish Borderers, from their Welsh origin, than Fin Maccoul and Gow Macmorne, who seem not, however, to have been unknown, yielded gradually to the renown of Wallace, Bruce, Douglas, and other patriots, who so nobly asserted the liberty of their country. Beyond that period, numerous but obscure and varying legends refer to the marvellous Merlin, or Merrdin the Wild,and Michael Scott, both magicians of notorious fame......"

It is to these traditions, referred to here in another piece of writing, in which Scott demonstrates his own in-depth knowledge of the connections between the Ancient Welsh and Border Cultures, that we shall be turning our attention throughout this book. But first, we must examine Scott's relationship with his life-long friend and childhood companion, Adam Ferguson; a relationship which, as we shall see, was to determine the direction in which the Laird of Abbotsford's own literary career would ultimately progress. Before moving on, however, its worth noting, finally, that, as well as the parallels previously drawn between historical circumstances along the Border during the Heroic Golden Age of Border Minstrelsy, which, as we shall see in due course, reached its zenith during the fifteenth and sixteenth centuries, the incidents immortalized in Scott's *Lay of the Last Minstrel* above, which relate to the kidnap of a young Stuart Prince, are mirrored in certain definite respects, once again, by the traditions that have come down to us in connection with the boyhood of the Dark Age hero, Emrys; himself one of Arthur's own illustrious ancestors.

The Legend of Emrys likewise features in our story, as does the line of de Brus, whose most famous descendant, King Robert I, was himself sprung from one of the most prominent noble families of the Borders; the Bruces of Annandale. In view of this, it should come as no surprise that this great "hero" of Scottish independence should have been involved in an assassination not dissimilar to the one lamented by Llywarch in connection with the death of Urien of Rheged; which involved his own cold blooded murder of John "The Red" Cumin; himself the one time Regent of Scotland, in the Dominical Church of Dumfries; as a means of dispensing with his greatest competitor for the Scottish Crown.

Bruce's assistants in this heinous homicide were likewise two other prominent Border Barons, Kirkpatrick and de Lindsay, whose families were to suffer a terrible retribution for their crimes; in accordance with a contemporary prophecy, some fifty-two years later; when de Lindsay's son, James, murdered Kirkpatrick's successor for some unknown reason; "and was afterwards executed by order of King David II"; as Sir Walter informs us, yet again, in the pages of the *Minstrelsy*.

"The story of the murder" Scott then continues, "is thus told by the Prior of Lochlevin" in the poetical compositions of the Chronicler Wyntoun:

"That ilk yhere in our kynryk
Hoge was slayne of Kilpatrik
Be schyr Jakkis the Lyndessey
In-til Karlaveroc; and away
For til have bene with all his mycht
This Lyndyssay pressyt all a nycht
Forth on hors rycht fast rydand.
Nevyrtheless yhit thai hym fand
Nocht thre myle fra that ilk place:
Thare tane and broucht agane he was
Til Karlaveroc, be thai men
That frendis war till Kirkpatrick then;
There was he kepyd rycht straytly.
His wyf passyd till the King Dawy,
And prayid him of his realte,
Of Lauche that scho mycht serwyd be.
The King Dawy than also fast
Till Dumfres with his curt he past,

At Lawche wald. Quhat was thare mare?
This Lyndessay to deth he gert do thare."

As one would expect, in the pages of Scott's *Minstrelsy,* we find another composition, written, once again, "in imitation of the Ancient Ballad", which focusses on this terrible slaying. Entitled *The Murder of Caerlaveroc*, on account of the fact that the killing took place at Caerlavroc Castle, another of the numerous locations that we shall be visiting in the chapters that follow, this "modern" ballad is the work of Scott's friend and correspondent Charles Kirkpatrick Sharpe; another Borderer with Jacobite associations and a native of the very region- the Western Marches- where these events are known to have taken place.

In this way, Scott and his circle, Kirkpatrick Sharpe, Leyden, J.B.S. Morrit, and others, established themselves as the true modern successors of the Border Minstrels of the fifteenth and sixteenth centuries; through their own contemporary writings in the *Minstrelsy*; thus continuing this unbroken tradition into the modern era. But now, without further ado, we must turn our attention to another of Scott's circle, whose own contribution to the Laird of Abbotsford's literary development has never been fully appreciated by any of Sir Walter's biographers to date: The soldier, singer and tale teller, Adam Ferguson; Scott's *Merry Knight.*

Illustration 2): "Scott's image of the Border Minstrel": Nineteenth century engraving, taken from Adam and Charles Black's 1899 edition of "Castle Dangerous".

Chapter Two

From Kamtschatka to Huntley Burn

"One Monday mornin' when we set sail,
The wind did blow a heavy gale;
To fight the French it was our intent,
Through smoke and fire, through smoke and fire,
And it was a dark and gloomy night......"

Old English ballad.

In Sir Walter Scott's journal entry for March 19th 1827 we find the following reference:

"Set about my labours, but enter Captain John Ferguson from the Spanish Main, where he has been for three years. The honest tar sat about two hours, and I was heartily glad to see him again. I had a general sketch of his adventures which we will hear more in detail when we can meet at kail-time".

"Scott was generally in high spirits at dinner, though he ate little; " writes his biographer, the novelist, John Buchan. He "had no fixed seat at table but would drop into any place vacant. The company did not sit long when the cloth was drawn, but joined the ladies in the library or drawing-room, where about ten o'clock a light supper was served. Sometimes they danced reels, and on most evenings there was music, when Adam Ferguson would sing "Johnnie Cope" and Anne or Sophia" (Scott's two daughters) "Kenmure's on and awa".

Thus we are presented with the image of the Border Laird, at home in his baronial hall, listening to his family, and his loyal retainers- Adam Ferguson was the tenant of Scott's other Border property at Huntley Burn and the brother of his seafaring friend the "honest tar", recounting the heroic deeds of his Nation's historic past:

Amongst those fortunate enough to be a guest at such gatherings was my Grandfather's Grandfather, Robert Ferguson M.D. (1799-1865); Physician to H.M. Queen Victoria: The Great-Nephew of Adam Ferguson L.L.D. (1723-1816), the great philosopher, the friend of Hume, Gibbon and Adam Smith and the father of Sir Adam Ferguson, Scott's lifelong friend, Robert Ferguson M.D. owed his social position not only to Scott, but also to Queen Victoria's fascination with all things Scottish: A fascination which itself was to have its roots in the romance of the Waverley Novels.

As a boy, and as a young man, Robert made frequent visits to Scott's residence at Abbotsford, and wrote extensively of such visits in later life.

The "....real friend and much loved companion of Scott", my ancestor writes, whilst describing the Author's Circle, "was Sir Adam Ferguson.....his schoolfellow and playmate".

"Shrewd, joyous, a bon-vivant, an unrivalled observer, an unparalleled narrator, Scott always said that could Adam print his face with his stories he need not have written. Scott, himself abounding with every kind of anecdote, never spoke in Sir Adam's company but to draw him out. If he took a walk with you he could relate things which he observed and which you missed. He had every quality of a great dramatist. He seized on the essence of things. He was equally apt for fun or wit. He could make you roar or weep. His anecdotes were full of marrow, pith, sap of human nature. They were endless; for he had no repertory to be produced in driblets and for chosen occasions....."

"I have seen Sir Walter listening entranced as Adam Ferguson was describing some trait of battle he had witnessed by himself; and as the interest gathered he has jumped up from his chair and joined the imaginary host in the melee, clapping his hands and shouting and stamping about with prodigious vigour."

Elsewhere he tells us of how Adam Ferguson could "Somehow use" this "power of raising and fixing the imagination in man" to a similar degree with animals: "The excellent and quaint Lord Eldin (John Clerk) had a favourite jackdaw, which was permitted whenever there was company to come to dessert and walk up and down the table and pick for himself. Adam Ferguson volunteered to make him talk, and began instanter to utter certain sounds which very speedily withdrew the bird from his food, and produced from him a counterblast, to the exquisite delight and astonishment of the host, who shouted, "Eh Adam kens the Daw langige- he kens the Daw langige"; the colloquy continuing till the laughter of the guests silenced both actors. Sir Adam then gave us the substance of their talk, much after the fashion of those ancient ballads so common and so characteristic in Scotland- like "The Twa' Corbies".

This extract, from the writings of one of Scott's own intimates, serves to illustrate just to what extent Scott had managed, during the course of less than a generation, to etch these ballads into the public consciousness. Amongst the other numerous guests who likewise witnessed these musical entertainments was the American author Washington Irving, who writes of a conversation with the Laird of Abbotsford in which the latter "....went on to expatiate on the popular songs of Scotland. "They are part of our national inheritance", said he, "and something that we may truly call our own. They have no foreign taint; they have the pure breath of the heather and the mountain breeze. All the genuine legitimate races that have descended from the Ancient Britons, such as the Scotch, the Welsh and the Irish, have national airs. The English have none, because they are not natives of the soil, or, at least, are mongrels. Their music is all made up of foreign scraps, like a harlequin jacket, or a piece of mosaic. Even in Scotland we have comparatively few national songs in the eastern part, where we have had the most influx of strangers. A real old Scottish song is a cairn gorm- a gem of our own mountains; or rather, it is a precious relic of old times, that bears the national character stamped upon it; like a cameo that shows what the national visage was in former days before the breed was crossed." These last comments of Sir Walter's are of particular relevance with respect to those traditional ballads and airs collected by Robert Burns.

In view of their lyrical content then, it is perhaps thoroughly unsurprising that so many of the songs sung at Scott's fireside should still be popular today, both north and south of the Border: *Johnny Cope,* for example, which is concerned with the celebrated defeat of the Government Army under Sir John Cope at the Battle of Preston Pans in 1745, an engagement in which, as we have already seen, Scott's friend, Stewart of Invernahyle, is known to have taken an active role, was recorded in recent years by the late Ewan MacColl. Likewise, *The Twa' Corbies* has also been re-recorded, during the

Modern Folk Revival, by one of the many bands that he himself was to influence during the course of his own long and varied career. As we have also seen, both of these songs were themselves amongst those in Adam Ferguson's repertoire. Others are known to have included the celebrated *Laird of Cockpen;* and in Lockhart's biography of Sir Walter we catch many glimpses of Scott's *Merry Knight.*

Captain, later Admiral, John Macpherson Ferguson, Scott's "honest tar", was Sir Adam Ferguson's younger brother. At twelve, he had gone to sea, enlisting as a "first class volunteer" aboard the Caesar. In 1801 he was involved in the Battle of Copenhagen, aboard the Victory. Scott's authorized biographer, Lockhart, refers to him as being "a favourite lieutenant of Lord Nelson", and in O'Byrne's *Dictionary of Naval Biography* we find numerous references to him bearing "a conspicuous part in a multitude of very dashing exploits".

About the time that his brother joined the ship's company of the Victory, Adam first enlisted in the Army; in the 58th Regiment. Previous to this, like Sir Walter, who likewise would have followed the drum, if it had not been for the already mentioned childhood sickness that left him lame for the rest of his life, he had served in the ranks of the Edinburgh Volunteers. This fact is worth mentioning, in view of the overall bardic theme of this work, for, amongst the contemporary compositions that also found their way into the pages of Scott's *Minstrelsy,* was the author's own *War-Song of the Royal Edinburgh Dragoons:*

"To horse! To horse! The standard flies,
The bugles sound the call;
The Gallic navy stems the seas,
The voice of battle's on the breeze,
Arouse ye one and all!

"From high Dunedin's towers we come,
A band of brothers true;
Our casques the leopard's spoils surround,
With Scotland's hardy thistle crown'd;
We boast the red and blue......"

Scott's lyrics, with their references to *Dunedin*, the Caer Eidyn of Aneirin's *Gododdin*, at once remind us of the Dark Age poetical epics of North Britain;

which we looked at in the last chapter. The inclusion of *The War Song,* together with several other contemporary compositions "in imitation of the ancient ballad", confirms the compiler of the *Minstrelsy* as the true successor, as has previously been suggested, of the ancient bards and minstrels of the Dark and High Middle Ages. For, in addition to preserving the traditional songs of his forefathers, it was always the preserve of the *Sovereign Bard,* the King's own personal songsmith, to compose his own verses in the ancestral heroic metre of his forebears.

And this, as we shall see, is precisely what Scott can be shown to have done, not only with his *War Song of the Royal Edinburgh Dragoons,* but also with many of his other lyrical compositions. In view of this, it is also highly appropriate that, in his notes to the version of the *War Song* that were eventually to appear in the expanded edition of the *Minstrelsy* edited by Henderson, Scott tells the reader of how these lyrics were "written during the apprehension of an invasion"; before quoting from the celebrated speech of the Ancient Caledonian Chieftain, Galgacus, leader of the confederation of tribes that fought the invading Romans, under Julius Agricola, during the First Century A.D.:

"On then, into action; and as you go, think of those that went before you and those that shall follow".

Amongst the other modern compositions included in the pages of Scott's *Minstrelsy* is *The Curse of Moy* by J.S.B. Morrit; which is described by its editor as "a Highland Tale". Its story, Scott informs his readers in his notes, "is founded on an ancient Highland tradition that originated in a feud between the Clans of Chattan and Grant". Consisting of some forty-nine verses, this poem is perhaps one of the influences that Scott absorbed at this time which were to have a bearing on his own later composition of *The Lady of the Lake;* a poem which will figure in the biographical notes that now follow in relation to Scott's lifelong friend Adam, later Sir Adam, Ferguson.

At this point we must turn our attention to some of Scott's extensive correspondence with his old school friend, whilst the latter was serving as an officer in Wellington's Army during the Peninsular War. During the course of the above exchange, which concerns the lyrical content of some of Scott's earlier narrative poems, these self same bardic themes feature throughout; as does the Laird of Abbotsford's constant use of the heroic metre; as a means of exhorting his fellow countrymen to carry out heroic acts in defence of their country; just as Llywarch (ie. Lyulph), Aneirin and Galgacus had done before.

As has already been seen, Adam Ferguson first obtained a commission in the British Army at about the time his brother joined the Navy. And, following various "chances and changes", as Lockhart puts it, he was eventually to rise to the rank of captain. In a letter to Scott from St. Heliers, Jersey, dated 4th March 1807, he writes of how he is "......every day more and more convinced that the military profession was my predestined one......Whether I shall live to arrive at the rank of Field-Officer time must show. Failing this consummation of all military happiness, and though the worst might come to the worst- that I be left adrift a half-pay captain- I think, with a very little farm on the banks of the Tweed between Peebles and Selkirk......I could pass my time very much to my liking....." As we shall see shortly, Adam's aspirations in this direction would one day be fulfilled, a matter, which, as will also be noted in due course, is of some considerable significance in relation to our story. [1]. (See notes to chapters.)

In 1808 he joined the 101st Regiment. When we hear of him again he is writing to Sir Walter from Lisbon; the date at the top of the letter being 31st August 1811. Previous to this he had taken part in Wellington's defence of Portugal, which had involved the construction of the Lines of Torres Vedras, a network of palisades and fascines centred upon the three strategic points of Torres Vedras, Sobral and Lisbon:

"I was so fortunate to get a reading of *The Lady of the Lake,* when in the Lines of Torres Vedras", he writes to Sir Walter, "and thought I had no inconsiderable right to enter into and judge of its beauties, having made one of the party on your first visit to the Trosachs. While the book was in my possession I had nightly invitations to evening parties, and, I must say, though not conscious of much merit in the way of recitation, my attempts to do justice to the grand opening of the stag hunt were always followed by bursts of applause, for this canto was the favourite amongst the rough sons of the fighting 3rd Division. At that time supplies were scanty, and in gratitude I am bound to declare that to the good offices of "the Lady", I owed many a nice slice of ham and rummer of hot punch."

Sir Adam's commanding officer through probably the most significant part of his campaigning in Spain was Sir Edward Packenham, brother-in-law of the Iron Duke and ancestor of Lady Elizabeth Longford; whose biography,

Wellington: The Years of the Sword, first published in 1969, is still a landmark publication in the field of Napoleonic history, more than thirty years after its first appearance in print. After distinguishing itself under Picton at Bussaco, and fighting at El Bodon, Ciudad Rodrigo and Badajoz, the 3rd Division was to take part in the most significant action of the Campaign at the Battle of Salamanca; where, at 5p.m. on the afternoon of 22nd July 1812, their commander was to be responsible for initiating "Wellington's master stroke"; in the words of his latter day descendant:

"At the end of the attack begun by Packenham, two French divisions were irreparably broken and a third (Brennier's) disabled; indeed, over a quarter of Marmont's army was defeated. It was this action which inspired a Frenchman to say that "at Salamanca Wellington beat 40,000 men in forty minutes."

Another of Scott's poetical works which was highly popular amongst Adam's comrades in the Duke of Wellington's army was *The Vision of Don Roderick*, a copy of which he was to receive as a gift from his old school friend. In another letter, in which he writes to thank the Laird of Abbotsford for this much appreciated present, we hear of how he was particularly delighted by "the stanzas announcing the approach of the British fleets and armies". He then continues by assuring his correspondent "that the Pats are to a man enchanted with the picture drawn of their countrymen and of the great man himself. Your swearing in the true character of a minstrel, "shiver my harp and burst its every chord" amused me not a little. Should it be my fate to survive,.." he then adds, "I am resolved to try my hand on a snug little farm either up or down the Tweed, somewhere in your neighbourhood, and on this dream many a delightful castle do I build...."

Again, Sir Adam writes to Scott of his desire to take up the profession of Border Farmer, and again we are given another glimpse of Scott as the successor to Llywarch and Aneirin: For, once again, in the lyrics of *The Vision*, the poet exhorts his readers to take up arms against their enemy, the French.

"And O! Loved warriors of the Minstrel's land!
Yonder your bonnets nod, your tartans wave;
The rugged form may mark the mountain band,
And harsher features, and a mien more grave;
But ne'er in battle-field throbbed heart so brave
As that which beats beneath the Scottish plaid,

And when the pibroch bids the battle rave,
And level for the charge your arms are laid,
Where lives the desperate foe, that for such onset stayed!
"Hark! From yon stately ranks what laughter rings,
 Mingling wild mirth with war's stern Minstrelsy,
His jest while each blithe comrade round him flings,
 And moves to death with military glee:
Boast, Erin, boast them! tameless, frank, and free,
 In kindness warm, and fierce in danger known,
Rough Nature's children, humorous as she:
 And He, yon Chieftain- strike the proudest tone
Of they bold harp, green Isle!- the Hero is thine own."

Unfortunately for Adam, like so many of Erin's "Pats" to whom he here refers, he would be taken prisoner during "the Hero", Wellington's, retreat from Burgos in 1812. On his release in 1814, with Napoleon safely exiled on the Island of Elba, he would return to his native Scotland, where he was to take up residence in 1817; together with his three beloved sisters, at the mansion house of Toftfields; which they renamed Huntley Burn, as tenants of the Laird of Abbotsford. His dream of settling down as a Border Farmer had finally come true.

Now, having established his one time schoolfriend in the vicinity of his own palatial residence, Scott set about gleaning from Sir Adam every morcel of information relating to every possible aspect of his previous military experiences and incorporating them into the pages of his novels. Once again, his endeavours in this direction could be said to be in line with the circumstances under which many of his predecessors, who had likewise expounded the Heroic Bardic Tradition in previous centuries, had gone about their work when composing verse or telling stories which related to the heroic exploits of the martial icons of their own Nation's immediate, and distant, historical past.

Perhaps one of the greatest heroic poets that Scotland has every produced was the celebrated *Blin' Harry the Minstrel,* the late fifteenth century people's bard, so called, owing to his having been blind, who came to excel as the author of his great poetical biography of the Mediaeval Scottish rebel William Wallace. In many respects, this Scottish Homer, whose own Classical Greek counterpart was likewise unsighted, was the forerunner of Sir Walter in every respect; particularly when one considers the manner in which both Scott's writings and Blin' Harry's poetry were to capture the popular imagination. Indeed, the imagery borrowed from Scott and so cleverly utilized by Mel Gibson in his production of *Braveheart,* has its own antecedents in the original re-telling of the first great Scottish struggle for independence from England; composed by Blin' Harry around about the year 1460.

As we have already seen, the Laird of Abbotsford would himself have undoubtedly joined the army had it not been for a childhood illness, which, although certainly less debilitating in many respects than the blindness which was to afflict the author of *Wallace,* was to prevent him from enjoying the military career he is believed to have so greatly desired by his contemporary descendant, Dame Jean Maxwell-Scott. So, like the Blind Minstrel, Scott was forced to content himself with listening to his friends recount their own experiences of warfare at his dinner table or his fireside; and using them for the model upon which to base his own historical fictions; much like the manner in which Blin' Harry was to take the oral traditions of his own time, in particular those relating to the exploits of William Wallace, and turn them into heroic poetry of his own composition.

Lady Elizabeth Longford notes the extensive experience of seige warfare gained by the veterans of Wellington's 3rd Division during the Peninsular War in her biography of the Iron Duke. And, in view of this, it is perhaps hardly surprising that, amongst the pages of chapter twenty five of Sir Walter's *Old Mortality,* itself one of his most celebrated Border Novels, set in the time of James Grahame of Claverhouse, Viscount Dundee, we find one of the best descriptions of seige warfare, as it would have been conducted during the era of muzzle loading firearms, to have appeared in print in any work of fiction during the entire history of British literature.

As for the novel itself, which was to appear in print as the first work in a series of volumes entitled *Tales of my Landlord,* in a letter dated 22nd November 1816, Scott writes to his friend Morritt as follows:

".......But to descend from Shakespeare, his bust and cabinet, to matters of humbler import, you will receive in a day or two the *Tales of my Landlord.* The last is, I think, the best I have been able to execute, although written by snatches and at intervals......"

Some months earlier, in another letter dated 12th March 1816, this time to Adam Ferguson, Scott first makes the suggestion that the latter settle close to his own residence in the Borders; at the previously mentioned mansion house of Toftfields:

".....Now you and your sisters might comfortably inhabit this mansion during summer, and it would be admirable shooting quarters, near enough to us and others to be quite sociable, and distant enough to be perfectly independent. This is a plan for future consideration, but it affords us a prospect of laying our auld grey prows together, as we used to do our young rattlepates."

We shall be looking at this particular sequence of correspondence with respect to another point of relevance at a later stage in our story. In the meantime, it is important to note that, as we have already seen, it is most likely that, as a direct result of this social interaction, Sir Adam's own previous military experiences, and the latter's recounting of them at Scott's dinner table and fireside, some of Sir Walter's most spellbinding literary portrayals of fictional military engagements came into being; a fact attested to in the writings of my own ancestor; Robert Ferguson M.D.

Just a few weeks previously, on 22nd February 1816, Adam had suffered a grave tragedy when his Father, Professor Adam Ferguson (1723-1816), had passed from this world into the next. The death of this old gentleman had marked the end of an era, for whilst he had lived he was, during the last years of his life, the sole survivor of a circle of intellectuals that had included the philosopher David Hume, the economist Adam Smith, William Robertson the historian, Joseph Black the scientist, John Home the playwrite, Hugh Blair the Divine and Allan Ramsay the painter; himself the son of the poet and balladeer who was to influence Scott.

Old Professor Ferguson lived in a house on the outskirts of the City, in an area so remote that it was to become known as "Kamtschatka" to his friends, after the region in Siberia. And, it was under the roof of this, his school playmate's abode, that the young Walter Scott was to meet the poet Robert Burns, the hero who he idolized, in the winter of 1786/7: "As for Burns", he would later write, "I was a lad of fifteen in 1786/7, when he first came to Edinburgh, but had sense and feeling enough to be much interested in his poetry, and would have given the world to know him; but I had very little acquaintance with any literary people, and still less with the gentry of the west country, the two sets that he most frequented. Mr. Thomas Grierson was at that time a clerk of my father's. He knew Burns, and promised to ask him to his lodgings to dinner, but had no opportunity to keep his word, otherwise I might have seen more of this distinguished man. As it was, I saw him one day at the late venerable Professor Ferguson's where there were several men of literary reputation, among whom I remember the celebrated Mr. Dugald Stewart. Of course we youngsters sate silent, looked and listened. The only thing I remember which was remarkable in Burns' manner, was the effect produced upon him by a print of Bunbury's, representing a soldier lying dead on the snow, his dog sitting in misery on the one side, on the other his widow, with a child in her arms. These lines were written beneath,-

> "Cold on Canadian hills, on Minden's plain,
> Perhaps that parent wept her soldier slain;
> Bent o'er her babe, her eye disolved in dew,
> The big drops, mingling with the milk he drew,
> Gave the sad presage of his future years,
> The child of misery baptized in tears."

Burns seemed much affected by the print, or rather the ideas which it suggested in his mind. He actually shed tears. He asked whose lines they were, and it chanced that nobody but myself remembered that they occur in a half forgotten poem of Langhorne's called by the un-promising title of *The Justice of the Peace*. I whispered my information to a friend present, who mentioned it to Burns, who rewarded me with a look and a word, which, though of mere civility, I then received, and still recollect with very great pleasure.

"His person was strong and robust: his manners rustic, not clownish; a sort of dignified plainess and simplicity, which received part of its effects perhaps from one's knowledge of his extraordinary talents. His features are represented in Mr. Nasmyth's picture, but to me it conveys the idea that they are diminished as if seen in perspective. I think his countenance was more massive than it looks in any of the portraits. I would have taken the poet, had I not known what he was, for a very sagacious country farmer of the old Scotch school- ie. none of your modern agriculturalists, who keep labourers for their drudgery, but the douce gudeman who held his own plough. There was a strong expression of sense and shrewdness in all his lineaments; the eye alone, I think, indicated the poetical character and temperament. It was large, and of a dark cast, and glowed (I say literally glowed) when he spoke with feeling or interest. I never saw such another eye in a human head,

Illustration 7): Contemporary engraving, by Finden, of Abbotsford Hall during the time of Scott's actual residence there.

though I have seen the most distinguished men in my time. His conversation expressed perfect self-confidence, without the slightest presumption. Among the men who were the most learned of their time and country, he expressed himself with perfect firmness, but without the least intrusive forwardness; and when he differed in opinion, he did not hesitate to express it firmly, yet at the same time with modesty. I do not remember any part of his conversation distinctly enough to be quoted, nor did I ever see him again, except in the street, where he did not recognize me, as I could not expect he should. He was much caressed in Edinburgh, but (considering what literary emoluments have been since his day) the efforts made for his relief were extremely trifling.

"I remember on this occasion I mention, I thought Burns' acquaintance with English poetry was rather limited, and also, that having twenty times the abilities of Allan Ramsay and of Ferguson, he talked of them with too much humility as his models; there was doubtless national predeliction in his estimate."

"I need not remark on the extent of knowledge", continues Scott's biographer, Lockhart, "and justness of taste, exemplified in his early measurement of Burns, both as a student of English literature and as a Scottish poet. The print over which Scott saw Burns shed tears is still in the possession of Dr. Ferguson's family, and I had often heard him tell the story, in the room where the precious relic hangs, before I requested him to set it down in writing...."

And so it was that the Laird of Abbotsford encountered Burns, on the first and last time that they were ever to meet. Burns was to exert a considerable influence upon Scott, and, as we shall see, in a future chapter, was himself, like the Ragged Lion, a successor to the ancient bards of old in the true sense of the word. As we have seen during the course of the last chapter, it was the role of the ancient bards not only to preserve the ancient poetical compositions and songs of their ancestors, but also to compose similar lyrics of their own.

Often these lyrics, in the case of the songs that were sung at least, would consist of new verses composed to old traditional tunes. This is one of the key elements in Burns's own work as a songsmith. Of the countless examples of words that Burns composed to traditional airs the best known include *Ye Banks and Braes,* which he wrote to the tune of an old air called *The Caledonian Hunt's Delight; My Love is like a Red, Red Rose,* which is only

Illustration 5): Zeitter's engraving of the famous Nasmyth portrait of Robert
Burns referred to in Scott's own autobiographical fragments.

partly of his composition, whilst the air is a modernized version *of Low Down in the Broom*; and perhaps his most famous set of lyrics, apart from *Auld Lang Syne, Scots, Wha Hae;* which are composed to an old air called *Hey Tuttie Tattie*.

In addition to this, Burns, like Scott, was a collector of ballads; amongst the most famous of the fine examples of the traditional Scottish ballad that he collected being *Macpherson's Rant*. The song, which tells the story of a latter day Robin Hood, who was captured at Keith Market and executed at the Cross at Banff in 1700, was itself as popular amongst the ranks of the Duke of Wellington's Highland troops as Sir Walter's own poetry. Another of the songs which Burns was also to collect, this time whilst among the same Border peasants who Scott himself was to obtain so many ballads from in later years, was the immortal *Tam Lin*. One of the most famous and important Border Ballads, the earliest printed edition, which appears in the 1792 volume of Johnson's *Musical Museum*, was itself collected by the famous Alloway poet.

Entire chapters in this book are devoted to Burns, and to the song to which I have just referred. In the meantime, it is sufficient to add that, like Burns, Scott was likewise to indulge in the composition of numerous modern lyrics to ancient tunes, as well as reworking old traditional songs that had been partially forgotten by the communities from which he had collected them. An example of the last category are the very fine verses that he added to the ballad *Jock O' Hazledean*; whilst under the impression that all but the first verse had been irrecoverably lost. Another set of lyrics that he was to compose to a traditional air were those of *Bonnie Dundee*, himself one of the principal characters in the novel *Old Mortality:*

> *"To the Lords of Convention 'twas Claverhouse spoke,*
> *'ere the King's Crown go down there are crowns to be broke,*
> *So each cavalier that loves honour and me,*
> *Let him follow the bonnets o' bonnie Dundee......"*

As we saw in the introduction, Scott's own Jacobite predecessor, "Beardie", was himself a follower of Dundee, so it is worth making a short digression here, just as a means of illustrating just how important an icon he was in the Laird of Abbotsford's historical hall of fame. In A.N. Wilson's masterly biography of Scott, *The Laird of Abbotsford,* which, quite rightly, John Carey of the Sunday Times describes as a work in which the writer "traces the man

Illustration 4): J.B. Lane's engraving, after Sir Henry Raeburn, of Professor Adam Ferguson, 1723-1816, whose own circle of intimates, who were to include John Home, the celebrated "Author of Douglas", were to exert a formative influence upon the young Sir Walter Scott.

in the works with a novelist's insight", the author quotes Lockhart's account of Joseph Train's visit to Scott's Edinburgh house, as a means of indicating the significance of Dundee in the author's great intellect; his campaigns having formed the backdrop for some of the most celebrated lyrics contained in the Border Minstrelsy:

"He found him at work in his library, and surveyed with enthusiastic curiousity the furniture of the room, especially the only picture, a portrait of Graham of Claverhouse. Train expressed the surprise with which everyone who had known Dundee only in the pages of the Presbyterian Annalists, must see for the first time that beautiful and melancholy visage, worthy of the most pathetic dreams of romance. Scott replied, "that no character had been so foully traduced as the Viscount Dundee- that thanks to Woodrow, Cruickshanks, and such chroniclers, he, who was every inch a soldier and a gentleman still passed among the Scottish vulgar for a ruffian desperado, who rode a goblin horse, was proof against shot, and in league with the Devil."

One is here reminded of Scott's own description of one of the Lairds of Ellangowan in another of his celebrated Border novels, *Guy Mannering*, who had "joined Clavers at Killie-Krankie. At the skirmish of Dunkeld..." Scott continues, "he was shot dead by a Cameronian with a silver button (being supposed to have proof from the Evil One against lead and steel), and his grave is still called the "Wicked Laird's Lair".

In addition to composing lyrics in honour of Bonnie Dundee, Scott would also write similar verses dedicated to his close friends, like the following lines written in honour of Sir Adam Ferguson; to be sung to the tune of the Jacobite air *Come ower the Sea, Charlie.*

"Come ower the Tweed, Adam,
    Dear Adam, Sir Adam,
Come ower the Tweed, Adam,
    And dine with us all.
We'll welcome you truly,
    And stuff you most duly,
With broth, greens and bouille
    In Abbotsford Hall,
    Come ower the Tweed Adam."

Illustration 3): "The Merry Knight", 1930s photographic facsimile of W. Nicholson R.A.'s portrait of Sir Adam Ferguson taken from Symington's "Unpublished Letters of Sir Walter Scott", 1932.

In view of the pair's closeness, and in view of the fact that Adam's Father had played a principal part in making possible Scott's single lifetime encounter with Burns, it is perhaps unsurprising that "When Walter Scott determined", as my ancestor writes, "to settle on the borderland, the scene of all his studies which formed his mind, he persuaded his old schoolfellow and friend, Sir Adam Ferguson, to become his tenant of a small farm house refitted, just under the Eildon Hills, and amid the traditions of Thomas the Rhymer.

"The tenants of Huntley Burn, as the estate is called, were three brothers, batchelors, and three maiden sisters, all in middle age, and all of very salient characteristics of mind and person. The three brothers had all embraced the military profession, had therefore seen much. They had been separated from each other almost from early youth, and when they at last met they were new to each other in every respect, save in a strong family attachment. Sir Adam had served in the Peninsular and had there been made prisoner and sent to France. Colonel Ferguson had gained his honours and a moderate competency in India; and Admiral Ferguson, who had served under Nelson, remained afloat almost without intermission during the Napoleonic Wars.

"Each of these men was 6 feet and upwards, bony, spare, and powerful. Each had his own peculiarity. The Admiral, who was really a handsome man, encouraged the bluntness of expression and the demeanour of a sailor of that day, but united it with a deep religious feeling. The Colonel was the most imperturbable being I ever knew. He was cheerful under every possible infliction or affliction; not from indifference, but apparently from constitution. He had been hit in battle, and kept whistling and fighting till he fainted......"

"Sir Walter Scott, who got hints from every thing and person, obtained from him much that he valued and used in his description of Indian scenes; just as he based the nautical part of the *Pirate* from information extracted from the Admiral. The Colonel, however, had the advantage over his younger brother of being a most graphic penman."

On September 16th, 1827, Sir Walter was to make the following entry in his *Journal*: "The Ladies went to Church; I, God forgive me, finished the *Chronicles* (of the Canongate) (2: See notes to chapters) with a good deal of assistance from Colonel Ferguson's notes about Indian affairs. The patch is, I suspect, too glaring to be pleasing; but the Colonel's sketches are capitally good....."

Illustration 8): Worthington's 1827 engraving of Wilkie's genre painting of Scott and his family in the garb of "South Country Peasants."

Amongst the numerous Indian anecdotes to be found nestling amongst the pages of the Waverley novels is the following reference, which appears once again in the pages of *Guy Mannering,* and which refers to the participation in a hunt of one Captain Brown, who we encountered earlier, in the first chapter:

"Once the fox, thus persecuted from one stronghold to another, was at length obliged to abandon his valley, and to break-away for a more distant retreat, those who watched his motions from the top slipped their greyhounds, which excelling the fox in swiftness, and equalling him in ferocity and spirit, soon brought the plunderer to his life's end.

"In this way, without any attention to the ordinary rules and decorums of sport, but apparently as much to the gratification both of bipeds and quadrupeds as if all had been followed, four foxes were killed on this active morning; and even Brown himself, though he had seen the princely sports of India, and ridden a-tiger-hunting upon an elephant with the Nabob of Arcot, professed to have received a day's excellent amusement....."

Amongst Colonel James and Sir Adam's own circle of friends was Sir John Macpherson, former Governor General of India; and himself amongst Scott's own very numerous correspondents (see J. Alexander Symington, *Some Unpublished Letters of Sir Walter Scott*, Basil Blackwell, Oxford, 1932. pp.98). Macpherson himself, like the fictitious Captain, had actually hunted tigers with the Nabob of Arcot, a fact which serves to illustrate still further the extent to which Scott relied upon the testimony of those who had lived, travelled and indeed fought, in those far flung corners of the Empire, about which he had only read in books, when compiling the numerous volumes of his Waverley Novels.

In addition to becoming the Skipper's godfather, hence the "honest tar's" full name of John Macpherson Ferguson, the former Governor General was also the guardian of the teenage Robert Ferguson M.D.; himself the author of the above quoted description of the tenants of Huntley Burn; as previously noted in the opening paragraphs of this chapter. Amongst the young Robert Ferguson's other intimates was the American writer Washington Irving, whose *Abbotsford and Newstead Abbey* (published Henry J. Bohn, London, 1850), has already been quoted above in connection with traditional Scottish airs. Like Irving's other friend, Sir David Wilkie, who painted Scott and his Family, together with Sir Adam, in his celebrated oil sketch, "The Abbotsford Family", which now hangs in the National Gallery of Scotland, Irving himself was amongst Scott's numerous visitors to Abbotsford.

Amongst the pages of Irving's *Abbotsford and Newstead* we also find the author describing Scott's attachment to Scottish popular songs, in the context of his previously mentioned Jacobite sympathies: "These songs", wrote Irving, "were much relished by Scott, notwithstanding his loyalty; for the unfortunate "Chevalier" has always been a hero of romance with him, as he has with many staunch adherents of the House of Hanover, now that the Stuart line has lost all its terrors......"

Irving was amongst those fortunate enough to witness the regular musical entertainments that took place at Abbotsford and which I have also previously described in this chapter. And, in addition to this, and whilst visiting Abbotsford in August 1817, shortly before the arrival there of his friend Wilkie, the American traveller was given a tour of the surrounding countryside by its celebrated Laird. During the course of this tour, Scott was to point out, "at a distance, the Eildon Stone. There in ancient days," Irving was to continue, "stood the Eildon Tree, beneath which Thomas the Rhymer, according to popular tradition, dealt forth his prophecies, some of which still exist in antiquated ballads."

And, it is to the antiquated ballads to which Irving here refers that we must now turn our attention, for the central character at the hub of this last mentioned bardic cycle is himself in all probability the greatest Border Minstrel who ever existed: The legendary singer, songsmith, prophet and mystic, Thomas of Erceldoune.

Chapter Three

True Thomas Sat on Huntlie Bank........

"I was at Ertheldoun
with Thomas spak y thare
there herd y rede in roune
who Tristrem gat and bare
who was King with croun
who him fostered thare......."

Fourteenth Century Metrical Romance

In his introduction to the *Ancient Ballad of Thomas the Rhymer* in the *Minstrelsy of the Scottish Border,* Scott describes the mediaeval master poet Thomas of Ercildoune by informing his readers of how "Few personages are so renowned in tradition as Thomas of Ercildoune, known by the appellation of "The Rhymer". Uniting, or supposed to unite, in his person the powers of poetical composition and of vaticination, his memory, even after the lapse of five hundred years, is regarded with veneration by his countrymen......"

It is perhaps for this reason then that many years previous to the appearance of *Waverley*, and "while yet unknown as a poet", Scott "had commenced a prose tale upon the legendary story of Thomas the Rhymer....." [1]. Scott himself describes his original intention with regard to the above composition as being one in which he had "nourished the ambitious desire of composing a tale of chivalry, which was to be in the style of *The Castle of Otranto,* with plenty of Border characters, and supernatural incident", in the 1829 introduction to that year's edition of *Waverley*; previously quoted in an earlier chapter. In an appendix to the same introduction an old fragment of this attempted romance is also presented, and in it, in embryonic form, we find many of the key elements that were to resurface in Scott's later novels.

The historical backdrop upon which the writer sets the scene is that of the High Middle Ages, and the fragment begins with the arrival of an English knight in a Border village that has just been ravaged by his fellow countrymen- much to the consternation of the local inhabitants. Again, Scott can be seen, even at this early stage in the development of his prose style, to be looking towards writing for an English audience. This romance, "which was to have been entitled Thomas the Rhymer", never got beyond the first chapter. However, in the same appendix in which the fragment of his unfinished novel appears, Scott informs his readership of how, although "No more of the proposed tale was ever written;" the "author's purpose was that it should turn upon a fine legend of superstition, which is current in the part of the Borders where he had his residence; where, in the reign of Alexander III of Scotland, that renowned person Thomas of Hersildoune, called the Rhymer, actually flourished. This personage, the Merlin of Scotland, and to whom some of the adventures which the British bards assigned to Merlin Caledonius, or the Wild, have been transferred by tradition, was, as is well known, a magician, as well as a poet and prophet. He is alleged still to live in the land of Faery, and is expected to return at some great convulsion of society, in which he is to act a distinguished part- a tradition common to all nations, as the belief of the Mahomedans respecting their twelfth Imaum demonstrates....."

The reason why this fragment and the attached notes are so important is because they hold the keys to Scott's most singular obsession: The roots of his beloved Border Ballads in the Ancient British Bardic Tradition of old. As we see here, Scott compares Thomas of Ercildoune to the mytho-historical character Merlin the Magician; and it is therefore significant that both Scott and Thomas were the successors of the ancient tradition to which Merlin himself was the heir; a tradition that can be traced back to the Pre-Christian inhabitants of the region where both Scott and Thomas were later to reside; and which in turn can be shown to be firmly founded upon ancient Druidic beliefs.

In order to understand just to what degree Scott was obsessed with Thomas the Rhymer I must draw the reader's attention, once again, to the writings of Washington Irving, whose *Abbotsford and Newstead* I quoted at the end of the preceeding chapter: "Late in the evening of 29th August 1817", Irving writes, "I arrived at the ancient little border town of Selkirk, where I put up for the night. I had come down from Edinburgh, partly to visit Melrose Abbey and its vicinity, but chiefly to get a sight of the "Mighty Minstrel of

70

the North." I had a letter of introduction to him from Thomas Campbell the poet, and had reason to think, from the interest he had taken in some of my earlier scribblings, that a visit from me would not be deemed an intrusion."

During the course of his visit to Abbotsford Irving was to be given a tour of the surrounding countryside by its Laird, as we have also seen during the course of the previous chapter. And, after being shown the site of the celebrated Eildon Tree, under which True Thomas is said to have uttered his famous prophecies, the pair "turned up a little glen, with a small burn or brook whimpering and dashing along it, making an occasional waterfall, and overhung in some places with mountain-ash and weeping-birch. "We are now", said Scott, "treading classic, or rather fairy ground. This is the haunted glen of Thomas the Rhymer, where he met with the queen of fairy land, and this is the bogle burn, or goblin brook, along which she rode on her dapple grey palfrey, with silver bells ringing at the bridle."

"Here", said he, pausing, "is Huntley Bank, on which Thomas the Rhymer lay musing and sleeping when he saw, or dreamt he saw, the queen of Elfland:-

> *"True Thomas lay on Huntlie Bank;*
> *A ferlie he spied wi' his e'e;*
> *And there he saw a ladye bright,*
> *Come riding down by Eildon Tree.*
>
> *Her skirt was of the grass green silk,*
> *Her mantle o' the velvet fyne;*
> *At ilka tett of her horse's mane*
> *Hung fifty siller bells and nine......."*

Here Scott repeated several of the stanzas, and recounted the circumstance of Thomas the Rhymer's interview with the fairy, and his being transported by her to fairy land:-

> *"And 'til seven years were gone and past,*
> *True Thomas on earth was never seen".*

"It is a fine old story" said he, "and might be wrought up into a capital tale".

"Scott continued on, leading the way as usual, and limping up the Wizard Glen, talking as he went, but as his back was toward me I could only hear the deep growling tones of his voice, like the low breathing of an organ, without distinguishing the words, until pausing, and turning his face towards me I found he was reciting some scrap of Border Minstrelsy about Thomas the Rhymer. This was continually the case in my ramblings with him about his storied neighbourhood. His mind was fraught with the traditionary fictions connected with every object around him, and he would breathe it forth as he went, apparently as much for his own gratification as for that of his companion.

> "*Not hill, nor brook, we paced along,*
> *But had its legend or its song.*"

"His voice was deep and sonorous, he spoke with a Scottish accent, and with somewhat of the Northumbrian "burr" which, to my mind, gave a doric strength and simplicity to his elocution. His recitation of poetry was, at times, magnificent."

Thus Irving gives us a description of Scott as the true bardic shaman; at one with the landscape and the traditions of its people; just as Merlin and the Rhymer had been before him. As we shall see in a later chapter, the Ancient Bardic Tradition of old was not only concerned with recounting the heroic deeds of Princes and Kings. It was also concerned with both landscape and environment; for its true origin can not only be traced back as far as Druidic times, but to the prehistoric shamanistic world of animism and the worship of nature spirits. This will be looked at again in detail further on, in the meantime, let us return once again to Washington Irving's description of The *Wizard of the North;* and his ancient ancestral locality: We now join them in the vicinity of Sandyknowe, the location of Scott's Grandfather's Border farm, to which he had been sent in early childhood when afflicted with the aforementioned illness that was to leave him lame for life.

"Not far from Sandy Knowe, Scott pointed out another old border stronghold standing on the summit of a hill, which had been a kind of enchanted castle to him in his boyhood. It was the tower of Bemerside, the baronial residence of the Haigs, or de Hagas, one of the oldest families of the Border. "There had seemed to me", he said, "almost a Wizard spell hanging over it, in consequence of the prophecy of Thomas the Rhymer, in which, in his young days, he most potently believed:

"Betide, betide, whate'er betide,
Haig shall be Haig of Bemerside".

"Scott added some particulars which showed that, in the present instance, the venerable Thomas had not proved a false prophet, for it was noted that, amid all the changes and chances of the Border, through all the feuds and forays and sackings, and burnings, which had reduced most of the castles to ruins, and the proud families that once possessed them to poverty, the tower of Bemerside still remained unscathed, and was still of the ancient family of Haig.

"Prophecies however often insure their own fulfillment. It is very probable that the prediction of Thomas the Rhymer has linked the Haigs to their tower as their rock of safety, and has induced them to cling to it, almost superstitiously, through hardships and inconveniences that would, otherwise, have caused its abandonment."

Scott's obsession with the haunts of Thomas of Ercildoune was one of the primary motivations at the root of his purchase of huge tracts of land in the vicinity of Huntley Bank and the Eildon Hills; a venture which would eventually contribute significantly to his own financial ruin and untimely death as he worked himself into a state of complete and utter exhaustion trying to pay off the debts he had incurred as a result of this unwise speculation. It was also the main reason for his tenants, the Fergusons, renaming the old mansion house of Toftfields "Huntley Burn". For, the house itself is within a very short distance of Rhymer's Glen, and the Bogle Burn flows within yards of the Merry Knight's former residence; which still bears the name that he and his siblings gave it some one hundred and eighty years ago.

As for True Thomas himself, the ancient ballad from which Irving recounts Sir Walter having recited those immortal verses appears amongst the pages of the *Minstrelsy*; in a version slightly different to the one more recently recorded by Steeleye Span on their folk rock album "Now We Are Six" some twenty years or more ago. The latter version of the song holds more in common with the rendition of the ballad published by Robert Jamieson in his *Popular Ballads and Songs* (Edinburgh, 1806) and referred to by James A. H. Murray in his *Romance and Prophecies of Thomas of Ercildoune* (1875). According to Murray, "Jamieson's copy apparently came from the same source as Scott's." Murray then quotes from a letter in which the above source is referred to by a correspondent of Thomas Percy Bishop of Drumore, author of the celebrated *Reliques of Ancient English Poetry;* another work which, as has already been noted, was to exert a considerable influence upon the young Sir Walter Scott:

"Mr. Jamieson visited Mrs. Brown on his return from Aberdeen, and obtained from her recollection five or six ballads and a fragment......The greatest part of them is unknown to the oldest persons in this country. I accompanied Mr. Jamieson to my friend Scott's house in the country, for the sake of bringing the collectors to a good understanding. I then took on me to hint my suspicion of modern manufacture in which Scott had secretly anticipated me. Mrs. Brown is fond of ballad poetry, writes verses, and reads everything in a marvellous way. Yet her character places her above the suspicion of literary imposture; but it is wonderful how she would happen to be the depository of so many curious and valuable ballads."

The two differing versions of the ballad can now be compared below, as Jamieson's rendition of the first two verses of this song are placed alongside those of Scott as they were previously quoted from Irving's account of his visit to Abbotsford:

"True Thomas lay o'er yonder bank	*"True Thomas lay on Huntlie Bank*
And he beheld a lady gay	*A ferlie he spied wi' his e'e*
A lady that was brisk and bold	*And there he saw a lady bright*
Come riding o'er the fernie brae.	*Come riding down by Eildon Tree."*

"Her dress was of the grass green silk	*"Her dress was of the grass green silk*
Her mantle O' the velvet fyne	*Her mantle o' the velvet fyne*
At ilka tate of her horse's mane	*At ilka tett of her horse's mane*
Hung fifty siller bells and nine."	*Hung fifty siller bells and nine."*

In fact, if the truth be known, Mrs. Brown's version of these lyrics, which Scott used in his compilation of the *Minstrelsy,* was not the only rendition of the ballad that he had been able to gain access to; as his own notes in the pages of the collection show: It had in fact been originally "obtained from a lady residing not far from Ercildoune"; but was later corrected and enlarged by using references from Mrs. Brown's MSS.

It is Scott's collation and editing of so many of the ballads that he published that has led many later writers to accuse him of re-writing them; as a means of undermining his integrity as a scholar. In fact, as Professor Child was to show in the decades that followed, many different versions of these ballads existed; not only in Scotland, and in England, as we shall see in a following chapter, but in places like America too. The one thing that is certain, however, is that, despite the elaborations that inevitably occur with regard to all unwritten, "living", oral traditions, all of the different versions contain distinct parallels that show them to have evolved out of the same ultimate body of original source material, of ancient, and ultimately "unknown" (ie. unprovable) origin; as far as attributing the root compositions to any one specific individual is concerned.

In addition to this, exactly the same can be said of an ancient metrical romance, attributed by Scott and others to the Rhymer himself. The original source in which Scott found this old epic poem, which he later published as *A Metrical Romance of the Thirteenth Century by Thomas of Ercildoune, called the Rhymer, from the Auchinleck MS by Walter Scott esq. Advocate;* and which was printed by James Ballantyne for Archibald Constable and Co., Edinburgh, and Longman and Rees, London; 1804; was Auchinleck MS W.4.1. in the Advocates Library. This MS also contains a vast amount of other material, all of which is not only related, in terms of origin and provenance, to the *Tristrem*, but is also connected with the Border Minstrel Tradition that ultimately evolved out of the ancient Bardic traditions of Llywarch, Aneirin and the other great Dark Age British poets encountered during the course of the first and second chapters of this book.

The exact relevance of the material now listed to the ballads in the *Minstrelsy* will be dealt with stage by stage in the chapters that follow. In the meantime, it is sufficient to say that the most relevant sections of the abovementioned MS to our particular story are Section 37, which contains *The Romance of Sir Tristem* which Scott himself published:Section 7, which consists of *The Legend or Romance of Owain Miles*, which "contains the adventures of Sir Owain, a Northumbrian Knight, in St. Patrick's purgatory in Ireland"; Section 27, which is headed *Of Arthur and of Merlin*; and *King Orfeo*.

This last item, which Scott points out is a version of the "story of Orpheus and Eurydice converted into a romance of Faery" is also quoted by the Author of Waverley in the pages of the Minstrelsy, as we shall see later. In addition to this, the Arthurian piece that makes up Section 27, and which is described by Scott as a "long and curious romance", "may be", says the author, "the Gret Gest of Arthour, described by Winton, to Hucheon of the

Awle Royale. It contains all the earlier history of King Arthur and the Chivalry of the Round Table, but is left unconcluded by the author or transcriber."

The attribution of authorship of a metrical romance centred around the legend of Sir Tristrem is what connects Thomas of Ercildoune with the entire corpus of Arthurian tradition; and thus proves him beyond any reasonable doubt to be the mediaeval Border successor to Merlin and Aneirin; not to mention Taliesin; who is also another of the British Bards who we shall be looking at elsewhere in this treatise. The link with Sir Tristrem not only connects Thomas with the British Arthurian Tradition, but also with Brittany; and in geographical terms gives him an association, as we shall see further on, with the very region from which Scott's own ancestors might ultimately have migrated originally: The old Northern British Kingdom of Rheged.

In view of this it is therefore appropriate that the Eildon Hills should also be linked with an Arthurian legend of their own: A legend which states that Arthur and his Knights lie buried in a secret cavern under the earth and in the immediate vicinity of Huntley Bank and the Eildon Tree. Thus, the ritual landscape around which Scott took Irving on his guided tour becomes interconnected with a whole host of other ritual centres which can all be shown to have similar associations, in terms of their links with Ancient Bardic Tradition, to those possessed by the ancient haunts of Thomas of Ercildoune: Alderley Edge in Cheshire, for example, is another site where Arthurian heros lie waiting for Doomsday; and Pentonville Heights, in North London, which has a longstanding tradition with the magician Merlin, has similar connections of its own.

In a similar way, the closing verses of Scott's version of the Ballad of Thomas the Rhymer possess certain key elements which are common to both the Ancient Cymric Bardic Tradition and the mytho-historical cycles with which Merlin himself is associated. For, upon Thomas's arrival in Fairy Land, where he is to serve the Queen of the Fairies for seven years, he is given the fruit of a magical apple tree as his reward:

> "Syne they came on to a garden green,
> And she pu'd an apple frae a tree-
> Take this for thy wages, true Thomas;
> It will give thee the tongue that can never lie."

In the ancient Welsh *Black Book of Carmarthen*, an old Bardic poetical tract entitled *Afallennau*, or *The Apple Trees*, associates this genus with the gift of prophecy:

> *"Sweet Apple Tree with gentle flowers,*
> *Which grows in the earth, its branches unequal in length,*
> *The Wild Man fortells the tidings which will come......"*

Again, as we shall see, in another, later, chapter, this poem contains references to the territories bordering the old Kingdom of Rheged; not to mention a whole host of Northern British Dynasts who are all associated with the poetry of the Llywarch Hen and Aneirin Cycles; as well as the accompanying genealogies which have already been looked at in the opening chapter. But most important of all, in the ancient Bardic *Triads of Ireland*, which are derived directly from the Pre-Christian three line verses that the Druids composed as part of their oral tradition, the Apple and the Hazel, both of which are associated in the ancient texts with the art of poetic seership, are "the only two sacred trees for the wanton felling of which death is exacted."[2]

In Robert Graves's *White Goddess*, the great Celticist and classical scholar tells of how "The seven noble sacred trees of the grove particularized in a seventh-century poem appended to the ancient Irish Law "Crith Gablach" were: birch, alder, willow, oak, holly, hazel, apple...." Elsewhere, he makes mention of the fact that the apple tree was "the tree of immortality.....", before posing the following questions: "Where did King Arthur go to be healed of his grievous wounds? To the Isle of Avalon, the secret "island of Apple-Trees". With what talisman was Bran summoned by the White Goddess to enter the Land of Youth? With a silver blossomed apple branch from Emain in which the bloom and the branch were one". He then goes on to inform his readers of how "The Island of Emain, the Goidelic Elysium is described thus in a poem by Ragnall, son of Godfrey King of the Isles:

> *"An amaranthine place is faery Emain:*
> *Beauteous is the land where it is found,*
> *Lovely its rath above all other raths,*
> *Plentiful apple trees grow from that ground....."*

"Oisin, when taken to the same Land of Youth by Niamh of the Golden Hair, sees his weird first as a hornless fawn pursued by a red-eared white hound, but then in its own shape, royally dressed and mounted on a white horse in pursuit of a beautiful girl upon a dark horse; in her hand is a golden apple."

And, it is Merlin or Myrddin no less who is accredited with authorship of the poem *Afallennau*. In view of this, it is therefore appropriate that in writing of his own literary intentions when attempting to compose his unfinished prose tale based upon the romantic legends of Thomas of Ercildoune, Scott should have compared the Rhymer to Merlin. It is also worth noting then, that like Thomas, Merlin is himself also associated with the magical, although some say unlucky, thorn tree.

In Murray's *Romance and Prophecies of Thomas of Erceldoune,* we find the following references to "The Rhymer's Thorn", an ancient tree which, according to a Mr. James Wood of Galashiels, had formerly stood in "a garden belonging to the Black Bull Inn....." "It was a large tree," he says, which sent out its roots "in all directions ," and thus "absorbed much of the growing power of the soil," so that the then landowner of the pub "set his son to cut the roots all around, and clear the garden of them. This was the spring of 1814, and the thorn which had defied the blasts of probably 900 years, now shorn of its roots, succumbed shortly after to a violent westerly gale. It was immediately replanted, with several cartloads of manure dug in around it; but, notwithstanding all the efforts of the people to keep it alive, it never took root again. In 1830 the ground on which it stood came into the possession of the late John Spence, writer, Earlstoun, who built a high wall around the garden, leaving a square opening near the top to mark the site of the tree."

The reason why the local populace were so anxious to keep this ancient tree alive, is on account of one of the Rhymer's own prophetic couplets, also referred to by Murray:

> *"This thorn-tree, as long as it stands,*
> *Earlstoun shall possess a' her lands."*

In speaking of these lines, Murray informs the reader of how "The lands originally belonging to the community of Ealrston have been, in the course of time, alienated piecemeal, till there is scarcely an acre left;" this last quotation having been taken by Murray from the writings of Robert Chambers.

Chambers also makes note of how "The Rhymer is supposed to have attested the infallibility of his predictions by a couplet to the following effect:

> "*When the sant goes abune the meal*
> *Believe nae mair o' Tammie's tale......*"

In plain English, that it is just as impossible for the price of the small quantity of salt used in the preparation of porridge to exceed the value of the larger quantity of meal required for the same purpose, as for his prophecies to become untrue."

To return once more to the writings of Scott, we hear, once again, in the pages of the *Minstrelsy,* of how "The grave of Merlin is pointed out at Drumelziar, in Tweedale, beneath an aged thorntree. On the east side of the churchyard the brook, called Pausayl, falls into the Tweed; and the following prophecy is said to have been current concerning their union:

> "*When Tweed and Pausayl join at Merlin's grave,*
> *Scotland and England shall one monarch have.*"

On the day of the coronation of James VI the Tweed accordingly overflowed, and joined the Pausayl at the Prophet's grave......"

The source from which Scott claims to have originally obtained this tradition is none other than Pennicuik's *History of Tweedale,* p.26. He then goes on to make the following observation, which I myself have already set out to prove during the course of this chapter and those that have preceeded it, when he says that "These circumstances would seem to infer a communication betwixt the south-west of Scotland and Wales, of a nature peculiarly intimate; for I presume that Merlin would retain sense enough to choose, for the scene of his wanderings, a country having a language and manners similar to his own."

We shall be examing these links again further on. But first we must travel back downstream along Sir Walter's beloved River Tweed, to the vicinity of Huntley Bank and the Eildon Hills once more. And, in so doing, we shall take a journey into the supernatural dimension of the Otherworld realm of the Fairies. [3]

Chapter Four

The Wee Wee Man

"Twas down by Carterhaugh, Father,
  I walked beside the wa,
And there I saw a wee wee man,
The least that eer I saw.

His legs were scarce a shathmont lang
  Yet umber was his thie;
Between his brows there was ae span,
And between his shoulders three.

He's taen and flung a meikle stane,
  As far as I could see;
I could na, had I been Wallace wight,
Hae lifted it to my knee.

"O wee wee man, but ye be strang!
  Where may thy dwelling be?"
It's down beside yon bonny bower;
Fair Lady, come and see."

"On we lap, and away we rade,
  Down to a bonny green;
We lighted down to bait our steed,
And we saw the Fairy Queen.

With four and twenty at her back,
  Of ladies clad in green;
Tho the King of Scotland had been there
The worst might hae been his queen.

On we lap, and away we rade,
  Down to a bonny ha';

The roof was o the beaten goud,
The floor was of chrystal a'.

And there were dancing on the floor,
Fair ladies jimp and sma',
But in the twinkling o an eye,
They sainted clean awa......"

This ballad, a version of which, like *The Twa' Corbies,* was likewise
recorded by "Steeleye Span", on their 1973 album "Parcel of Rogues", the
title of which, appropriately, was taken from that of an old proscribed
Jacobite song attributed to Robert Burns, is one of the most important ballads
to be gathered by Scott and incorporated into the pages of the various
editions of his *Border Minstrelsy.* It originally appeared in volume 2 of the
1802 edition of the work, on page 234 [1], where it was appended to the lyrics
of another ballad, *The Young Tamlane;* which has already been mentioned in
chapter 2 in reference to Burns, and which will, as previously seen, feature
elsewhere in this work; but was subsequently dropped from future editions;
which is a pity; in view of its lyrical content. The fundamental reason for *The
Wee Wee Man's* signficance is, that like the ballad of Thomas the Rhymer,
which concerns a meeting with the Queen of the Fairies, it likewise also
takes the reader, or listener, into the realm of the Fairies; and in so doing
transports us back to a time long before the advent of either Christianity or
Druidism and into Britain's primordial shamanistic past.

The worship of, and conversation with, Fairies was an integral part of rural
culture in Scotland, both in the Borders themselves as well as farther north in
the Highlands; right up until the era in which Scott himself was writing.
Many of the early ballads that the Author of *Waverley* was to acquire,
directly from the mouths of the inhabitants of these remoter parts of the
countryside, were obtained through his acquaintance with the poet, novelist
and celebrated *Ettrick Shepherd,* James Hogg (1770-1835). Hogg is
significant in one major respect, in that he himself was the living
embodiment of the Border Fairy Tradition: A tradition which is to play a
major part in our story.

For one of the best descriptions of this curious, and at times controversial,
character, we will now turn our attention to the pages of the works of John
Buchan; whose celebrated biography of Scott has already been quoted at an
earlier juncture:

"This Hogg came of interesting stock, for there had been witches on the paternal side, and his maternal grandfather, Will o' Phawhope, was the last man on the Border who had spoken with the fairies. It was a promising source for balladry, and the ballads were duly forthcoming- some verses of *The Outlaw Murray,* and the whole of the sixty-five stanzas of *Auld Maitland,* taken down from his Mother's recitation....."

In a letter to Scott dated 30th June 1802, Hogg describes his Mother as "a living miscellany of old songs...." "I never believed she had half so many,....." he then continues, "until I came to a trial. There are none in your collection of which she hath not a part, and I should by this time have had a great number written for your amusement,- thinking them all of great antiquity and lost to posterity- had I not luckily lighted upon a collection of songs, in two volumes, published by I know not who, in which I recognized about half a score of my Mother's best songs almost word for word......"

Elsewhere in the same letter Hogg descibes the wildness of his locality, and the environment in which these ancient fragments had been preserved, by word of mouth, for generations:

"Many indeed are not aware of the manners of this place; it is but lately emerged from barbarity, and till this present age the poor illiterate people in these glens knew of no other entertainment in the long winter nights than in repeating and listening to those feats of their ancestors which I believe to be handed down inviolate from father to son for many generations, although no doubt, had a copy been taken of them at the end of every fifty years, there must have been some difference which the repeaters would have insensibly fallen into, merely by the change of terms in that period. I believe it is thus that many very antient songs have been modernized, which yet to a connoisseur will bear visible marks of antiquity. The Maitlen (the *Auld Maitland* of the *Border Minstrelsy),* exclusive of its mode of description, is all composed of words which would, mostly every one, both spell and pronounce in the very same dialect that was spoken some centuries ago......"

Curiously enough, the man who originally introduced Scott to the Ettrick Shepherd was one William Laidlaw, who is also of major significance in our story; the fundamental reason being that he himself is living proof of the assertions previously made throughout the preceeding pages: That the Border ballads which Scott collected are themselves directly descended from the ancient bardic traditions of the Cymru of "Y Goggledd"- North Britain. The name "Laidlaw", according to a tradition preserved by the family itself in former times and repeated in the pages of numerous works on the origins of British surnames, originally denoted that the family had, in the far distant past, dwelt in the vicinity of the Shropshire town of Ludlow. One of the earliest progenitors of the family, which has resided for the most part in the old county of Selkirk, in the vales of Ettrick and Yarrow, since at least the thirteenth century, was one "William of Lodelawe"; who in 1296 was recorded as having been accused of concealing horses from the English.

The town of Ludlow lies just a few miles east of Offa's Dyke, which, in the Dark and early Middle Ages, marked the border between the old Saxon Kingdom of Mercia and the Welsh Principality of Powys. In view of the fact that the original place of origin with which the family of Laidlaw is accredited with migrating from, at some point before 1296, is itself located on the English side of the Border, it would seem curious, at this particular juncture, to find a member of that family acting in a way which would seem to be overtly hostile to the English; when first we encounter the Laidlaws in the earliest written records and traditions available to us. However, a brief examination of the known origins of some of the other local families provides us with vital clues as to why this should be so.

Approximately the same distance away from Ludlow as the ancient border with Mercia, in a southerly direction, is the old Herefordshire town of Leominster; located on the River Lugg. And, just a few miles downstream, on the banks of the same waterway, is the village of Bodenham; the ancient ancestral home of a local gentry family; the Bodenhams of Rotherwas.

Although the original documents possessed by that family during the last century, and from which the genealogy of Bodenham of Rotherwas, as it appears in the 1837 edition of Burke's *History of the Commoners*, was originally derived, take their pedigree only as far back as the twelfth century, when "Hugh de Bodham, alias de Bodenham", was "Lord of Bodenham Rogeri, in the county of Hereford, temp. Stephen and Henry II", Duncomb's *History and Antiquities of Herefordshire,* published in 1812, claims that Roger de Bodenham, Lord of Bodenham in "the time of Edward the Confessor", was, like the ancestors of several other local Welsh Border Families, such as the Hornyolds and the Griffiths of Garn, descended from "some of the chiefs" of the old Saxon nobility.

The same source also makes mention of the fact that Bodenham is a name which denotes that the local inhabitants of the village, and possibly their landlords, the de Bodenhams themselves, were of both British (ie. Cymric or Welsh) and Saxon origin. It is therefore quite probable then that the Laidlaws were of ancient Cymric stock too, and it is perhaps this ethnicity which was to prompt the family's original migration to North Britain. Dr. Heinrich Harke of the University of Reading's work on the ethnic affiliations of those interred in some of the earliest Anglo-Saxon cemetaries unearthed in recent years may provide further clues as to the complexities surrounding inter-racial marriages between native Britons and Teutonic immigrants during the Dark Ages; associations which in turn may have had some kind of bearing upon the composition and dispersal of later Mediaeval populations. So, in view of the evidence already looked at, in relation to Merlin and Arthur's links with the region to which the ancestors of Clan Laidlaw were to migrate, it is by no means improbable that the twelfth and thirteenth century inhabitants of the same locality were themselves aware of being possessed of a similar ethnic origin, to the one previously described, of their own.

This, in itself, would explain why, throughout contemporary records from the great Tudor and Plantagenet eras of Border warfare, several of the most prominent clans involved in the feuds and struggles which so epitomized this fascinating period of strife and conflict in the history of both nations, appear as having been possessed of surprisingly fickle allegiences; being neither wholly loyal to either side. In a document dating from July 1583, itself quoted extensively by both James Reed and the novelist George Macdonald Fraser in the latter's own 1971 study of Border history, *The Steel Bonnets,* we find "A note of the gentlemen and surnames in the Marches of England and Scotland".

Under the heading of the "West Marches", we find the following list of names: "England; gentlemen- Musgraves, Loders, Curwenes, Sawfelde. Surnames.- Graemes, Rutlitches, Armestrongs, Fosters, Nixons, Tailors, Stores. Scotland; Maxwells, Johnstons, Urwins, Grames, Bells, Carlills, Battison, Litles, Carrudders....."

As will be noted from this list, the name Graeme, or Grame, appears to have been used by the inhabitants of both sides of the Border. Similarly, in the ballad of *Jamie Telfer of the Fair Dodhead,* another key set of lyrics from Sir Walter's immortal collection, we find a narrative which is referred to by Reed as describing "the complexities of Border loyalties and allegiences"; in a

84

situation in which the "English band" at the centre of the action is apparently portrayed as "picking up its information on the northern side of the Border". (See Reed, James: *The Border Ballads*, Spredden Press, 1991, pp. 104-107).

Elsewhere, amongst the pages of the *Minstrelsy*, we find the Author of *Waverley* commenting upon how "The men of Tynedale and Reedsdale, in particular, appear to have been more frequently tempted by the rich vales of the Bishoprick of Durham, and other districts which lay to the southward, than by the rude desolation of the Scottish Hills."

The key element in this complexity of inter-clan and cross Border allegiance and feud appears to have been that like Arthur, Merlin, Llywarch and Urien, the Borderers of the Great Heroic Golden Age of the fourteenth and fifteenth centuries, men like the Outlaw Murray and Kinmont Willie, were neither Scottish nor English, but Britons. We shall look further at the Cymric origins of several key Border families during the course of our study, in particular that of Johnston or Johnstone; a Clan which features in many of the ballads collected in Scott's *Minstrelsy*. Similarly, the Shropshire origins of the Laidlaws will be looked at again in a future chapter, in relation to a local version of a Scottish ballad incorporated into Scott's *Minstrelsy;* located by Professor Child; himself likewise the discoverer of an American version of the same song.

In the meantime, let us return to the writings of Scott, where we find him commenting, once again, amongst the pages of his *Minstrelsy*, in his introductory essay to *The Young Tamlane,* on the geographical location at which the Fairy encounter alluded to in the song at the head of this chapter is supposed to have happened:

"Carterhaugh is a plain, at the confluence of the Ettrick and Yarrow, in Selkirkshire, about a mile above Selkirk and two miles below Newark Castle; a romantic ruin which overhangs the Yarrow......The peasants point out upon the plain those electrical rings which vulgar credulity supposes to be traces of the Fairy revels......."

Scott now goes into some detail as regards the legends surrounding the events related to in the previously mentioned ballad of *The Young Tamlane,* before recounting how one of the most famous" Fairy frolics" that is alleged to have taken place in the vicinity is said to have occurred during the eighteenth century:

"The victim of Elfin sport", he says, "was a poor man, who, being employed in pulling heather upon Peatlaw, a hill not far from Carterhaugh, had tired of his labour and laid him down to sleep upon a Fairy Ring. When he awakened he was amazed to find himself in the midst of a populous city, to which, as well as to the means of his transportation, he was an utter stranger. His coat was left upon the Peatlaw; and his bonnet, which had fallen off in the course of his ariel journey, was afterwards hanging upon the steeple of the church of Lanark. The distress of the poor man was, in some degree, relieved by meeting a carrier whom he had formerly known, and who conducted him back to Selkirk by a slower conveyance than had whirled him to Glasgow. That he had been carried off by the Fairies was implicitly believed by all, who did not reflect that a man may have private reasons for leaving his own country and for disguising his having intentionally done so."

To understand more of what is alleged to have happened in Scott's account of the circumstances under which this man is supposed to have been transported, in an instant, to a location many miles away, I now propose to refer the reader to a peculiar legend which refers to the existence of unseen trackways which supposedly run right across the ancient rural landscape of Britain and Ireland. This particular legend is quoted, second hand, by one of the greatest contemporary writers on such subject matter, John Michell; author of *The View Over Atlantis, City of Revelation* and numerous other titles too multitudinous to list here.

According to Michell, "The peculiar legend of unseen tracks running straight across country aroused the interest of J.D. Evans-Wentz, who in the early part of this century travelled widely among the Celts of Britain and France, collecting fairy stories and other relics of the old mythology. In several parts of Ireland he heard about the fairy paths. These paths, sometimes preserved only in local memory, were said to be the routes of seasonal processions. On a certain day the fairies passed through the land, and anyone who stood in their way might be struck dead or taken off never to return. A man whose house happened to be situated on a Fairy Path must on that day leave his front and back door open, for it was unwise to obstruct the fairy parade. In his book, *The Fairy Faith in Celtic Countries,* Evans-Wentz tells how he asked an Irish seer for an explanation of the fairy paths and was told that they were lines of some kind of magnetic current, whose exact nature had lately been forgotten......"

Elsewhere, Michell continues by informing the reader of how "In Australia and North America the dragon lines are creation paths, haunted by the gods and by the great primeaval serpent, the ancestral guardian of all living things. In Ireland they are the roads of the fairies. In some parts of the world they can still be seen from the air, although their origin is obscure and even their existence is no longer remembered by the people through whose country they run.....In fact they are sun paths, for they are so set that a traveller walking down a certain line at the equinox or solstice would see the sun rising or setting on the horizon straight ahead....."

As we shall see in the next chapter, these ancient trackways have an additional purpose, a purpose which also provides us with clues as to the exact origin of the name of "Scott" itself. In the meantime, before moving on, it may be noted that, despite Scott's own scepticism as regards the actual substance of some of the legends he was to encounter during the course of his editing and publication of the *Minstrelsy,* he noted them down and included them in his narrative nevertheless; being anxious to preserve even the most far fetched of the traditions that he was to encounter for posterity; and in order that future generations of scholars might learn from his researches. Sir Walter, after all, was a product of the Scottish Enlightenment: Through his relationship with the Fergusons he was to come into contact with such luminaries as the scientists Joseph Black and James Hutton; not to mention Dugald Stewart, Adam Smith, John Home, and Hugh Blair.

In view of this, it is hardly surprising that, intellectually speaking, we find him leaning towards modern rationalist thought when recounting some of the Fairy traditions associated with the Plain of Carterhaugh and the surrounding area. However, the fact that he went so far as to set out these legends, peculiar to the neighbourhood through which his own ancestors had ridden and fought for centuries, in spite of such intellectual prejudices, is perhaps truly indicative of his devotion to meticulous scholarship. More than a century was to pass before Evans-Wentz was to put pen to paper. A fact which shows quite clearly the extent to which the Laird of Abbotsford was truly ahead of his time in terms of the pioneering work he was to do in the field of study that he had chosen. All things considered then, it is perhaps unsurprising that both the ballads and the folklore with which they are associated feature incidentally throughout all Scott's novel writing; and could indeed be described as the hidden undercurrent that permeates all of the fictional literary output he was to be responsible for; in the decades following the publication of his *Minstrelsy of the Scottish Border*.

But now, let us return, once again, to the ancient ballad which gives this particular chapter its title. For, it is in Scott's celebrated version of this traditional song, which is the variant referred to in Lowry Charles Wimberley's *Folklore in the English and Scottish Ballads* (publ. Dover Press, New York, 1965), that we are informed, in verse three, of how the Wee Wee Man of the title has picked up and "flung a meikle stane", a large boulder, and flung it as far as the singer can see. The balladeer then continues by telling her listeners of how, even if she had been "Wallace wight", or "Wallace the brave" in the old Scottish dialect, she'd never "Hae lifted it to" her knee.

As Michell himself explains in his *View Over Atlantis,* currently available as the revised and updated *New View Over Atlantis* through Thames and Hudson, the principal characteristic of all of these ancient "sun paths" or "fairy paths", is that they run in perfectly straight lines. And, strange as it may seem, the ballad of *The Wee Wee Man,* as Scott recorded it and as it appears in the first edition of the *Minstrelsy,* may well preserve within its verses the route of one of these ancient paths; located in the immediate vicinity of where the mysterious encounter with the little man is alleged to have occurred.

A short distance north east of Carterhaugh, towering some four hundred feet above the confluence of Ettrick Water and the River Tweed, is Meigle Hill; atop of which is a gigantic boulder known as "Wallace's Putting Stone". And this, we may suppose, could well be the self same "meikle stane" that our fairy midget is alleged to have hurled across the landscape. If a straight line is drawn on the map from the Plain of Carterhaugh, in the direction of Meigle Hill, it passes directly through this mighty rock and on up to an ancient hill fort overlooking Leader Water in Lauderdale; far to the north. A similar alignment can be found to pass right the way through Peat Law, where the fairy kidnapping, previously described by Scott in the pages of the *Minstrelsy,* is said to have taken place. This alignment, likewise, continues northwards, passing through the Cairn atop of Mains Hill a few miles west of the fort above Leader Water. The various alignments that link the Plain of Carterhaugh to a multitude of ancient sites in the area will be examined in depth further on. In the meantime, it is worth noting that the evidence given above may well provide another equally rational explanation for the strange circumstances related in the lyrics of this obviously ancient folk song; in that its storyline may contain what is effectively a series of hidden ciphers relating to ancient landscape alignments.

Again, we shall be looking at the ancient science of landscape alignment, with particular reference to how it relates to the ballads and folk traditions collected by Scott, at a later stage. Suffice to say that extensive scientifically oriented research carried out over the past few decades has revealed that many ancient prehistoric sites were laid out in such a way as to act as astronomical calendars; possibly for use in the planting of annual crops. Similarly, as previously shown in the above quotations from the writings of John Michell, many of the trackways that ran between such sites were likewise laid out using astronomical know how.

In addition to this, many of them, being set out in perfectly straight lines, were invariably sited on the shortest route between one or more locations. Perhaps this last fact lies at the root of the strange tale of the fairy kidnapping alleged to have taken place on Peatlaw. The fact that the traveller is recounted as having been transported from one place to another in an instant may well be a hidden reference to his being possessed of some secret knowledge; doubtless attributed to his having conversed, like Will O' Phawhope, with the Little People; which enabled him to navigate from one location to another by using ancient folk memories of prehistoric landscape alignments marking the shortest route from "A" to "B"; and which were possibly preserved in the form of ballad or folk song.

On another level entirely, it may also not be uninteresting to note that in certain parts of Scotland human beings are not only alleged to have conversed or ridden off with the Fairies, but some are even supposed to have married into the Fairy Race. To illustrate the relevance of this particular phenomenon in relation to our story I now propose to make another brief digression which centres upon the life of Robert Ferguson M.D. (1799-1865); who, as we have already seen, was the Great Nephew of Professor Adam Ferguson; the Merry Knight's father; as well as being the author of the previously quoted anecdotes that have appeared transcribed during the course of the preceeding chapters.

Amongst Robert Ferguson's own publications was his *Puerperal Fever* (1839), and *Diseases of the Uterus and Ovaria* in *Tweedie's Library of Medicine*. According to his entry in the Dictionary of National Biography, he was also one of those who attended Sir Walter Scott in 1831 "when he passed through London in broken health on his way to Naples, and again in 1832 on his way back". Some fourteen years later, in 1846, he was to marry, as his second wife, Mary Lowther Macleod, daughter of the Chief of Clan Macleod of Dunvegan on Skye; and it is in reference to this particular lady's ancestry that I now propose to draw the reader's attention to certain specific aspects of the Ancient Celtic Fairy Tradition.

Young Robert Ferguson first came into contact with the people of Skye through his guardian, Sir John Macpherson, (1745-1821), one time Governor General of India; whose own father was the Revd. John Macpherson (1710-1765), the Minister of Sleat. In addition to becoming acquainted with Dr. Johnson during the course of the latter's famous tour of the Hebrides in the company of James Boswell, the older Macpherson was the author of a remarkable and rare work on the *Origin, Antiquities, Language, Government, Manners, and Religion of the Ancient Caledonians, their Posterity, the Picts, and the British and Irish Scots* published in 1768. These last mentioned facts will be seen to be of particular relevance further on, when we examine the Ferguson Family involvement in the publication of Macpherson's *Ossian;* and its relationship to Scott's work as a writer of narrative poems.

According to the unpublished writings of a near relative, in whose house I have recollections of being shown a portrait of Scott's " Honest Tar" by Sir John Watson-Gordon in early childhood, "Robert Ferguson M.D. first saw the lady who became his second wife sketching on Skye. He hurried back and told his host and hostess that he must meet this beautiful young woman, to be told that it would be impossible except perhaps a bow at a Ceilidh as the Macleod was very strict with his daughters. To my great grandfather Robert M.D., the word impossible did not exist. He met her, and met her again. The old Chief died and his son, as Chief and brother of Mary Macleod of Macleod saw Robert M.D. With the greatest politeness he informed him he could not agree to the marriage. He reckoned without his sister, who told him she respected him as Chief and head of her Clan and would always love him as her brother, but she was going to marry Robert Ferguson M.D."

As to this lady's illustrious ancestry, the original thirteenth century progenitor of Clan Macleod was one Leod, a descendant of the old Norse kings of Man and the Isles. He himself, according to tradition, is said to have married a Fairy Princess. In an oft quoted genealogical tradition, that makes its appearance time and time again in the numerous Clan histories that have appeared in print in connection with the Chiefs of Macleod, and which is taken from an old fourteenth century manuscript, we are told of Leod's initial encounter with his Fairy Bride [2]:

90

"Mic Leoid, a tthaid, Clanna Leod, fri Lara agus i thainig a sioth broghaibh a riocht Lara, ionnus gorug triar mac, ar a ffiul sliocht."

"Leod, from whom (descend) the Clan Leod, by Lara, and she came from the Fairy Palaces in the shape of a Lara, so that she bore three sons, of whom there are descendants."

The Fairy Tradition was until comparatively recently still a powerful influence amongst the folklore of the inhabitants of the Island, even in our own century, and the present Clan Chief is still in possession of a Fairy Flag; which is said to have been given to Leod by his Fairy wife; when, after twenty years of marriage, she was forced to return to Fairyland. Again, the legends associated with this liason involve references to specific sites in the landscape which are alleged to have close elemental associations with the Fairy Folk. It was at Fairy Bridge, about three miles or so from the Chief's castle, that the Fairy Princess bade farewell to her human spouse; giving him, in recognition of their former union, the abovementioned Fairy Banner; which, she promised, when waved, would summon Fairy help in times of extreme danger.

According to legend, the Flag could only be waved on three occasions; and it is of particular interest that, in 1600, during the wars between the Macleods and the Macdonalds of Sleat, the Flag was not waved; despite the desperate situation that the Clan was in; owing to the fact that in the minds of the Macleod's Clansmen, there was a great deal of concern that to do so would bring down some terrible retribution upon those who attempted to summon Fairy assistance to their aid a fourth time.

Of the three occasions that there are on record of the Flag being used to invoke the Fairy magic that it is alleged to possess, two instances of its use are said to have taken place in battle; one at the Battle of Waternish, in 1580, and the other about a century before at the Battle of Glendale. It is also said to have warded off a cattle plague, which promptly ceased.

In order to to give the reader some idea of the importance of this banner to the Macleods of Skye, it is worth noting that, like the Hereditary Pipers to the Chiefs of the Macleods, the Mac Cruimins, the office of Standard Bearer to the Clan Chief was likewise passed on from one generation to the next; having remained in one family for some three centuries or so. Murcha Breac, who fell at the Battle of Bloody Bay in 1480, a decade before Glendale, was himself interred in the same grave on Iona as the Chief at whose side he himself was slain; and the Standard Bearer was always given an armed escort of twelve men; hand picked for their bravery and valour; and all sworn to lay down their lives in defence of the Fairy Banner.

Before going any further it is also worth mentioning that in the pages of the *Minstrelsy,* in the previously quoted from *Introduction to the Young Tamlane*, Scott also goes into some detail with regard to alleged liasons between human beings and those of Fairy origin. "Gervase of Tilbury" he says, "assures us that in his days the lovers of the Fadae, or Fairies, were numerous, and describes the rules of their intercourse with as much accuracy as if he had himself been engaged in such an affair. Sir David Lindsay also informs us that a leopard is the proper armorial bearing of those who spring from such intercourse, because that beast is generated by adultery between a pard and a lioness. He adds, that Merlin, the prophet, was the first who adopted this cognizance, because he was "borne of faarie in adultre, and right sua the first duk of Guyenne was borne of a fee; and therefoir, the armes of Guyenne are a leopard......."

We shall be examining the Fairy origins of the Macleods yet again in a future chapter; and we shall also be looking at Merlin's ancestry in specific detail elsewhere in this book. In the meantime, before going back to the ballads, it is necessary to draw the reader's attention to the reference, in the previously given Gaelic pedigree, to Leod's wife having come from "the Fairy Palaces in the shape of a Lara". It has been suggested that the word "lara" is a corruption of "lair", which translated means "a young mare". In order for the reader to understand more fully the significance of the last statement I must now draw his or her attention to the writings of the twelfth century Norman chronicler, Gerald of Wales: In the third part of his *History and Topography of Ireland*, Gerald writes of "a new and outlandish way of confirming Kingship and Dominion". (3)

"There are some things" he says, "which, if the exigencies of my account did not demand it, shame would discountenance their being described. But the austere discipline of history spares neither truth nor modesty.

"There is in the northern and farther part of Ulster", he continues, "namely in Kenelcunnil, a certain people which is accustomed to appoint its King with a rite altogether outlandish and abominable. When the whole people of that land has been gathered together in one place, a white mare is brought forward into the middle of the assembly. He who is to be inaugurated, not as a chief, but as a beast, not as a king, but as an outlaw, has bestial intercourse with her before all, professing himself to be a beast also. The mare is then killed immediately, cut into pieces and boiled in water. A bath is prepared for the man afterwards in the same water. He sits in the bath surrounded by all his people, and all, he and they, eat of the meat of the mare which is brought to them. He quaffs and drinks of the broth in which he is bathed, not in any cup, or using his hand, but just by dipping his mouth into it round about him. When this unrighteous rite has been carried out, his Kingship has been conferred."

In order to understand, first of all, what it is we are being told, it is important to realize that Gerald of Wales, a Christian monk, is giving us a description of a pagan ritual associated with the shamanistic initiation of a sacral king. It is not only probable, but quite definite, that his description of the tribal chieftain having sexual intercourse with an animal is a deliberate misrepresentation; much like the maligning of the Tartars by western chroniclers. It is quite probable that the ancient inhabitants of the part of Ulster that he describes worshipped the horse as a sacred animal. It is also likely that when a new chief was inaugurated a feast was held at which horse flesh was consumed. It is also probable that the chief himself was married to a priestess of the cult of the sacred horse to which he and his tribespeople were wont to offer sacrifice; and this is where the genealogy of Clan Macleod can give us clues as to what actually happened.

As we have already seen, Leod's wife is supposed to have come before him in the shape of a young mare. It is therefore of interest that in several places along the Western Seaboard of Britain itself, most notably at Padstow in Cornwall and Minehead in Somerset, the townspeople still perform annual dances in which a hobbyhorse is paraded around the town with various individuals, whose families have lived in the area for generations, taking turns to dance inside it. It is quite probable then that Leod's wedding to his Fairy wife took place in the form of some kind of ritual to that previously described; and that the tribal customs practised by her ancestors, were, like those of the Ulster tribespeople previously referred to, a remnant of an ancient shamanistic past.

And, in view of the fact that both the Fairy Queen and the Wee Wee Man of Scott's Border ballads seem to have taken their human companions to the Fairy realms on horseback-hence the references to steeds in both sets of lyrics, it would appear that, as has already been asserted, the ancient songs that Scott himself was to recover were in some way the last fragmentary remains of some lost shamanistic heritage. Thus, it can be said to be the case that the Laird of Abbotsford was, as has already been suggested, the true nineteenth century successor to the Ancient Bards of "Y Gogledd"; as well as their prehistoric shaman forbears.

The initiate in all "primitive" societies is an individual who has mastered all of the ancient folklore of the tribal people to which he belongs. This is what Scott effectively did, whether knowingly or unknowingly, consciously or unconsciously. And, as a means of adding further weight to my argument, it is also worth pointing out that the people responsible in such societies for supervising the instruction of each generation of shamanistic initiates are themselves possessed of hereditary connections with the transmission of such primeval folk traditions. This in itself is precisely what James Hogg, his Mother and the numerous other ballad singers that Scott encountered during the course of his extensive travels, across the ritual landscape which Merlin and Thomas the Rhymer had frequented many centuries before him, were. Likewise, William Laidlaw could claim a similar pedigree: A pedigree which we will look at again when we next examine the shamanistic traditions touched on in this chapter in yet another religio-mythological context; in yet another cycle of ballads.

Chapter Five

The Sun, the Serpent and the False Knight on the Road

"Old King Cole was a merry old soul,
And a very old soul was he.
He called for his pipe,
And he called for his bowl,
And he called for his fiddlers three......"

Old Traditional Nursery Rhyme

In the preceeding chapter we looked at ancient prehistoric solar or "Fairy" paths; and how some of the invisible landscape alignments that fall into this particular category of phenomenon are alluded to in the ballad of *The Wee Wee Man*. During the course of my examination of the significance of such alignments I referred the reader to the writings of John Michell; who, throughout his numerous works refers to the orientation of many prehistoric religious centres as being specifically designed to invoke the power of the Earth Spirit- the Serpent or "Dragon" that symbolizes the ancient primordial creative energy of the Universe.

As we saw in Chapter 4, the Plain of Carterhaugh, itself the scene of many a Fairy encounter in the folklore of the Border Peoples, is located at a point where a large number of these "Fairy Paths" converge. As well as the two previously examined during the course of the last chapter, another of these alignments, which is directly in line with the central peak of the three Eildon Hills, divided in legend by the magical invocations of Scott's kinsman, the Wizard and Astrologer Michael Scott, passes straight through the course of the Bogle Burn; where we earlier found Sir Walter in conversation with the American writer Washington Irving. We shall be joining Scott and Irving again shortly, as they wander about the ancient archaeological remains of the

Laird of Abbotsford's domestic locality; remains, which, as we shall see, provide clues as to Scott's own Clan origins.

Perhaps the abovementioned legend of Sir Michael's wizardry hints at the latter's own knowledge of the existence and significance of these ancient alignments. For, close to his own one time residence, a similar alignment runs from an old abandoned motte, overlooking Howden, Philiphaugh and the Valley of Ettrick Water, through Carterhaugh and on to the ancient Yarrow Stone; which lies in the shadow of Mountbenger Law. As we shall see, during the course of the somewhat lengthy chapter that now follows, the existence of these Fairy Paths provides us with definite clues as to the true authenticity of the Ancient Ballad of True Thomas, as it appears in the Minstrelsy. During the course of this chapter I shall be examining certain passages in this ballad at length. I shall also be presenting the reader with a vast amount of inter-connected mythical, historical and other material; as a means of proving, beyond any reasonable doubt, that what Scott recovered, when he collected this ballad, was a true bardic survival; from the most ancient time.

The reason, quite simply, why this should be necessary, is because certain individuals, who shall remain nameless, have attempted to cast doubt on Scott's integrity as a scholar in these matters; as well as upon the integrity of his sources; claiming that when Scott went out in search of ballads for his *Minstrelsy,* the locals knew he was coming and exaggerated the traditions he had come to collect in order to exact more money from him. This, I am afraid, is far from the case, and, as anyone who reads and understands what follows during the course of this chapter will come to realize, is absolutely ridiculous.

Of course, Scott did not get every single fact right. This, however, was no fault of his own. For, just as science has advanced considerably since the time when he himself wrote, so too has the field of scholarship in which he himself was very much a pioneer. A couple of Scott's mistaken conclusions will be examined during the course of what is to follow. However, I must state, before elaborating any further on such matters, that the reason why I shall be referring to these very minor errors at all is to give the reader some more vital clues as to what it was that Scott had stumbled upon, when first he discovered, in an old forgotten manuscript, the mediaeval metrical romance attributed to Thomas the Rhymer; that he himself would later publish.

Before arriving at that particular point in our story however, I intend to take the reader on a journey similar to the one that True Thomas was to take, in the company of the Fairy Queen: A journey to the Magical Fairy Garden, where the Rhymer was to be offered the fruit of the Sacred Apple. The purpose of this journey is to show the reader how, both in the British Dark Age and the early Anglo-Saxon Period, the dynasties that ruled over Glastonbury's Vale of Avalon, which, I conjectured, is in all probability the location of this magical garden previously alluded to, were also connected with the North British Dynasts of "Y Goggledd"; who have featured, and will continue to feature, throughout this book; as well as their Northumbrian counterparts.

During the course of this journey we shall also be looking at the traditional customs of both areas, as a means of further strengthening the validity of this previously outlined hypothesis. In addition to this, we shall likewise be looking at clues which might possibly identify the species or genus of tree to which the celebrated Eildon Tree, under which True Thomas would encounter the Fairy Queen, and under which he sang forth his prophetic rhymes, belonged. But first of all, I now propose to take the reader back into the realms of the Fairy Paths; in order to find clues as to Sir Walter's own genealogical origins.

In view of the connections that I have already made between the Welsh Marches, particularly the area around Ludlow, where the Laidlaws of Ettrick and Yarrow are supposed to have originated, and the Scottish Border Country, where Scott was to collect so many of his ballads, it is perhaps significant that the writer in whose footsteps John Michell was to follow was himself a Herefordshire man born and bred; and the person responsible for the invention of the pinhole camera and Watkins Exposure Meter. The man who first noticed the significance of our Ancient British Trackways, and who later wrote a book on the same subject, was the brewer, manufacturer and pioneer photographer Alfred Watkins. It is therefore important to realize that the phenomenon previously described in the words of John Michell, from whose writings I have quoted from extensively, namely, the traditional method of landscape alignment used by the Ancient Britons for setting out their religious centres, can be shown to be firmly rooted in Astronomical and Geodetic Science. And, it is perhaps for this reason that it was a Victorian light industrialist and manufacturer, from a brewing and scientific background, as opposed to an artist or sentimentalist, who first re-discovered this long lost science.

Before looking into Watkins, his theories, and their relevance to Scott, however, it is worth noting that Michell was amongst the first to draw the public's attention to the fact that "The belief,......that civilization in Britain began with the Romans, has blinded us to the significance of those remarkable straight lines which can be found on almost every large scale map and which are commonly marked "Roman Road". The extent of these roads and the amazing accuracy of their alignments have caused considerable speculation; but, for want of a better theory, it has generally been assumed that they were built by the Romans to consolidate their conquest, while their straight lines are supposed to have been the product of typical Roman ruthlessness and efficiency."

"In fact," Michell continues, "it can be shown that the system of straight roads is far earlier than the Roman Invasion. In the first place, they occur in Ireland, a country which never suffered Roman occupation, in just the same way as they appear on the English map. Secondly, the Celts were noted charioteers, and would scarcely have been without the paved roads necessary for running their vehicles; and finally, archaeological excavation has shown that many roads, previously considered to be of Roman origin, are prehistoric tracks which the Romans later repaired or resurfaced. Beneath the Roman surface of the Foss Way, Ermine Street and Watling Street, excavators have uncovered the paving stones of earlier roads, at least as well drained and levelled as those which succeeded them."

After presenting yet more facts, Michell finally concludes that "When the Romans came to Britain they must have found traces of a vast system of straight tracks......Where stretches of these old tracks ran in useful directions, the Romans.....used them for transport". As we shall see, this theory is of particular relevance to what we will be looking at further on.

As for Watkins himself, he was born, in 1855, at Hereford; just a stone's throw from the Bodenhams' seat at Rotherwas; the son of a local brewer. His intimate knowledge of the local Herefordshire landscape, which he was to refer to time and time again in his writings, just as Sir Walter was to refer to the geography and topography of the Scottish Borders in his, was acquired as a result of of his employment as a brewer's representative, or outrider, in his youth. Many years later, at the age of sixty-five, he was to perceive, in a flash of inspiration, what he himself was to come to believe was the significance of the prehistoric alignments previously referred to: A phenomenon that he was to name "The Ley System" in his two published works *Early British*

Trackways and *The Old Straight Track;* which appeared in 1922 and 1925 respectively. In view of the fact that, as we shall see shortly, Watkins's own theories provide us with clues as to the exact origin of the name of "Scott", it is an interesting coincidence that this original flash of inspiration is alleged, by his biographers, to have occurred at Bredwardine, on the River Wye, just a few miles upstream from Hereford and Rotherwas. Another interesting coincidence is that in Scott's first novel, *Waverley*, one of the fictitious families that are drawn into the drama are the Lowland Lairds of Bradwardine.

Whatever prompted Scott to choose such a name for some of his fictional characters is beyond the scope of this book. What is certain though is that in the pages of *The Old Straight Track* we find Watkins referring to Scott's own origins, in a quotation from the writings of one J.G.Wood who ".....finds the place-name element "Scot" frequently occurring all over England in such names as "Scot's Hole", "Scot's Hill", "Scotland Bank", etc., has nothing to do with the northern nation, but simply indicates the shelter or lookout place of the watcher or scout, and associates the name with.......touts or beacons."

In consideration of this it is also significant that the two prehistoric alignments that I referred to originally, which converge on Carterhaugh, link a series of hill tops together in perfect straight lines. It is also worth mentioning that in ancient time it was customary to use beacons, or fires, lit on top of such commanding locations, for the purpose of communication, or at particular points in the ancient ritual calendar, such as the Festival of Beltane; itself associated with Bel, a god of fire. In more recent times such practices were carried on in times of emergency, such as when the Spanish Armada arrived off the Devonshire Coast in the Reign of Queen Elizabeth the First.

"If any doubt is felt as to the identity in origin or meaning of "Scot" and "Scout",....." Wood is quoted as saying, in concluding an essay which appeared in the Woolhope Club "Transactions" of 1920, p.198, ".....reference may be made to the arms of Sir Walter Scott, in which the sinister supporter is a black man holding a lighted torch in the position for lighting the beacon; and the motto is "Watch Weel". The closing chapters of "*The Antiquary*" also seem to indicate a more than casual interest in the history and practise of signalling by beacon fires."

Surprising as this may seem, Wood's assertion that the original progenitor of the name of Scott may have been given his name as a result of his holding some position in the Borders which involved him working as either a scout, or a signalman, who might have used beacon fires either to summon his fellow Borderers to assemble, before conducting a raid into enemy territory, or else warn his neighbours of the sighting of a body of hostile troops, is attested to by archaeological remains. For, as has already been seen, the area in which Scott was to make his home is dominated by the Eildon Hills; a series of peaks which are themselves associated with the legends of King Arthur and his Knights of the Round Table. Of the three peaks that make up the Eildon Hills, the northernmost is occupied by an ancient hill fort which is described by A.H.A. Hogg in his *Guide to the Hill-Forts of Britain* (published Paladin, 1984), as being "one of the largest hill forts in Scotland". Hogg also conjectures that the site may well have been the old capital of the Celtic tribe known as the Selgovae; who allegedly gave their name to the nearby town of Selkirk, where, centuries later, Sir Walter himself was to preside over the local Court of Justice.

The hill fort itself developed in three separate stages, starting first of all as a small 0.7 hectare enclosed site, oval in shape, which was originally placed on the summit of the hill. Later, another rampart was added, which enclosed slightly over 3 hectares; before the fort was expanded to its full 16-hectare capacity. The remains of hut circles attesting to its occupation, not only in times of danger, but on a full time settled basis, show this site to have belonged, in its final stages, to a class of settlement known to archaeologists as "Oppida". With the establishment of a large Roman fort at the northernmost foot of the hills c. 80 A.D. however, the British habitation of this site ceased permanently. Interestingly enough, it seems probable that it is this Roman fortified structure that Washington Irving refers to in his previously quoted account of his perambulations in the company of his celebrated host:

"A further stroll among the hills brought us to what Scott pronounced the remains of a Roman camp, and as we sat upon a hillock which had once formed part of the ramparts, he pointed out the traces of the lines and bulwarks, and the praetorium, and showed a knowledge of castramentation that would not have disgraced the antiquarian Oldbuck himself. Indeed, various circumstances that I observed about Scott during my visit concurred to persuade me that many of the antiquarian humours of Monkbarns were taken from his own richly compounded character, and that some of the scenes and personages of that admirable novel were furnished by his own neighbourhood......."

Directly above the Roman fort, on the summit of the northernmost peak of the Eildons, the Romans constructed a signal station, and in view of what we have already seen in the above given quotations taken from the Garnstone Press edition of Michell's *View Over Atlantis,* in connection with how they constructed their military roads on top of trackways that were already there, it is not improbable that the original 0.7 hectare enclosed site, which gradually developed into a fully occupied settlement, had been used in Pre-Roman times as a signal or beacon station as well; and that the landscape alignments alluded to in the lyrics of *The Wee Wee Man* were likewise part of an overall signalling network in which this was a key location.

Michell's theories as regards Roman routeways are echoed in A. Wainwright's *Old Roads of the Eastern Lakeland,* published in 1985 by the Westmorland Gazette. In a section on the ancient road across Moor Divock; which appears on page 21 of this fascinating little publication, Wainwright echoes Michell's theories exactly, when he explains how "There has long been doubt about the origin of the swathe cut through the bracken of Moor Divock between the foot of Ullswater and and Heltonhead at the base of Loadpot Hill. Not in doubt is the existence of a track along here ages before the Romans laid their High Street across a depresssion in the Moor: They must have been mightily surprised to find an abundance of traces of a much earlier civilization, stone circles, tumuli, standing stones and burial mounds in close proximity on the moor (all still to be seen today) being evidences of its occupation by prehistoric man.

"These ancient monuments were linked by a primitive path, but today this footway is as wide as a modern road and although its surface is of grass and gravel there appears to be metalling in some sections. Some antiquarians attribute this development of the road in its present proportions to the Romans, who were the only roadmakers in the district before late mediaeval times; another opinion is that it was indeed the work of the early natives, there apparently being relics of an ancient avenue of boulders, possibly a continuation of...." a "stone avenue at Shap....." "Nobody knows for sure...." Wainwright concludes, "It is a mystery not likely to be solved."

To the east lies the town of Appleby-in-Westmorland, which is likewise located on an old Roman road; and which is also the venue for the annual

101

Illustration 10): Branxholme Castle, Co. Roxburgh; one of the many seats of
the Scotts of Buccleuch, from another contemporary engraving c.1814.

Appleby Horse Fair; a traditional gypsy festival. We shall be returning to the
subject of this ancient institution in a later chapter, when we look once again
at the origins of the Laidlaws. And, approximately the same distance away,
in a westerly direction, is the Vale of St. John, the locality in which Scott was
to set his *Bridal of Triermain*. But in order to find another clue as to the exact
origins of the original ancestor of the name of Scott we must travel north, to
an area just south of Carlisle known as Inglewood Forest.

When dealing with this same subject matter in Chapter One, I quoted the
tradition preserved in the verse history of Sir Walter's kinsman, Captain
Walter Scott of Satchells; the seventeenth century poet, historian and
genealogist; which claims that one "John of Galloway", who was given the
appellation "Scot" by King Kenneth in the late tenth century, was
accompanied in his migration from Galloway to Rankleburn by another

individual; also of Ancient North British stock. The name by which this last individual appears to have been known was "Wat English" or "Wat the English"; and it seems that he may have been John Scot's brother.

As to the fate of this Wat English, the editor of the 1786 edition of Satchells's verse history makes the "following conjecture concerning his posterity:" "Wat's place of residence being fixed at Bellanden, upon the south side of the Forrest of Rankleburn, betwixt Buckleugh and Branxholm, it may not be improbable that the surname of English, given him by Kenneth, might have been some how corrupted into that of Inglish or Inglis. Perhaps Inglis of Branxholm, Branshaw, Whitlaw, Whitrigs, Goldilands, Todishaw, Todholes, & c. was one of the descendants of this Wat English".

Interestingly enough, it is this last piece of speculation which provides us with a vital clue as to the true origins of the original progenitor of Clan Scott. For, as we saw in the opening chapters, he and Wat English are supposed to have arrived in Branxholme from Galloway; but were ultimately descended from amongst the British population of the old Kingdom of Rheged around Carlisle. It is also significant then, in view of this, that during the Dark Ages a great deal of intermarriage appears to have taken place, in certain specific areas, between native Britons and the recently arrived Angles and Saxons. As has already been seen, Bodenham in Herefordshire appears to have been a settlement where just such a mixed population resided. It is therefore quite probable then that the population of Inglewood near Carlisle, "Ingle" being indicative of the presence of Angles or Saxons, were either mixed or intermarried with the local Cumbrians in this era. This makes it likely that both John Scott and Wat English had already acquired their surnames before their legendary encounter with King Kenneth III in the Forest of Rankleburn. And, in view of the fact that Kenneth is known to have ruled Scotland in the Tenth Century, it seems not improbable that John and Wat migrated to Branxholm and its environs as a result of the extensive Viking Raids that had begun in the late eighth century; and which were to continue for hundreds of years.

We shall look at the relevance of the Norse Incursions and the impact of Scandinavian Culture upon Scotland generally in a coming chapter. In the meantime, it is safe to say that John Scott's ancestors were in all probability "scouts" or watchmen; who may well have assisted the inhabitants of Cumbria in looking out for the dreaded longships that menaced the western coasts of Britain at this time; before their first recorded descendant migrated north east, to found the Dynasty of Buccleuch in the Tenth Century. Further proof of the validity of these assertions is provided by the presence of "Ingle" names in Galloway also, two fine examples being the village of Ingleston, just north west of Dumfries, and another locality of the same name just south east of Castle Douglas.

To the north, as one makes one's way through Nithsdale and Annandale in a more easterly direction, several more Roman roads run across the high country. Beside one of these roads, at a location roughly equidistant from the ruined Tower of Raecleugh in the Lowther Hills to the West, and Hart Fell and Arthur's Seat in the east, themselves two more locations associated in legend with Merlin the Magician, is another Roman signal station like the one previously referred to in connection with the Roman and Pre-Roman earthworks which at one time dominated the immediate vicinity of the Eildon Hills. Was this another location at one time connected with the original progenitors of Clan Scot, in the days before their supposed migration from Galloway?

Additional evidence which would give credence to the validity of such speculations is manifest in the fact that the man who John Scot, "the Signalman", and his "brother", Wat English, found living at Branxholme and Rankleburn when they arrived there was one "Brydine" [1]. The latter name would appear to belong to someone possessed of identical ethnic origins to our two Gallovinian brothers; "Brydw" being a British name, whilst "Ine" is clearly of Saxon origin.

Returning once again to Scott's own residential locality, and his beloved Eildon Hills, proof that the previously scrutinized alignments in the vicinity of Carterhaugh and Meigle Hill were once part of an ancient ritual landscape is provided by other local place names; which would appear to be indicative of the validity of all of my previously made assertions in connection with these phenomena: Both of these solar paths, or "Ley Lines" as the author of *The Old Straight Track* refers to them, terminate far to the north east; in the vicinity of Hillhouse; near Leader Water. One terminates at Headshaw Hill, the other at a nearby hill fort. If these two sites are joined up by drawing a straight line directly through them on the map, they can be found to be directly aligned with an ancient settlement at Blythe; to the south east. Blythe itself is located on another alignment which runs in a southerly direction through Dod Mill, Dods and an ancient prehistoric stone known as "The Dod's Corse Stone"; and it is here that we find our proof.

104

In Watkins's *Old Straight Track*, in the same chapter as the author makes mention of "Scott" or "Scot" names, he also puts forward the hypothesis that the original "Ley Men" responsible for the laying out, and maintenance, of these ancient pathways were likewise referred to as "Dodmen". The gigantic chalk figure at Wilmington in Sussex, otherwise known as "The Long Man", is supposedly a representation of one of these ancient landscape architects. For, in each of his hands he allegedly carries what is supposedly a gigantic sighting rod. It is therefore interesting to note, in view of this, that, in modern English, the name for an old man who needs two walking sticks to get about is a "dodderer"; he himself being referred to as a "doddering old man". This fact is noted by Watkins, who also adds that the definition of the English word "dodge" means to move something, or oneself, "to and fro, or backwards and forwards or up and down".

What this would appear to imply is that these "dod-men" moved up and down these ancient pathways, either as guardians, or maintenance men; possibly as a mixture of both; as will be seen below in the verses of another ballad which I shall shortly be examining. The name "Dodd" probably originates from the same source as the word "Druid", which, in Welsh, appears as "der wydd", a compound of the words "dar", superior, and "gwydd", a priest or inspector [2]. In some later place names the word "Dodman" became corrupted to "Deadman"; such as at "Deadman's Hole" in Norwich- "Hole", Watkins suggests, being a word for lane. However, as we shall see presently, this name has another significance all its own.

This corruption of "Dodman" to "Deadman" may well have lead to another distortion, encouraged, quite possibly, by the newly established Christian Church. For, running south from Berwick-on-Tweed, in the direction of Corbridge and Hadrian's Wall, is another great "Roman" road known as "The Devil's Causeway". Local place names however would appear to link it to our Druidic Dodman; a fact attested to by the naming of nearby "Doddington Moor"; with its network of stone circles, cup-and-ring marked rocks and ancient fortifications. Similarly, as it crosses Horton Moor it passes a region littered with yet more prehistoric remains, closely resembling those previously described by Wainwright in relation to the road across Moor Divock.

In view of this unfortunate corruption from "Dodman", to "Deadman", to "Devil Incarnate", the lyrical content of the ballad which now follows can perhaps be better understood: Entitled *The False Knight on the Road*, the verses here transcribed appeared originally in the pages of Motherwell's *Minstrelsy;* previously referred to at the beginning of this book in connection with the "Twa' Corbies". A further fact that is worth noting is that the editor of the above publication discovered this particular version of the ballad in Galloway. A very fine rendition of this song appears on an early "Steeleye Span" L.P. entitled *Please to See the King.*

"O Whare are ye gaun?"
  Quo the fause knicht upon the road:
"I'm gaun to the scule,"
  Quo the wee boy, and still he stude.

"What is that upon your back?"
  Quo the fause knight on the road:
"Atweel it is my bukes",
  Quo the wee boy, and still he stude.

"What's that ye've got in your arm?"
  Quo the fause knight on the road:
"Atweel it is my peit",
  Quo the wee boy, and still he stude.

"Wha'a aucht thy sheep?"
  Quo the fause knight on the road:
"They are mine and my mither's",
  Quo the wee boy, and still he stude.

"How monie o them are mine?"
  Quo the fause knight on the road:
"A' they that hae blue tails",
  Quo the wee boy, and still he stude.

"I wiss ye were on yon tree:"
  Quo the fause knight on the road:
"And a gude ladder under me",
  Quo the wee boy, and still he stude.

"And the ladder for to break:"
  Quo the fause knight on the road:

106

"And you to fa down",
  Quo the wee boy, and still he stude.
"I wiss ye were in the sea:"
  Quo the fause knight on the road:
"And a gude bottom under me",
  Quo the wee boy, and still he stude.

"And the bottom for to break",
  Quo the fause knight on the road:
"And ye to be drowned",
  Quo the wee boy, and still he stude......."

The structure of the ballad shows it to have been originally composed in a manner closely resembling the classic bardic style; the entire compositional layout being indicative of its versification in the ancient Celtic classical mode. Such lyrical "conversation pieces" occur time and time again throughout Gaelic, or Erse, and Old Welsh literature. In the Ossianic Cycles, for example, the questions asked of Graidhne by Fionn MacChumail possess a similar structure; whereas amongst the Welsh Bardic Poetical Traditions of the Heroic Golden Age we find a poem that recounts a conversation between Taliesin and Merlin; preserved in the Black Book of Carmarthen. As we shall see in due course, some of the other ballads that we shall be looking at during the process of our investigations possess similar properties. One of the reasons for this is because they may have been sung as duets, *The Two Magicians*, which we shall encounter further on, being a good case in point.

In view of the evidence presented by Watkins and others which we have examined above, it is by no means impossible that the "fause knight" on the road was originally a "Dod-Man"; as opposed to a brigand or highwayman; as one might be led to believe by the lyrical content of the ballad in its present, and possibly highly corrupted, state. It is clear from the method of versification that the ballad represents some long forgotten initiatory inquisition from indiginous mythic tradition; in view of the similarities between it and the bardic poetry previously alluded to in the preceeding paragraph. Unfortunately, however, due to the pagan nature of the "Dodmen" themselves, they were to become the victims, in a sense, of later Christian propagandists; who sought to demonize them at all costs. And, it is this Christian propaganda that was to result in the complete loss of many ballads; as well as the obscuration and distortion of many more.

Even in Scott's own time the Ragged Lion was himself encountering many difficulties, due to this unfortunate factor. In a letter to George Ellis, who was likewise at that time engaged in a similar line of research to himself, and addressed and dated "Lasswade Cottage, 20th April 1801", Scott writes as follows:

"My Dear Sir- I should long ago have acknowledged your instructive letter, but I have been wandering about the wilds of Liddesdale and Ettrick Forest, in search of additional materials for the *Border Minstrelsy*. I cannot, however, boast much of my success. One of our best reciters has turned religious in his later days, and finds out that old songs are unlawful. If so, then as Falstaff says, is many an acquaintance of mine damned......"

It is generally accepted that the "fause knight" is none other than "False" or "Old" Nick- the Devil. It is most likely that the "villain" of the ballad was transformed into an evil inquisitor only as a result of late corruptions in the lyrics. For, in Pre-Christian times the Scot or Dod-Man would doubtless have been viewed as a benevolent influence; keeping the ancient British trackways safe for the lonely traveller.

Another example of a "Devilish" Dod-Man, who has been demonized in such a way as to confirm as fact my previously set out speculations, as a direct result of what would appear to be the machinations of interfering Christians, can be found lurking amongst the legends associated with the Maiden Stone; an ancient Pictish symbol stone located at Chapel of Garioch in Gordon; itself a classic cross slab of pink granite. Legend has it that it is the petrified remains of a daughter of the Laird of Balquhain; who, having made a wager with a stranger that she could bake a good supply of bread before he could build a road to the top of nearby Bennachie, discovered that the man she had made the bet with was none other than the Devil himself; who finished the road before it was done and came back to claim his reward. As she fled before him she was transformed into stone. [3].

If the truth be known it is probable that another, ancient, pagan, as opposed to Christian, symbol stone existed here, along with a connected trackway like those previously described by Wainwright and others, which in some way had connections with rituals associated with offerings of bread of some kind. Pagan rituals could once have been enacted either at a Pre-Christian stone which may well have stood here before the erection of the Christian cross slab, or in its immediate vicinity, along the lines of the ancient May Customs still extant at Callendar in Perthshire as late as 1794. A contemporary account quoted by Michael Dames in his *Avebury Cycle* (publ. Thames and Hudson, 1977), describes this ritual in such a way as to show it to have a distinct connection with a famous incident recounted by Asser, biographer of King Alfred the Great; whose "Life" has become an important part of English folklore.

"A big oatmeal cake is cut into portions, one being blackened with charcoal from the fire. The pieces are then put into a bonnet, and everyone, blindfolded, draws out a portion. Whoever draws the black bit is the devoted person who is to be sacrificed to Baal, whose favour they mean to implore, in rendering the year productive of the sustenance of man and beast, although they now pass from the act of sacrificing and only compel the devoted person to leap three times through the flames."

Whether any real life ritual sacrifices such as this ever took place is a matter of debate. It is more probable that, like at the annual "Burning of the Bartle" at West Whitton in North Yorkshire, the victim was in all probability a thief, a shirker or a sodomite. Whatever actually happened, the burning of oat or barley cakes was a common practise in ancient Celtic folklore. According to legend King Alfred the Great is supposed to have burned his historic cakes at Athelney, in Somerset. His fortress there, located on the tidal River Parrett, is just twelve miles from Glastonbury Tor; and like Glastonbury, Avebury, and Cadbury Castle, equated by some with the mythical Camelot, Alfred's fortress is located on what is perhaps one of the most important "solar paths" in the British Isles: The so-called "Great Dragon Line", which runs from St. Michael's Mount in Cornwall, to Bury St. Edmunds in Suffolk; and which is astronomically aligned with both the May Day Sunrise and the November Day Sunset. No coincidence then that Alfred should burn his cakes on an ancient site that lines up with the May Day Sunrise at which his Perthshire counterparts would burn theirs. No coincidence either that he should have an ancient Briton, St. Swithun, for a mentor in his youth. St. Swithun's name is directly derived from the ancient Welsh "Syweddyd", which also finds expression in the name "Swithold", who appears in the following quotation from Shakespeare: [4]

"Swithold footed thrice the wold,
He met the Night-Mare and her Nine Fold,
Bid her alight and her troth plight,
And aroynt thee, witch, aroynt thee!"

The Night Mare here is none other than the previously encountered sacred horse, worshipped long before Christianity; and of which the Elfin Queen's Fairy Steed, in the ballad of Thomas the Rhymer, is just one manifestation. As we will now see, the manner in which she is greeted by Thomas is considerably less disrespectful than the welcome accorded her in the writings of the "Bard" of Stratford:

"True Thomas he pull'd aff his cap,
And louted low down to his knee,
"All hail thou mighty Queen of Heaven,
For thou peer on earth I never did see."

"O no, O no, Thomas", she said;
"That name does not belang to me;
"I am but the Queen of fair Elfland,
"That am hither come to visit thee.

"Harp and carp, Thomas," she said;
"Harp and carp along wi' me;
"And if you dare to kiss my lips,
"Sure of your bodie I will be".

"Betide me weal, betide me woe,
"That weird shall never danton me,"
Syne he has kissed her rosy lips,
All underneath the Eildon Tree.

"Now, ye maun go wi me", she said;
"True Thomas, ye maun go wi me;
And ye maun serve me seven years,
Thro' weal or woe as may chance to be."

She mounted on her milk-white steed;
She's ta'en true Thomas up behind;
And aye, whene'er her bridal rang,
The steed flew swifter than the wind.

O they rade on, and further on;
The steed gaed swifter than the wind,

Until they reached a desert wide,
And living land was left behind.

"Light down, light down now, True Thomas,
And lean your head upon my knee,
Abide and rest a little space,
And I will show you ferlies three.

"O see ye not yon narrow road,
"So thick beset with thorns and briers?
"That is the path to righteousness,
"Though after it but few enquires.

"And see ye not that braid braid road?
"That lies across that lily leven?
"That is the path of wickedness,
"Though some call it the road to Heaven.

"And see ye not that bonny road,
"That winds about the fernie brae?
"That is the road to fair Elfland,
"Where thou and I this night maun gae.

"But, Thomas, ye maun hold your tongue,
"Whatever ye may hear or see;
"For, if you speak word in Elflyn land,
"Ye'll ne'er get back to your ain countrie."

O they rade on, and farther on,
And they wade through rivers aboon the knee,
And they saw neither sun nor moon,
But they heard the roaring of the sea.

"It was mirk mirk night, and there was nae stern light,
And they waded through red blude to the knee;
For a' the blude, that's shed on earth,
Rins through the springs o' that countrie."

This section of the ballad recounts the circumstances surrounding Thomas and the Fairy Queen's journey to Elfyn Land. The last verse gives us another clue as to the secret location of this magical lost paradise, where it is said that "a' the blude that's shed on earth, Rins through the springs o' that countrie......" As we saw in a previous chapter, the references to the magical apple tree in the next verse, denote that their destination is none other than the mythical Isle of Avalon- Sacred Glastonbury in the Somerset Levels.

In the shadow of Glastonbury Tor is Chalice Well, an ancient sacred spring which is supposed to have gushed forth from the ground when St. Joseph of Arimathea struck it with his staff. Joseph, the legendary Grail Keeper who is said to have brought Christianity to Britain in 37 A.D. when he founded the first church on the site of what was later to become Glastonbury Abbey, is likewise associated with a sacred thorn tree; a genus with which both Thomas and Merlin have their own connections. The staff with which he divined the spring beneath Chalice Well was made of Mediterranean thorn. And, it is said that the thorn trees that can be found all over nearby Wearyall Hill are descended from this very staff; which took root when Joseph planted it in the ground. But most interesting of all is the fact that the waters of Chalice Well itself are so rich in iron that wherever they flow the rocks are stained red, as if with blood; just like the springs in this ballad.

On the face of this evidence it is safe to conclude that the Ballad of Thomas the Rhymer, as Scott and his associates collected it, from Mrs. Brown's M.S. and the recitation of some of the other locals, was an ancient fragment of almost incalculable provenance. It is clear that it is of Pagan origin, for in it, the Queen of Elfland declares herself for who she is when hailed as a Heavenly being by the hero of the ballad. And, given the fact that both it, and the previously examined ballad of *The Wee Wee Man,* contain hidden cryptic references to the phenomenon later referred to as "The Ley System" by Alfred Watkins, more than a century after Scott's publication of his versions of these two ballads, it is beyond question that the Laird of Abbotsford made some discovery of almost incalculable significance when he collected these lyrics; that even he himself was totally unaware of. This assertion is given even greater credence when one considers that the ballad of *True Thomas* contains references to the sacred spring at Glastonbury in a completely pagan, as opposed to Christian context. These references are unique in any legendary source; and it is even more incredible that they occur in a ballad cycle connected with an area hundreds of miles away from the Vale of Avalon itself.

112

I now propose to examine some of the other important factors that link up with all of the material previously examined; which will in turn shed more light upon the little known connections between the North British Dynasties of "Y Goggledd" and the inhabitants of the Isle of Avalon and the Somerset Levels during the Dark Age and Early Mediaeval Periods. Once again, we shall find definite proof of these associations in the poetry of the early Welsh Bards. And, yet again, we shall find more historical, mythological and genealogical links between both areas and the Kings of the West Saxons; who were to succeed their North British counterparts as guardians of these ancient traditions.

As we saw earlier in this same chapter, Alfred the Great hid out from the Danes in the Sea Moors around Glastonbury; and it was here that he burnt the cakes. In the preceeding chapter we looked at the legends surrounding the existence of the magical Fairy Paths, which have now been identified as Watkins's celebrated "Ley System". The references in the ballad of *True Thomas* to the magical roadways shown to the Rhymer by the Queen of the Fairies are doubtless another distant folk memory of this ancient forgotten system; just like the hidden language in the albeit corrupt ballad of *The False Knight Upon the Road* with its inquisitional elements akin to some of the Ancient Erse poetry preserved in the Ossianic Cycles.

The writer and historian Mary Caine, who has spent some considerable time researching into the origins of Alfred's West Saxon Dynasty, puts forward the hypothesis that Alfred's Line could claim Celtic descent, noting that his ancestor, Cerdic, who, interestingly enough, provided the model for Cedric of Rotherwood in Scott's *Ivanhoe,* possesses a name which is directly derived from "Caradoc"- an old Welsh name. She also makes mention of the significance of the fact that Alfred should have as his principal Royal advisor a Welsh monk named Asser, who was himself none other than the brother of Morgan Hen; a Prince of South Wales; according to Cymric records.

This tradition is echoed in the writings of W.A.S. Hewins, who, by some strange coincidence, was to edit the papers of one Colonel Charles Whitefoord, who, like Invernahyle, the romantic Highlander whose stories were to so greatly influence the youthful Laird of Abbotsford, was not only a veteran of the '45 Rebellion, but, in addition to being captured by Sir Walter's friend, was later to provide the real life model for the character of Colonel Talbot in Scott's novel *Waverley.* [5]. One of Hewins's more obscure publications is his *Royal Saints of Britain,* ".....showing their genealogical

113

connections: The relation of the Early Saints to the Story of Glastonbury, and some of the characters in the Arthurian Romances"; which he privately published at the Chiswick Press in 1929.

According to Hewins, the area lying roughly between Worcester and the Avon Valley, the area which, as we have already seen, was inhabited in later times by the Bodenhams and various other ancient families who could likewise claim noble Saxon descent, was ruled by a dynasty known as the Wisseans, or Hwiccas; whose lineage may well have sprang from both the Anglo-Saxon Royal Houses as well as the line of Ambrosius Aurelianus; a famous Dark Age Welsh ruler; thus making them related to King Arthur. One of Alfred's wife's ancestors, Wigmund Prince of the Hwiccas and King of Mercia, was himself a scion of this illustrious line; being a descendant of Prince Osric- "Osric Rex"; founder of the old diocese of Worcester.

According to a genealogy that is given by Hewins, Osric himself was not only Prince of the Hwiccas, but was also the nephew of Queen Osritha of Northumberland. This fact is of particular relevance to our story, for the Saxon Kings of Northumbria were successfully able to extend their kingdom as far north as Edinburgh and the River Forth at this time; whilst also holding sway over all the territory later to become associated with the legendary Thomas the Rhymer.

These facts are noted by Scott himself, who, in his introduction to the Metrical Romance of Sir Tristrem, already mentioned during the course of a previous chapter, tells his readership of how, in those times, "The disputed frontier, instead of extending across the island, as the more modern division of England and Scotland, appears to have run longtitudinally, from north to south, in an irregular line, beginning at the mountains of Cumberland, including the high ground of Liddesdale and Teviotdale, together with Ettrick Forest and Tweedale; thus connecting a long tract of mountainous country with the head of Clydesdale......"

The previously alluded to fact that, during the era in which the above described frontier, as it is referred to by Scott, was actually in existence, the Kings of Northumberland were themselves related to a dynasty of Saxon nobles, whose territory included Glastonbury, now becomes all the more interesting in view of what the Author of Waverley also discloses in connection with Thomas the Rhymer's own ancestry; elsewhere in the same introductory essay. As regards the quite obvious Celtic elements of which the

114

Sir Tristrem is itself clearly made up, the Ragged Lion makes the following comments:

"There occurs here an interesting point of discussion: Thomas of Ercildoune, himself probably of Saxon origin, wrote in the Inglis, or English language, yet the subject he chose to celebrate was the history of a British chieftain. This, in a general point of view, is not surprising. The invaders have in every country, adopted, sooner or later, the traditions, sometimes even the genealogies, of the original inhabitants; while they have forgotten, after a few generations, those of the country of their forefathers. One reason seems to be, that tradition depends on locality. The scene of a celebrated battle, the ruins of an ancient tower, the "historic stone" over the grave of a hero, the hill and valley inhabited of old by a particular tribe, remind posterity of events which are sometimes recorded in their very names. Even a race of strangers, when the lapse of years has induced them no longer to count themselves as such, welcome any fiction by which they can associate their ancestors with the scenes in which they themselves live, as transplanted trees push forth every fibre that may connect them with the soil to which they are transferred. Thus every tradition failed, among the Saxons, which related to their former habitations on the Elbe; the Normans forgot, not merely their ancient dwellings in Scandinavia, but also their Neustrian possessions; and both adopted, with greedy ardour, the fabulous history of Arthur and his chivalry, in preference to the better authenticated and more splendid atchievements of Hengist, or of Rolf Granger, Conqueror of Normandy. But this natural disposition of the conquerors to naturalize themselves, by adopting the traditions of the natives, led, in the particular situation of the English Monarchs after the Conquest, to some curious and almost anomalous consequences."

Is this the reason why, as Mrs. Caine explains in her *Glastonbury Zodiac, Key to the Mysteries of Britain,* "Cerdic's ancestors were Bron, Beldig and Odin- or Bran, Belin and Gwydion- British god-kings to a man"; or is there some other explanation; more in line with the previously set out suppositions connected with the genealogical researches of Hewins and others? We shall return to Scott's introduction to the *Sir Tristrem* again in a later chapter. In the meantime, as a means of elucidating further upon the cryptic ciphers contained in the ballad of *True Thomas,* let us re-commence our exploration of Ancient Celtic Tree Lore; an esoteric system that finds expression throughout this ballad; with particular reference to the sacred or magical apple tree in the Fairy Garden to which the Rhymer himself is transported.

115

Illustration 11): Goldieland Tower, Roxburghshire, the ancient, by then ruined, Border stronghold, as Scott himself would have known it c.1814.

As we saw earlier, the only other tree which is accorded equal status with the apple in Ancient Irish Druidic and Bardic Lore is the hazel. This last mentioed tree is itself associated with an ancient sacred well, just like St. Joseph's Sacred Thorn previously referred to; this time located in Ireland and referred to by Robert Graves:

"The nut in Celtic legend is always an emblem of concentrated wisdom: something sweet, compact and sustaining enclosed in a small hard shell- as we say: "this is the matter in a nut-shell". The Rennes Dinnschenchas, an important early Irish topographical treatise, describes a beautiful fountain called Connla's Well near Tipperary, over which hung the nine hazels of poetic art which produced flowers and fruit (ie. beauty and wisdom) simultaneously. As the nuts dropped into the well they fed the salmon swimming in it, and whatever numbers of nuts any of them swallowed, so many bright spots appeared on its body. All the knowledge of the arts and sciences was bound up with the eating of these nuts,......."

The salmon here are likewise the Irish counterparts of the Welsh Salmon of Knowledge. Graves then goes on to tell us of how, "In England, a forked hazel stick was used until the 17th cent. for divining not only buried treasure and hidden water.....but guilty persons in cases of murder and theft. In the Book of St. Albans (1496 edn.) a recipe is given for making oneself as invisible as if one had eaten fern-seed, merely by carrying a hazel-rod, a fathom and a half long with a green hazel twig inserted in it."

Perhaps the sighting rods carried by our "Dodman" or "Deadman" for laying out his "Sun Paths" were made of hazel? A clue to the possibility of this being so is provided by another of his names: The "Coleman", "Coelman" or "Colman". The MacColmans are a Sept of Clan Buchanan of Loch Lomond; and both the Buchanans and the neighbouring Clan of Colquhoun have an age old association with St. Kessog; who is himself linked in tradition with Monks' Island in the Loch. The clan badge and lucky plant of Colquhoun is the hazel, and there is evidence to suggest that in far distant times both the MacColmans and the Colquhouns worshipped the sacred hazel. As Graves points out, in ancient bardic or druidic divinatory alphabets, the "letter Coll was used as the Bardic numeral nine- because nine is the number sacred to the Muses and because the hazel fruits after nine years. The hazel was the "Bile Ratha", "the venerated tree of the Rath"- the Rath in which the poetic Aes Sidhe" (the Fairies) lived. It gave its name also to a god named Mac Coll or Mac Cool (the Son of the Hazel) who according to Keating's *History of Ireland*, was one of the three earliest rulers of Ireland, his two brothers being Mac Ceacht (son of the plough) and Mac Greine (son of the Sun)......."

This last fact is of particular significance, for, amongst the Welsh and Bretons, "Coel" is another aspect of "Hoel", the Sun God. The so-called "Heel" stone at Stonehenge, which is aligned to the Midsummer Sunrise, was originally sacred to "Hoel" or "Cole"; and we also have good reason to believe that Dodman or Deadman's "Hole" is likewise a corruption of the same name. In Welsh bardic tradition the goddess Elen, who features in *The Mabinogion*, was the mythical daughter of Old King Cole or Coel, to whom the famous "Sarn Elen" or "Causeway of Elen" that traverses Wales was originally dedicated. It was also in her honour that the sacred trackways or

117

Illustration 12): Dore's "Castle of Astolat", illustrating the romantic image of the ancient British trackway as an integral part of the Arthurian and Mediaeval landscape.

"Sun Paths" of Britain were originally laid out; and it was likewise with her too that the ancient megalithic "Hele" stone was also associated.

So how is all this connected with Thomas the Rhymer and the Eildon Hills? The answer to this question lies in the "Life" of another obscure Celtic Saint, that of St. Collen; who, like Old King Coel or Cole and the Colquhouns, is likewise linked with the sacred hazel. Collen himself is one of the most elusive Celtic Saints of the Dark Age Period; the main source for his biography being a sixteenth century M.S. of late origin. He is represented as being the founder of churches at Llangollen in Clywd, in Wales, Colan in Cornwall, and Langolen in Finistere in Brittany; and is also associated with Glastonbury in Somerset. But most interesting of all is the fact that an old Welsh bardic genealogical manuscript entitled *Bonedd y Saint*, or *The Lineage of the Saints*, which was compiled during the twelfth century according to modern reckoning, although the earliest surviving copy dates from about a hundred years later, makes Collen a descendant of a dynasty from Eastern North Britain; seated at Traprain Law in East Lothian.

In addition to this, Collen is also made a descendant of the real life "Old King Coel"; whose descendants also included King Urien of Rheged and the British bard Llywarch Hen. It is therefore no coincidence then, that the poem *Geraint ap Erbyn* or *Geraint son of Erbin*, which I compared in the opening chapters of this book to some of Scott's own poetical works, should, in addition to being attributed to Llywarch Hen, be concerned with a battle which took place upstream along the same tidal river, the Parrett, at "Llongborth", Langport, south east of Glastonbury, as the one on which Alfred burnt his cakes:

> *In Llongborth I saw the rage of slaughter,*
> *And biers beyond number,*
> *And red stained men from the assault of Geraint.....*

> *In Llongborth I saw the edges of blades in contact,*
> *Men in terror and blood on the pate,*
> *Before Geraint, the great son of his Father.*

> *In Llongborth I saw the spurs*
> *Of men who would flinch from the dread of the spears,*
> *And the drinking of wine out of the bright glass.*

In Llongborth I saw the weapons
Of men, and blood fast dropping,
And after the shout, a fearful return.........

Thus, in Dark Age times, we find a North British Bard singing of a battle fought within a short distance of the Isle of Avalon; whilst he himself can be shown to be physically related to a line of Princes ruling from a fortified stronghold just a few miles north of the Rhymer's sacred Eildon Hills; who can in turn be shown to be the ancestors of a Welsh saint who is himself likewise linked with Glastonbury's Avalonian Levels. Similar connections indeed to the ones previously outlined with regard to the links between the Hwiccas or the Wiseans, Alfred the Great's West Saxon Line and the Dynasty of Northumbria in the centuries that followed.

All these links lead one to ask as to whether the original Eildon Tree was a Sacred Hazel used by Thomas to guide himself back from the Sacred Isle of Avalon after Seven Years? Or, had the Queen of the Fairies schooled him in the poetic arts and imparted to him the secrets of the "Dod" or "Coleman"? Or, did Thomas himself become an initiator, like the dreaded "False Knight on the Road" after his Solar Quest to the mythical Garden of Sacred Apples?

Whatever the answers to these questions, the fact that St. Collen has proven links with Brittany provides another possible answer as to why Thomas of Ercildoune should have concerned himself with composing a metrical romance centred upon the deeds of the Arthurian Knight, Sir Tristrem; other than the one previously provided by Scott. Sir Tristrem can be proven to have unquestionable links with Scotland, Cornwall, Wales and Brittany; as will be noted throughout the chapters that follow. He can thus be shown to have definite connections with all of the areas with which St. Collen also has an association; and, in addition to this, his lover, Iseult, is represented as the neice of Prince Morholt, the brother of the Queen of Ireland, by the twelfth century romancer Beroul.

St. Collen, meanwhile, is noted in certain sources as being descended from an Irish Prince named Matholwch in some of the previously mentioned biographical material relating to him. Are "Morholt" and "Matholwch" one and the same, one name being a French Mediaeval rendition of a Dark Age Welsh original? If so, this might provide us with many of the answers that we are looking for. "Morholt" and "Matholwch" will appear in a later chapter; during the course of which I shall try and get nearer to the truth.

120

In the meantime, another reason why Thomas the Rhymer may well have concerned himself with the legend of an Arthurian hero, apart from the latter's well documented Scottish associations, is more than likely due to the fact that a hundred years or so before the Rhymer composed the metrical romance that Scott later published, the Royal Dynasty of Scotland had united itself with the Royal House of Brittany. Murray, in the introduction to his *Romance and Prophecies*, shows that we have good reason to believe that Thomas of Ercildoune was actually born at some point between 1212 and 1220 A.D. Fifty years or so before his birth, an Anglo-Norman noble named Conan le Petit, Earl of Richmond in Yorkshire, had passed away. Conan le Petit's other title, to which he could lay claim as a result of the marriage of his father, Alan Niger, son of Stephen Comte de Penthievre, to Bertha, daughter of one Conan le Gros, was Comte de Bretagne: Count of Brittany. Conan le Petit's marriage to Margaret, daughter of Henry Earl of Huntingdon and sister of William the Lyon, King of Scots (1165-1214), was to bring about this union; the end result of which was the popularization in Scotland of the Arthurian Romances which the migrating Cymry had taken to Brittany with them centuries before.

We shall be looking at the links between Wales, Cornwall, Cumbria, Galloway and Brittany- or "Lesser Britain", over and over again throughout this book. At present, it is sufficient to say that during the break up of the Roman Empire and the Saxon Invasions that followed, a huge number of British nobles migrated to Brittany en masse. With them went many of the myths and legends of the old Cymry; including the forerunner of a Mediaeval romance which was to be retold over and over again in the following centuries.

Before revealing the name of this romance, it is worth mentioning that through his Father's marriage to Bertha, Conan le Petit could trace his ancestry back, through that of his Grandfather, Conan le Gros, who was himself the son of Alain Fergaunt (Red Beard) Comte de Bretagne, all the way to the late Fourth Century; when his Mother's ancestor, Conan Meriadec, an ancient British Chieftain from the very Borderlands where Scott's own Clansmen would hold sway in centuries to come; had accompanied the rebel Roman Emperor Magnus Maximus on his fateful military expedition to the Continent; from which neither of them had ever returned.

121

According to the genealogies published by Hewins in his *Royal Saints of Britain*, Alain Fergaunt's own ancestor, Conan le Tort, Comte de Rennes, son of Juhel Berenger Comte de Rennes (fl. 930-937), was Father-in-Law of Richard Duke of Normandy; Grandfather of William the Conqueror; who could himself claim Breton descent through the latter's marriage to Conan le Tort's daughter Judith. And this, in all probability, more than any of the reasons previously given by Scott, is the principal explanation as to why the Arthurian Traditions became so popular at William's Court; as well as those of his successors. It would also explain why, amongst the old heroic Arthurian fables contained in the Auchinleck M.S. from which Scott recovered the *Tristrem*, there is "A list of names of Norman Barons occupying three pages......" of which Scott comments in the introduction to his edition of the *Metrical Romance* that he published, that there ".....is no hint of the purpose of this list, which is perfect."

Before rounding this chapter off I feel that it is necessary to inform the reader that it is not the purpose of this particular line of enquiry to attempt to trivialize Scott in any way. Indeed, quite the opposite is the case. There were many qestions about the origins of Thomas's metrical romance that he himself was unable to answer. All of the traditions that we have looked at in this chapter have been intended to show, first and foremost, that there is a definite link between Ercildoun or Earlston, in the Borders, and Glastonbury in Somerset; and that this is the secret location of the Fairy Garden to which Thomas was taken. Thus, by providing the reader with answers with which Scott himself was unable to provide the readers of his generation, it is hoped that he or she might better understand the Laird of Abbotsford's great achievement in the preservation of his Border Ballads for future generations.

As for Scott's original intention in publishing the *Sir Tristrem*, we can now turn to the explanation afforded us by Lockhart in the first volume of his biography of the *Laird of Abbotsford,* Ch. 12, p.364.

"Whether the story of Tristrem was first told in Welsh, Armorican, French or English verse, there can, I think, be no doubt that it had been told in verse, with such success as to obtain very general renown, by Thomas of Ercildoune, and that the copy edited by Scott was either the composition of one who had heard the old Rhymer recite his lay, or the identical lay itself. The introduction of Thomas's name in the third person as not the author, but the author's authority, appears to have had a great share in convincing Scott that the Auchinleck M.S. contained not the original, but the copy of an

English admirer and contemporary. The point seems to have been rendered more doubtful by some quotations in....Warton's History of English Poetry; but the argument derived from the enthusiastic exclamation "God help Sir Tristrem the knight- he fought for England", still remains; and stronger perhaps even than that in the opinion of modern philologists, is the total absence of any Scottish or even Northumbrian pecularities in the diction.

"All this controversy may be waived here. Scott's object and delight was to revive the fame of the Rhymer, whose traditional history he had listened to while still an infant among the crags of Smailholme. He had already celebrated him in a noble ballad; he now devoted a volume to elucidate a fragment supposed to be substantially his work; and we shall find that thirty years after, when the lamp of his own genius was all but spent, it could still revive and throw out at least some glimmerings of its original brightness at the name of Thomas of Ercildoune."[3]

No, far from trying to undermine Scott's work both as a writer and a scholar, I have sought, by showing the above given section of the *Ballad of True Thomas* to be a genuine fragment of bardic lore, akin to those that can still be found amongst the ancient traditions of both Wales and Ireland, to portray Scott as he really was: The Wizard of the North, and the true successor to Thomas himself. This is necessary, in view of recent attempts, by those totally unversed in such traditions, to reduce Scott's collecting and editing of the ballads of his beloved Borderland to a kind of antiquarian form of musical and lyrical tourism.

And now, as I bring this chapter to a close, I shall reveal the name of the Mediaeval Romance that first found its way into Europe as a result of the great Dark Age migrations to Brittany: It is none other than the *Romance of Tristan* or Tristrem. For, besides the Beroul version to which I have already referred, the German Romancer, Gottfried Von Strasbourg (fl. 1210) also composed a version of the same story that Thomas of Ercildoune was to turn into a metrical romance later in the same century. The source from whence Gottfried's "Tristan" was itself derived was none other than "Thomas of Britain". In view of the fact that Gottfried was writing at about the time that Thomas of Ercildoune was born, Thomas of Britain cannot possibly be him. What is certain though is that the two are connected, not only through their mutual preoccupation with the Romance of Tristan or Tristrem; but also through a definite mutual ethnicity; and possibly a common genealogical origin as well.

123

This last connection would appear to link the common ancestors of Thomas of Ercildoune, and some of the other Border Clans, with Gottfried's *Thomas of Britain*. Before going too deeply into this, however, we must return once again to Scott's Border ballads; where more clues as to the origins of the Laird of Abbotsford, as well as the Rhymer himself, are to be found.

Chapter Six

The Brig O' Dread

From Whinny-muir when thou mayst passe,
Every night and alle;
To Brig o' Dread thou comest at laste;
And Christe receive thye saule.....

A lyke-Wake Dirge

During the course of the previous few chapters we have charted, what might be, for the ordinary lay reader, who is acquainted with Scott only through his poetry and his novels, some pretty unfamiliar territory. The intricacies of the history of the Dark Ages, the Princes and Bards of "Y Goggledd", King Alfred's West Saxon Dynasty, Alfred Watkins's "Ley System" and all of the other subjects that have been covered during the course of the preceeding pages, must be understood in order for one to be able to grasp the true significance of many of the ballads that Scott collected; as well as the context in which they were originally composed. Of particular relevance is the Arthurian material, for it is only by gaining an understanding of this last subject that we can really begin to understand Scott the man and Scott the writer generally. From a psychological point of view, the chivalric code that runs right the way through Scott's writings, prose and poetical alike, came directly from the Arthurian Romances that he was to devour with relish throughout his entire life; as we shall see from the following extract from the already much quoted writings of Washington Irving; in which he describes an evening at Abbotsford spent with the Ragged Lion in a "quaint looking apartment, half study, half-drawing room."

"Scott read several passages from the old Romances of Arthur, with a fine deep sonorous voice, and a gravity of tone that seemed to suit the antiquated black letter volume. It was a rich treat to hear such a work read by such a person, and in such a place; and his appearance, as he sat reading, in a large armchair, with his favourite hound Maida at his feet, and surrounded by books and reliques, and Border trophies, would have formed an admirable and most characteristic picture. When I retired for the night, I found it almost impossible to sleep: The idea of being under the roof of Scott; of being on the Borders on the Tweed; in the very region which had, for some time past, been the favourite scene of romantic fiction; and, above all, the recollections of the ramble I had taken, the company I had taken it, and the conversation which had passed, all fermented in my mind, and nearly drove sleep from my pillow......"

Appended to the *Ancient Ballad of Thomas the Rhymer* in Scott's *Minstrelsy* are two further episodes in the story, composed and edited by Scott himself, from amongst the numerous traditions relating to True Thomas's life and the poems he composed. In the third part of the story, composed in its entirety by Scott, all of the Arthurian, and other elements, previously explored in relation to the Rhymer's Legend, rise to the surface in what is perhaps one of the best composed of Scott's lesser known poetical works:

True Thomas rose, with harp in hand,
  When as the feast was done;
(In Minstrel strife, in Fairy Land,
  The elfin harp he won).

Hush'd were the throng, both limbs and tongue,
  And harpers for envy pale;
And armed lords lean'd on their swords,
  And hearken'd to the tale.

In numbers high, the witching tale
  The prophet pour'd along;
No after bard might e'er avail
  Those numbers to prolong.

Yet fragments of the lofty strain
  Float down the tide of years,
As bouyant on the stormy main
  A parted wreck appears.

He sung King Arthur's Table Round:
  The warrior of the Lake;
How courteous Gawaine met the wound,
  And bled for ladies' sake.

But chief, in gentle Tristrem's praise,
  The notes melodious swell;
Was none excelled in Arthur's days,
  The knight of Lionelle.

For Marke, his cowardly uncle's right,
  A venomed wound he bore:
When fierce Morholde he slew in fight,
  Upon the Irish shore.

No art the poison might withstand;
  No medicine could be found,
Till lovely Isolde's lilye hand
  Had probed the rankling wound.

With gentle hand and soothing tongue
  She bore the leech's part;
And while she o'er his sick bed hung,
  He paid her with his heart.

O fatal was the gift, I ween!
  For, doom'd in evil tide,
The maid must be rude Cornwall's queen,
  His cowardly Uncle's bride.

Their loves, their woes, the gifted bard
  In fairy tissue wove;
Where lords, and knights, and ladies bright,
  In gay confusion strove.

The Garde Joyeuse, amid the tale,
  High rear'd its glittering head;
And Avalon's enchanted vale
  In all its wonders spread.

Brangwain was there, and Segramore,
  And fiend-born Merlin's gramarye;
Of that fam'd wizard's mighty lore,
  O who could sing but he.......?

A passage more illustrative of Scott's obsession, or "fixation", even, for want of a better word, with all things Arthurian one could not hope to find. And, in view of this, it is therefore appropriate, that we now return to the subject of the MS. collection of Romances numbered W.4.1 in the Advocates' Library in Edinburgh; from which, as we have already seen, Scott was to recover the *Sir Tristrem* of Thomas of Ercildoune. As we have also seen, it is in the same manuscript that we find the previously referred to legend of "Sir Owain"; who Scott describes, in the pages of the *Minstrelsy,* as "a Northumbrian Knight"; who, "after many frightful adventures in St. Patrick's land of purgatory, at last arrives at the bridge, which, in legend, is placed betwixt purgatory and paradise." Scott then quotes the following passage from this legend, which, like that of *Sir Tristrem,* is likewise composed in poetical form:

The fendes han the knight ynome,
  To a stinkard water thai ben ycome,
He no sigh never er non swiche;
  It stank fouler than ani hounde,
  And mani mile it was to the grounde,
  And was as swart as pitch.

And Owain seigh ther ouer ligge,
  A swithe strong naru brigge:
The fendes seyd tho;
  Lo! sir knight, sestow this?
This is the brigge of paradis,
  Here ouer thou must go.

And we thee with stone prowe
  And the winde thee schal ouer blow,
And wirche thee full wo;
  Thou no schalt for all this unduerd,
Bot gif thou falle a midwerd,
  To our fewes mo.

And when thou art adown yfalle
  Then shall com our fellawes alle,
And with her hokes the hede;
  We schal thee teche a new play:

Thou hast served us mani day,
  And into helle thee lede.

Owain biheld the brigge smert,
  The water ther under blac and swert,
And sore him gan to drede:
  For of othing he took yeme,
Never mot, in sonne beme,
  Thicker than the fendes yede.

The brigge was heigh as a tour,
  And as scharpe as a rasour,
And naru it was also;
  And the water that ther ran under,
Brend o' lightning and of thonder,
  That thocht him michel wo.

There is no clerk may write with ynke,
  No no man no may bethink
No no maister deuine;
  That is ymade forsoth ywis,
Under the brigge of paradis,
  Halvendel the pine.

So the dominical ous telle,
  Ther is the pure entrae of helle,
Seine Poule berth witnesse;
  Whoso falleth of the brigge adown,
Of him nis no redempcioun,
  Noither more nor lesse.

The fendes seyd to the knight tho,
  Ouer this brigge might thou nowght go,
For the noneskines nede;
  Fle peril, sorwe, and wo,
And to that stedether thou come fro,
  Wel fair we schal thee lede.

Owain anon be gan bithenche,
  Fram hou mani of the fendes wrenche;

God him saved hadde;
He sett his fot upon the brigge,
No feld he no scharpe egge,
No nothing him no drad.

When the fendes yseigh tho,
That he was more than half ygo,
Loude thai gun to crie;
Allas! Allas! that he was born!
This icht knight we have forlorn
Out of our baylie.

This poem is important for two reasons. Firstly, because certain key elements, such as the *Brig o' Dread* feature in some of the Border ballads amongst Scott's unique collection; and secondly, the presence of Sir Owain, in part of the Auchinleck M.S. Collection, gives us a vital clue as to the true identity of Thomas of Ercildoune and the origins of the *Sir Tristrem* in the self same collection.

Dealing first of all with the references to the *Brig o' Dread* in the ballads collected in the *Minstrelsy*, the particular song in which we find them is the *Lyke-Wake Dirge*, which, as Scott informs us, in the notes to the above, "is a sort of charm sung by the lower ranks of Roman Catholics, in some parts of the north of England, while watching a dead body previous to internment. The tune is doleful and monotonous, and, joined to the mysterious import of the words has a solemn effect." For anyone who is familiar with the arrangement of this song by the 'sixties band "Pentangle", Scott's assessment of the dirge is a thoroughly accurate appraisal. Elsewhere in the introductory notes to his version of the ballad, Scott continues as follows:

"Passages similar to this dirge are also to be found in *Lady Culross's Dream* as quoted in the second dissertation prefixed by Mr. Pinkerton to his *Select Scottish Ballads.....*" And, elsewhere in the same introductory essay, Scott also informs his readers of how, "The late Mr. Ritson found an illustration of this dirge in a MS. of the Cotton Library, containing an account of Cleveland, in Yorkshire, in the Reign of Queen Elizabeth....." which, he says, "was kindly communicated to the editor by Mr. Frank, Mr. Ritson's executor....."

130

So, here we see that the basic themes, that find expression in the previously quoted passages from *Sir Owain*, not only find parallels in the Border ballads themselves, but also in the traditional folk songs of other regions of the British Isles, such as those here referred to; which had been sung since the earliest times as part of the funerary rituals and night vigils for the departed common to those places, from the very dawn of Christianity; and with their roots in the pagan religions that had preceeded it. Such rituals are referred to in the abovementioned Cotton M.S. discovered by Ritson. And, in other parts of England similar customs have, since time immemorial, been an integral part of indiginous folk tradition. Since at least the Middle Ages, for example, the Staffordshire town of Bilston held an annual watch or wake service in honour of the dead. Such customs would, more often than not involve an all night vigil, which would usually be held, by candlelight, in the local church yard; and frequently on the feast day of the saint to which the church itself was dedicated.

Interestingly enough, the all night vigil was likewise often an integral part of the training and initiation of a Mediaeval Knight; after which he would be given his spurs. And, it is therefore significant that such practises were in themselves symbolic of a kind of death and rebirth; another recurring theme in many of the traditional folk customs peculiar to the British Isles. For, as *Sir Owain* passes over the "Brig o' Dread" he is being subjected to an initiatory process similar to those previously described; and it is therefore of interest to note that, amongst the ancient Pre-Christian Celtic Peoples of Britain, religious initiation ceremonies, many of which were of an overtly occult nature, were likewise a key factor in the training of a young warrior; much as survival skills are taught to members of the modern day Special Air Service Regiment.

Of the ancient pugilistic schools that once existed in Britain, probably the most famous of all was that of the Amazon Princess Sgathach; who is herself associated with the ruined fortress of Dunscaith on the Isle of Skye; until recently the property of Godfrey James MacDonald of MacDonald; Chief of the Name and Arms of MacDonald. It was to Skye that Cu Chulain, probably the most famous legendary warrior hero in old Irish mythology, was sent to be instructed by Sgathach; "in the Land of Shadows". The fact that, in the legends which recount this particular episode in this archetypal warrior's life, Cu Chulain has first to cross the Plain of ILL Luck, and travel through the "Perilous Glen", in order to find his way into Sgathach's kingdom, shows that definite parallels exist between this cycle of myths and those in which we encounter Sir Owain. For, as he reaches his destination, he comes to the "Bridge of Leaps, beyond which", is the territory of the warrior queen.

With his arrival on the hither side of the Bridge of Leaps, Cu Chulain encounters "many sons of the Princes of Ireland, who were come to learn feats of war" from Sgathach; and who our hero finds "playing hurley on the green". It is at this point that we are reminded of the warrior customs of Scott's ancestral Borderlands, as they are described by him in the introduction to the *Minstrelsy:*

"For smaller predatory expeditions the Borderers had signals and places of rendezvous peculiar to each tribe. If the party set forward before all the members had joined, a mark cut in the turf or on the bark of a tree, pointed out to the stragglers the direction which the main body had pursued. Their warlike convocations were frequently disguised, under pretence of meetings for the purpose of sport. The game of football, in particular, which was anciently, and still continues to be, a favourite Border sport, was the means of collecting together large bodies of Moss-Troopers previous to any military exploit.

When Sir John Carey was warden of the East Marches the knowledge that there was a great match of football at Kelso, to be frequented by the principal Scottish riders, was sufficient to excite his vigilance and apprehension. Previous also to the murder of Sir John Carmichael it appeared at the trial of the perpetrators that they had assisted at a grand football meeting at which the crime was concerted."

From this passage we can gather that not only are there parallels to be found between the legendary tracts contained in the Auchinleck M.S. and Celtic Mythology, but that there are also quite definite connections between the ancient customs of the Borders and those allegedly practised by the Ancient Celtic Warrior Elite of the Heroic Golden Age. This in itself is just one of the many reasons why Scott's compilation of the *Minstrelsy* was, and is, so important. For, not only did he collect the ballads of the Borders themselves, but he also recorded the ancient customs with which so many of them were, and had been associated.

Before returning to Skye once again, where, it will be remembered, we encountered another bridge from one world to the next, the Fairy Bridge, where the first Chief of Macleod was given his Fairy Flag, it is also worth

132

noting that the Sir Owain of the Auchinleck M.S. was never a "Northumbrian knight", as is claimed in the poem from which the above quoted passages were taken. He was in fact the son of Urien of Rheged, and a relative of the bard Llywarch Hen. And, what is more, he features in two other important texts, one of Welsh origin, and the other a twelfth century French romance composed by Chretien de Troyes; itself entitled *Yvain*. The Welsh text is none other than *The Mabinogion*, one of the most famous pieces of early Welsh literature in existence. And, amongst the collection of romantic tales of which it is composed is a story entitled *Owein or the Countess of the Fountain*; where, we encounter not only Owain or Owein himself, but also one "Kynon son of Clydno"; who appears, not only in the verses of the *Gododdin*, but also in the Welsh Triads.

In the *Triads* Kynon is mentioned as being the lover of one of Urien's daughters, whilst the *Gododdin* notes his presence at the Battle of Catraeth; as well as mentioning him as being the son of one of the Kings of Caer Eidyn- Edinburgh. And so, once again, we are brought back to the territory with which I have attempted to familiarize my readers throughout the precceding chapters: The Dark Age Poetry of the Bards of North Britain. It is therefore of interest, in view of this, that Jeffrey Gantz, in his notes to the Penguin edition of *The Mabinogion*, makes note of the fact that the "Yvain", "Perceval" and "Erec" of Chretien bear a distinct similarity to the "Owain", "Peredur" and "Geraint" of the above Welsh collection. And, just as the central character in the *Owain* can himself be connected with the dynasties of "Y Gogledd", so too can the heros of the other two epics: Peredur son of Evrawg is cited in the old Welsh genealogies of the Middle Ages as being a member of a British Dynasty that formerly ruled York, whilst Geraint is the same hero of whose praises we have already heard Llywarch Hen sing. Although not a descendant of "Old King Coel", like Owain, Kynon, Peredur or Llywarch himself, the fact that he features in the poetical compositions of a Northern bard shows him to be linked with all the other heros herementioned.

But to return once again to Cu Chulain's adventures on Skye, upon his arrival at "The Bridge of Leaps, which is described as "very narrow and very high", and as crossing "a gorge where far below swung the tides of a boiling sea" [1], "in which ravenous monsters could be seen swimming", he is told that not one of the other warriors there assembled has so far managed to cross the bridge, for, in the words of Ferdia mac Daman the Firbolg, "there are two feats that Sgathach teaches last, and one is the leap across the bridge, and the other the thrust of the Gae Bolg....." (a deadly spear technique). Nevertheless, undaunted, Cu Chulain attempts to leap the bridge, which he eventually succeeds in doing on his fourth attempt; and enters the fortress of Sgathach.

There is evidence to suggest that, just as the three previously referred to romances of Chretien's are French versions of earlier Welsh or Breton originals, so too is the legend of "Sir Owain" a later "Christianized" version of the tale of the Bridge of Leaps. As we shall soon see in the pages that now follow, proof of this is provided by the fact that, previous to his trials at the "Brig o' Dread", Owain is said to have been in "St. Patrick's Land of Purgatory". In fact, as will soon be made clear, the character of St. Patrick in the abovementioned poem is a Christianized version of a far more ancient and primordial legendary figure.

One of the most famous bodies of primeaval Scottish Gaelic Folk Literature, which, like the ballads collected by Scott, had existed as an essentially oral poetical medium until comparatively recent times, are the poems of the Cycle of Ossian son of Fingal; himself probably the most celebrated of all the Ancient Gaelic Master Poets. And, amongst the myriad of heroic characters who feature throughout this heroic cycle is Cu Chulain.

Strangely though, despite the fact that the historical Ossian would have been dead long before St. Patrick was ever born, he likewise features in these self same poetic cylces; many of which were collected and translated by James Macpherson (1736-1796); who travelled the Highlands at a time when many of the oral traditions relating to the Ossianic cycles were still extant in their purest unwritten form. Macpherson, like Scott, was accused by his critics of re-writing many of the traditions that he was to recover; just as Iolo Morgannwg, the eighteenth century Welsh Bard of Liberty, was to be in connection with his researches into Cymric Folk Tradition in the decades that followed.

In"A Dissertation concerning the Poems of Ossian", which appeared in the 1785 edition of his *Poems of Ossian*, Macpherson makes mention of the fact that, despite the fixing of "the death of Fingal in the year 286" in the Irish Ossianic poetical cycles, which are closely related to those of Scotland, his son Ossian "is made contemporary with St. Patrick; who preached the gospel in Ireland about the middle of the fifth age. Ossian, though, at that time, he must have been about two hundred and fifty years of age, had a daughter young enough to become wife to the Saint. On account of this family connection, Patrick of the Psalms, for so the Apostle is emphatically called in the poems, took great delight in the company of Ossian, and in hearing the great actions of his family. The saint sometimes threw off the austerity of his profession, drunk freely and had his soul properly warmed with wine, to receive with becoming enthusiasm, the poems of his father-in-law."

Of course, in reality, St. Patrick was never acquainted with the historical Ossian, neither was he ever married. What has happened in the case of this tradition is that the Christian scribes who wrote down many of the ancient bardic traditions of their forefathers, incorporating Christian elements into their newly re-edited texts, despite their pagan origins, as a means of furthering the cause of their own religion, often to the complete detriment of historical fact, have tampered with it. Therefore, it is by no means beyond the realms of possibility that the character of "St. Patrick", in the legend of "Sir Owain" is most probably an old pagan hero.

In view of the fact that the name "Padrogyl" frequently occurs in many of the ancient Pre-Christian sources to which I here refer, we have good reason to suppose that this old pagan hero might originally have provided the archetypal model for the individual who is supposed to have married Ossian's daughter; before the inclusion of a Christian saint in the re-edited manuscript sources previously referred to above. In Welsh tradition Padrogyl is identified at times with St. Petroc; Petroc being none other than the Cambro-Cornish version of the Irish Patrick; thus providing us with further evidence to substantiate our previously drawn conclusion. This theory is given yet more back up when it is realized that, as regards "Sir Owain" himself, another pagan hero who likewise features in the very same Irish heroic cycles as those in which we previously encountered Cu Chulain, is one Owen mac Duracht: Owen in this instance being a Gaelic rendition of the Cymric Owain. [2]

So, now that we have established the parallels between the Irish Heroic Cycles, the Mediaeval Romance of "Sir Owain", and the ballads contained in the *Minstrelsy*, let us move on to the clues that are to be found with regard to the true identity of Thomas of Ercildoune, which lie buried in these same ancient traditions. First of all, there is the tale of Oisin's journey, in the company of Niamh of the Golden Hair and on the back of a fairy steed, to the Land of Youth. We touched on this myth before, in Chapter 3, where I identified this magical paradise with the same one to which Thomas the Rhymer is taken by the Fairy Queen in the ballad of *True Thomas*.

Included among the many supposed descendants of Oisin or Ossian's Father, King Fingal, are the Macintyres of Islay. Amongst the people of Islay too there persisted, up until the last century, a local legend, mentioned by J.F. Campbell in his *Popular Tales of the West Highlands, Orally Collected,* published by Alexander Gardner in 1893, associating Thomas with the hill of Dumbuck; Dun-a-bhuic, the Buck's Hill near Dumbarton (Dunbreaton, or Mount Breaton ie. of the Bretons/Britons.) Like Lothian and Thomas's own locality this region was ruled by North British Dynasts during the Dark Age Period; themselves recorded also in the genealogies and poems of the North British Bards. And, in view of this fact then, it is not altogether surprising that we should find Thomas central to one of the local traditions which states that he "is supposed to be still living, enchanted in Dumbuck.....and he appears occasionally in search of horses of a peculiar kind and colour. He pays for them when they are brought to the hill; and the vendor sees enchanted steeds and armed men within the rock......"

Amongst the local population, it is always been said of Thomas:

Nuair a thig Thomas an riom 's a chuid each,
Bidh latha nan creach an Cluaidh.....

When Thomas of power and his horse shall come,
The day of plunderings will be in Clyde.

A similar legend, involving King Arthur and his Knights sleeping inside a hill, just like they are alleged to do beneath the Eildons, and the purchase of a horse, this time by Merlin, is associated with a hill at Alderley Edge in Cheshire. It is therefore of interest that Thomas's name is supposed to have been "Learmont", "Learmond", "Leirmonth" or "Learmonth"; after the lands of Learmonth in Berwickshire. And, in view of the fact that the word "Lair", as we saw in Chapter 4, is an old Erse word for a "young mare", the name of this location, and indeed Thomas of Ercildoune's own surname, might refer to it being situated on or near "The Hill of the Young Mare"; where Thomas's family might originally have taken up their residence. Indeed, the Moncreiffes of that ilk derive their name from the celebrated "Monadh Craoibhe", the "Hill of the Sacred Bough"; which was an ancient Pictish stronghold. Their family badge is a sacred oak, symbol of the ancient Druids, so it is therefore not impossible that the name "Learmont" was likewise derived from some similarly ancient sacred site.

But to get closer still to the Thomas of Islay legend, and indeed to the original author of the Romance of Sir Tristrem, I now propose to draw the reader's attention to another ancient Welsh genealogy which appears in the previously mentioned Mediaeval manuscript *Bonedd y Saint- The Pedigree of the Saints.* In Section 54 of this M.S. we find a genealogy tracing an obscure Welsh saint, one "Idloes", who is made the son of a certain "Gwdnabi"; and the grandson of "Llawvrodedd Varfog" or "Varchog".

Further on in the same M.S. we find the genealogies of two more of Llawvrodedd's sons: Efadier and Gwrial, whose names appear in Section 85. This last tract notes that their Mother is identified as "Archvedd" or "Archwedd", who is claimed to be "verch Arthur"- the daughter of King Arthur of the Britons.

So, who are these obscure Celtic saints? Well, the possibility exists that "Gwydnabi" is a corruption of Gwyddno Garanhir; a semi-mythical British Prince who features in the legends associated with the Bard Taliesin; himself in many ways another Dark Age equivalent of Thomas the Rhymer. In addition to possessing a magical hamper, itself cited by the Bards as being amongst the original "Thirteen Treasures of Britain", on account of the fact that if sufficient food for one person was placed inside it, when it was opened again it could feed a hundred, Gwyddno Garanhir is also portrayed as the ruler of a vanished kingdom: Legend associates him with a now petrified forest which is still visible in the shallows of Cardigan Bay, the so-called "Cantref y Gwaelod"- the "Sunken Cantref"; a Dark Age version of the Lost Continent of Atlantis.

Similar legends are associated, in Cornwall, with the Trevelyan Family, the original progenitor of whom is alleged to have jumped on horseback to escape the tidal wave that sank the now lost Kingdom of Lyonesse, part of which joined Land's End to the Isles of Scilly. Originally Lyonesse is supposed to have included Cornwall, Brittany and Galloway; and it is therefore of interest that, like the Trevelyans, whose coat-of-arms bears the image of a half submerged horse, the Johnstones of Annandale, another famous Border Clan who feature throughout Scott's *Minstrelsy*, in connection with the numerous feuds and wars that have taken place between the families of that region, also have a horse likewise placed on their own coat-of-arms; the other heraldic beast with which it appears being the lion; a symbol associated with both King Arthur himself, as well as the Lost Kingdom of Lyonesse. As we have already seen, Sir Tristrem himself likewise has links with Cornwall, Brittany and Galloway; so it therefore comes as no surprise that in *Beroul's Romance of Tristan,* Lyonesse should be cited as Tristan's own native land.

A few miles to the south west of the Johnstone's original power base, which was centred around their stronghold at Lochwood, just to the north of Johnstonebridge and in the shadow of Hart Fell, is the so-called "Mote of Mark". This ancient hill fort, which looks out into the Urr Water Estuary as it opens out into the Solway Firth, is associated in legend with King Mark of Cornwall, Tristan's uncle and the husband of his lover Iseut in Beroul's "Romans". A few miles further west, up the same coastline, is "Trusty's Hill Fort", a location which is also connected with Tristan in local mythology.

The key myth which connects all of these families and all of these locations is the legend of Lost Lyonesse, which, as we have already seen, is likewise connected with the emblem of the sacred horse; which is in turn linked not only with the myths surrounding the deeds of Thomas the Rhymer, but also with all of the ancient Fairy traditions previously looked at. But how does this relate to Gwyddno Garanhir, who, as we saw above, was our original connection with all of this?

Put simply, Taliesin's original bardic patron was, according to legend, Elphin, Gwyddno Garanhir's son; who, in some of the Taliesin Cycles, I refer in particular to those recounted by Graves in his *White Goddess,* is portrayed as the nephew of Maelgwyn, King of Gwynedd. Maelgwyn himself is one of the most famous Welsh Princes of the Sixth Century; and appears throughout contemporary Dark Age sources; most notably in the writings of the sixth century monk, Gildas the Wise; and in the Chronicle of Nennius; where the date of his death is given as 547. In the last mentioned text Maelgwyn is noted as having succeeded Arthur as High King of Britain, following the Battle of Camlann in 537, where the latter is reputed to have fallen. And, in view of the fact that Elphin is made nephew to Maelgwyn, it would make him a contemporary of Urien of Rheged; in whose honour Taliesin is known to have made many compositions. Urien's cousins were all present at the terrible battle of Arderydd, in 573, which would make all of the dates in the chronicles seem to fit in with historical and mythological fact.

In the legends recounted by Graves Elphin is imprisoned by Maelgwyn at Dyganwy near Llandudno; at that time the capital of Gwynedd. Taliesin sets out to rescue him, something he succeeds in doing by first enlisting the help of Maelgwyn's own chief bard, Heinin; in order to secure his release. The method by which he is able to do this is by first entering into a magical bardic contest with the bards of Gwynedd; which begins with him putting a spell on them "so that they could only play "blerwm blerwm" with their fingers on their lips like children"; whilst he recited a long "riddling poem, the Hanes Taliesin", which they were unable to understand". (3).

The answer as to why Maelgwyn would want to kidnap his nephew in the first place, however, is the key question; in that it provides us with the true identity of Tristan himself. For, in another Welsh bardic genealogical manuscript, entitled *Bonedd yr Awyr,* which deals primarily with the pedigrees of the Welsh Princes of the Great Heroic Age, which is calculated as having ended in 664 with the death of Cadwaladr King of Gwnedd, we find a direct reference to Tristan. Unfortunately, due to the fact that this particular M.S. is part of a collection of genealogical manuscripts of very late origin, which are collectively known as the *Hanesyn Hen* series of manuscripts, certain textual corruptions are now present in the primary sources available to us; which have found their way in there as a result of constant re-editing.

The particular tract in which Tristan is mentioned by name is entitled "Ach Cadwaladr o Gogail", and basically gives a series of pedigrees of the mothers of various Princes of Gwynedd; starting first of all with Cadwaladr and working back to Maelgwn. The section with which we are concerned, or rather, sections with which we must concern ourselves, relate to the mother of Maelgwn's son and successor, Rhun, the mother of Maelgwyn himself and his own Grandmother.

"Mam Rhun ap Malegwn", the document reads, "Gwallwen verch Afallach".

This tract effectively identifies Rhun's mother as being one "Gwallwen daughter of Afallach". This fact is interesting, first of all because, if the legend of Taliesin is correct, and Maelgwyn was Elphin's Uncle, then this woman, whoever she was, could well have been his Mother's sister. What is doubly interesting is that "Afallach" literally translated, means "Lord of Avalon". Or, to put it more accurately, "Lord of the Sacred Vale of the Apples". Which, as we have already seen in Scott's "Ballad of True Thomas", is the ultimate destination of Thomas the Rhymer on his magical journey in the company of the Queen of the Fairies.

This section of the manuscript in turn is followed by another pedigree, which reads as follows:

"Mam Maelgwyn Gwynedd, Meddyf ferch Faeldaf m. Dylan Draws o Nankonwy."

This genealogy makes Maelgwyn Gwynedd's Mother the daughter of Faeldef, which is none other than the female form of the Pictish name "Fidach", and the Grandaughter of "Dylan Draws" of Nankonwy: "Nankonwy" being none other than a late Welsh rendition of "Novantia"; the old tribal territory of the Novantae. As we saw in the opening chapter, this ancient province was originally located where Galloway is now; a fact which now draws Maelgwyn's dynasty well and truly into the picture with respect to the old Kingdom of Lyonesse and all of the other related localities and families referred to earlier in this chapter.

And, coincidentally, "Dylan Draws" is a late Cymric corruption of of the Pictish name "Drust" or "Drystann" (ie. Drustanus); which is itself the Dark Age forerunner of the Mediaeval "Tristrem" or "Tristan". On the face of this then, what the above given facts would appear to suggest is that Tristan himself was of Pictish origin. And, coincidentally, at Trusty's Hill, one of the two outcrops that lie either side of the entrance into the hillfort is carved with three Pictish symbols: The classic double Z-rod, together with two mythical beasts. In late Roman times this area was part of the old northern border province of "Valentia"; and the Life of St, Ninian, founder of the nearby diocese of Candida Casa at Whithorn in Wigtownshire, attests to him converting the Pictish population of this region as early as the fifth century; a fact that is attested to by the Venerable Bede.

So, on the face of this evidence, Tristan or Sir Tristrem was most definitely a Pict. But, as we shall see, the Drustanus or Tristan of this genealogy was not the only person of that name to whom Maelgwn of Gwynedd was related:

"Mam Meddyf merch Tallwch ap Kwch m. Kychwein," the manuscript continues, "chwaer y Drystann"; thus giving Meddyf a brother, "Drystann".

This pedigree names Meddyf's father as "Tallwch", whose name is clearly a Welsh rendition of the Pictish "Talargan". He in turn is made the son of one "Kwch", whose name is likewise a Cymric version of the Pictish "Circiu"; and the next name in the pedigree is likewise a Brythonic equivalent of "Ce

Circinn". Both of these names are derived from two of the seven mythical Pictish heros who supposedly founded the seven Pictish Kingdoms of Transmarine Scotland; which then went on to give rise to the Seven Ancient Mormaerships of Alba during the early Mediaeval Period: Angus, Atholl, Strathern and Menteith, Fife, Mar and Buchan, Moray, and Caithness and Sutherland.

The final genealogical tract which I now propose to deal with is probably the most interesting, however, for in it we are given the genealogy of Maelgwyn's father, Katwallawn or Cadwallon Llawhir- "the Generous".

"Mam Katwallawn llawhir, Prawst ferch Tithlym Prydyn".

This makes Cadwallon's mother the daughter of Talorgen the Pict. More interesting than this though is the fact that the earlier, and more textually reliable Jesus College Manuscript 20, which dates from the Fourteenth Century and which is currently in the Bodleian Library in Oxford, gives the following genealogical information regarding the ancestry of Cadwallon and his brother Einyawn:

"Einyaw a Katwallawn llawhir, deu vroder oedynt, ac eu dwy vam oedynt chwioryd, merchet y Didlet brenhin Gwydyl Fichti ym Pywys".

This pedigree makes the two brothers descendants, in the female line, of the Irish speaking Picts of Powys- "Gwydyl Fichti ym Pywys". The reason why this tract is so interesting is because it connects a southern Welsh Kingdom, which at one time straddled the entire Mercian Border, from Gwynedd in the north to Gwent in the south, with Gaelic speaking northern Picts. The Kingdom of Powys was to fragment in the Middle Ages into the Kingdoms of Powys and Arwystli, or "Twixt Wye and Severn". And, it is to a place not so very far from Offa's Dyke, on the English side of the Border, in close proximity to the latter of these two aforementioned regions, that we find a reference in the pages of Watkins's *Old Straight Track:*

"Visiting the Hermitage adjoining Courtfield, Herefordshire (the birthplace of Cardinal Vaughan)", Watkins writes on page 189 of the above, "....I found it not only to be on an unmistakeable sighting mound, but precisely on a ley (detailed in my earlier book as through the Bewell Well), which, south of the Wye, runs as follows: Palace Ford, Dinedor Camp (which towers above the Bodenham's now vanished country seat at Rotherwas), Caradock Homestead

141

(Caradoc being the name of many an ancient British Prince), Pict's Cross, Hom Green Cross, Walford Church, Leys Hill, Hermitage at Courtfield, Speech House......"

In Cadwallon's time the border of the territory of the Middle Angles lay far to the east, and the location here described as "Pict's Cross" by Watkins, as well as being the site, no doubt, of a cross slab similar to the one at Chapel Garioch in Gordon looked at during the course of a previous chapter, is that ruled over by his Pictish ancestors. And now we come to the clue as to why Maelgwyn, Cadwallon's son, should want to kidnap Elphin in the first place: I have previously conjectured that he was perhaps a son of Maelgwyn's wife's sister. There is, however, another explanation as to who he was, the alternative being that he could just as easily have been the son of Maelgwn's own sister.

Whatever the exact relationship, Elphin was almost certainly descended in the female line from the Ancient Kings of the Picts; just like Tristan. Evidence that this was in fact the case is provided by the fact that Maelgwyn's own son, "Bridei filius Mailcon", appears on the ancient Pictish regnal lists as King of the Picts between 556 and 586 A.D. And, in view of the fact that the Picts possessed an electoral system of monarchy, which devolved upon matrilinear descent, ie. anyone descended through the female line from the Pictish Royal House could be elected king, Elphin may well have possessed a similar pedigree; and this may have constituted the principal reason as to why Maelgwyn should want to kidnap him.

In view of this, and assuming that it was the case that Maelgwn kidnapped Elphin in order to prevent him from being elected King of the Picts, it is indeed of great interest that, in some versions of the Pictish regnal lists, "Bridei filius Mailcon" is preceeded by two other kings who ruled only briefly. One of these monarchs is referred to in a very corrupt text as "Galam Cennaleph". Many of the surviving Pictish Regnal lists are extremely fragmentary in nature, and in view of the fact that no written copies were ever fully compiled in the Picts' own language, the extant manuscript sources having been penned for the most part in either Latin or Gaelic, it is by no means beyond the realms of possibility that this particular name is a corrupted version of "Elphin map Gwyddno"; whose own Father's name I have previously conjectured as having been corrupted to "Gwyddnabi" in another manuscript.

As to the real truth of the matter, we will never know for sure. What we can be certain of, however, is that Tristan himself was most definitely of Pictish descent and came from an area in Galloway that may well have provided a temporary home to Sir Walter Scott's ancestors, in the wake of their original exodus from Cumbria and before their settlement in the immediate vicinity of Branxholme; if the testament of Scott of Satchells is to be believed.

We can also be sure, in view of the legends concerning the "Cantref y Gwaelod", that Elphin's own ancestors, like Tristan in Beroul's *Romance*, had some kind of a link with the ancient Kingdom of Lyonesse. In all probability this "Lost Kingdom" was some kind of Pictish confederation that existed before the arrival of the other ancient British peoples in these western reaches of Britain; for the Pictones, who Caesar mentions as having inhabited parts of the western seaboard of Gaul were likewise almost certainly of Pictish descent; and may well have been connected with this same, lost, maritime Kingdom of greatest antiquity.

But the real sting in the tail is the fact that, in the middle of the Fifth Century, at the behest of King Arthur's own Grandfather, Ambrosius Aurelianus, Cadwallon Llawhir's Grandfather, a chieftain named Cunedda, the ancestor of St. Collen, who featured in an earlier chapter, migrated to Wales from the territory of the Manau Gododdin in eastern North Britain. Tradition has it that he came with a group of his sons, whose names appear in the manuscript from which I previously quoted the pedigrees given above relating to Drustanus; directly beneath the genealogy of Cadwallon's Mother; recounted above; and under the heading "Meibion Cunedda Wledig": "The Children of Cunedda Wledig". In view of this, it is therefore no coincidence that another Welsh poem, dedicated to the praises of Cunedda, should begin as follows:

I am Taliesin, ardent in song,
I will extol baptism........

The only loose end that now needs to be dealt with revolves around my identifying Llawvrodedd and Archwedd the daughter of Arthur as being possible parents of Gwyddno Garanhir. If Gwyddno was a contemporary of Maelgwyn, then Llawvrodedd and Arthur would likewise have lived contemporaneously with one another; which makes it unlikely that Llawvrodedd married the latter's daughter. However, in some of the more obscure bardic tracts uncovered by the eighteenth century antiquarian scholar Iolo Morgannwg, there is another individual whose name bears a distinct resemblance to that of Llawvrodedd; and who, in addition to being the latter's son, could have been about the right age to have married Archwedd. This individual is referred to in the texts as "Llovas Llaw Dino". The name looks very much like a corruption of "Llawvrodedd" and "Gwyddno", just as "Dylan Draws" is a corruption of "Drustanus"; and in the original texts from which the manuscripts extant in Iolo's time were ultimately copied the name could have read "Gwyddno ap Llawvrodedd": "Gwyddno son of Llawvrodedd". In other words, Gwyddno's genealogy, that of his father, Llawvrodedd, and indeed, that of a brother of his bearing the same name, may all have got mixed up together as a result of some confused re-editing of the sources in which they appear.

To understand how these texts came to be corrupted in the first place it is important to realize that these genealogies were originally transmitted orally, from generation to generation, by the Bards. And, as a result, when some of them eventually came to be written down, a certain amount of corruption occurred. In the case of Llovas Llaw Dino or Llawvrodedd, however, the scribe may have had a very valid motivation for wanting to obscure certain facts relating to his descendants; particularly if he himself was in any way related to them. The reason for this is because the same ancient tracts which refer to Llovas Llaw Dino by name attest that he was the alleged assassin of of Urien of Rheged; claiming that he had been hired to do the deed by Morcant Bulc; another North British Chieftain. And, if this really was the case, the names in the genealogies of the three obscure Welsh saints mentioned above may have been tampered with as a means of disguising their relationship to the murderer of so mighty a hero. A monastery likewise would doubtless have been seen as a fitting place to send such an individual's descendants in those far off times into the bargain.

Further evidence which may give credence to these theories can be found in a little referred to Triad, also recovered by Iolo, in which the Three Great Herdsmen of Britain are identified as Gorwennydd, Gwydion ap Don and Llawvrodedd. The same tract also makes mention of the fact that Llawvrodedd is supposed to have tended the cattle of a North British Prince named Nudd Hael. And, in the old Welsh genealogies, Nudd Hael is made both a contemporary, and indeed a relative, of a Prince named Rhydderch Hael; himself mentioned elsewhere, in the writings of Nennius, as being one of the three princes who joined Urien in his campaign against the Saxons mentioned in the opening chapters of this book; during the course of which he was to meet his death.

144

Considering these last facts, Llawvrodedd the younger, who is mentioned as a knight in Iolo's sources, may well have been Gwyddno's younger brother. Further evidence that would tend to suggest that he was is provided by the fact that, like Gwyddno, he was the possessor of another of the Thirteen Treasures of Britain: A magical knife which was alleged to serve for twenty men seated at table simultaneously. This legend bears a distinct similarity to the one which relates to Gwyddno's magical hamper; and would therefore tend to suggest that the two legends are related. In addition to this, it should also be remembered that there are no fewer than two Gwyddnos, the other being Gwyddno ap Cawrdaf, and three Elphins, the two who likewise have not so far featured here being the sons of Urien and Gwyddno ap Cawrdaf respectively, all living pretty much contemporaneously with one another.

Taking all of this into account, it seems possible that all of them were in some way physically related to each other. And, if this was the case, it is by no means impossible that Urien's principal rival, Morcant Bulc, had been exploiting some kind of inter-dynastic rivalry when he skillfully engineered the death of Urien. As to the relevance of all of this to Scott's *Minstrelsy,* and, in particular the traditions he collected in relation to the deeds of Thomas of Ercildoune, in order to understand the interconnectedness of all of this, we must return once again to the legend of Sir Owain; and the *Brig o' Dread.*

As we saw earlier, the Dynasty of Maelgwn Gwynedd, which originally migrated to Wales from Traprain Law in East Lothian, just a few miles north of Ercildoune, were physically related to the real life Drustanus who provided the model for the Tristan or Sir Tristrem of the Arthurian Romances. In addition to this, the same dynasty is alleged in the above quoted genealogies to have had marital associations with Avalon- the magical paradise to which the original author of Scott's metrical romance of *Sir Tristrem* was taken, in legend, by the Fairy Queen. It is therefore significant that St. Dunstan, the alchemist Abbot of Glastonbury Abbey, who will himself feature again and again throughout our story, was baptized at Tootle Bridge on Avalon's River Brue; surely some sort of ancient initiatory ceremony; especially when one considers that according to legend Arthur's funeral barge passed this way on its journey to his final resting place.

Further downstream is Pomparles Bridge, where the Brue divides into three separate streams in the shadow of Glastonbury's Wearyall Hill. It was here, according to one legend at least, that the sword Excalibur was returned to the

Lady of the Lake, from whom it was originally obtained. Similarly, in the pages of *The High History of the Holy Grail*, the questing knights must pass the test of the Three Bridges in order to enter the Grail Castle: "They were right great and right horrible to pass. And three great waters run below". (4). Again, the parallels between these legends and that of Sir Owain's test at the "Brig o'Dread" are immediately apparent.

Elsewhere in Glastonbury's immediate environs, and on another ancient waterway that traverses the Somerset Levels, we encountered Alfred the Great burning his cakes. Further upstream along the same river, and directly above Langport, where Geraint ap Erbin fought his great battle against the Saxons, is Pict's Hill; clearly denoting a hidden connection between Tristan's Picts and Somerset; the old Kingdom of the Gewissae. Were the Saxon "Gewissae" descended, in the female line, from the "Gwydyl Fichti" of Pict's Cross and Pict's Hill? Who knows? If they were it would explain why we encountered King Alfred conducting a quasi-pagan May Day ritual that we know to have been indiginous to Perthshire, itself located in one of the most important of the Seven Ancient Pictish Kingdoms, in the heart of the English West Country.

This possible connection between the Picts and a West Saxon King draws us, once again, to the writings of Sir Walter Scott and the introductory notes to his *Sir Tristrem:* "The Saxon Kingdom of Bernicia," he writes, "was not limited by the Tweed, but extended, at least occasionally, as far north as the Frith of Forth....." And, elsewhere, amongst the writings of the Revd. Richard Augustin Hay, we are told of how the area around Rosslin, just south of Edinburgh, was, in the time of Donald I King of Scots (635-642), the abode of a Pictish Prince named Asterius; whose daughter Panthioria is said to have married that self same monarch (5). Thus, in Scott's own writings, as well as those of another, lesser, author, we find references to definite links between the northernmost Saxon Kingdom and the territories of the Ancient Picts, which in themselves would not only tend to suggest that both the Pictish and Northumbrian Dynasties were in some way inter-connected, but would also appear to be indicative of Scott's *Ancient Ballad of True Thomas*, as collected by him from the manuscript of Mrs. Brown and the oral traditions of his ancestral locality, being a genuine fragment of ancient bardic narrative composition. (6). Such facts would tend to put all the wild accusations of forgery on Scott's part to shame.

Before finally concluding this chapter, however, it is worth asking one more question: What is the significance of the apparent parallels between certain key elements in both Arthurian Metrical Romance, and the ballads which Sir Walter collected? To find the answer to this we must turn to another key work which, as we have already seen, was itself to exert a formative influence upon the young Laird of Abbotsford; and which, as has also been noted, was one of the collections which ultimately inspired him to publish his own collection of Border Ballads in the *Minstrelsy:* The 1765 publication *Reliques of Ancient English Poetry, consisting of old heroic ballads and songs, and other pieces, of our earlier poets;* by Thomas Percy; Bishop of Dromore.

In it, following an essay "On the Ancient Metrical Romances & C.", there is to be found a whole collection of ballads, many of which have been based entirely upon incidents in Mallory and other famous Mediaeval Arthurian Chroniclers. It therefore follows that this presence of Arthurian influences in Scott's ballads denote that the body of primarily Arthurian literature that found its way into the Auchinleck M.S. was in all probability part of the same corpus of original bardic source material that ultimately gave rise to both it, and to the ballads with which it is connected: The bulk of that literary reservoir being of a definite Pre-Christian origin.

We shall be looking at some more material of this nature in the next chapter. In the meantime, it only remains for me to add that amongst the metrical romances alluded to in Percy's previously mentioned essay is one entitled "Sir Gawan and Sir Galaron of Galloway". Again, we find further evidence of links between the old Pictish Principality of Galloway and King Arthur's court in one of the ballads contained in the "Reliques"; thus providing us with yet more proof of the validity of the assertions already outlined during the course of this chapter. We shall be returning to Galloway once again in due course, in the meantime, let us look at the exploits of a member of another Border Clan who feature throughout the pages of Scott's *Minstrelsy:* "The Gallant Grahams........."

Chapter Seven

Hughie the Graeme

Gude Lord Scroope's to the hunting gane,
   He has ridden o'er moss and muir;
And he has grippit Hughie the Graeme,
   For stealing o' the Bishop's Mare.

Now, good Lord Scroope, this may not be!
   Here hangs a broad sword by my side;
And if thou canst conquer me,
   The matter it may soon be try'd.

I ne'er was afraid of a traitor thief;
   Although thy name be Hughie the Graeme,
I'll make thee repent thee of thy deeds,
   If God but grant me life and time.

Then do your worst now, good Lord Scroope,
   And deal your blows as hard as you can!
It shall be tried within an hour,
   Which of us two is the better man.

But as they were dealing their blows so free,
   And both so bloody at the time,
Over the moss came ten yoemen so tall,
   All for to take brave Hughie the Graeme.

Then they hae grippit Hughie the Graeme,
   And brought him up through Carlisle town;
The lasses and lads stood on the walls,
   Crying, "Hughie the Graeme, thou'se ne'er gae down!

Then hae they chosen a jury of men,
    The best that were in Carlisle town;
The twelve of them cried out at once,
    "Hughie the Graeme, thou must gae down!"

Then up bespak him gude Lord Hume,
    As he sat by the judge's knee,-
"Twenty white owsen, my gude lord,
    If you'll grant Hughie the Graeme to me."

"O no, O no, my gude Lord Hume!
    Forsooth and sae it mauna be;
For, were there but three Graemes of the name,
    They suld be hanged a' for me."

'Twas up and spake the gude Lady Hume,
    As she sat by the Judges knee,-
"A peck of white pennies, my good lord judge,
    If you'll grant Hughie the Graeme to me."

"O no, o no, my gude Lady Hume!
    Forsooth, and so it mustna be;
Were he but the one Graeme of the name,
    He suld be hanged high for me."

"If I be guilty," said Hughie the Graeme,
    "Of me my friends shall have small talk";
And he has louped fifteen feet in three,
    Though his hands were tied behind his back.

He looked over his left shoulder,
    And for to see what he could see;
There he was aware of his old father,
    Came tearing his hair most piteously.

"O hald your tongue, my father", he says,
    "And see that ye dinna weep for me!
For they may ravish me o' my life,
    But they cannot banish me fro' heaven hie.

149

"Fare ye weel, fair Maggie, my wife!
The last time we came ower the muir,
'Twas thou bereft me of my life,
And wi' the Bishop play'd the whore.

"Here, Johnie Armstrong, take thou my sword,
That is made o' the metal sae fine;
And when thou comest to the English side,
Remember the death of Hughie the Graeme".

With regard to the actual historicity of this ballad, the late Ewan MacColl, in his *Folk Songs and Ballads of Scotland* (publ. Oak Publications, 1965), quotes the writings of Stenhouse, who says that according "to tradition", "Robert Aldridge, bishop of Carlisle about the year 1560, seduced the wife of Hughie Grame, one of the bold and predatory chiefs, who so long inhabited the debateable land on the English and Scottish Border. Grame being unable to bring so powerful a prelate to justice, in revenging himself made an excursion into Cumberland and carried off, inter-alia, a fine mare belonging to the bishop." "It is a pity", MacColl adds, in his notes to this ballad, "that historical facts do not substantiate this excellent story."

Having examined Scott's version of the ballad, which is transcribed above, we shall now compare it with that of MacColl, which is given below; and which can be shown to provide further clues as to the true origins of the lyrics themselves; as well as the probable identity of Hughie the Graeme. As for the version of the song previously given, Scott has the following to say about it in his notes in the *Minstrelsy:*

"In Mr. Ritson's curious and valuable collection of legendary poetry, entitled *Ancient Songs,* he has published this Border ditty from a collation of two old black-letter copies, one in the collection of the late John, Duke of Roxburghe, and another in the hands of John Bayne esq. The learned Editor mentions another copy, beginning *Good Lord John is a hunting gone.* The present edition was procured for me by my friend Mr. W. Laidlaw, in Blackhouse, and has been long current in Selkirkshire. Mr. Ritson's copy has occasionally been resorted to for better readings."

What follows now is the MacColl version of the ballad. The reader will note that the chorus contains a reference to *Londonderry.* In this instance we can be assured that the location which is here referred to is most likely

Londonderry just south-east of Catterick, in North Yorkshire- the "Catraeth" of the "Gododdin" in Ancient Welsh poetry.

The Laird o' Hume he's a huntin' gane,
Over the hills and mountains clear
And he has ta'en Sir Hugh the Grame
For stealin' o' the Bishop's mear.

Chorus: *Tay ammarey, O Londonderry,*
Tay ammeray, O London dee.

"They hae ta'en Sir Hugh the Grame
And led him down through Strievling toon,
Fifteen o' them cried oot at ance,
"Sir Hugh the Grame he must gae doon!"

"Were I to die", said Hugh the Grame,
"My parents would think it a very great lack",
Full fifteen feet in the air he jumped
Wi his hands bound behind his back.

Then oot and spake the Lady Black,
And o' her will she was right free,
"A thousand pounds, my lord, I'll gie,
If Hugh the Graeme set free to me".

"Haud your tongue, ye Lady Black
And ye'll let a' your pleading be!
Though ye would gie me thousands ten,
It's for my honour he would die."

Then oot it spak her Lady Hume
And aye a sorry woman was she,
"I'll gie ye a hundred milk white steeds
Gin ye'll gie Sir Hugh the Grame to me".

"O haud your tongue, ye Lady Hume,
And ye'll let a' your pleadings be!
Though a' the Grahams in this court,
He should be hanged high for me."

He lookit ower his left shoulder,
It was to see what he could see,
And there he saw his auld faither,
Weeping and wailing bitterly.

"O, haud your tongue, my auld faither,
And ye'll let a' your mourning be!
For if they bereave me o' my life,
They canna haud the heavens frae me!"

"Ye'll gie my brother, John, the sword
That's pointed wi' the metal clear
And bid him come at eight o'clock,
And see me pay the Bishop's mear.

"And brother, James, tak' here the sword
That's pointed wi' the metal brown,
Come up the morn' at eight o' clock
And see your brother putten down.

"Ye'll tell this news to Maggie, my wife,
Neist time ye gang to Strievling toon:
She is the cause I lose my life ,
She wi' the Bishop played the loon."

Of the closing verses, Scott makes the following comment: "Of the morality of Robert Aldridge, Bishop of Carlisle, we know but little, but his political and religious faith were of a stretching and accomodating texture. Anthony a' Wood observes that there were many changes in his time, both in church and in state, but the worthy prelate retained his offices and preferments during them all."

Elsewhere, when attempting to identify the hero of the ballad himself, Scott informs his readership of the following: "I find no traces of this particular Hughie Graeme of the ballad; but from the mention of the Bishop, I suspect he may have been one of about four hundred Borderers against whom bills of complaint were exhibited to Robert Aldridge, Lord Bishop of Carlisle, about 1553, for divers incursions, burnings, murders, mutilations, and spoils with them committed (Nicolson's "*History*", Introduction, p.lxxxi).

There appear a number of Graemes in the specimen which we have of that list of delinquents.

"There occur in particular,

Ritchie Grame of Bailie,
Will's Jock Grame,
Fargue's Willie Grame,
Muckle Willie Grame
Will Grame of Rosetrees,
Ritchie Grame, younger of Netherby,
Wat Grame, called Flaughtail,
Will Grame, Nimble Willie,
Will Grame, Mickle Willie,
with many others......."

In view of the fact that Hughie is nowhere to be found on this list of members of his Clan, who appear in contemporary records linking them with the other key figure associated with the "historical" traditions connected with this ballad, it seems likely, in fact, it is defintely true to say, that Ewan MacColl's previously made assertions are indeed correct. So who was Hughie the Graeme? Did he ever exist? And, what is the significance of the ballad?

Well, to begin with, the ballad may be a romantic tale combining several strands of historical truth, and conjoining them into one fiction. As has already been substantiated, the brigandage to which the inhabitants of the Border counties were subjected by certain members of this Clan during the sixteenth century is itself undisputed; and is indeed well documented. And, as we shall see later on, in Chapter Twenty One, another important member of the Clan was himself to be remembered in the lyrics of yet another of the many ballads that feature in the *Minstrelsy*.

The ballad in question is *The Gallant Grahams*, which concerns itself with the Ducal House of Montrose, the most senior branch of Clan Na Graimach; and the defeat of James Graham, the great Marquess of Montrose, one of Scott's icons in a number of ways, at the hands of the Parliamentary army during the Civil Wars. Scott's version of this mighty ballad, which he gathered "from tradition, enlarged and corrected by an ancient printed edition entitled *The Gallant Grahams of Scotland*, to the tune of *I will away, and I will not tarry,* furnished by Joseph Ritson, concludes with the execution of Montrose; who was "sentenced to be hanged by the neck, cut down, disembowelled, beheaded and quartered."

After defending himself at his trial, before all his tormentors, Montrose composed his own metrical prayer for recitation at his execution, which, as will be seen below, bears a certain resemblance, in some definite respects, to verse fourteen of the ballad collected by Scott; and verse nine of that given by MacColl [1]:

Let them bestow on ev'ry Airth a Limb;
Open all my veins, that I may swim
To thee my Saviour, in that Crimson Lake;
Then place my par-boil'd Head upon a Stake;
Scatter my Ashes, throw them in the Air:
Lord (since Thou know'st where all these Atoms are)
I'm hopeful, once Thou'll recollect my Dust,
And confident Thou'lt raise me with the Just.

So, perhaps the ballad of *Hughie the Graeme* has had more than one historical strand incorporated, or interwoven, into its lyrical content; as has previously been suggested. Or, perhaps, like some of the ballads that have previously been examined during the course of this book already, it possesses a deeper meaning; which lies concealed far beneath its surface. Even at first glance there are certain key elements within each of the two previously given versions which differ considerably. From the point of view of geography, for example, Scott's version is set in Carlisle, whilst MacColl's is centred upon Stirling; in the old Mormaership of Menteith; in traditional Highland Graham Country; where Aldridge and his cronies would have had no jurisdiction. And it is at this juncture that we find our first clue as to the true nature of some of the deeper, latent, undercurrents lurking in the background; elements far more subtle than those that one would merely expect to find if one were just to take the lyrics at face value.

In Sir Rupert Ian Moncreiffe's vast and exchaustive work on Scottish Clan history, *The Highland Clans* (publ. Barrie and Jenkins, 1982), the author expounds the now popularly held opinion that the Grahams belonged, originally, to the "Anglo-Norman aristocracy, and derived their surname from the lordship of an English manor, the "grey home" called "Graegham" in the Domesday Book."

This is certainly the case with regard to the Lindsays, who trace their origins right the way back, through William de Lindsay of Ercildoune (fl.1133-47), to the Norse Jarl Ivar of the Uplanders; a celebrated Norwegian raider. It is also true of the Sinclairs, whose ancestors, like those of William Wallace, likewise arrived in Scotland as a direct result of the marriage of St. Margaret of England to Malcolm Canmore, King of Scots.

The Setons can also be shown to have originally arrived in England in the army of William the Conqueror, before migrating north; as did the original ancestors of the Chiefs of Clan Fraser; one of whom appears on the Roll of Battle Abbey; prior to their arrival in Scotland along with a whole host of Norman, Flemish and Breton Barons: The Bruces of Annandale were amongst this influx of continental blood, as were the ancestors of the Royal House of Stuart; who claim descent from Flaald, hereditary Steward of Dol in Brittany (fl.1080). The Hays are also of Norman origin, deriving their name from La Haye, in the Contentin Peninsular. But for the Grahams, there are several other plausible explanations as to their origins; all of which have a bearing, as we shall see, upon the lyrical content of the two versions of this ballad previously given.

In R.R. McIan's *The Clans of the Scottish Highlands,* first published in 1845, but still a classic work in certain definite respects and a true treasure trove of anecdotal information, we find the following tradition concerning their Clan History:

"The Gallant Grahams have acted so chivalrous and important a part in the annals of Scottish history, as to have well merited that appellation. Their traditional origin is of the highest antiquity, the ducal family of Montrose tracing its descent to the fifth century. The Emperor, Antoninus, had raised a fortified wall of extraordinary strength from sea to sea, in the vain hope that it would preserve the conquered provinces from the dread incursions of the Scots, but Graeme who commanded the confederated tribes, broke through this useless defence, which from him became afterwards known as "Graeme's dyke". The name was indicative of the fierceness of the man, Gruamach or Gramach being applied to one of stern, forbidding look and manner, the term whence is derived the Gothic "grim".

"Any satisfactory record," the writer then continues "of the several generations who succeeded this hero, filling up the interval between him and William de Graeme, who lived in the reign of David I and is witness to the foundation of the abbey of Holy Rood, in 1128, cannot be expected, but from this ancestor they are regularly authenticated."

Upon reading the above one is instantly reminded of the previously quoted extracts from Scott's introduction to the *Minstrelsy*, which appeared in the opening chapters, as regards the inhabitants of the Manau Gododdin; as well as the desperate struggles and conflicts that were to take place along the frontier region at the twilight of the Roman Empire. These are the tribesmen who constituted the "first wave of the torrent which assaulted, and finally overwhelmed, the barriers of the Roman power in Britain"; those self same Picts, whose "Gothic" tongue was a "dialect of the Teutonic" by Scott's reckoning. It is therefore interesting, in view of all these facts, that in Southern Britain, also, several earthworks of similar scale should exist which are all called either "Grimsdyke" or "Grim's Ditch". And, in view of Scott's previously referred to assertion, that at least some of the Pictish dialects spoken in Britain in those far off times were related to the Germanic Linguisitic Group, it worth noting that "Grim", according to the reckoning of certain modern historical writers, most notably Brian Branston, was a colloquial "nickname" for Odin or Woden amongst the Dark Age Saxons. Branston, writing in his classic work on Anglo-Saxon deism *The Lost Gods of England* (publ. Thames and Hudson, 1984), asserts that the fact that such earthworks were associated with him in this way, attests to "the awe in which Woden was held as the supposed creator of these vast ramparts, while at the same time suggesting the popular nature of his cult in that here a nickname is used."

Now, as we shall see, in the pages that follow, the association with "Grim" possessed by these mighty banks and trenches may well ante-date the arrival of the Saxons by some several centuries. For, amongst the numerous examples of ancient earthworks that came to be named after Grim by the incoming Saxons during the Dark Ages are Grim's Ditch at Aldworth in Berkshire, Grimsbury Castle at nearby Hermitage, Grim's Ditch at Mongewell in Oxfordshire, and two other earthworks of the same name, one running between Evenlode and Glyme in the same county, and another in the Chilterns. Modern archaeology has come to associate these sites with the arrival in Britain of Belgic tribes from the Continent during the Iron Age. And, it is therefore not altogether surprising that similar defensive structures are peculiar to Scotland also; as the following extract from the previously quoted letter from Scott to George Ellis that I referred to in an earlier chapter attests:

156

"I have been rather an observer of detached facts respecting antiquities, than a regular student. At the same time, I may mention one or two circumstances, were it but to place your elephant upon a tortoise. From Selkirkshire to Cumberland, we have a ditch and bulwark of great strength, called the Catrail, running north and south, and obviously calculated to defend the western half of the island against the inhabitants of the eastern half. Within this bulwark, at Drummelzier, near Peebles, we find the grave of Merlin, the account of whose madness and death you find in Fordun. The same author says he was seized with his madness during a dreadful battle on the Liddle, which divides Cumberland from Scotland. All this seems to favour your ingenious hypothesis, that the sway of the British Champion (Arthur) extended over Cumberland and Strathcluyd, as well as Wales. Ercildoune is hardly five miles from the Catrail......."

In view of the fact that, here in the Scottish Borders, a similar series of defensive ramparts is here referred to as "The Catrail", by Scott, thus inferring that, like most of the structures of this particular category in Southern Britain, they too are linked with the Belgic confederation of tribes referred to as "The Catuvellaunii", themselves in the vanguard of the resistance to the Roman invaders under Caesar and his successors, it is safe to assume that the association of all such earthworks with Grim, or "Gruamach", is of a much earlier provenance than the Anglo-Saxon Era. For example, we know for definite that the Saxons connected these sites with Grim on account of the fact that they were so in awe of them that they thought that the only possible explanation for their existence was that they had been brought into being by some kind of superhuman agency. In their case, it was the god Grim who they thought was responsible; just as the Dark Age Britons came to asssociate the ramparts of Cadbury Castle in Somerset with the Magician Merlin.

On the face of this then, it is far from impossible that, in a similar way, the Picts likewise came to connect such mighty constructions with one of their own warrior heros. A hero who, like Cu Chulain, was attributed with possessing semi-supernatural warrior skills. The name "Girom" or "Giromsolus", for example, appears throughout the Pictish King Lists; as do names like "Tarain". The last given name is linked by Marjorie O. Anderson in her *Kings and Kingship in Early Scotland* (publ. Scottish Academic Press, Edinburgh and London, 1980), with "the Gaulish thunder-god Taranis whose cult seems to have been widespread in Britain."

So, given the fact that the incoming English possessed a god of their own named Thunor, who was himself the equivalent of Taranis; and that they also claimed that their lines of Kings, from those of the West Saxons and Bernicians to those of the East Angles, Middle Angles & C., were all descended from Odin; as well as a whole line of divine or semi-divine god kings, it is by no means impossible that the Picts likewise possessed similar beliefs. This, from the evidence that we have, is most likely, in view of the fact that many of the names on certain versions of the Pictish King Lists are prefixed with what may be the "throne" or coronation name of "Bruide"; which Moncreiffe of that ilk identifies with the male manifestation of the pagan goddess Brigid; thus inferring that each of the Pictish rulers took on a kind of divine, or semi-divine status upon their accession. The Morayshire Clan, Brodie of Brodie, are themselves connected with this pagan archetype, and are in turn universally acknowledged to be of Pictish origin. Taking this into consideration then it is not unreasonable to conclude that the Graemes or Grahams may claim a similar antiquity for their own Clan. If this should indeed turn out to be the case then, Hughie the Graeme is not an actual historical character at all, but an ancient Pre-Christian pagan archetype, who has found his way into this ballad on account of his exalted status amongst the people of the Borders, as well as those of the Menteith region of Strathern; itself a Pictish stronghold since the earliest of times and the location where he is placed in the MacColl version of the ballad. Perhaps the newly religious ballad singer to whom we saw Scott refer in a previous chapter knew this, and perhaps this is why he considered ballads to be "unlawful". We shall never know for sure.

The opening verses of the Scott ballad recount a legendary duel between Lord Scrope and Hughie the Graeme. During the latter's subsequent trial we find the appearance of certain key characters, involved in certain archetypal situations, that show, first of all, that both of the above given ballads must have come out of the same corporate body of original source material- the presence of Lady Hume in both ballads being a classic case in point. The second thing that the reader will also notice is that there is an overtly pagan element in both sets of lyrics. The key to this last point is that, like the account of the survival of a form of sacral kingship in Northern Ireland well into the Middle Ages which appears in the previously quoted from extract from the writings of Gerald of Wales, the theft of this particular horse has an overt association with sex. For in this instance Hughie the Graeme has allegedly stolen the Bishop's horse or mare on account of the latter's infidelity with his own wife.

In reality, Hughie would only have had to have gone to the Bishop's clerical superiors to get justice for what is allegedly supposed to have happened; so that what we have here is definite proof that these lyrics contain within their composition a hidden wealth of archetypal folk traditions whose true origins can only be really guessed at. A vital clue as to what these folk traditions were, exactly, can be found concealed within the structure of some of Britain's most ancient traditional customs. As we saw in the last chapter, certain ballads, such as *The Lyke Wake Dirge*, have definite links with many of the traditional folk customs enacted annually across the British Isles. Similarly, a duel between two archetypal heros is at the centre of many a traditional folk play; just as it is in the case of Scott's version of the *Ballad of Hughie the Graeme*.

A valid case in point is the Rottingdean Mummers' Play, enacted each year at Rottingdean in Sussex, by members of the celebrated folk singing Copper Family and friends. The Copper Family Tradition will come under scrutiny in Chapter Twenty Two. In the meantime, it is worth noting that at Antrobus in Cheshire an annual performance likewise takes place of a metrical folk play, centred on a mythical duel between "King George" and "Black Prince", and itself enacted by the Antrobus Soul Cakers.

At Marshfield in Gloucester a similar play is performed in which the duellists are "King William" and "Little Man John". At Antrobus, however, which is just a stone's throw from Alderley Edge, which is associated in local legend with both Merlin and the purchase of a horse, as we likewise saw in the last chapter, we have the added attraction of the appearance of Dick the Wild Horse during the course of the performance. It therefore follows then that the original duel that the two heros may have been involved in might well have been over the ownership or possession of a sacred horse. And, in view of the link between the sacred horse itself and the Ancient Fairy Religions, it may also not be impossible that the horse in question was in fact a priestess of the cult of the sacred horse; for whose hand in marriage our duellists were competing.

At Kingston in Surrey, a site linked with Glastonbury and Alfred's Dynasty of the West Saxons, owing to the fact that it is home to the celebrated Coronation Stone, upon which they were seated in order to be enthroned, in a fashion not dissimilar to that in which the Scottish Kings were formerly crowned at Scone, there was, until quite recently, an annual football game, held every year in the town market place; which took place every Hocktide.

According to legend, this custom originally started on account of a duel between two rival Saxon nobles, over the love of Merton's Fair Maid; a story that is at the heart of the town's oldest suviving folk myth.

According to Mrs. Mary Caine, whose writings I quoted earlier in connection with the genealogical origins of the West Saxons, Kenwhal, King of the West Saxon Dynasty in 672 A.D. was killed by a love rival named Kynard; himself possibly equitable with "Cenred", father of "Ine", King of Wessex between 688 and 726. Both Kenwhal and Kynard are known to have been cousins, a fact confirmed in Kingstonian legend; and it is therefore curious that, in addition to a variant spelling in which the former of these two noblemen's name is spelt "Cenwalh", there are two known, recorded, descendants of Cynric, grandson of Cerdic, in the earliest documentary sources available to us. Cerdic, who as we saw earlier was himself the original model for Cedric of Rotherwood in Scott's *Ivanhoe,* was ancestor of King Alfred the Great, who, curiously enough, has a connection with the sacred horse all of his own; a connection which likewise ties in with yet another of Sir Walter's novels.

Alfred's place of birth, according to his biographer, Asser, was at Wantage, in the county of Berkshire. In a legend referred to in connection with the nearby village of Uffington, where the remains of an Iron Age camp, associated with the Belgic tribes previously referred to in connection with the Grimsdyke and other connected earthworks, lie close to a mighty chalk figure of a horse, Alfred is claimed to have summoned the Saxons to do battle with the Danes. The instrument with which he is supposed to have done this is itself a massive megalithic boulder, almost certainly connected with some sort of prehistoric pagan worship, which is located close to Uffington Camp and nearby Whitehorse Hill; and which is bored through with holes into which he is supposed to have blown. The resulting sound is claimed to have been the means by which he summoned his army, but in more ancient times the sound may have issued forth as part of some ancient ritual in some way connected with the cult of the sacred horse.

Close by is Wayland's Smithy, a site associated with yet another "Lost God" of the Anglo-Saxons, according to Branston. The ancient megalithic structure, which only came to be linked with a Saxon deity in Dark Age times, is in turn associated with a series of folk legends which may well be connected with the Cult of the Sacred Horse; in that it is supposedly a place where unshod horses mysteriously appear with freshly crafted shoes, if the phantom smith who resides at the site is placated with an offering of a silver

160

penny. Curiously, the legend of Wayland and his links with this ancient site feature in the plot of one of the Laird of Abbotsford's own novels, the Elizabethan "Kenilworth". As regards the mythical associations we have already looked at, however, could these connections be in some way indicative of some lost affiliation between Cerdic's Line and the Ancient Picts, a half forgotten connection even in Alfred's own time? We can only guess without proper documentary proof. There is however a vital clue to be found in the ancient Kingstonian legends previously referred to.

Following the slaying of Kenwahl or Cenwalh, his followers marched all the way to Merton, decapitated Kynard or Cenred, and kicked his head all the way back to Kingston. Originally, the game was played between the two villages of Kingston and Merton. In later times it became confined to Kingston's Apple Market, with Kingston Bridge and the Clattering Bridge, which passes over the Hoggsmill Brook, a small tributary of the Thames, as the two opposing goal posts. Again, in view of the archetypal associations with bridges outlined in the last chapter, it is perhaps fitting that two bridges should provide the boundaries of the pitch. A curious anecdote which relates to this story can be found amongst the pages of the Anglo-Saxon Chronicle, where, for the year 672, there is an entry which specifically states that after Cenwalh's death, his Queen, Seaxburgh, ruled for a year in his stead. Christopher Brooke, in his *Norman and Saxon Kings*(publ. B.T.Batsford 1963), states quite adamantly that this situation had hithertoo been unheard of prior to these events, and such a set up never occurred again in the history of Wessex Kingship.

In view of this, it leads one to ask the question, were the two rival dynasts fighting over a British heiress, herself possibly descended from a local dynasty with Pictish connections, like those previously encountered in Herefordshire during the course of the last chapter? The name "Seaxburgh" may be a corruption of the Gaelic "Sadb", a name associated in Ossianic Tradition with Ossian's own Mother; herself the daughter of Bodb the Red. The landscape in which many of the Ossianic legends are rooted is located for the most part along the Western Seaboard of the Scottish Highlands; an area in which, as we have already seen, the sacred horse was a symbol of power associated with the Fairy Faith from the earliest times. And, in view of the fact that many of the long abandoned ramparts and fortifications that litter the British landscape were associated with a Pictish hero or god long before becoming linked with Odin, if my previously outlined hypothesis is correct, it is not altogether impossible that, following the departure of the

161

Roman legions from British soil during the late fourth and early fifth centuries, isolated pockets of these wild northerners, whose many incursions into areas south of Hadrian's Wall are well recorded in ancient texts, may have remained settled on lands in the south previously abandoned by the Imperial Citizenry or migrants to Brittany.

As for Seaxburgh, a possible clue to her identity, or at least the identity of the archetype with which her own ethnic associations were to result in her acquisition of the name by which she has come to be known in the pages of the Anglo-Saxon Chronicle, might well lurk amongst the lyrics of another ballad; more local to the area around Kingston and Merton and set just a stone's throw from St. Bride's Church in Fleet Street; a fourth century foundation built over the remains of an earlier Roman shrine; which has links with a Christianized aspect of the archetype with which the Ancient Pictish Throne Name, Bruide, is itself inextricably linked. As the reader will now note, this ballad, likewise, contains certain stylistic similarities in common with the two previously given versions of Hughie the Graeme that I have set out in the preceeding pages. Again, I shall be giving the reader two versions of this ballad as well; so that, once again, comparisons can be made between them. The ballad in question, which is known variously as *Georgie* or *Geordie*, appears in the pages of the *Penguin Book of English Folk Songs*, edited by Ralph Vaughan Williams and A.L. Lloyd. It also forms part of the incomparable repertoire of the American folk singer Doc Watson, whose own Father-in-Law's Family preserved a traditional Mountain Fiddle Style version of this ballad for several generations.

In an earlier chapter we looked at the links enjoyed by the Laidlaws of Ettrick, from whom Scott's friend and assistant William Laidlaw was himself descended, with the Shropshire town of Ludlow. At a similarly earlier juncture we also touched briefly on a matter concerning further musical connections between these two areas. Of particular relevance to these last mentioned associations is the discovery by Scott and his associates of the haunting fragment *The Wife of Ussher's Well;* another of the ballads incorporated into the *Minstrelsy* and one which we shall be looking at again in full during the course of a later chapter. In view of this, it is an interesting coincidence that, not only was a version of this ballad to turn up in Shropshire, a fact related in the voluminous writings of Professor Child, but another American folk singer, the 'sixties icon Joan Baez, was to discover another rendition of the ballad on the other side of the Atlantic in an Appalachian version in some ways not at all dissimilar to the version of

Geordie likewise rediscovered, and in part recovered, by the incomparable Doc Watson.

As we shall also see, in the notes that follow the two versions of the ballad of *Geordie* which now follow, there are also certain lyrical elements within this ballad that would appear to connect it, not only with "Hughie the Graeme", as has previously been suggested, and will indeed be shortly illustrated, but also with the West Country as well. The last mentioned fact would tend to suggest that at one time all of these songs were part of a single corporate body of bardic literature, with its origins lost in the far off mists of time.

In the chapters to come we shall be looking at further West Country connections with the orally preserved ballads collected by Scott; ballads such as *Lord Thomas and Fair Annie*, which, as well as having links with several of the ballads collected by Bishop Percy, also has a connection with a song collected just a short distance from where we found Alfred burning his cakes in an earlier chapter. This same group of ballads likewise have a connection with the traditional folk singing of the Copper Family of Rottingdean in Sussex; whose music and mumming were touched on in connection with the Antrobus Soulcakers at an earlier stage of this same chapter; something else that will be further scrutinized in the closing chapter of this book. But now, without further ado, I shall present the reader with the American version of the ballad of *Geordie* or *Georgie:*

As I walked over London Bridge,
One misty mornin' early,
I heard some fair young maiden say
"Lord spare me the life of Georgie!

"Go saddle me up my milk white steed,
And bridle him so gaily!"
Then ride away to the King's High Court;
And plead for the life of Georgie.

So she rode all day, and she rode all night,
'till she was wet and weary,
Then combing back her long yellow hair,
She plead for the life of Georgie.

Then Georgie rode up and he plead for himself,
He says "I never murdered any,
But I stole sixteen of the King's best steeds,
And sold them in Romamy!"

Then the oldest lawyer at the bar
Says, "George I'm sorry for you,
But your own confession condemns you to die,
May the Lord have mercy on you!"

If I was over on yonder hill,
Where kisses I've had plenty,
With my sword and my pistol by my side,
I'd fight for the life o' Georgie.

As Georgie was a walking through the streets,
He bid farewell to many,
Then he bid farewell to his own true love,
Which grieved him worse than any.

Georgie was hanged with a golden chord,
Just like you've never seen any,
For he was a member of the Royal Race,
And loved by a virtuous lady".

As the reader will have noticed, this ballad contains certain key stylistic elements in common with both the previously given versions of *Hughie the Graeme;* most notably, the theft of a horse or horses, and an ensuing trial where various individuals plead for the life of the hero; before he is eventually executed. In Scott's version of the ballad there is the added dimension of a duel between two heros, and, in view of the implications of this last mentioned factor, something which we have already looked at during the course of this chapter, the fact that, towards the end of the ballad of *Georgie* the singer discusses fighting a duel to win the hero a reprieve, these lyrics may well constitute evidence that this ballad was likewise in some way connected with ancient folk customs not dissimilar to those already looked at with respect to Antrobus in Cheshire and Marshfield in Gloucestershire.

Of the exact nature and circumstances of these folk customs, we can only guess. However, the fact that they may well have some sort of association with sacral kingship, of the particular kind practised by the ancient prehistoric inhabitants of these islands, and the rituals connected with it, is hinted at by the reference to Geordie or Georgie being "a member of the Royal Race." With respect to this particular aspect of the last given verse, the name "Romamy" may in itself be a corruption of "Romany", a fact which, once again, may be what is being hinted at by the references to the duel and to Georgie being a member of the Royal Race. The Gypsies of the British Isles still conduct physical contests in the "election" of their self-styled "Gypsy Kings". Amongst the most notable "Kings of the Gypsies" to have come to the fore in recent decades is the celebrated Bartley Gorman, a fighting descendant of a long line of champion pugilists; who is himself noted for contesting the title "King" or "Champion" of the Gypsies with Johnny Fletcher, on the death of the late Uriah Burton; his universally acknowledged predecessor.

Although it is historical fact that the vast majority of the true Romany population of Europe as a whole are physically descended from the old Indo-Aryan Warrior Caste, driven out of the Indian Sub-Continent by invading Moslem armies a millennium or so ago, previous to this various travelling castes are known to have existed in Europe; with particular associations with the crafting of metals and the trading of horses. In Britain especially such people may well have had links with sites such as Wayland's Smithy and Uffington Castle, two locations which we have already looked at in connection with the ballads examined during the course of this chapter. And, in view of this, and in view of the references throughout these ballads to the theft of horses in particular, a recurring feature in all of the songs that we have looked at so far in chapter seven, it is by no means impossible that the group of ballads here examined may also have some sort of connection with the customs and rituals of such travelling peoples.

Another interesting factor which cannot be overlooked is the reference to "London Bridge" in the opening verse of the ballad of *Georgie*. This is important for a variety of reasons, the most obvious of which is the reference to both "London", as well as "Londonderry" in MacColl's version of the ballad of *Hughie the Graeme*. On another level however, London Bridge is itself located close to the site of an ancient, undoubtedly megalithic, stone, not unlike the Coronation Stone at Kingston; where some sort of enthronement ritual may have been conducted in prehistoric times. Half remembered folk memories of such events appear to have filtered down into the writings of Shakespeare, who portrays the Sussex rebel Jack Cade, a kind

165

of fifteenth century version of Ken Livingstone in a number of ways, as
having himself "elected" king after striking London Stone with his rod or
cane; in the historical drama "Henry VI". It will also be noted that there are
some additional parallels in the second version of the above given ballad,
which now follows, with MacColl's lyrics previously transcribed. This
ballad, itself entitled *Geordie*, as opposed to *Georgie*, was taken originally
from the repertoire of one Charles Neville of East Coker in Somerset in the
early nineteen hundreds, and can be used to illustrate that all of the above
given ballads are themselves in some way connected.

As I came over London Bridge
One misty morning early,
I overheard a fair pretty maid
Lamenting for her Geordie.

"Come bridle me my milk-white horse,
come bridle me my pony,
That I may ride to London's court,
To plead for the life of Geordie."

And when she entered in the hall,
There was lords and ladies plenty,
Down on her bended knee she did fall,
To plead for the life of Geordie.

"Oh Geordie stole no cow nor calf
Nor sheep he never stole any,
But he stole sixteen of the King's wild deer,
And sold them in Bohenny."

"Oh, two brave children I've had by him,
And the third lies in my bosom,
And if you would spare my Geordie's life,
I'd freely part from them every one."

The judge looked over his left shoulder,
And said: "I'm sorry for thee.
My pretty fair maid, you come too late,
For he's condemned already."

"Let Geordie hang in golden chains,
Such chains as never was any,
Because he came of the royal blood,
And courted a virtuous lady."

"I wish I was in yonder grove,
Where times I have been many,
With my broad sword and pistol too,
I'd fight for the life of Geordie."

An arrangement of this historic ballad was recently recorded by Jo Freya on a compact disc collection marketed through the "Past Times" chain of novelty stores under the title *The Traditional Songs of England.* In the sleeve notes to the collection, the compiler of the above, with reference to the judge looking over his left shoulder, writes that "It was customary for the judge to look over his left shoulder when passing the death sentence (the left- Latin "sinister"- being associated with evil)......" Again, as we saw in MacColl's version of *Hughie the Graeme,* the ballad hero is observed as looking over his own left shoulder as the sentence of death is passed.

Williams and Lloyd, in their notes to the same ballad, point out that versions of this song likewise exist in Scotland too. The reference to "Bohenny" in the last given version is doubtless indicative of a connection with Bohennie, close by Braes o' Lochaber; an area where Alexander Gordon, 3rd Earl of Huntley, is noted as having acquired much new territory during the late fifteenth and early sixteenth centuries. They also note how the Scottish sets "...differ considerably from the English ones, for in them the hero is not a thief but a nobleman, thought by some scholars to be George Gordon, Earl of Huntley, who suffered royal displeasure when he showed clemency towards a Highland robber in 1554."

In view of this last mentioned fact, it is worth noting that, in the search for the true origins of this ballad, we are now fast approaching the territory of Sir Walter's favourite songsmith, Thomas of Ercildoune. For, strange as it may seem, he too has a connection with the Gordons, a link which revolves, once again, around his own legendary prophecies.

The 3rd Earl of Huntley's brother, Sir William Gordon, who fell at the Battle of Flodden in the year of George, the 4th Earl's birth, was ancestor of the Gordons of Gight; whose tower house of Gight Castle, now a sad and

167

decaying ruin, stands above the steep bank of Ythan, close to the hamlet of Stonehouse; near Methlick. The Rhymer is said to have predicted that "when the herons leave the tree, the lairds of Gight shall landless be". In 1787, the herons of Gight, that had inhabited the castle, much like the ravens at the Tower of London, for centuries, deserted the place for nearby Haddo. Soon after, Lady Catherine Gordon, mother of Scott's unfortunate friend, Lord Byron, the poet, and herself the thirteenth "Laird" in a line stretching back to 1479, was forced to sell Gight Castle; in order to pay the gambling debts incurred by her husband, "Mad Jack" Byron.

Gight Castle is not the only stronghold in this area which has connections with Thomas the Rhymer. There is also a link with Fyvie Castle, which, in 1338, was granted to Sir James Lindsay, Earl of Crawford. This connection is of interest on account of the fact that Sir James is cited as being a descendant of Sir William de Lindsay, Lord of Crawford and Ercildoune, whose father and grandfather had both been in possession of the lands of Ercildoune during the twelfth century. The connections between Thomas and Fyvie revolve around the following verses, taken from the Rhymer's legendary metrical prophecies:

Fyvyns riggs and towers,
Hapless shall your mesdames be,
When ye shall hae within your methes
Frae harryit Kirk'slands stanes three;
Ane in Preston's tower;
Ane in my Ladye's bower
and ane below the water yett;
And it shall never get.

George Seton in his *History of the Family of Seton,* (publ. Edinburgh, 1896), recounts the following traditions with regard to Fyvie's connections with Thomas the Rhymer.

"In my notice of Fyvie Castle" he writes, "I neglected to mention an interesting relic still preserved in the ancient stronghold, to which reference is made in the......" Prophecies "of Thomas the Rhymer. Like others of a similar kind, it is supposed to have been a boundary mark abstracted from ravished churchlands, and carrying a curse to the descendants of successors of sacrilegious robbers. Be this as it may, it is somewhat strange that although Fyvie has been transmitted through three or four families for many

168

successive generations no male heir has been born at the castle for five hundred years."

It is interesting to note that soon after the Lindsays acquired the castle it passed by marriage into the hands of the Prestons, to whom line five in the above quoted prophetic stanzas refers. In the sixteenth century the castle was purchased by Sir Alexander Seton, who, like the Lindsay Family, was connected by marriage to the Earls of March, who gave their name, "Earlston", to the Ercildoune of True Thomas.

"Two of the three stones" Seton claims, "are said to have been found, but one beneath the "water yett" is still unaccounted for." According to one source quoted by Seton, a stone was formerly "preserved in the castle and shown as one of the three weird stones". Seton then also relates how his source maintains that the stone is referred to as "the dripping stone", for, he says, "it is asserted that this stone at times gives out a quantity of damp as to half fill the bowl in which it is kept with water, while at other times it absorbs the whole. It is not known how or even when this mysterious stone came to occupy the place it now does."

Elsewhere in the same work Seton also recounts how "Mr. Ferguson of Kinmundy informs us that the "dripping stone"- sometimes called "the weeping stone"- used to be kept in the uppermost room in one of the towers and he saw it on two different occasions. On the one occasion the bowl was nearly full of water, and the stains on the floor showed that it sometimes overflowed. On the other occasion the bowl was dry and the stone encrusted with a white salty efflorescense."

In view of all the connections made in chapters three to five of this book, it is worth noting that Fyvie Castle lies just a short distance north east of Chapel of Garioch and Bennachie; which featured in the previously recounted legends relating to the Maiden Stone. These locations are all deep in the old tribal territories of the Northern Picts, and in the sixth century nearby Turriff was the capital of a Pictish Prince. This considered, it would appear that the possibility exists that the great body of bardic literature to which the ballads that we have been looking at during the course of this chapter once belonged was of Pictish origin. The fact that the English version of the *Geordie* ballad previously referred to was acquired at a location situated on a tributary stream of the River Yeo, which in turn runs into the River Parrett, which, as we have already seen, flows past a place called "Pict's Hill" would only seem to confirm this. It is also relevant that the River Parrett, which we looked at in connection with the idea of "The Otherworld Bridge" in the last chapter, flows past East and West Lydford; where it is bridged once again by an old Roman road which may well have been built over a more ancient British trackway of the Watkins variety.

Strangely enough, East and West Lydford, or Ludford, has an association with London, in that, according to legend, London was at one time called "Caer Lud", after a semi-legendary Ancient British Prince named "King Lud"; who supposedly built its walls. Whatever the archaeological evidence, or lack of it, to substantiate this particular part of the legend of London's supposed prehistoric foundation, Lud is known for certain to have been the name of a Celtic god, much like "Grim" and Taranis. So, it is not impossible that he was not only worshipped by the ancient prehistoric inhabitants of the site where the Romans were later to build their city of Londinium, but also by those who in former times lived both at Lydford and Ludlow; from whence the Laidlaws of Ettrick are supposed to have migrated at some point before 1296 A.D.

According to one folk tradition, quoted by John Morris in his *Age of Arthur,* Lud is supposed to have been buried atop of London's Ludgate in the statue of a bronze horse. In view of this, the reference in verse two of the English version of *Geordie* to bridling a pony gives us a subliminal link with the ancient British goddess "Epona"; who is herself connected with the cult of the sacred horse- the latter being her totem animal (see T.G.E. Powell, *The Celts,* Thames and Hudson, 1980). And, in view of all of these last made connections, it is not beyond the realms of possibility that Leod, the original progenitor of Clan Macleod on Skye, who we encountered in connection with my previously made references to Fairy origins and sacral kingship in the Western Isles, may have been the last of a line of sacral kings; contemporaneous with those referred to by Gerald of Wales; who originally worshipped a manifestation of Lud; as well as his equine female consort. Confirmation of this last fact can be found once again in the pages of McIan, where we find the following references to the origins of his Clan:

"It is universally acknowledged", says the writer in Douglas's Baronage, "that the Macleods are descended of the Norwegian Kings of Man; but the chronicle of that island does not afford satisfactory authority for this supposition. We much more readily believe that they are the descendants of the ancient inhabitants of the Western Highlands, an origin which is surely as honourable as a derivation from these insular invaders.....The lands in Skye, where the Chiefs of this Clan have so long resided, were obtained by marriage with a daughter of Mac Arailt, a Norwegian settler." So perhaps then, it is through the Mac Arailts that the Macleods can claim their ancient Norse descent, whilst Leod himself was of Pictish origin; a fact which may well find confirmation with the presence of the name "Lutrin" in some of the Pictish King Lists. This last given name may well be a kind of primeaval double barrelled name along the lines of "Leod Tharan". Moncreiffe's extensive researches would appear to be indicative of Pictish Kings using both personal and sacral or "god" names; so it is indeed possible that this particular line of speculation will indeed stand up to further scrutiny.

So what does all this imply in relation to Scott, and his collection of Border Ballads? Put simply, in the pages of the first chapter, I made it clear beyond any reasonable doubt that it is my considered opinion that Scott's collection and collation of these ballads constitutes what is perhaps his greatest literary achievement. When one considers that the evidence here presented, both in this chapter, and those that have preceeded it, would appear to indicate that, like the *Sir Tristrem*, which can be proven, by reference to Cymric records, to have been composed around the legendary deeds of an Arthurian Knight of proven Pictish descent, some of the ballads that Scott collected and incorporated into the *Minstrelsy* constitute the lost fragments of an ancient undiscovered body of Pictish literature, Scott's discoveries in this field are perhaps unique. And, without his efforts in this direction the ballads that he collected, and the ancient literary heritage of which they are an albeit late, and to a large extent corrupted, manifestation, would almost certainly have been lost to us forever.

It is universally acknowledged that Pictish culture left no written literature behind it whatsoever. The only recognized writings in existence which historians attribute to them with any certainty is the Pictish King List. Bearing in mind that, like the Welsh, the Scots and the Irish, they must have had some kind of oral literary heritage of their own, it is not impossible that at least fragments of this now lost bardic tradition may have found their way into the ballads and customs of later folk tradition. This in turn would tend to give further credence to the ideas and theories previously set out during the course of the preceeding pages.

Before moving on and leaving behind the *Hughie the Graeme* cycle of ballads, it is worth noting, for the record, that in Williams and Lloyd's notes to their version of *Geordie,* they inform their readers that "In the English versions, which may be re-makes of the Scottish, the main character is always an outlaw. An old black letter ballad names him as George Stoole of Northumberland, who was executed in 1610; but even in its "robber" form (if that is the more recent) the song probably pre-dates the 17th cent. Mr. Neville's tune is related to the well known air *Searching for Lambs.*

Geordie has been found in oral tradition also in Sussex, Cambridgeshire, Somerset, Norfolk, Suffolk, Surrey, Dorset and Yorkshire."The great antiquity of the ballad here asserted by Williams and Lloyd adds still further credence to the theories previously set down during the course of this chapter, despite the limitations of these two writers' knowledge with respect to the ancient bardic tradition.

With particular regard to the duelling element present in both the Scott version of *Hughie the Graeme* and the above referred to version of *Geordie,* it has already been noted that the Picts possessed an electoral monarchy, involving the periodic election of descendants from their ancient sacral line of kings. In view of the fact that these princely descendants of Pictish royalty must all trace their lineage matrilineally in order to qualify for election to supreme kingship, it is quite possible that there was a considerable amount of competition amongst the various tribal warrior castes prevalent amongst the different tribal cultures peopling Pre-Roman Britain for the hand in marriage of these Pictish heiresses. That physical conflicts must have occurred at one time or another over the course of time between the various factions competing for their favours was therefore inevitable. And, in view of all of the evidence thus far presented during the course of this chapter, it is not impossible that one or more of these conflicts provided the initial inspiration at least for some of the elements incorporated into the original storyline of the ballad or metrical romance from whence both of these ballads ultimately proceeded.

The fact that Williams and Lloyd successfully connect this ballad with Yorkshire gives us a link with an identical game to the old Kingston Football Game already looked at; played every January 6th at Haxey on Humberside. Although the object for which the two village teams are competing is not a ball as such, but a leather tube known as "The Hood", the annual game of Haxey Hood can be proven to have an identical origin to the Surrey game previously described. The hood to which the title of the game owes its name was originally the headgear of another Fair Maid- in this instance Lady

Mowbray; and there is also evidence to suggest that at one time the game also incorporated some kind of ritual sacrifice or execution into it; much like the execution of Kenwahl of Kingston's murderer. This considered then, it is safe to say that the leather tube, like Kingston's football, was almost certainly, in former times, the head of an executed murderer or adulterer.

The reason why I have made the point that the individual may have been an adulterer is that, owing to the fact that the consorts of these Pictish heiresses were invariably individuals who had been specially selected, due either to their military prowess or on account of their possession of some other great skill or talent, for another individual to be caught in adultery with one of these noblewomen, the tribal or Druidic heirachy whose honour had thus been besmirched would almost certainly have demanded their execution. In the Ossianic Tradition the legend of "Diarmuid and Grainne" may well preserve another record of just such a set of circumstances.

According to tradition, Grainne's husband, Fionn, was the elected captain of the Fianna of Erin, a military band much like those previously referred to in the chapter on the "Brig o' Dread". Diarmuid, who elopes with Fionn's wife eventually dies as a result of pricking his heel on the bristles of the Boar of Ben Gulban. The legend here related may well be indicative of Diarmuid having been executed by yet another military elite for whom there are also definite records, both in classical and Celtic sources; for the bristles here referred to may well be symbolic of the spears of the ancient warrior caste known as the "Gaesatae" or spearmen; who feature in the writings of Polybius; themselves ancestors of Clan Fegusson; whose name is derived from "fear", a man, and "geis", a spear; and whose Kilkerran Sept carry three boars' heads on its coat of arms. A similar group of individuals may well have provided the inspiration for the ten yoemen who assist in the arrest of *Hughie the Graeme* in Scott's version of the ballad.

As one might expect, Haxey on Humberside is just a short distance from Grimsby, which is just one of many locations throughout Yorkshire where names associated with "Grim" are to be found. These include Grimston Garth, home since the twelfth century of the de Grimston Family, one of whom witnessed the foundation charter of Meaux Abbey in 1135, Grimston Fields Farm, several locations known as Grimston Grange, two Grimston Hill houses, together with two Grimstons, Grimston Manor Farm, Grimston Moor, Grimston Park, Grimston Wood, Grimston Brow, Grimsworth Dean Beck, Grimthorpe Manor and Grimthorpe Wood.

The presence of all of these sites would tend to suggest that there may well be evidence to support the persistent tradition in Scotland, a tradition to be found in the writings of Hector Boece (1465-1536) and the metrical history of Scotland by William Stewart that it inspired, that, following the disintegration of the old Roman Empire, large swathes of territory as far south as Humberside, fell into the hands of the Picts and Scots. These traditions, as we shall see, may have further relevance to some of Scott's other ballads, particularly the related legend that Westmorland acquired its name through a connection with a warrior chieftain from the old Pictish Kingdom of Moray.

Strangely enough, there is a connection between Westmorland and Gipsy Hill in what is now the London suburb of Upper Norwood; in that it is the former location of the Westmorland Society for the benefit of children born in London whose families originally came from Westmorland. Many of the gypsy families who for centuries parked their caravans on Gypsy Hill, some of whom were visited by Samuel Pepys in the year 1668, had connections with the traditional horse fair at Appleby-in-Westmorland going back many generations; and it is with roving Romany bands such as these that the ancestors of William Laidlaw may well have made their way north in the early Middle Ages. Perhaps the original "Bohenny" of the English version of *Geordie* referred originally to the Celtic settlement at nearby Banstead, which, in its turn, may derive its name from the Fairy "Ben Sidhe"; from whence we obtain the word "Banshee".

Perhaps it was for a banshee's favours that Hughie the Graeme fought and lost his duel. Perhaps it is she who is the real Lady Hume, or else Lady Black, whose name, Black, or Blake, is, according to Watkins, another of the Coel or Scott names associated with the Dodmen. And, needless to say, it is this last mentioned fact that takes us straight back to the Scottish Borderlands from where we started out originally. For, the village of Hume lies just a few miles north west of Learmouth, the district from which the Rhymer's own clan are said to have emanated. Directly above East and West Learmouth is Blake Law, a hill, the name of which may well indicate that the dodmen once used it for orienting their ancient sacred alignments.

Directly south of Learmouth the countryside rises up to a level plateau, atop of which is Hoselaw Loch. A long straight road, possibly built over the top of an ancient prehistoric trackway, runs past the loch; having first passed across a gradual incline called "Horse Rigg"; terminating at Frogden. Frogden itself lies directly above Kale Water, which runs north west up to Grahamslaw; where there are located both ancient caves and an ancient stone that may have been an old mark stone at one time; indicating the site of an ancient boundary or "ley line". Is this the original homeland of Hughie the Graeme or Graham? And, was the original poetical forerunner of the ballad that recalls his death at one time part of the repertoire of Thomas of Ercildoune?

Whatever the connections between the real or imaginary Hughie the Graeme and the landscape referred to above, the myths and folk traditions that we have looked at during the course of this chapter have definite links with one of Melrose's most ancient traditional customs; which died out at the turn of the century. In the centre of the town square is the ancient "Mercat Cross", where, to this very day, the "marriage ball" is kicked off by newly wed brides. In ancient times such a gesture would be the signal for the commencement of the traditional "E'en Ba' Game", a football game in many ways not dissimilar to the ancient Kingston football game and its counterpart played at Haxey in Humberside. Did the Melrose football game, like its southern equivalents, once have a connection with the election of sacral kings? We will never know for sure, for its true origins are lost in the mists of time, but the evidence afforded us by the ballads and traditions that the town's most celebrated resident collected at the dawn of the industrial era would appear to indicate that this is indeed the case.

Chapter Eight

Light Down, Light Down, Cospatrick Brave

Light down, light down Corspatrick brave,
And I will shew thee curses three,
Shall gar fair Scotland greet and grane,
And change the green to the black livery.

Thomas the Rhymer part second
Altered from ancient prophecies.

In the introductory notes to his own "noble ballad", contained within the *Minstrelsy* and in which, according to Lockhart, the Author of *Waverley* "celebrated" the legendary Thomas of Ercildoune, Scott informs his readership of how the sage's principal patron "Corspatrick (Comes Patrick), Earl of March, but more commonly taking his title from his castle at Dunbar, acted a noted part during the wars of Edward I in Scotland....."

Elsewhere in the *Minstrelsy*, an entire ballad is dedicated to the memory of this illustrious individual:

Cospatrick has sent oe'er the faem;
Cospatrick brought his ladye hame;
And fourscore ships have come her wi',
The ladye by the grene-wood tree.

There were twal' and twal' wi' baken bread,
And twal' and twal' wi' gowd sae reid,
And twal' and twal' wi bouted flour
And twal' and twal' wi' the paramour.

Sweet Willy was a widow's son,
And at her stirrup he did run;
And she was clad in the finest pall,
But aye she let the tears down fall.

"O is your saddle set awrye?
Or rides your steed for you owre high?
Or are you mourning, in your tide,
That you suld be Cospatrick's bride?"

"I am not mourning, at this tide,
That suld I be Cospatrick's bride;
But I am sorrowing, in my mood,
That I suld leave my mother good.

"But, gentle boy, come tell to me,
What is the custom of my countrie?"
"The custom thereof, my dame," he says,
"Will ill a gentle lady please."

"Seven Kings' daughters has our lord wedded,
And seven kings' daughters has our lord bedded,
And he's cutted their breasts frae their breast-bane,
And sent them mourning hame again."

"Yet, gin you're sure that you're a maid,
Ye may gae safely to his bed;
But gif o' that ye be na sure,
Then hire some damsell o' your bour."

The ladye's called her bour maiden,
That waiting was into her train;
"Five thousand merks I'll gie to thee,
To sleep this night with my lord for me."

When bells were rung, and mass was sayne,
And a' men unto bed were gane,
Cospatrick and the bonny maid,
Into ae chamber they were laid.

"Now speak to me, blankets, and speak to me, bed,
And speak, thou sheet, enchanted web;
And speak my bonny brown sword, that winna lie,
Is this a true maiden that lies by me?"

"It is not a maid that you hae wedded,
But it is a maid that you hae bedded;
It is a leal maiden that lies by thee
But not the maiden that it should be."

O wraithfully he left the bed,
And wraithfully his claiths on did;
And he has ta'en him through the ha',
And on his Mother he did ca'.

"I am the most unhappy man,
That ever was in Christen land!
I courted a maiden, meik and mild,
And I hae gotten nothing but a woman wi' child."

"O stay, my son, into this ha',
And sport ye wi' your merrymen a';
And I will to the secret bour,
To see how fares wi' your paramour."

The carline she was stark and sture,
She aff the hinges dang the dure;
"O is your bairn to laird or loun,
Or is it to your Father's groom?"

"O hear me, Mother, on my knee,
Till my sad story I tell to thee:
O we were sisters, sisters seven,
We were the fairest under heaven.

"It fell on a summer's afternoon,
When a' our toilsome taks was done,
We kast the kevils us amang,
To see which suld to the grene-wood gang.

"O hon! alas, for I was youngest,
And aye my weird it was the hardest!
The kevil it on me did fa'
Whilk was the cause of a' my woe.

"For to the grene-wood I maun gae,
To pu' the red rose and the slae;
To pu' the red rose and the thyme,
And deck my mother's bour and mine.

"I hadna' pu'd a flower but ane,
When by there came a gallant hende,
Wi' high-coll'd hose and laigh-coll'd shoon,
And he seemed to be sum kingis son.

"And be I maid, or be I nae,
He kept me there till the close o' day;
And be I maid, or be I nane,
He kept me there 'till the day was done.

"He gae me a lock o' his yellow hair,
And bade me keep it ever mair;
He gae me a carknet o' bonny beads,
And bade me keep it against my needs

"He gae me a gay gold ring,
And bade me keep it abune a' thing."
"What did ye wi' the tokens rare,
That ye gat frae that gallant there?"

"O bring that coffer unto me,
And a' the tokens ye shall see."
"Now stay, daughter, your bour within,
While I gae parley wi' my son".

O she has ta'en her thro' the ha'
And her son began to ca';
"What did ye wi' the bonny beads,
I bade ye keep against your needs?

"What did ye wi' the gay gold ring,
I bade you keep abune a' thing?"
"I gae them to a ladye gay,
I met in grene-wood on a day.

"But I wad gie a' my halls and tours,
I had that ladye within my bours;
But I wad gie my very life,
I had that ladye to my wife."

"Now keep, my son, your ha's and tours;
Ye have that bright burd in your bours:
And keep, my son, your very life;
Ye have that ladye to your wife."

Now, or a month was come and gane,
The lady bore a bonny son;
And 'twas well written on his breast bane,
"Cospatrick is my father's name."
O row my ladye in satin and silk,
And wash my son in the morning milk.

As in the case of *Hughie the Graeme*, which was at the centre of the last chapter, no historical facts whatsoever exist to substantiate the story around which this ballad is centred. The lyrics themselves contain key elements which they hold in common with many similar "romantic" ballads, being full of references to "red roses" and "the grene-wood"; as well as incorporating into their general storyline the classic imagery of Mediaeval Romance. Once again, however, just like the ballad of *Hughie the Graeme*, there is evidence to suggest that there may be some connection between this ballad and the lost literary traditions of the Ancient Picts.

In verse seven, appropriately enough, we find reference to how Cospatrick has both wedded and bedded the daughters of seven kings. Surely these are the seven sub-kings previously referred to throughout the preceeding chapters? And, elsewhere in the ballad we find references to the casting of "kevils", or lots, amongst the ballad bride and her six sisters. The word "kevil" may well be derived from the sacred Gaelic tree name "Coll", which we have already encountered previously at an earlier juncture.

It is now generally recognized that the Druids undoubtedly possessed sacred divinatory tree alphabets, akin to the old Norse and Teutonic Runes. Amongst the Gaels these letters appear to have been referred to as "Ogham", on account of their association, since the earliest times, with Ogma mac Breas, a legendary warrior akin to Hercules, whilst in Welsh tradition a similar system appears to have existed known as "Coelbren y Beirdd"; or the Coelbren of the Bards. As we have already seen, the name "Coel", in Welsh, is likewise connected with the Sacred Hazel; and it is therefore quite probable that, just as hazel rods or wands were used in divination, so too were hazel sprigs incised with sacred tree letters. If this was indeed the case, it was doubtless with a bunch of these self same divinatory sprigs that the ballad heroine referred to in these verses "cast kevils", together with her six sisters, in order to decide who should enter into the "grene-wood" in order to collect roses, sloes and wild herbs; a symbolic act which doubtless held some sort of primeaval shamanistic significance to the original composer of this ballad; as well as the latter's audience. The seven sisters too would seem to indicate some sort of connection or other with the star constellation associated with the seven legendary nymphs collectively known as the Pleiades; which is itself known to have been revered by the peoples of many ancient civilizations.

It is at this point that we at last encounter a rational explanation, amongst the lyrics of one of the most enigmatic ballads to appear in the *Minstrelsy*, for an obscure reference relating to one of Scott's own highly individual, some would even say peculiar, methods of working. In the opening chapters we looked at the Shortreed Family account of Scott's journeys out into the wild Border landscape in search of materials for his collection. When asked by his son as to whether or not Scott took any note books or similar items with him during the course of these travels in the remoter parts of the countryside, Shortreed snr. was heard to reply that, as far as he was aware, the Laird of Abbotsford had none that he ever saw, whilst simultaneously adding that they "had neither pens, nor ink, nor paper."

"But", he is noted as recollecting, "we had knives and they served the turn just as weel, for we took bits o' Cuttings wi' them, frae a broom Cowe, or an aller, or a hazel-bush, or whatever else might be at hand, and on thae bits o' stick (maybe tway or three inches lang they were) he made a variety o' notches, and these were the only memoranda I ever saw him take or have, of any of the memorable spots he wished to preserve the recollection of, or any tradition connected wi' them. And when he had notched them they were just

181

slipt into our pockets, a' heads and thaws. When we cam hame frae some o' our trips, I hae seen us have a'maist haill wallets fu' o' them- wud aneuch to mend a mill as Burns says. I coudna think what he meant by this at first, and when I asked him what a' thae marked sticks were for, he said, "these are my log-book, Bob!"

Revived interest in the ancient origins of the Ogham, Coelbren and other related alphabets only really began in earnest in this century; most particularly with the publication of Robert Graves's writings on the subject. Previous to this such subject matter was confined purely to the fringes of minority interest. In view of this it is by no means impossible that Scott himself may have come across some ancient Border equivalent of the Welsh and Gaelic systems, possibly in an ancient manuscript text now no longer extant; and which he never wrote about in any published essay; possibly because he could not envisage it being taken seriously. In an earlier chapter I took a direct quotation from the *Minstrelsy* with respect to the ancient system of marks cut into the turf or the bark of trees by Border Reivers as secret signals to their fellow clansmen. Could these doubtless secret sigils have had some connection with an ancient system of divinatory alphabets, referred to here in the ballad of *Cospatrick,* which were in some way connected with the Welsh and Irish ones previously referred to? We will doubtless never know for sure. All that we can say for certain, is that Scott's method of using such a means of cutting notches into sprigs of hazel and other sacred woods appears to fit in with what we know about the bardic and druidic uses of Ogham and Colebren. Nothing else can be said on the matter, other than the fact that, if this really is what Scott was doing, his nickname of "The Wizard of the North", was justly deserved.

But what of Cospatrick, the historical hero with whom, over the course of time, this most ancient ballad eventually came to be associated? Well, from Scott's point of view the Earls of Dunbar and March were one of the most important feudal families to hold sway along the marches of his beloved Scottish Borderland. We have already touched upon their relationship with Thomas of Ercildoune, the prophet and poet who they are known to have patronized- hence his association with Ercildoune or Earlston, the "ton", "town" or seat of the Earls of March. More important than this though, Cospatrick and his sires can be shown to have claimed descent, not only from the Anglo-Saxon nobility, like the Bodenhams of Rotherwas in Herefordshire, but also from the old royal line of Wessex; King Alfred the Great's own dynasty. (See Appendix 3, Table 4).

This in itself would do much to explain one of the reasons why, in Thomas of Ercildoune's *Sir Tristrem*, the author is quoted, by Scott, Lockhart and others, as having exclaimed, as "his hero joins battle with Moraunt", [1]

"God help Tristrem the Knight
He fought for Ingland....."

This particular aspect of Ercildoune's *Sir Tristrem* is touched on in Scott's previously quoted from correspondence with George Ellis, which appears in volume one of Lockhart's biography. Here, the Author of *Waverley* comments to his correspondent of how "This strain of national attachment would hardly have proceeded from a Scottish author, even though he had laid his scene in the sister country....." Although a good supposition, this theory can perhaps be dismissed, when one recognizes that this Scottish author's principal patron was a nobleman whose Anglo-Saxon ancestry was considered important enough, by both the bard himself, as well as his lord and his family, to warrant the insertion of such a reference in the verses of his metrical compositions.

Strangely enough, in terms of Scott's own writings, this very same bloodline, that of the Earls of Dunbar and March, almost certainly provided the historical model for the Saxon lineage of Rowena, Scott's heroine in what is perhaps his most famous novel, *Ivanhoe*. Central to the plot of the novel is the romance between the hero himself and Rowena, who is described in the author's narrative as being a Princess of an ancient Saxon line. This fact is of particular relevance when it is considered that the first Earl of March to be named "Gospatrick" or "Cospatrick" was himself the son of Algatha, a grandaughter of King Ethelred the Unready; showing how, amongst the pages of one of his most culturally significant novels, Scott was to draw upon influences firmly rooted in his own Border heritage.

On his Father's side, Cospatrick was descended from the old Kings of Scots. The son of Maldred of Cumbria, whose brother, King Duncan, was allegedly murdered, in reality justly slain, by King Macbeth, Cospatrick's own links with the Anglo-Saxon Royal Line is perhaps explanatory to a still further degree as to why there should be so many connections between the traditions of Wessex and those of the Border Marches over which his descendants were to rule; something which has already been explored at an earlier juncture. As for Macbeth, we shall be looking at his reign and the alleged "usurpation" of Duncan's crown in a future chapter. In the meantime, it is sufficient to note that, contrary to the supposedly "historical" traditions which find expression in Shakespeare, Macbeth was neither a usurper nor a murderer; but was in fact the last justly elected King of Scotland.

Maldred's wife was the daughter of Uchtred, Prince Bishop of Chester-le-Street and sometime Earl of Northumberland; the date of whose death is believed to have been about 1016. Uchtred's own line will be looked at again in a future chapter, in connection with their links with the real life model for the legendary outlaw Robin Hood; another of the characters who features in the pages of *Ivanhoe*. Uhtred's wife is identified in written sources as one "Elgive", sister of Edmund Ironside; himself viewed by many of the disaffected Anglo-Saxon nobles of the early Eleventh Century as being the last legitimate King of England; whose own death, as well as that of his Father, Ethelred, is known to have taken place in the same year as that of Uchtred or Uhtred.

Again, we shall be looking at some of the historical elements incorporated into the plot of *Ivanhoe* in more detail in a future chapter. In the meantime, with regard to Maldred's own ancestry, he himself could claim descent in the male line from the ancient hereditary Abbots of Dunkeld; itself located in Atholl; which, as we have already seen, was in former times one of the old Pictish sub-kingdoms or Mormaerships. Perhaps this is how an ancient ballad which contains definite Pictish elements, as evidenced by certain key verses which have been analysed during the course of this chapter, came to be associated with a nobleman of Saxon descent. It is a hypothesis that should indeed be considered.

An additional series of factors which would do much to support, and indeed substantiate, this last made hypothesis in turn, revolve around the Arthurian mythological cycles; which, when examined closely, show themselves, in a large number of cases, to be of a far earlier provenance than the Dark Age period when the actual historical characters with which they are associated are known to have lived. Sir Lancelot, for example, has been shown by scholars working in this field to have archetypal links with the Celtic god Lugh, whose spear, or "lance", may have given rise to this hero's name in the romantic poetry of the High Middle Ages. Certainly, there are no references to anyone actually called "Lancelot" in the old Welsh Arthurian texts; showing the name of Guinevere's courtly lover to have a far later origin than one would otherwise expect.

In the previous chapter we looked at certain elements in the ballad of *Hughie the Graeme* which might tend to provide us with clues as to the exact attitude, within Pictish society, towards those caught in adultery with an heiress of one of the Pictish Royal or noble lines. In view of this it is not altogether impossible that the reference in verse seven of *Cospatrick,* as to how the hero of the ballad has cut off the breasts of each of his seven brides, might denote the kind of punishment that a Pictish heiress could herself expect, if she too were found to have transgressed the ancient laws of the bardic "Fili", or judges.

In view of what we have seen here, and elsewhere throughout this book, the apparent connections between these ancient ballads, and the culture of the Picts, would make the"Sir Tristrem" of Thomas of Ercildoune one of the most important bardic survivals of the High Middle Ages. The reason for this revolves around the fact that the provable Pictish ancestry of the hero of the romance provides us with a bridge, in the form of the "Tristrem" itself, between the ballads, which can likewise be shown to have definite connections with the author of that story, and the Ancient Pictish civilization; from amongst whose nobles we have documentary proof for Drustanus or Tristan's descent.

Scott seems to have had some idea of the "Sir Tristrem's" true significance, a fact which is in all probability due to the attribution of authorship of this metrical romance to Thomas of Ercildoune himself. Proof of this last made assertion is found in Lockhart's statement that both Scott, and his friend John Leyden, who was to assist him greatly in his editing of the *Minstrelsy,* had originally intended to give the *Tristrem* "......not only a place, but a prominent one, in the *Minstrelsy of the Scottish Border.* Unfortunately, this was not to be the case, owing to the fact that, as a result of Scott's already quoted from, and extensive, correspondence with Ellis, the "......doubts and difficulties which Ellis suggested,.....though they did not shake Scott in his opinion as to the parentage of the romance, induced researches which occupied so much time, and gave birth to notes so bulky that he eventually found it expedient first to pass it over in the two volumes of the Minstrelsy which appeared in 1802, and then even in the third which followed a year later; thus reserving Tristrem for a separate publication; which did not take place until after Leyden had sailed for India."

Cospatrick Earl of Dunbar and March's Anglo-Saxon descent is also significant for political reasons; a fact which may also explain the reference to *Ingland* in the Rhymer's *Sir Tristrem*. For, at the heart of all English attempts throughout the Middle Ages to interfere in the affairs of Scotland, and Scottish attempts to resist that interference, is the descent of the Scottish Kings from King Malcolm III's second marriage to St. Margaret of Scotland; herself the grandaughter of Edmund Ironside. And, it was the ultimate Anglo-Saxon, as opposed to Norman, descent of the Scottish nobility, the Scottish Royal House being descended from the most senior branch of the old Wessex Royal Line, that was the original source of much of the friction; whilst being a considerable source of pride to the Scottish nobles at the same time.

All these things considered then, it is quite feasible that Cospatrick Earl of March's pride in Saxon descent eventually led to Thomas of Ercildoune incorporating the above given reference to the supposed English connections of the hero of his metrical romance into lines of his versifications; his principal motivation for so doing being for the purpose of his patron's own personal gratification. We shall be looking more closely at the descent of the Kings of Scots from St. Margaret of England in the chapter that follows, when we examine the work of one of the poets and songsmiths best known for his celebrations of the heroic acts of Bruce and Wallace; two Scottish patriots at the forefront of the national conflicts alluded to in the previous paragraph. One final note on the ballad of *Cospatrick* which is worth drawing the reader's attention to, revolves around the possibility that, like the original ballad of *Hughie the Graeme* referred to in the previous chapter, the original Mediaeval forerunner of the eighteenth century lyrics here presented may well have formed part of the repertoire of Thomas the Rhymer himself; much like the "Tristrem" at the heart of our story.

Chapter Nine

John Barleycorn Must Die

"There were three Kings into the east,
Three Kings both great and high,
And they hae sworn a solemn oath
John Barleycorn should die.

"They took a plough and ploughed him down,
Put clods upon his head,
And they hae sworn a solemn oath
John Barleycorn was dead."

These verses, which concern the growing and harvesting of the barley crop, which is then turned into alcohol, and which simultaneously recall ancient folk memories of possible human sacrifices, like those associated with the Cult of Tammuz in Near Eastern Culture, come from one of the finest examples of Robert Burns's own re-renderings of a traditional ancient ballad. In the opening pages of Scott's son-in-law Lockhart's biography of Burns, a work which he was to dedicate jointly to Scott's friend, James Hogg and Allan Cunningham, the poet and biographer of the artist David Wilkie, the author describes this composition as "a good old ballad, very cleverly new modelled and extended;" whilst adding that, in his opinion, the *Death* and *Elergy of Poor Mailie* deserve more attention.

As we saw in the opening chapters of this book, the poet Robert Burns was to exert a considerable influence upon the mind of the young Walter Scott. It is therefore perhaps no coincidence then that in childhood Burns himself was exposed to many similar influences to those with which Scott was to come into contact under his Grandfather's roof whilst convalescing in the Borders. As a child, Burns's first contact with poetry came from his Mother's own "inexhaustible store of ballads and traditionary tales", with which she is said to have "nourished his infant imagination."

Unfortunately, we are not in possession of anything like the amount of information available to us in connection with Burns's Mother's family as we are with Sir Walter's own illustrious ancestry; so tracing the exact origins of the oral culture to which he was exposed at this time of life is not so easy as it is with that into which the infant Sir Walter was first immersed at Sandyknowe.

Another of the storytellers with whom Burns was to come into contact early in life was an old woman named Betty Davidson, who is described as having "filled his infant mind with popular legends" in the pages of the *Dictionary of National Biography*. In view of this then it is hardly surprising that, following the failure of his farm at Ellisland towards the end of the 1780s, Burns began to devote much of his time to the collecting and rewriting of many popular old songs and ballads.

One of the first pieces of written literature which was to leave an indellible impression upon Burns was a borrowed copy of a biography of William Wallace, which was perhaps to inspire some of his most famous lyrics, which appear in the song *Scots, Wha Hae*:

Scots wha hae wi Wallace bled,
Scots wham Bruce has often led,
Welcome to your gory bed,
or to victorie!

Now's the day and now's the hour;
See the front o' battle lour;
See approach proud Edward's power,
Chains and slaverie.

Wha will be a traitor knave?
Wha can fill a coward's grave?
Wha sae base as be a slave?
Let us turn, and flee!

Wha for Scotland's King and Law
Freedom's sword will strongly draw,
Freeman stand or freeman fa',
Let him follow me!

By oppression's woes and pains,
By your sons in servile chains,
We will drain our dearest veins,
But they shall be free!

Lay the proud usurpers low!
Tyrants fall in every foe!
Liberty's in every blow!
Let us do, or dee!"

Such sentiments can be found, expressed over and over again, throughout Scott's own voluminous writings; and place the Laird of Abbotsford and his own lyrics firmly in the same heroic bardic tradition that Burns himself had formerly continued. The central point of relevance of both these lyrics, and their composer, to our own story, however, revolves around the previously made connections between the bardic repertoire of Thomas of Ercildoune, and the Cymro-Breton traditions in which I have shown it to be rooted; traditions with which Wallace's own ancestors would doutbless have been familiar in view of their Welsh extraction. Wallace, together with Bruce, are the two most important figures in Mediaeval Scottish history; and it is as a direct consequence of this that the bardic traditions cultivated under the roofs of the noble families from which they descended were to have an important impact upon the development of Scottish literature; and its minstrel tradition in particular.

As for Burns himself, his own family's origins provide us with certain clues as to how the ancestors of William Wallace, hero of *Braveheart* and *Scots Wha Hae*, found their way into Scotland to begin with; a fact of some significance for a variety of reasons. Burns's Father, William, who, like his ancestors, spelt his name "Burnes", came originally from Kincardineshire; where the family held the farm of Clockenhill on the Dunottar estate of Earl Marischal Keith; who had suffered attainder for his part in the Rising of 1715. It was his family links with the Earls Marischal that led to Burns's own convictions that his relatives had suffered in the Jacobite Cause.

As far as is ascertainable, Marischal Keith's ancestors derived their own name from the lands of Keith in the parish of Humbie in East Lothian; not so very far from Scott's own ancestral Borderlands. Humbie itself lies on a tributary of "Birns Water", one of a whole host of small rivers that run down off the Lammermuir Hills in a notherly direction. And, it is therefore not inconceivable that the poet's ancestors originally derived their name from this locality; before migrating to Kincardineshire from the very region where their aristocratic landlords originally held the lands from whence they too obtained their identity. As we saw in an earlier chapter, in a direct quotation from Scott's own correspondence with Ellis, the whole of this region was at one time under Anglo-Saxon dominion; and it is therefore not inconceivable that the name "Burnes" denotes that the poet's own ancestors were originally of Bernician origin; just as the Border Clan of Burnes, themselves native to the Scottish Middle Marches, may well have claimed a similar ethnicity.

The reason why this should be the case is due to the fact that, with the arrival of St. Margaret in Scotland, a wholesale migration of Edmund Ironside's followers took place; as many disaffected Saxons travelled over the Border with her; bringing with them certain Celtic elements from elsewhere. Of these, most, if not all, were Bretons who had followed the Normans to England; and Welshmen from the Western Marches. Most of the last mentioned appear to have migrated from the very area bordering Shropshire and Hereford and Worcester where we have previously encountered the Saxon dynasty of the Hwiccas; as well as a contingent of Picts and various families, such as the Bodenhams of Rotherwas, for whom a combined Cymric and Saxon origin has been claimed by genealogists. And, on the face of this, and other evidence later to be presented in our text, it is not unreasonable to suppose that the original metrical romance upon which Thomas of Ercildoune was to base his own, later, *Sir Tristrem,* was originally introduced into the very Scottish Borderlands where Thomas himself would one day reside, as a direct result of this migration.

In view of what we have already seen in connection with the Bodenhams, it may also not be uninteresting to note that there are definite genealogical and marital connections, to be found amongst genuine documentary sources, that are still extant and which show both the Earls of Northumberland and the Scottish Royal House to have had links with Wales through the Normano-Breton Marcher Lords in the period directly after St. Margaret's marriage to Malcolm III of Scotland. The one key element of population in Scotland at this time, whose arrival in the north coincides with this very era, is the Welsh element to which William Wallace's own ancestors are known to have belonged. These migrating Welshmen appear to have made their way into Malcolm's Kingdom as a direct result of two key factors. The first of these appears to have involved a dynastic link between some of them and Edmund Ironside's noble Mercian followers; a faction who can also be shown to have

190

had close links with Northumberland at this time. The second important connection between Wales and Scotland in this era involves some legendary associations relating to the supposed descendants of Banquo, the semi-mythical adversary of King Macbeth.

The legend of Banquo is almost certainly an ancient folk memory, like the fragmented traditions incorporated into Blind Harry's metrical "life" of William Wallace; and provides us with vital clues as to how the Mediaeval Welsh ethnic minority in Scotland, of whom the original "Waleis" ancestor of Sir William was one, established themselves north of the Border originally. The legendary tradition expanded upon by Shakespeare recounts how, following a prophecy that Banquo's descendants would one day supplant Macbeth's dynasty as the Royal House of Scotland, the two former friends quarrelled; Banquo being slain and his heir Fleance driven into exile by King Macbeth.

These semi-mythical traditions also relate how Fleance, after escaping from his ordeal at the hands of Macbeth's assassins, eventually married the daughter of King Gruffyd ap Llywelyn of Wales. Their son, the same legendary sources maintain, was himself none other than Walter the Young Welshman; supposed ancestor of the Stuart or Stewart Dynasty. Unfortunately, these legends diverge considerably from true historical reality, for, as we have already seen, the Stewarts were originally of Breton descent; a fact that has already been noted during the course of a previous chapter. The real relevance of these legends however is that they are indicative of some definite link between Wales and Scotland at this time; a link which would ultimately result in the establishment of Clan Wallace in the latter kingdom; and the formation of Thomas of Ercildoune's "Tristrem".

As we shall now also see, this particular group of folk myths are not the only set of legendary traditions linking the Welsh element in the Mediaeval Scottish population to the House of Stuart. For, another such association is itself supposedly meant to have existed between one of William Wallace's own direct male ancestors and the House of Stuart; during the reign of King David I of Scots. As we shall see shortly, these legends also specifically relate to some of the wholesale migrations that are known to have taken place within Scotland during the course of the Mediaeval Period; something which we will be returning to yet again in a future chapter.

According to the most celebrated of all of Wallace's biographers, Blind Harry, Wallace's ancestors migrated north with the Fitzalans, from whom the House of Stuart were themselves to descend, from an area in Shropshire close to where the Border Laidlaws are alleged to have had their own ancestral homeland. Legend has it that the mother of Walter, the first Stewart, was a Warenne of Shropshire; and that Walter himself may have wooed a Welsh cousin with the aid of Richard Wallace, the great-grandfather of Malcolm Wallace; the great Scottish patriot's father.

Unfortunately, like some of the historical traditions we have already looked at in connection with the ballads, not to mention the House of Stuart, there is no actual historical evidence to support this story whatsoever. It is definite fact that Ricardus Wallensis held lands in Ayrshire under Walter the Steward; and that he gave his name to Riccarton; a few miles north of Ayr and Alloway, where Burns's own Father was to migrate from the north in the centuries that followed. It is also a fact that some of the other families native to this same region can be shown to have been of Welsh origin too; most notably the Montgomerys; who likewise emigrated from a place not far from the Cambro-Shropshire Border.

When it comes to the ancestry of the House of Stuart, however, the historical facts and the legend diverge considerably. The pedigree of the Stuart Dynasty that later came to rule Scotland, and eventually England as well, following the ascent to the throne of Robert the Steward as Robert II King of Scots, is well documented; and there is much additional evidence to substantiate the facts given amongst the documents still in existence, which relate to the numerous descendants of Walter the Steward and the hereditary Stewards of Dol, in Brittany. Foremost amongst those descendants is the present Earl of Moray, one of whose ancestors was the "Bonnie Earl of Moray" of ballad fame; and whose ancient pedigree appears amongst the pages of *Burke's Peerage*.

According to the genealogy of the House of Moray, as it is given in *Burke's,* Walter Fitz Alan, first Great Steward of Scotland, married one Eschyne de Molle, who, it is believed, was the daughter of Malcolm, the first Hereditary Doorward of Scotland. It is generally reckoned that their son, Alan Fitz Walter, was the common ancestor of all of the noble lines of Stewart throughout the Scottish Kingdom. Walter Fitz Alan's own father, meanwhile, Alan Fitz Flaad, feudal Baron of Oswestry and Sheriff of Shropshire as Vicecomes for King Henry I of England, was married to one Aveline, the daughter of Arnulf, Seigneur de Hesdin in Picardy. So, on the face of this evidence, it would appear that there are no historical facts available to us which would substantiate the legend recounting the supposed links between the House of Stuart and the Shropshire Warennes; which supposedly relate to the connections between the FitzAlans and William Wallace's own ancestors.

As far as is ascertainable, the only provable connections that exist between the Wallace's of Ayrshire and the Warennes relate to Sir William Wallace's own links with John de Warenne (1231-1304), who had been appointed guardian of Scotland by King Edward I of England. John Earl of Warenne's daughter, Isabel, was, according to a pedigree preserved in the pages of the Revd. William Betham's *Genealogical Tables of the Sovereigns of the World*, published in 1795, the wife of John Baliol King of Scots (1292-1296), whose reign was brought to a premature end following his defeat by Edward Plantagenet. The same pedigree refers to Warenne's mother as being a natural daughter of William Earl of Pembroke, thus indicating that in all probability the links between Wales and the powerful Earls of Warenne are of considerably later origin than the abovementioned legends would appear to attest. On another level, John de Warenne's grandson, and successor, is mentioned as having held the Earldom of Menteith, in addition to those of Warenne and Surrey; and it is therefore not insignificant, in view of the fact that the de Warennes are linked in legend with the House of Stewart, that the legitimate Scottish holders of this title were the descendants of Alan Fitz Walter, 2nd Heriditary Steward of Scotland.

Before looking into the background of the Stewart Earls of Menteith, however, it is worth noting that de Warenne may have been appointed guardian of Scotland by Edward I, on account of his predecessors' marital links with the Scottish Royal House, and not the Hereditary Stewards; as the legend might suggest. As we shall see shortly, Henry Earl of Northumberland, the son of David I King of Scots and ancestor of John Baliol, married a relative of the Warennes at about the same time as Wallace's ancestors are said to have been involved in the betrothal of a Shropshire Warenne to an ancestor of the Stewart Royal House. (2). Is this the real marriage, now half forgotten, that the fragmented folk traditions collected by Blind Harry originally referred to? It is indeed an interesting hypothesis.

We shall be examining the English Baronies of the de Warennes at a later juncture, in Chapter 22, when we look at the links between the English folk traditions of Sussex and those of the Scottish Borders in the concluding chapter. In the meantime, let us return to the subject of the Stewart Earls of Menteith, from whence we originally digressed. The first of the family to hold the title was Walter, son of Walter, 3rd Hereditary Steward of Scotland; who was invested with the Earldom in 1260 in right of his wife, Mary; Countess of Menteith in her own right and younger daughter and co-heiress of Maurice, 3rd Earl of Menteith. Walter was also Sheriff of Ayr after 1263, and can therefore be shown to have had connections with the region where Wallace's own family held lands just nine years or so before the date of the latter's own birth.

Walter's son and successor in the title, Alexander, 6th Earl, took part in the invasion of England by the Scottish nobles in 1296, was amongst those captured after the English victory at Dunbar, and was forced to do homage to King Edward I, together with many of his fellow prisoners, following a period of imprisonment in the Tower of London. His son, Alan, was a supporter of Robert the Bruce and died in captivity in 1308. Alan's daughter, Mary, passed the Earldom on to her husband, Sir John Graham, 9th Earl of Menteith; and their daughter and heiress, Margaret Graham, Countess of Menteith, "carried the Earldom with its caput at Doune Castle", according to Burke's Peerage, to her fourth husband, "Robert Stuart Duke of Albany, by whom she was ancestress of the Earls of Castle Stewart and Moray".

More interesting than this though is that Walter the Steward's brother, who succeeded his father as Feudal Baron of Oswestry, Sheriff of Shropshire and Castellan of Shrewsbury, was the direct male line ancestor of Edmund Fitz Alan of Arundel; who married Alice de Warenne, sister of John Earl of Warenne and Surrey, later in the fourteenth century. It is therefore quite probable that all of the legendary connections between the Wallace Family, and that of Warenne, which are referred to in the compositions of Blind Harry the poet, in fact originally related to the links between the Earls of Surrey, and the Hereditary Stewards' English cousins, the Fitz Alans, a generation later.

So how does all this relate to the arrival of Clan Wallace, the Anglo-Cymric Metrical Romance Tradition, or the poet Robert Burns's ancestors on the Scottish side of the Border? Well, to find the answers to these questions we must return once again to the lands of Keith in East Lothian; from whence the ancestors of the Earls Marischal are known to have taken their patronymic designation. Tradition asserts that the family originally acquired the portion of Keith known as "Keith-Hervey", so called on account of it being owned by Herveus, Hervey or Herve, who is stated as being the original progenitor of the Family of Keith, in the reign of King David I.

The south east portions of Keith, however, did not fall into the family's hands until the marriage of Phiip de Keith, a contemporary of William the Lion, to Eda, daughter and heiress of Hugh Lorens; who had inherited them from her Mother, Eda; daughter and heiress of Symon Fraser; from whose name this particular part of Keith was in times past called "Keith Symon". Of the Frasers, McIan's "Clans of the Scottish Highlands" has the following to say with respect to their origins:

"Of the Norman descent of this clan it is asserted there can be no doubt whatever, and the Roll of Battle Abbey is cited as evidence that the knight from whom the Frasers are descended came over in the army of William the Conqueror, 1066. The exact period when the posterity of this warrior obtained a settlement in Scotland is not spoken of with so much confidence, but the convenient circumstance of David I having married an English Princess, is fixed upon for the establishment of her countrymen on the lands of the native Scots....."

The English Princess to whom King David is known to have been wed was herself none other than Matilda, daughter of Waltheof Earl of Northumberland; who is himself reckoned as being the great-grandson of Uchtred of Northumbria; husband of Edmund Ironside's sister Elgive and the ancestor of the Earls of March; patrons of Thomas of Ercildoune. Uchtred also appears to have been styled ruler of Bernica, and it is therefore not impossible that both the Keiths and the Frasers were originally of Norman or Breton origin; and that they, together with the poet Burns's own Bernician ancestors, might have established themselves in the vicinity of the lands of Keith at this particular historical juncture; adding another plausible dimension to the Burns question.

David I's son by his marriage to Matilda, who also married Simon St. Liz or de Seint Liz, by whom she had, along with various other children, Waltheof Abbot of Melrose (1148-1159), was Henry Earl of Northumberland; whose own son, David Earl of Huntingdon, was ancestor of both John Baliol and Robert Bruce. Another genealogical anecdote which also has a bearing on this particular part of our story is the fact that Matilda's sister was the alleged wife of Raoul de Toeni, or Ralph de Toesny as he is sometimes called. The

195

de Toenis were the builders of a famous abbey near Bretuil in Normandy, and were lords of Landal and ancestors of the Albini Family; who were in turn to pass the Earldom of Arundel down to the English branch of the FitzAlans. And, in addition to this, Raoul de Toeni's Father, Roger de Toeni, was connected with the Breton Comtes de Porrhoet. Also, his brother Robert de Toeni, or Robert de Stafford as he is also known, married the sister of William FitzOsbern; who, together with Comte Alain Fergent, commanded the Breton contingent at the Battle of Hastings.

In view of the links that we have already looked at as regards the intermarriage between the Breton nobility and the Dukes of Normandy, it must come as no surprise that Waltheof Earl of Northumberland was likewise married to a neice of William the Conqueror. It is also unsurprising then, in view of the connections that have already been proven to have existed between the old English province of the Hwiccas and the Saxon Royal House of Northumbria, that the de Toenis should have possessed lands in Herefordshire; along with their estates in Lincolnshire, Leicestershire and various other counties.

William Fitz Osbern was to become Earl of Hereford after the Conquest, and it is therefore also of some significance that his wife's mother, Helena, wife of Roger de Toeni, should herself have been the daughter of one Herve Fitz Morvan; whose own father was the Breton Comte de Leon; whose dynasty was one of several families of note to be possessed of legendary associations with the original Tristan of the Mediaeval Romances. The intermarriage between the de Toenis and the Saxon Earls of Northumberland at this time may well have occurred as a direct result of the longstanding connections between Northumbria and the Western Marches; connections that almost certainly have a bearing upon the exalted place of the Pictish hero of a Breton romance in the Bardic traditions of the Scottish Borders: That hero being none other than True Thomas's *Sir Tristrem*.

On the face of the above evidence then, it is also not in the least bit impossible that the Sir Tristrem legends found their way into the Scottish Borders as a direct result of the links between the de Toenis and the Scottish nobility at this time; and that the ancestor of the family of Keith, like the Breton Herve Fitz Morvan, could himself claim a similar ethnic origin. As for the ancestor of Clan Fraser having been present at the Battle of Hastings, the author of McIan's "Clans" continues as follows: "No record is found decisive of this opinion....", whilst adding that "the name of the reputed founder of this Clan, as it stands on the Norman Roll, is Frisell, and we find the Latin and Saxon Chroniclers presenting the various orthographies of Frazier, Freshele, Fresale, Frizil, & C."

As we saw earlier, in the centuries that followed the original influx of Anglo-Norman, and indeed Breton blood, into Scotland in the aftermath of the Battle of Hastings, the Keiths were to acquire extensive estates in Kincardineshire; just south of Aberdeen. In view of the apparent links between the Frasers and the lands of Keith, where, like the Earls Marischal, they were to acquire their earliest Scottish possessions, it is unsurprising that some of them would also acquire lands in the vicinity of Aberdeen too. Prominent amongst these was Sir Alexander Fraser, who was to found the port of Fraserburgh some three hundred years or so after the family first appears in written records. Another interesting and relevant anecdote is the fact that one of the most able, and indeed most famous, members of the Clan during the Mediaeval Period was probably Sir Simon Fraser; who fought alongside Wallace at the Battle of Rosslyn in 1302; like many of their Anglo-Norman Scottish contemporaries.

As the reader will now have gathered, I have taken everything full circle and arrived back where I started out a few pages previously, in connection with the great Scottish patriot William Wallace; leader of the rebellion against Edward I. It is significant also that the point at which I bring him back into my narrative centres on the Battle of Rosslyn. The reason why this last fact is so important is because the first of the Anglo-Norman nobles to enter Scotland during the reign of Malcolm III was one William St. Clair; himself a direct male line descendant of Richard II Duke of Normandy. William de St.Clair's father had, together with his two brothers, opposed the succession of William "the Bastard", Conqueror of England, to the Dukedom; and it is perhaps as a direct result of this fact that William was to go into exile in Hungary with the future St. Margaret of Scotland; a fact which would in turn lead to his acquisition of the Earldom of Rosslyn.

After the conquest of England by William and his Norman army, St. Margaret was sent to Scotland to be married off to King Malcolm III. William de St. Clair was to accompany her, as was the alleged founder of another great Scottish clan, Maurice, "....a Hungarian, who accompanied Edgar Aethling" (the legitimate heir to the Saxon Royal House of Wessex and the rightful King of England) "and his sister Margaret into Scotland". (3). The clan which Maurice is alleged to have founded was that of Na

197

Drumainich- Clan Drummond; which allegedly derives its name from the lands of Drymen in Stirlingshire; where he and some of his descendants were to settle in the years that followed his first setting foot on Scottish soil.

Amongst Maurice's numerous descendants was one Malcolm Beg Drummond, who, in the year 1220, is on record as having made a gift of the Barony of Uardross to the parsonage of Inchmohome in the island on the Lake of Mentieth; which became a priory in 1238 and thenceforth the burial place of the Drummonds. It was here, in April 1263, that Malcolm Beg's grandaughter, Margaret, married David II of Scots; and thus became Queen of Scotland. Similarly, his Great-Grandaughter, Anabella, would later marry the future Robert III King of Scots; and so become ancestress of the future Kings of Scotland and the United Kingdom. As we will now see, the above marital links between these two families may shed light on the legend of Banquo's Line previously recounted at an earlier juncture.

As we noted at the beginning of this same chapter, legend associates the Stewart Royal House with descent from Banquo; Macbeth's celebrated adversary. In view of the fact that Walter the Steward could in no way have been descended from Fleance, it is worth speculating as to whether or not the alleged descent of the Stuart Kings from Banquo was acquired as a result of intermarriage between the Drummonds and the Scottish Royal Line.

As we have just seen, Maurice, founder of Clan Drummond, accompanied the Saxon Margaret to Scotland. In addition to this, the old Saxon House of the Hwiccas, as well as being connected by marriage, as we shall see shortly, with the Royal Dynasties of Wales, was also linked with the Earls of Northumberland; as well as the de Toenis; themselves possessed of numerous Breton connections. Thus, in addition to the ancestors of Wallace, a descendant of Banquo's Line whose own progeny might well have intermarried with the Chiefs of Drummond, may well have accompanied St. Margaret on her journey north; either from Wales or Northumberland; and that this is perhaps how the Stuart descent from Banquo came into being. Perhaps there is another explanation, or perhaps this legend is pure fiction, like so much of the mythology that has been woven around Macbeth; who was, to all intents and purposes, the last true King of Scots.

We shall be looking at Macbeth and his legacy in Scotland more fully in a later chapter. In the meantime, it is worth noting that, like the Drummonds, the Stewarts too are possessed of ancient historical associations with the

Priory of Inchmohome; in that Walter Earl of Menteith, the son of Walter 3rd Hereditary Steward, still lies buried in the Priory ruins. These links may well be indicative of a certain closeness between the Stewarts and the Drummonds, before the two families became intertwined as a result of the abovementioned marital unions towards the end of the thirteenth century. Perhaps, at the root of these links, was some, now long forgotten, link between Clan Na Druimainich and Wales. Unfortunately, this is something upon which we can only speculate. However, in view of the fact that, as we have already seen, Walter Earl of Menteith's grandfather's father, Walter the Steward, became associated with the Wallaces on account of their mutual links with Wales, it is perfectly feasible that the association between Walter the Steward's descendants and Clan Drummond occurred as a direct result of similar Cymric connections to those possessed by William Wallace's predecessors.

In William Wallace's own time Walter Earl of Menteith was likewise Sheriff of Ayr; a fact which in itself may well be indicative of close links between a region which had by this time been settled by Maurice's heirs, and one where there was by now a Welsh ethnic minority established within the population. These last mentioned facts may indeed lend further weight to the previously set out theories.

Although, as we saw earlier, there were no marital links at this time between the Fitz Alans- ancestors of the Stuart Dynasty, and the de Warennes, a fact which can be proven beyond any reasonable doubt, there was a definite connection between the Earl of Warenne and Surrey's Family and the Scottish Royal House during the very period when William Wallace's ancestor is said to have been living on lands that he held under Walter the Steward. The monarch who Walter the Steward served, David I, was the father of Henry Earl of Northumberland; himself the ancestor of the de Brus, Stuart and Baliol claimants to the throne in the centuries to follow. And, as was seen earlier, Henry of Northumberland's wife, Ada, was herself the youngest daughter of the de Warenne Earl of Surrey.

In view of this last revelation then, it is almost certain that the fragmented traditions recorded in the writings of Blind Harry the Minstrel in fact refer to Wallace's ancestor being involved in the marriage contract between Ada de Warenne and the Earl of Northumberland; the negotiations over which he may well have assisted the first Hereditary Steward in bringing to a satisfactory conclusion. If this is what happened, it might imply that Richard

Wallace was sent on a mission to Shropshire, where Walter the Steward's Fitz Alan cousins then held sway; to bring all of this about. If this is what occurred, it would seem to indicate that the Wallace Clan were already established in Scotland before the arrival of the first Hereditary Steward. Circumstantial evidence which may be indicative of this is provided by the fact that Raoul de Toeni appears to have been married to Henry of Northumberland's aunt.

Raoul de Toeni's brother, Robert de Stafford, is known to have given Wrottesley and Liventon to Evesham Abbey in the year 1072. One of the witnesses to this charter was Osbern Fitz Richard; who, as we saw above, was to distinguish himself fighting alongside the Comte de Bretagne at the Battle of Hastings. His father, Richard Fitz Scrob, was married to a daughter of Robert Fitz Wimark or Guiomarc'h; who, although a Breton, was the holder of lands in Hereford and Worcester long before the Norman Conquest and as far back as Edward the Confessor. More interesting than this though is the fact that Osbern Fitz Richard himself was married to Nest, the daughter of the Welsh King Gruffydd ap Llywelyn; who died in 1063.

In view of the fact that Robert de Stafford's sister Adelisa married Osbern's son, William, it shows the de Toenis to be linked by marriage, not only to the Royal Line of Scotland, but also to a Welsh Royal Dynasty into the bargain. Interestingly enough, it is this self same Welsh dynasty that the exiled Fleance is said to have married into; a fact which is in turn in keeping with everything that we already know about the links between the Welsh Marches and the North East of England, where King Duncan of Scotland's sons were likewise to take refuge from their own father's killer, at this very same time. And, of further relevance is the fact that Fleance himself is generally believed to have fled to Wales via Northumberland during the very years when St. Margaret's future husband was himself residing on the English side of the Northumbrian Border. Further proof of these associations, which would tend to support all of the previously set out theories, as regards the connections between the Scottish Borders and the Welsh Marches at the time when St. Margaret Aethling arrived in the North, shortly after the Norman Conquest, is provided by the fact that both Robert de Stafford and Osbern Fitz Richard, as well as being contemporaries of St. Margaret, can be shown to have been possessed of extensive Welsh connections.

The central thrust of this last piece of evidence revolves around Osbern Fitz Richard's own marriage to a Welsh Princess, for that Princess was herself the daughter of a marriage between a Welsh Prince and the daughter of Aelfgar, Earl of the East Angles in 1053; who was to succeed as Earl of the Mercians in 1057. Aelfgar in turn could trace his ancestry back, through his father, Leofric Earl of Leicester, the husband of the semi-legendary Lady Godiva, to the now familiar Dukes of the Hwiccas; rulers of the Saxon province straddling the Welsh Borders; who have featured throughout this and the preceeding chapters in connection with Glastonbury and the Royal House of Wessex. More important than this though is the fact that Ealdgyth, the daughter of Aelfgar, was herself the sister of Morkere, Earl of Northumberland in 1066; who, as well as being Osbern Fitz Richard's brother-in-law, is known to have taken an active role in the rebellion of the Saxon thegn Hereward the Wake against Norman rule.

So, in the year 1066, there was a Saxon Earl governing in Northumberland who was himself the brother-in-law, not only of a Welsh Prince, but also of a Norman baron whose Breton ancestors had held lands in Hereford and Worcester in the time of Edward the Confessor. In view of these facts it is more than probable that, amongst his own retinue, Morkere maintained Welsh mercenaries; and that amongst these mercenaries were, quite possibly, the ancestors of William Wallace; as well as one or more descendants of Banquo or Fleance.

Contemporary records show a relative of Morkere named Owen, himself likewise descended from the union of a Welsh mother and a Saxon father, to have been fighting, together with his brother Outred, in the war band of Hugh Lupus; the Norman Earl of Chester. Both of these men are also known to have commanded under the Earl of Shrewsbury in Anglesey in 1098. After seeing service in the ranks of various Norman war bands, Owen was to become ancestor of the Griffiths of Garn, a prominent Welsh gentry family; after marrying into a Welsh dynasty and settling on the Welsh side of the frontier.

In a similar way, it seems more than likely that, in the case of many of Ironside's supporters in the North East, much of the same sort of thing happened following St. Margaret's emigration to Scotland. The followers of Ironside, of whom Owen's own grandfather was one, in addition to opposing Harold, also viewed St. Margaret's descendants as the legitimate successors of the old House of Wessex in the aftermath of her brother's death, and the ending of Alfred's dynasty in the direct male line. And, it is therefore probable, as I have already pointed out, that Robert Burns's own ancestors were amongst those to travel north into Scotland from the old Saxon Kingdom of Bernicia at this time; if they were not already settled there.

This theory is given further strength in view of what we know about Owen's grandfather Outred, who is mentioned in documentary sources as being one of the followers of Leofric Earl of Mercia (1026-1057). His wife is described in some genealogies as being the widow of Edmund Ironside himself; and it is generally reckoned that she is identifiable with Ealdgyth, daughter of Edwin (K.1039), the brother of Leofric and the uncle of Aelfgar Earl of the East Angles; Morkere of Northumberland's father. And, amongst the supporters of the rebellion led by Edwine Earl of Mercia, Morkere's older brother, in 1062, was Owen's father, Eadwine. To many, Edward the Confessor was viewed as a usurper on account of his Norman blood; and the fact that he was descended from Aethelred the Unready's second marriage to a daughter of the Duke of Normandy.

So what do all of these facts show, in relation to our story and Sir Walter's Scott's lifelong obsession with Border Minstrelsy? Well, as we have already seen, the eleventh century ruling dynasties of Wales can be shown to have intermarried, not only with the Saxon nobles of the old provinces of Mercia and the Hwiccas, but also with the Normano-Breton Marcher Lords who succeeded them as the dominant force on the Welsh Borders in the years following the Conquest. It is therefore probable that there were, amongst the entourages of the various Welsh Princes who married into these noble houses at this time, Welsh bards or minstrels who introduced various aspects of the already popular Arthurian legends into the repertoires of their English and Normano-Breton counterparts; as a direct result of these alliances.

If this could defintely be shown to have been the case, it would tend to suggest that the Western Marches were the original cradle of the primordial metrical romance upon which Thomas of Ercildoune's *Sir Tristrem* was itself ultimately based. As has already been noted, the *Sir Tristrem,* although composed in English, can be shown to have been based on Cambro-Breton bardic traditions. The one area where Welsh, Saxon and indeed Breton influences appear to have become intermingled, first of all, was in the old territory of the Hwiccas.

And, it would therefore seem likely, given the provable genealogical and marital connections between Northumbria and both the Mercian and Normano-Breton aristocracy, in the second half of the eleventh century, that this bardic tradition originally found its way north from the very location from whence the abovementioned noble families originally hailed.

Although Scott's previously referred to, and indeed quoted from, correspondence with Ellis shows that neither of the two great scholars could come to a definite agreement as to who the original author of the *Sir Tristrem* was, there is circumstantial evidence to suggest that Scott may have believed that the bardic traditions that were to filter down to Thomas of Ercildoune may have originally emanated from the Welsh Marches: For example, in the *Thomas the Rhymer* fragment to which I referred during the course of chapter three, the English knight who Scott portrays as arriving in the recently ravaged Border village in which the opening scene is set is none other than Lord Lacy, Constable of Chester; a member of one of the very Marcher Families who carved out semi-autonomous lordships for themselves on the Welsh Borders during the early years of Norman rule: As well as the Lacys, Earls of Chester, and the Shropshire FitzAlans, other families involved, besides those we have already referred to, included the Gilberts, the Clares, and of course the Mortimers; one of whom would later usurp the power of the Plantagenet King Edward II.

In the opening conversation, at the beginning of Scott's fragmentary first chapter, we find Lord Lacy speaking with one of the local inhabitants of the village he has just entered, which is, as one would expect, none other than the village of Ercildoune; the residence of True Thomas himself. During the course of the above conversation, after it has been revealed that Lord Lacy is "travelling to the court of the King of Scotland on affairs of consequence to both Kingdoms....", the old man from Ercildoune is heard to exclaim: ".....God send your mission may bring back peace and the good days of our old Queen Margaret!"

"Amen, worthy Franklin," quoth the Knight- "Did you know her?"

"I came to this country in her train," said the Franklin; "and the care of some of her jointure lands, which she devolved on me, occasioned my settling here."

"And how do you, being an Englishman," said the Knight, "protect your life and property here, when one of your nation cannot obtain a single night's lodging, or a draught of water, were he thirsty?"

"Marry, noble sir", answered the Franklin. "Use, as they say, will make a man live in a lion's den; and as I settled here in a quiet time, and have never given cause of offence, I am respected by my neighbours, and even, as you see, by our forayers from England."

"I rejoice to hear it, and accept your hospitality- Isabella, my love, our worthy host will provide you a bed- My daughter, good Franklin, is ill at ease. We will occupy your house till the Scottish King shall return from his northern expedition......"

Thus, in a few lines of fictitious conversation, Scott makes the connection between the coming of St. Margaret, the Welsh Marches and the Scottish Borders that would appear to provide clues as to the true origins of the *Sir Tristrem*; as well as of his own knowledge of the same. At the same time he makes mention of the King of Scots being away on a northern expedition. This fact is also relevant, in that the wholesale Anglo-Norman settlement of the Lowlands, which began in earnest during the reign of David I previously mentioned, took place largely as a result of the rebelliousness of the northern provinces- in particular the old Mormaership of Moray.

The fundamental reason for these rebellions was the successful attempt, by Malcolm and St. Margaret's heirs, to do away with the ancient electoral system of monarchy that had prevailed in Scotland since the most ancient time- a system that can be traced right back to the Pictish period. It was their use of Anglo-Norman mounted knights and the castle technology that they possessed that led ultimately to the dominance of the Lowlands in later times, the use of English at the Scottish Court and the eventual supersedence of Gaelic Culture.

As for the *Sir Tristrem*, a few lines from which I have previously quoted at the head of Chapter Three, this metrical romance can itself be shown to hold certain key elements in common with the previously referred to Northern British epic *The Gododdin;* from which I have also quoted earlier in the text. As we saw earlier, the written version of Aneirin's poem is being recited to a scribe by a bard who has committed the original to memory. Likewise, with the *Sir Tristrem*, it is somebody else who is either writing or dictating Thomas of Ercildoune's original composition to whoever is writing it down.

It is also quite probable that True Thomas's original exerted a considerable influence in the succeeding century upon the likes of John Barbour (1320-

1395), himself the author of the metrical *Life of Robert the Bruce*; which was in many respects the forerunner of Blind Harry's *Wallace*. The Mediaeval Minstrel Tradition was still at its zenith at this time, as the following extract from a poem by Sir Richard Holland (fl.1420-1485), a cleric in the service of the powerful Border family of Douglas, will show. This verse, which is taken from a poem entitled *The Bard and other Entertainers at the Feast,* originally appeared in the celebrated *Book of Howlatt.*

Sae come the Ruke, with a rerd and rane roch,
A bard out of Ireland, with "Benachadee".
Said: "Gluntow guk dynydrach, hala mischy doch-
Rax her a rug of the roast, or sho shall ryme thee.
Mich macmory ach mach mountir moch loch-
Set her doun, give her a drink, what deil ails thee?
O dermyn, O Donall, O Dochardy droch.
Thir are the Ireland kingis of the Irishery:-
O Knewlyn, O Connochar, O Gregor MacGrane.
 The Sennachy, the Clarsach,
 The Ben Shene, the Ballach,
 The Crekery, the Corach,
  Sho kennis them ilkane.

This attempt to satirize a Gaelic speaking bard of the old school, a man immersed in the genealogical and historical traditions of the Ancient Gael, gives us clues as to how the Ancient Minstrel Tradition was gradually undermined to begin with. This poem was composed by a cleric, and it is doubtless due to the fact that the vested interests which he himself served could effectively monopolize the written word, that the ancient oral culture of the bards and minstrels was such a threat to, that we find him pouring scorn on the Irish poet who is here clearly the subject of his ridicule.

As for Blind Harry's *Wallace,* it is not improbable that this masterly piece of poetical narrative exerted a considerable influence upon both Burns and Scott. Thus, it can be shown that both Scott and Burns were the true inheritors, as I have already made clear elsewhere in the text, of a continuous bardic tradition that can be traced back through Blind Harry and John Barbour to Thomas himself; and thence to the Ancient Bards of the Dark Ages of whom Thomas was the 13th cent. successor.

Burns's patriotism, a sentiment inflamed no doubt by the writings of Barbour and Blind Harry, was at the heart of his composition of the lyrics of *Scots Wha Hae*; not to mention his collection and collation of so many of the traditional ballads and songs that he contributed to James Johnson's *Musical Museum*. We shall be looking at one of these songs again in a future chapter, in the meantime, before returning to the fate of our old friend John Barleycorn, it is worth quoting the final verses of one of Burns's most famous compositions as a last illustration of that patriotism:

O Scotia! my dear, my native soil!
For whom my warmest wish to heaven is sent!
Long may the hardy sons of rustic toil,
Be blest with health, and peace, and sweet content!
And O may Heaven their simple lives prevent
From luxury's contagion, weak and vile!
Then howe'er crowns and coronets be rent,
A virtuous populace may rise the while,
And stand a wall of fire around their much-lov'd Isle.

O Thou! who pour'd the patriotic tide,
That stream'd thro' great, unhappy Wallace's heart;
Who dar'd to, nobly, stem tyrannic pride,
Or nobly die, the second glorious part:
(The Patriot's God, peculiarly thou art,
His friend, inspirer, guardian and reward!)
O never, never Scotia's realm desert,
But still the patriot and the Patriot-Bard,
In bright succession raise, her Ornament and Guard!

As regards the Anglo-Norman Ascendancy, of which, effectively, both of the heros of *Scots Wha Hae* - Wallace and Brus alike, were themselves representatives, as far as the Ancient Gaelic aristocracy was concerned at least, it is interesting to note that it was not until Robert de Brus ascended the throne as rebel King of Scots, that his family were forced to renounce their lands in England. These included the old manor of Tottenham, in what is now North London; which from the 17th century onwards was to become known as "Bruce Castle".

It was almost certainly as a direct result of the establishment of this Anglo-Norman Ascendancy in Scotland that led to Thomas of Ercildoune's choice of the English language in composing his metrical *Sir Tristrem*. As we shall see shortly, there is evidence to suggest that True Thomas's ancestors were more closely related to those of William Wallace than they were to either the Earls of March or the Bruces. In the meantime, it is also worth remembering that the evidence here presented would appear to indicate that the possibility exists that the original romance upon which the Rhymer based his own epic poem may well have arrived on the Borders considerably earlier than the date previously suggested in chapter 5; although there is perhaps less direct evidence to support this last theory; the principal proof being of a circumstantial nature- something that we will hear more of in the chapters to follow. But now, without further ado, we must look again at the slaughter of young John Barleycorn, this time by his own cruel mother, at her well below the valley......

Chapter Ten

The Well Below the Valley

A gentleman was passing by,
He asked for a drink, as he got dry,
At the Well below the Valley O.
Green grows the lily O,
White among the bushes O.

My cup is full up to the brim,
If I were to stoop I might fall in
At the Well below the Valley O.
Green grows the lily O,
White among the bushes O.

If your true lover was passing by,
You'd fill him a drink as he got dry,
At the Well Below the Valley O.
Green grows the lily O,
Right among the bushes O.

She swore by grass, she swore by corn
that her true love had never been born
At the Well below the Valley O.
Green grows the lily O,
Right among the bushes O.

He said young maid your swearing wrong,
For six fine children you had born
At the Well below the Valley O.
Green grows the lily O,
White among the bushes O.

There's two of them by your Uncle Dan
At the Well below the Valley O.
Green grows the lily O,
Right among the bushes O.

Another two by your brother John
At the Well below the Valley O.
Green grows the lily O,
Right among the bushes O.

Another two by your Father dear,
At the Well below the Valley O.
Green grows the lily O,
Right among the bushes O.

If you be a man of noble scheme
You'll tell to me what did happen to them
At the Well below the Valley O.
Green grows the lily O,
White among the bushes O.

There's two buried neath the stable door
At the Well below the Valley O.
Green grows the lily O,
White among the bushes O.

Another two neath the kitchen door
At the Well below the Valley O.
Green grows the lily O,
Right among the bushes O.

Another two buried beneath the well
At the Well below the Valley O.
Green grows the lily O,
Right among the bushes O.

If you be a man of noble fame
You'll tell to me what'll happen me sel'
At the Well below the Valley O.
Green grows the lily O,
White among the bushes O.

You'll be seven years a ringin' the bell
At the Well below the Valley O.
Green grows the lily O,
White among the bushes O.

You'll be seven more a portin' in Hell
At the Well below the Valley O.
Green grows the lily O,
Right among the bushes O.

I'll be seven more a ringin' the bell,
But the Lord above me save my soul from portin' in Hell
At the Well below the Valley O.
Green grows the lily O,
Right among the bushes O......

This traditional Irish ballad, recorded in 1973 by the folk combo "Planxty", on their album of the same title, is included here for a variety of reasons. First and foremost, certain aspects of it are found paralleled in some of the ballads collected by Scott. In addition to this, the appearance of a noble stranger, seemingly with psychic powers of some kind, may denote that, once again, we have encountered our "der wydd" Druid dodman "inspector", who we met in chapter five, on one of his journeys up and down the Ancient Fairy Paths.

If this is the case, it will show conclusively, as I have already maintained, that most of the allegations made in the writings of Christian and Classical authors with regard to the Druids supposedly indulging in child sacrifice are most probably false. The fact that many of the prehistoric alignments previously referred to run directly through ancient wells would tend to suggest that this particular line of speculation is well founded. I shall present my readers with another ballad further on in this same chapter which would likewise tend to confirm this. In the meantime, it is worth pointing out that although some of the prehistoric inhabitants of the British Isles certainly did indulge in such bestial practises, it was almost certainly the aim of the more civilized Druids to keep such evil perversions in check.

In the Taliesin cycles, which we also looked at earlier, the child hero is pursued by the sow-goddess Cerridwen after accidentally tasting the forbidden Salmon of Knowledge. We shall be looking at this particular episode in these legendary cycles again shortly. In the meantime, it is worth asking the question as to whether or not the Well below the Valley is another sacred fountain like the one previously encountered in the legends associated with the nine hazels of poetic art. If this be so, then it is perhaps Cerridwen who we have encountered here too, sacrificing her own children in order to prevent them from unravelling the ancient mystical riddles that she herself has solved; for in the legends in which we come across Taliesin it is his own cruel mother who sets out to devour him in the first place. This last fact is of particular relevance in connection with the ballad which now follows.

Entitled *Lady Ann,* Scott writes of the version that he was to include in the *Minstrelsy,* which was, he says, communicated to him by his friend Mr. Kirkpatrick Sharpe of Hoddom, that "the general turn" of the ballad "seems to be ancient and corresponds with that of a fragment, containing the following verses, which I have often heard sung in my childhood:

She set her back against a thorn,
And there she has her young son born;
"O smile nae sae my bonnie babe!
An ye smile sae sweet, ye'll smile me dead."

And when that lady went to the church,
She spied a naked boy in the porch.

"O bonny boy, an' ye were mine,
I'd clead ye in the silks sae fine."
"O mither dear, when I was thine,
To me ye were na half sae kind."

Stories of this nature are very common in the annals of popular superstition", the Author of Waverley then continues, before recounting Kirkpatrick Sharpe's version of the ballad of *Lady Anne.*

Fair Lady Anne sate in her bower,
Down by the greenwood side,
And the flowers did spring, and the birds did sing,
'Twas the pleasant May-day tide.

But Fair Lady Anne on Sir William call'd,
With the tear grit in her e'e,
"O though thou be fause, may Heaven thee guard,
In the wars ayont the sea!"

Out of the wood came three bonnie boys,
Upon the simmer's morn,
And they did sing, and play at the ba',
As naked as they were born.

"O seven lang year wad I sit here,
Amang the frost and snaw,
A' to hae but ane o' these bonnie boys,
A-playin' at the ba."

Then up and spake the eldest boy,
"Now listen, thou fair ladie,
And ponder well the rede that I tell,
Then make ye a choice of the three.

"'Tis I am Peter, and this is Paul,
And that ane, sae fair to see,
But a twelvemonth sinsyne to Paradise came,
To join with our companie."

"O I will hae the snaw-white boy,
The bonniest of the three."
"And if I were thine, and in thy propine,
O what wad ye do to me?"

"'Tis I wad clead thee in silk and gowd,
And nourice thee on my knee."
"O mither! mither! When I was thine,
Sic kindness I could na see.

"Beneath the turf where I now stand,
The fause nurse buried me;
The cruel penknife sticks still in my heart,
And I come not back to thee".

This ballad, and the ballad from which Scott previously quoted a fragment in his introductory notes to *Lady Anne,* both hold much in common with another of the ballads collected and collated in this century by the late Ewan MacColl. Entitled *The Cruel Mother,* this song was also included in Professor Child's collection; and in his notes to the version which appear in his *Folk Songs and Ballads of Scotland,* from which I myself have previously quoted a version of *Hughie the Graeme* in an earlier chapter, MacColl points out that "Versions of this black ballad continue to be sung throughout the British Isles and North America."

A Minister's daughter in the North,
Hey, the rose and the linsie O,
She's fa'en in love wi' her Father's clerk,
Doon by the greenwood sidie, O.

She's courted him a year and a day,
Hey, the rose and the linsie O,
Till her the young man did betray.
Doon by the greenwood sidie, O.

She leaned her back against a tree,
Hey, the rose and the linsie O,
And there the tear did blin' her e'e,
Doon by the greenwood sidie, O.

She leaned her back against a thorn,
Hey, the rose and the linsie O,
And there twa bonnie boys has she born,
Doon by the greenwood sidie, O.

She's ta'en the napkin frae her neck,
Hey, the rose and the linsie O,
And made to them a winding sheet,
Doon by the greenwood sidie, O.

She's ta'en oot her wee penknife,
Hey, the rose and the linsie O,
And quickly twined them o' their life,
Doon by the greenwood sidie, O.

She's laid them 'neath a marble stane,
Hey the rose and the linsie O,
Thinking to gang a maiden hame.
Doon by the greenwood sidie, O.

She looked ower her faither's wa',
Hey the rose and the linsie O,
And she's seen they twa bonnie boys at the ba',
Doon by the greenwood sidie, O.

"O bonnie bairns,gin ye were mine
Hey, the rose and the linsie O,
I would dress ye in the silk sae fine,
Doon by the greenwood sidie, O."

"O cruel Mither, when we were thine,
Hey the rose and the linsie O,
We didna see ocht o' the silk sae fine,"
Doon by the greenwood sidie, O.

"O bonnie bairns,come tell to me,
Hey the rose and the linsie O,
What kind o'deith I'll hae to dee",
Doon by the greenwood sidie,O.

"Seven year a fish in the flood,
Seven year a bird in the wood.

Seven years a tongue to the warning bell,
Seven years in the caves o'Hell."

"Welcome, welcome, fish in the flood,
Welcome, welcome, bird in the wood.

"Welcome, tongue to the warning bell,
But God keep me frae the Caves o' Hell".

The parallels between this ballad and the previously given version of *The Well Below the Valley* are obvious; particularly as regards the references to the warning bell and the *Caves o' Hell*. Like the verses quoted by Scott in the notes to *Lady Anne,* there are, once again, references to the unlucky thorn tree which we encountered in connection with both Merlin the Magician and Thomas of Ercildoune; although in MacColl's *Cruel Mother* the presence of another species or genus of tree besides the thorn appears to be being hinted at also. More important than this though, and paralleling once again the Taliesin cycles, is the reference to what appears to be an attempt by the "Cruel Mother" to escape her punishment in Hell, when she is either turned or alternatively turns herself into a fish and then a bird.

As I have already pointed out, in the legendary cycles which are associated with the birth and life of the great Welsh master poet Taliesin, the young bard is chased by the goddess Cerridwen, after accidentally tasting the Salmon of Knowledge. In the ensuing chase he transforms himself into a hare, whilst his pursuer changes into a greyhound in an endeavour to catch him. He then plunges into a river in the shape of a fish, whilst she swims after him in the shape of an otter. Next they fly through the air as a bird pursued by a hawk; before Taliesin disguises himself as a grain of winnowed wheat on the threshing floor; which is swallowed by his pursuer in the guise of a black hen. In view of this, it would seem highly likely that all of the above given and quoted from ballads are ultimately rooted in the same source, and almost certainly evolved out of some ancient primordial corpus of pagan bardic literature; giving yet further credence to my previously made assertions that the male inquisitor in *The Well Below the Valley* is a Druid in disguise.

As for the true identity of those responsible for initiating the abominable sacrificial practises that lie at the heart of the underlying theme that runs through the storyline of all of these songs, a vital clue can be found in verse seven of *The Cruel Mother,* in which we hear of how the little boys who she has murdered have been buried by their mother under "a marble stane". To understand fully the significance of this last mentioned line, I now propose to take the reader back into the realms of Old Welsh Mythology once again. In a legend recounted by the ninth century Welsh Chronicler Nennius, whose writings constitute a major primary source for the study of the Arthurian

215

Period, a curious series of myths are recounted in relation to the early life of Ambrosius Aurelianus, otherwise known as "Emrys", father of Uthyr Pendragon and King Arthur's grandfather; a group of legends which we focussed on briefly in the opening chapter of this book.

Traditionally, Emrys is said to have been kidnapped in his youth by the scheming usurper Vortigern; a Romano-Briton who is held responsible by traditional Welsh historians for assisting the Saxon invasion of Britain on account of his employment of Anglo-Saxon mercenaries. This story, if it is actually true, illustrates the old saying that history often repeats itself, for the Battle of Melrose, which took place in 1526, and was fought "between the Earls of Angus and Home and the two chiefs of the race of Kerr on the one side, and Buccleuch and his clan on the other, in sight of the young King James V, the possession of whose person was the object of the contest....." seems to have been caused by a similar attempt to usurp the power of govenment to that in which the aforementioned Dark Age magnate, Vortigern, appears to have kidnapped the fifth century heir to the British throne; this time by a sixteenth century Border aristocrat.

The Battle of Melrose is also relevant to our story, for not only does it feature in the introduction to the *Minstrelsy*, but it also inspired those immortal lines of Sir Walter's previously quoted in chapter one, in connection with how

> "........gallant Cessford's life-blood dear
> Reeked on dark Elliot's border spear."

In the now largely forgotten writings of one of Sir Walter's own descendants [1] we find references to how "In the names of various localities between Melrose and Abbotsford, such as "Skirmish-field", "Charge-Law", and so forth, the incidents of the fight have found a lasting record; and the spot where the retainer of Buccleuch terminated the pursuit of the victors by the mortal wound of Kerr of Cessford (ancestor of the Dukes of Roxburghe) has always been called "Turn-again"........", a location which is to be found situated in the woods above Abbotsford House itself; a fact which was to influence considerably Scott's decision to acquire the original property that he was later to convert into his own very unique home.

Thus, in the mythical and symbolic elements incorporated within the storylines of the Border ballads, as well as the historical interconnectedness between bardic tradition, local legend, landscape and locality, we find a continuity which can be traced back over the course of countless generations, from the late seventeenth century, into the Dark Ages, the Pre-Roman Period and beyond. This continuity has been hinted at, referred to and illustrated throughout this book. But at no juncture does this timeless continuity manifest itself, in the modern era at least, than in the person, writings, and general character of Sir Walter Scott; last of the true bards.

But now, we must return once again to the legend of Emrys, who, although no doubt kidnapped in real life for a similar reason to the one which was to result in the Earl of Angus taking the young King James Stuart into custody more than a thousand years later, is referred to in legend as having been hunted down by Vortigern's masons on account of the fact that he was allegedly "a child without a father". The legend likewise recounts how his pursuers have the intention of killing their quarry and sprinkling the ground with his blood; thus invoking some kind of magical protection for the fortress that they plan to build upon the ground where he is to be slaughtered; as a means of warding off the destructive power of the elements.

Coincidentally, the way in which Vortigern's retainers detect the "child without a father", for whom they are looking, is by eaves-dropping upon the conversation of two boys involved in a football game; who appear to be quarrelling with one another. One of them is heard to say to the young Emrys, "You have no father, you will come to no good"; thus indicating to Vortigern's men that their quest is at an end.

Again, there are definite parallels between these legendary traditions and the subject matter of the previously given ballads. It is also worth noting that in the ballad of *Lamkin,* which also features in chapter one, the evil murderer of Lord Wearie's child is himself a mason and the builder of Balwearie Castle. More clues which would tend to suggest that the murder of the children by their "Cruel Mother" is a masonic one, besides the presence of the football game and the fact that her children are without a father, include their previously referred to burial beneath a "marble stane". Another relevant fact, as shall be noted later, is her own Father's clerical status, for, it is over his wall that she looks when she sees her ghostly deceased children at play; just as the woman in Scott's fragment finds her own naked child in the porch of a church; now come back to haunt her.

These elements contain echoes of an ancient English legend, this time from Reculver in Kent, which recounts how, on stormy nights, close to the old

Roman Saxon Shore Fort of Regulbium, the sound of crying babies can be heard upon the wind. Archaeologists involved in the excavation of the site unearthed the remains of sacrificed children close to the spot where this ghostly phenomenon is said to have occurred. And, as one might expect, it is believed that these babies were buried alive as part of some sort of perverted masonic ritual.

There is evidence to suggest that one of the causes of Vortigern's undoing was his employment of Saxon mercenaries in the chain of coastal forts referred to in Roman sources as the Forts of the Saxon Shore. It is therefore not impossible that the skeletons unearthed at Reculver have some link with the legend of Emrys; not to mention the contents of the above ballad. In order to see how the lyrics of a Scottish ballad can be linked with the ghostly children's cries of a Kentish legend however we must turn our attention to two later structures that now dominate the ruined remains of the bastions of Regulbium; which lie just a stone's throw away from where two of the most celebrated Saxon chieftains of the Dark Ages are said to have had their power base- the Island of Thanet.

On the edge of the sea stand the twin towers of a ruined Saxon church, all that remains of an ancient abbey first founded in the year 699. Another curious legend recounts how two spires were added to the original twin towers in the 16th century by the Abbess of the Benedictine nunnery of Davington, in honour of her twin sister who had died after the pair of them had been shipwrecked nearby. The Abbess herself was none other than Frances St. Clare or St. Clair, and it is the Scottish branch of the St. Clairs or Sinclairs, whose common ancestor first travelled to Scotland as St. Margaret's cup bearer, who, in the fifteenth century, were to become one of the foremost masonic families north of the Border, when,

"......in 1441 James II, King of Scotland, appointed (Sir William) St. Clair Patron and protector of Scottish Masons;....(this)....office was hereditary; (and) after his death, circa 1480, his descendants held annual meetings at Kilwinning...." [2].

Whether the masons employed by Frances St. Clare or St. Clair in the construction of the spires atop of the twin towers of Reculver indulged in similar ritual practises to those undoubtedly employed by Vortigern's architects, or not, nobody will ever know for sure. What we can say, however, is that the builders of another masonic structure, built by Sir

218

William St. Clair and first begun in 1446, were almost certainly involved in the preservation of certain masonic legends which can be shown in turn to possess certain parallels not only with the mythologies surrounding the kidnapping of the boy king Emrys, but also with the ballads previously referred to in this chapter. As we saw at an earlier juncture, the St. Clairs, upon their arrival in Scotland, were invested with the Barony of Rosslyn by King Malcolm III. And it was here, just five years after Sir William received his Royal appointment as patron and protector of Scottish masons, that work began on a masonic edifice which was to become the architectural embodiment of all of the above traditions. The structure in question was none other than Rosslyn Chapel, which stands perched on top of a gorge overlooking the North Esk Valley; just three miles south of Edinburgh. One of the most written about features of the chapel begun by Sir William is the so called "Apprentice Pillar". And, in an eighteenth century account of the chapel and its construction, we are told of

".....a tradition that has prevailed in the family of Roslin from father to son, which is,- that a model of this beautiful pillar having been sent from Rome, or some foreign place; the master mason, upon viewing it, would by no means consent to work off such a pillar, til he should go to Rome, or some foreign part, to take exact inspection of the pillar from which the model had been taken; that, in his absence, whatever might be the occasion of it, an apprentice finished the pillar as it now stands; and that the master, upon his return, seeing the pillar so exquisitely well finished, made enquiry, who had done it; and, being stung with envy, slew the apprentice".

Above Rosslyn Chapel's west door, a direction associated both with death, as well as the setting of the sun, is a carving of a young man with a gash in his temple; said to represent the murdered apprentice. Other effigies incorporated into the chapel's masonry include those of the master mason who slew him; as well as the victim's mother; called in masonic legend "The Widowed Mother"; whilst he himself is referred to as "The Widow's Son"; indicating that like Emrys in the story of Vortigern's masons, he too was a fatherless child. Similarly, in the ballad of *Cospatrick,* which we encountered in chapter eight, the ballad heroine is accompanied on her journey to her husband to be by "Sweet Willy", who is likewise referred to as a "widow's son" in verse three; no doubt indicating that, in addition to being tampered with by the church, these songs have also been altered at some stage by the meddling masonic brethren of the Anglo-Norman Ascendancy.

Interestingly enough, at Abbotsford, much of the "richly moulded" library ceiling is copied directly from the ornamentation at Rosslyn Chapel. Amongst the decorative motifs incorporated into this architectural curiosity are carvings of corn and other vegetation which might denote that, like the children in the ballad of *The Well Below the Valley,* whose own "Cruel Mother" swears oaths by "grass" and by "corn" that they had never existed, the murdered apprentice might well have been sacrificed to some sort of god of vegetation.

As for the "Cave of Hell" which features in MacColl's ballad, it is interesting to note that just a short distance from Rosslyn Chapel, in the North Esk Valley Gorge, is a cavern in the rock where Robert the Bruce is said to have taken refuge. The cavern is only accessible through a secret entrance, which can only be negotiated if one is lowered on a rope down into a well. Is this the "Cruel Mother's" "Cave of Hell" which can only be reached through a "Well below the Valley"? Is Rosslyn Chapel the place where the woman in Scott's fragment first encountered her murdered child? Is this the place in its sister ballad where MacColl's muderess's father once held his ministry? Whatever the answers to these questions, a superstitious person might conjecture that Sir Walter might have called down all the bad luck that affected him in later life upon himself, by copying the mouldings of his library ceiling from so unholy an edifice.

Another ballad, this time from England, and recorded in one of their own unique arrangements by folk rockers "Steeleye Span" on their 1975 L.P. *Commoner's Crown,* preserves an ancient folk memory of many similar practises to the ones previously encountered in the other ballads:

Four and twenty bonny bonny boys,
Playing at the ball,
Along came little Sir Hugh,
He played with them all.
He kicked the ball very high,
He kicked the ball so low,
He kicked it over a castle wall,
Where no one dared to go.

Chorus: *Mother, mother make my bed,*
Make for me a winding sheet,

Wrap me up in a cloak of gold,
See if I can sleep.

Out came a lady gay,
She was dressed in green.
"Come in, come in little Sir Hugh,
Fetch your ball again".
"I won't come in, I can't come in
Without my playmates all,
For if I should I know you would
Cause my blood to fall".

Chorus: *Mother, mother etc.*

She took him by the milk white hand,
led him to the hall,
Till they came to a stone chamber
Where no one could hear him call.
She sat him on a golden chair,
She gave him sugar sweet,
She laid him on a dressing board
And stabbed him like a sheep.

Chorus: *Mother, mother etc.*

Out came the thick thick blood,
Out came the thin,
Out came the bonny heart's blood
'till there was none within,
She took him by the yellow hair
And also by the feet,
She threw him in the old draw well
Fifty fathoms deep......

This ballad is centred upon the legendary martyrdom of Little St. Hugh of Lincoln, who was allegedly murdered in 1255, at the age of nine, by one of the city's Jews. The supposed culprit, one Koppin, was, after his "confession", executed along with eighteen others. In view of what we have already found in the lyrics of the other heregiven ballads that deal with this same dark and bloody subject matter, it is worth asking as to whether or not

Little St. Hugh was in reality the victim of a masonic murder; a murder in which his own cruel mother played an integral part? Like Rosslyn Chapel, Lincoln Cathedral contains a stone effigy of its own, which, like that of the murdered apprentice, belongs more to the world of the diabolical than the divine. The demonic "Lincoln Imp", a devilish creature, was placed in the Cathedral by the same malevolent masons who built the great castles that oppressed the subdued populace of England in the wake of William's conquest; not to mention the self same fortifications with which the war bands of the Anglo-Norman Ascendancy "pacified" the Highlands of Scotland on behalf of St. Margaret of England's heirs.

It is of relevance that football games feature not only in Steeleye Span's arrangement of *Little Sir Hugh*, but also in the versions of *Lady Anne* and *The Cruel Mother* published by Scott and MacColl. In an earlier chapter, itself primarily concerned with a ballad dedicated to the memory of another Hugh, "Hughie the Graeme", I put forward the hypothesis that a football game in which the head of a ritually put to death transgressor, whether rapist, murderer or adulterer, was used as a substitute ball, was almost certainly a common occurrence in prehistoric times. Perhaps a similar fate awaited the child molesting muderous hag of a cruel mother who is archetypally portrayed in the ballads that I have dealt with in this chapter.

Curiously, at Somerton in Somerset, just a few miles from Glastonbury and the Sacred Vale of Avalon, balls found in the rafters of the Mediaeval church roof show that football was once actually played inside the building itself. Perhaps the ballad of *Little Sir Hugh*, with its references to a ball being kicked over the wall originally recalled a game similar to this in which the boundary of the church yard marked the length and breadth of the pitch. The Kingstonian football game likewise took place in the shadow of the town's church; itself home to Kingston's ancient Coronation Stone. Similarly, at Haxey, where a not dissimilar "Hood" game has been played for centuries, the ritual customs which take place before the hood is pushed through the door of one village pub or another by a great heaving mass of rural masculinity, are centred on the ancient "Mounting Stone" a few feet from the village church.

As we saw in chapter seven, the lady who is traditionally credited with inspiring this ancient and undoubtedly pagan game was the wife of Sir John Mowbray. The de Mowbrays themselves were a scion of the Albini Family, whose ancestry sprang, as we saw in chapter nine, from the de Toenis. (See also Appendix 3, Table 3). The most senior branch of the family were Earls of Arundel until the title passed, in the thriteenth century, to the Fitz Alans of Oswestry; through marriage to an Albini heiress. As we also saw, the Fitz Alans sprang from the self same sires as the Stewart Kings of Scotland, and it is therefore of relevance to our particular line of enquiry that in the *Tristan* of Gottfried von Strassbourg, which is itself allegedly based upon the earlier romance of one *Thomas of Britain,* one of the principal characters is none other than Jovelin, who is described as "Duke of Arundel".

In view of this, it is an interesting fact that the first member of the Albini Family to hold the title "Earl of Arundel" was married to Queen Adeliza, the widow of Henry I and the daughter of Godfrey, Duke of Lorraine. Given the fact that Strasbourg is situated in the old German Duchy of Swabia, which, in both Gottfried and William, the first Earl of Arundel's time, bordered on what was then part of Godfrey's Dukedom, it is not beyond the realms of possibility that the "Tristan" legends found their way into Swabia as a direct result of the Albini Family's marital links with his daughter and co-heiress. Godfrey's other daughter, Joscelin, is cited by Betham as having married a member of the powerful Percy Family; whose descendants would later succeed as Dukes of Northumberland; a title originally held by the Albinis' relatives, the de Mowbrays.

If this is what happened, it would only serve to confirm the hypothesis already set out in the previous chapter, that the "Tistrem" legends, in their metrical form, arrived in the Scottish Borders as a result of the de Toeni Family's links with Northumberland. Another genealogical anecdote of particular relevance revolves around the fact that Lady Mowbray of Haxey Hood fame was herself descended from Osbern Fitz Richard's marriage to the daughter of King Gruffydd ap Llywelyn through her ancestor William de Braose.

The ballad of *Little Sir Hugh* may well place our Cruel Mother's probable execution on another Druidic ley line, by locating it in the precincts of what may have been a prehistoric sacred enclosure; before later tradition inserted the reference to a "castle wall". Certainly, many Norman castles were built directly on top of Druidic mounds that were already there, Windsor Castle being a fine example of this; and on page 146 of Watkins's *Old Straight Track,* we find references to traditional folk recreations being held at such places:

"Assemblies for recreation probably commenced quite early in prehistoric times, and the persistence of folk-memory as regards the type of spot at which they were held is illustrated by the fact that two or three years ago Caple Feast was revived to take place as of yore on the Wednesday in Whit week round Caple Tump, which is a large medium height tumulus......in an open space adjoining the church yard- with the road between- of King's Caple. I went to see and record it....but was a day too late, as the date had been altered....Round the Mound, the grass all nicely cut, there were signs where the stalls had been, and the shy village child playing on the horse block at the churchyard entrance told me how they had been dancing on the top of the mound the night before. Indeed, there were the modern signs of such outdoor recreation- confetti- to prove it,......And what a pretty circus-like ring it was, with its low parapet of earthen banking for sitting out, fine elms all round the rim, but none within!

Here, then, is a true survival of a folk meeting at the mound of amusement....."

Kingston's church and King's Stone are at the hub of a veritable vortex of ancient Druidic alignments, and the Kingstonian football game's traditional pitch was formerly located in the town's ancient apple market; directly outside the front door of the "Druid's Head" pub. On yet another level, the ballad of *Little Sir Hugh* also holds certain elements in common with another English folk song, this time collected from the repertoire of Mrs. Ford of Blackham, Sussex, in 1906:

"Mother, mother, make my bed,
And wrap me in a milk-white sheet,
And wrap me in a cloak of gold,
And see whether I can sleep.

"And send me the two bailies, likewise my sister's son,
That they may fetch me my true love,
Or I shall die before ever he can come."

The first three miles they walked,
The next three miles they ran,
Until they came to the high water side,
And laid on their breast and swam.

They swam till they came to the high castle
Where my lord he was sitting at meat:
"If you did not know what news I brought,
Not one mouthful more would you eat."

"What news, what news have you brought me?
Is my castle burnt down?"
"Oh no, your true love is very, very ill,
And she'll die before ever you can come."

"Saddle me on my milk-white horse,
And bridle him so neat,
That I may kiss of her lily lips
That are to me so sweet."

They saddled him his milk white steed
At twelve o'clock at night.
He rode, he rode till he met six young men
With a corpse all dressed in white.

"Come set her down, come set her down,
Come set her down by me,
That I may kiss of her lily, lily lips,
Before she is taken away."

My lady she died on the Saturday night
Before the sun went down.
My lord he died on the Sunday following
before evening prayers began.

My lady she was buried in the high castle
My lord was buried in the choir;
Out of my lady grew a red rose,
And out of my lord a sweet briar.

This rose and briar grew up together,
Til they could grow no higher,
They met at the top in a true lover's knot,
And the rose it clung round the sweet briar.

The first verse of Mrs. Ford's ballad is almost identical to the chorus of Steeleye Span's arrangement of *Little Sir Hugh*, as the reader will doubtless have observed; thus showing both songs to be in some way connected. And, in view of what we have already seen throughout this chapter, coupled with the lyrics themselves, it is worth asking as to whether or not it is the Cruel Mother who is here being asked to make for her child a winding sheet before putting him to sleep. The ballad *Mother, Mother make my Bed* also holds certain elements in common with one of Scott's other ballads from the *Minstrelsy*; a ballad in which the Cruel Mother makes yet another appearance: This song, entitled *Prince Robert*, is inserted directly after the ballad of *Cospatrick* in the edition of Scott's *Minstrelsy* revised by Henderson and referred to throughout this work.

Prince Robert has wedded a gay ladye,
He has wedded her with a ring;
Prince Robert has wedded a gay ladye,
But he darna bring her hame.

"Your blessing, your blessing, my Mother dear!
Your blessing now grant to me!"
"Instead of a blessing ye sall have my curse,
And you'll get nae blessing frae me."

She has called upon her waiting maid,
To fill a glass of wine;
She has called upon her fause steward,
to put rank poison in.

She has put it to her roudes lip,
And to her roudes chin,
She has put it to her fause fause mouth,
But the never a drap gaed in.

He has put it to his bonny mouth,
And to his bonny chin,
He's put it to his cherry lip,
And sae fast the rank poison ran in.

"O ye hae poisoned your ae son Mother,
Your ae son and your heir;

O ye hae poisoned your ae son, Mother,
And sons you'll never hae mair.

"O where will I get a little boy,
That will win hose and shoon,
To run sae fast to Darlinton,
and bid fair Eleanor come?"

Then up and spake a little boy,
That wad win hose and shoon-
"O I'll away to Darlinton,
And bid fair Eleanor come."

O he has run to Darlinton,
And tirled at the pin;
And wha was sae ready as Eleanor's sell
To let the bonny boy in?

"Your gude-mother has made ye a rare dinour,
She's made it baith gude and fine;
Your gude-mother has made ye a gay dinour,
And ye maun cum till her and dine".

It's twenty long miles to Sillertoun town,
And into Sillertoun ha'
The torches were burning, the ladies were mourning,
And they were weeping a'.

"O where is now my wedded lord,
And where now can he be?
O where now is my wedded Lord?
For him I canna see."

"Your wedded lord is dead", she says,
"And just gane to be laid in the clay;
"Your wedded Lord is dead", she says,
"And just gane to be buried this day."

"Ye'se get nane o' his gowd, ye'se get nane o' his gear,
Ye'se get nae thing frae me;

Ye'se no get an inch o' his gude broad land,
Tho' your heart suld burst in three."

"I want nane o' this gowd, I want nane o' his gear,
I want nae land frae thee;
But I'll hae the ring that's on his finger
For them he did promise to me."

"Ye'se no get the ring that's on his finger,
Ye'se no get them frae me;
Ye'se no get the ring that's on his finger,
An your heart suld burst in three."

She's turned her back unto the wa',
And her face unto a rock;
And there, before the Mother's face,
Her very heart it broke.

The tane was buried in Mary's kirk,
The tother in Mary's quair;
And out o' the tane there sprang a birk,
And out o' the tother a brier.

And thae twa met, and thae twa plat,
The birk but and the brier;
And by that ye may very weel ken
They were twa lovers dear.

In his notes to this version of the above ballad Scott has the following comments to make: "The last two verses are common to many ballads, and are probably derived from some old metrical romance, since we find the idea occur in the conclusion of the voluminous history of *Sir Tristrem*: "Ores veitil que de la tumbe Tristan yssoit une belle ronce verte et feuilleuse, qui alloit par la chapelle, et descendoit le bout de la ronce sur la tumbe d'Ysseult et entroit dedans." This marvellous plant was three times cut down, but, continues Rusticien de puise, "Le lendemain estoit aussi belle comme elle avoit cy-devant ete, et ce miracle etoit sur Tristan et sur Ysseult a tout jamais advenir."

Thus, in the pages of the *Minstrelsy*, we find Scott himself confirming my own previously made assertions, that both the ballads and the romances that he collected, for inclusion in the series of volumes that he published during the opening years of the last century, were once part of the same great body of bardic literature; some of which at least can be proven to be of Ancient Pictish origin. As to the full extent of Scott's own knowledge of all of this, we can only speculate. As the reader will have noted however, I myself have attempted, as far as possible, to assess the exact level of the Laird of Abbotsford's own awareness of the significance of the sources which he and his circle had discovered, from the surviving texts available to us.

Before rounding this chapter off it is important to remember that, in early and Pre-Christian times at any rate, a complex system of Bardism existed both in Britain and in Ireland. The classical author Posidonius of Apamea refers to the ancient "bardoi" as being amongst three categories, along with the "druides" and "vartes", in a complex religious caste system. In reality, as the great Celtic scholar F.J. Byrne makes clear in his *Irish Kings and High Kings* (Batsford, 1973), this system appears to have been even more diverse than this. Posidonius's Gallic Vartes correspond to a priestly rank referred to in Irish sources as a "Faith" or prophet. Beneath him in rank was the Fili, literally a "poet or seer"; amongst whose entourage we would find the Irish equivalent of the "bardoi" of Posidonius- the Bard; lower in rank and in effect an inferior poet, satirist or panegyrist.

Another function held by the "Faith" was that of judge, and this is almost certainly why, amongst the ancient ballads, there is in all probability preserved, as I have previously conjectured, the lost remnants of what was once an ancient indiginous bardic legal system. In all probability the three "Fiddlers" in the traditional nursery rhyme of "Old King Coel" were "Fili"-bardic poets.

Other categories within this extensive Bardo-Druidic heirachy are known to have included the Senchaid, a bardic genealogist who specialized in memorizing the lengthy poetical tracts tracing the descent of the nobility from the semi-mythical kings and heros of antiquity. Highest of all though were the Druids, the Celtic Magi; whose most superior rank was the Ollam-himself equivalent to a King or Bishop.

In view of this, it is by no means impossible that the semi-legendary Thomas of Ercildoune had, amongst his own entourage, a whole host of lesser, "inferior", minstrels. His prophetic powers would almost certainly seem to elevate him to the status of the Mediaeval equivalent of the old bardic "Faith", and this in itself would tend to suggest that it is not beyond the realms of possibility that, whilst the more "superior" works in Thomas's repertoire, such as the *Sir Tristrem*, were recited exclusively by Thomas himself, the "lesser" works in the vast corpus of bardic knowledge that he undoubtedly possessed were quite probably performed by his students. And, amongst those self-same "inferior" works were undoubtedly the forerunners of the ballads that Scott and his circle collected and included in the *Minstrelsy*. As for Mrs. Ford, the Sussex location where she is noted as having recited her version of *Mother Mother Make My Bed*, itself located not so very far from the Valley of the River Arun where the Albini Earls of Arundel held their lands, is given as Blackham; as I have already noted. This would tend to suggest that we have found another bardic tract on the site of one of the former haunts of our elusive Black, Blake or Dod Man. It may therefore not be uninteresting to note that in Michell's *View Over Atlantis* we find the following reference:

"In 1960 Mr. Charles Mountford travelled for three hundred miles across the Central Australian deserts with a group of native men on a seasonal journey to reanimate the spirit of the sacred centres along sacred lines. He found that each tribe looks after its own stretches of line, visiting the centres at the appropriate season, at each singing of a local episode in the history of creation. The successive rituals form what the aboriginals call a "line of songs", woven between the geomantic centres of their landscape. In his book *Winbaraku and the Myth of Jarapiri*, Mr. Mountford gives the reason for these seasonal journeys, "It is an aboriginal belief that every food, plant and animal......has an increase centre where a performance of the proper rituals will release the life essence or "Kurunba" of that particular plant or animal, and thereby bring about its increase."

Perhaps these ancient Aboriginal rituals, themselves thousands of years old, provide us with a clue as to the original shamanistic traditions in which our own ancient bardic heritage was itself rooted. The Aboriginal Songlines are the Australasian equivalent of the Fairy Paths that we examined in Chapter Five. Similarly, as I have already noted, in another earlier chapter, songs such as *Cospatrick* are full of references to expeditions into the "grenewood" to gather the fruits of the forest; a definite shamanistic preoccupation. "These centres" Michell continues, "all scenes of a certain incident in the great poem that describes the creation of life, are marked by some natural feature, a hill, rock or spring. Paintings on the rock walls, continually restored, show the undulating serpent, symbol of the current of life energy, and various sacred objects hidden nearby are decorated with a plan of the serpent's route across the landscape. The aborigines say that it is not the paintings themselves that procure the release of life essence but the rock on which they are drawn. It is the energy from these rocks that creates rain and fertilizes plants and animals. The paintings and ritual songs stimulate its flow and benefit the creatures with which the current of a particular spot is associated."

Curiously, the hills across Doddington Moor, where we encountered our "False Knight on the Road" earlier on in our journey, whilst traversing the Devil's Causeway, are littered with ancient rocks carved with "Cup and Ring Mark" symbols by the prehistoric inhabitants of this location. Is there some ancient link between these symbols and the Aboriginal customs previously described? Certainly some of the "Cup and Ring Mark" symbols indiginous to Britain bear certain distinct similarities to those employed by the Aborigines, so perhaps, at some point in the far, far distant past the two shamanic traditions evolved out of the same original cultural influences.

As for Mrs. Ford's husband, he is on record as having practised the smithcraft. This fact in itself gives us yet another link with the sacred Vale of Avalon, for Glastonbury's most famous Abbot, St. Dunstan, who, after baptism on the Brue went on to crown the Kings of Alfred's Wessex Line on Kingston's Coronation Stone, was, according to legend, at one time a practising blacksmith. At Mayfield, just a few miles down the road from Mrs. Ford's own locality, he is alleged to have engaged in a duel with the Devil; a magical contest in which "Old Nick" was to suffer pain and torment as the Saint gripped his nose with his glowing blacksmith's tongs. Mayfield too is a major ley centre and is directly aligned with the Long Man of Wilmington-the original "Dodman" referred to in the chapter on "The Sun, the Serpent and the False Knight on the Road".

As for the craft with which both St. Dunstan and Mr. Ford were themselves engaged, it is to a smithy that we shall be going on the next stage of our journey. In addition to being accredited with possessing the skills of the blacksmith, legend also portrays St. Dunstan as an alchemist. And, in the ballads and poetry that feature in the next chapter we will find definite parallels between these two ancient professions.

Chapter Eleven

The Song of Amergin

"Tha mise cuir mar gheasu oiribhse,
Bho sibh luchd freasdal mo cheardach
'S an conalan uare craicinn
'S a dhion o dhorus mo cheach...."

Duan na Ceardaich.

Amongst the vast corpus of Ancient Gaelic Bardic literature from the Heroic Golden Age are the Ossianic ballads of the Scottish Highlands. In the Hebrides, these ancient songs, which in times of old were sung to the accompaniement of "an instrument very like the lyre" to quote a classical source contemporaneous with Cicero [1], clearly the ancient clarsach, still exist as part of a living oral tradition.

One of the finest examples of these old bardic remnants is *Duan na Ceardaich* or *The Lay of the Smithy*, collected and published by Francis Collinson, author of *The Traditional and National Music of Scotland* (Routledge and Keegan Paul 1978) with the assistance of Margaret Fay Shaw; in 1954. This ballad tells the story of how Fionn, his son Ossian and grandson Oscar, together with three other Fenians, "fall in with a "monstrous smith" who possesses magical powers in the forging of weapons.....He agrees to make weapons for them on condition that these must be tempered in human blood, for which the band must draw lots to choose the victim. The lot falls upon Fionn himself. Fionn however finds the smith's mother, an old hag, and persuades her to go to the smithy. The smith, who is crouching behind the closed door waiting for Fionn, thinks it is Fionn who approaches, and as the hag enters the smithy, he plunges the sword through her body...."

From an historical point of view this ballad serves to remind us of the awe and reverence in which the smith was held amongst the ancient Celtic peoples of these islands.

For, as the smith himself is heard to say in verse three of this version of the Lay,

"I put spells on you, as you are folk dependent upon the work of the smith to follow me to the door of my smithy....."

The items upon which the "folk" who the smith puts spells on are dependent, of course, are the weapons that Fionn and his fellow Fenians seek to acquire. In view of how the Celts held swords, such as Arthur's "Excalibur", spears, such as that carried by Lugh, and other weapons that feature throughout their ancient mythologies with a reverence bordering on actual physical worship, it is not difficult to understand how the practitioner of smithcraft was himself equal in status to any Druid.

It is doubtless for this reason that in the ballad of *The Twa Magicians,* a version of which was collected by Motherwell, and included by Buchan in his *Ballads of the North of Scotland,* we find a smith engaged in the same kind of "shape shifting" activity. In the ballad, our hero, or anti-hero depending upon which point of view one holds, is seen to use a similar technique, whilst involved in a magical contest with a woman with whom he wants to indulge in sexual intercourse, to the one we saw Taliesin use earlier; during the course of the last chapter; in his endeavours to escape the clutches of pursuing Cerridwen; his own devouring mother.

The lady stands in her bower door,
As straight as willow wand;
The blacksmith stood a little forebye,
Wi hammer in his hand.

"Weel may ye dress ye, lady fair,
In your robes o red;
Before the morn at this same time,
I'll gain your maidenhead."

"Awa, awa, ye coal-black smith,
Would ye do me the wrang
To think to gain my maidenhead,
That I hae kept so lang!"

Then she has hadden up her hand,
And she sware by the mold,
I wudna be a blacksmith's wife
For the full o chest o gold.

"I'd rather I were dead and gone,
And my body laid in grave,
Ere a rusty stock o coal-black smith
My maidenhead shoud have."

But he has hadden up his hand,
And he sware by the mass,
I'll cause ye by my light leman
For the hauf o that and less."

O bide, lady, bide,
And aye he bade her bide;
The rusty smith your leman shall be,
For a' your muckle pride.

Then she became a turtle dow,
To fly up in the air,
And he became another dow,
And they flew pair and pair.
O bide lady bide etc.

She turned hersell into an eel,
To swim into yon burn,
And he became a speckled trout,
To gie the eel a turn.
O bide lady bide etc.

Then she became a duck, a duck,
To puddle in a peel,
And he became a rose kaimed drake,
To gie the duck a dreel,
O bide lady bide etc.

She turned hersell into a hare,
To rin upon yon hill,
And he became a gude grey-hound,
And boldly he did fill.
O bide lady bide etc.

Then she became a gay grey mare,
And stood in yonder slack,
And he became a gilt saddle,
And sat upon her back.

Wa she wae, he held her sae,
And still he bade her bide,
The rusty smith her leman was,
For a' her muckle pride.

Then she became a het girdle,
And he became a cake,
And a' the ways she turnd hersell,
The blacksmith was her make.
Wa she wae etc.

She turned hersell into a ship,
To sail out ower the flood;
He ca'ed a nail intill her tail,
And syne the ship she stood.
Wa she wae etc.

Then she became a silken plaid,
And stretchd upon a bed,
And he became a green covering,
And gaind her maidenhead.
Wa she wae etc.

The origins of this idea that the blacksmith, on account of his weapon making skills no doubt, is on a level footing with a Druid or magician doubtless stem from the time when the exact techniques of smithcraft were a closely guarded secret passed down from generation to generation by clans of brother craftsmen.

The warrior with the strongest and sharpest sword would like as not often defeat an opponent of equal skill on the field of battle; and this, it would seem, is one of the most likely reasons why the practitioners of these ancient arts were held in such high regard.

There is evidence to suggest that in Ancient Scotland the patrons of such craftsmen were the ancestors of the Chiefs of Clan MacDuff. The principal seats of the heads of this illustrious Clan are all located in Fife, and the old chiefs themselves are said to descend from the old hereditary Abbots of Abernethy. Abernethy itself is the site of an ancient monastery; the only remains of which are a great stone tower that stands directly beneath an Iron Age hill fort which was once a Pictish stronghold. Leaning directly against the wall of the monastic tower is an ancient Pictish symbol stone, incised with the image of a tuning fork flanked by a blacksmith's hammer and anvil; above a crescent v-rod.

Amongst the ancient privileges held by the Chiefs of Clan MacDuff is the right to place the crown upon the head of each new monarch of Scotland. So ancient, and indeed sacred, a right is this that when the sister of the Earl of Fife, the then chief, defiantly assisted in the coronation of King Robert the Bruce, her younger brother, being at that time completely in the power of the English King, Edward I had her placed in a cage and hung on the wall of Berwick Castle for some four years.

Curiously enough, the infamous Lady Macbeth, portrayed in Shakespeare's play as the principal instigator of the "murder" of the "rightful" King, Duncan, was herself the heiress of Clan MacDuff; and effectively Countess in her own right in accordance with the ancient Scottish system under which women too can inherit their male ancestors' titles and pass them on to their own offspring. In view of this it is perhaps interesting that in reality King Duncan met his death at a place called "Bothgowanan", literally, "The Hut of the Smith", located just outside of Elgin.

A tyrannical and unpopular king who had brought the country to the verge of ruin, Duncan had just suffered defeat at the hands of a rebel army led by the nobleman who would soon succeed him as ruler. Since the time of the Picts an electoral system of monarchy had existed in Scotland, and if a king were found to be unfit to rule he could be legally deposed, even killed, if he were to break the sacred bond of trust with his people. In view of this it is not unlikely that the defeated Duncan was either set upon, or possibly even handed over, to the smith or smiths who formerly resided at Bothgowanan and ritually put to death in a manner in which the monstrous smith in the ballad of *Duan na Ceardaich* plans to slaughter Finn or Fionn in order to temper his newly forged magical weapons in human blood.

Shakespeare's account of the rise and fall of King Macbeth is based entirely upon those of the monastic chronicles of the Roman Church. The system that Macbeth and his Queen, Lady MacDuff, represented was rooted in that of the Celtic Church and the Druidic tradition that it had succeeded. This is how many of the Scottish Clan Chiefs, most notably those of Clan MacNab-literally "The Son of the Abbot", came to be descended from the holders of old hereditary Abbacies. With Macbeth's death this system came to be stamped out altogether and the Church of Rome imposed upon the Highland Gaelic population by a new royal dynasty dominated by the Lowlands.

Interestingly enough, at Kingston in Surrey, where we earlier saw the deposition and ritual slaughter of a West Saxon usurper, there are connections with a Bishop's Palace and what once may have been an ancient smithy like the one doubtless located at Bothgowanan. As we saw previously, the one time Abbot of Glastonbury who was eventually to succeed as Archbishop of Canterbury and crown Wessex dynasts upon their coronation stone at Kingston, was himself associated with the skill of smithcraft. Before succeeding as Archbishop, Dunstan was also Bishop of London, and in Saxon times the principal residence of Bishops of London was located at Fulham; half way between Kingston and the old walled city. A curious legend relates how nearby Fulham church, the tower of which casts its shadow over the old Saxon Bishop's palace, was constructed, together with Putney Church on the opposite bank of the river, by two twin giantesses.

The legend tells of how the building of these two ecclessiastical foundations was carried out using "but one hammer" [2], which the sisters tossed from one side of the river to the other to the cries of "Put-nigh" and "Full home". When one of them dropped this legendary tool, it was repaired by a nearby hammer smith; who in legend gave the nearby London Borough of Hammersmith its name. Could these legends preserve some ancient atavistic folk memory of the existence of a site not unlike the one that I have previously conjectured was located at Bothgowanan in the vicinity of Putney and Fulham? A similarly sacred smithy was doubtless located at Abernethy in former times, where, likely as not, the ancient smiths of the hereditary Abbots whose right it was to crown each successive elected King of Scots forged the swords of those now almost forgotten monarchs before the coronation rituals associated with thheir enthronement could take place.

As we saw in the ballad of the *Twa Magicians*, the smith is referred to as a *Coal-black Smith;* a fact which doubtless connects him with the "Cole" and the "Black" men of "Blackham" (where we encountered a ballad singing wife of a Sussex blacksmith in the last chapter) and Coelbren fame. As for his swarthy complexion, our Abernethy smiths of Clan MacDuff are linked to the Gaelic "Dubh", which, in the words of MacIan's *Highland Clans*, "is descriptive of a black or dark coloured man".

But to return, once again, to the ballads from whence we have digressed, in another ballad, which, like a version of the *Twa Magicians,* was also recorded by "Steeleye Span", we encounter him again, this time in a song taken directly from the oral traditions preserved in the singing of one John Strachan:

"I am a forester of this land,
As you may plainly see,
It's the mantle of your maidenhead
That I would have from thee."

He's taken her by the milk-white hand
And by the leylan sleeve,
He's lain her down upon her back,
And asked no man's leave."

"Now since you've lain me down young man,
You must take me up again,
And since you've had your will of me,
Come tell to me your name."

"Some call me Jim, some call me John,
Begad it's al the same,
But when I'm in the King's High Court,
Erwillian is my name."

She being a good scholar,
She's spelt it o'er again,
"Erwillian that's a Latin word,
But Willy is your name."

Now when he heard his name pronounced,
He mounted his high horse,
She's belted up her petticoat,
And followed with all her force.

He rode and she ran
A long summer day,
Until they came by the river
That's commonly called the Tay.

The water it's too deep my love,
I'm afraid you cannot wade,
But afore he'd ridden his horse well in
She was on the other side.

She went up to the King's high door,
she knocked and she went in,
'Said one of your chancellor's robbed me,
And he's robbed me right and clean.

Has he robbed you of your mantle,
Has he robbed you of your ring?
No he's robbed me of my maidenhead,
And another I cannot find.

If he be a married man
Then hanged he shall be,
And if he be a single man
He shall marry thee.

This couple they got married,
They live in Huntly Town,
She's the Earl of Airlie's daughter
And he's the blacksmith's son.

This ballad, which concerns a liason between a blacksmith and the daughter of the Earl of Airlie, himself descended, as we saw in an earlier chapter, from the ancient Pictish Mormaers of Angus, takes us to the very region where a clan of smiths, themselves in all probability connected directly with those of Clan MacDuff, most probably did away with the defeated Duncan King of Scots. Huntly lies on the ancient road that runs up from Aberdeen, passing through the prehistoric ritual landscapes of the Urie and Don Valleys with their stone circles and other megalithic remains, in the direction of Elgin. From Elgin the road continues on, past Brodie Castle and Macbeth's Hill, where in legend the ghostly encounter with the Three Witches of Shakespeare's play is said to have taken place, to Cawdor Castle; itself just a short distance from the old stronghold of the same name that was actually standing at the time when Macbeth himself was Thane of Cawdor in Moray and Glamis in Angus. Again, the links between the hidden, subliminal references in the ballads and what we know about history are staggering.

As for the three witches, it is not impossible that they are a demonized manifestation of the seven singing maidens, who, in ancient times, would walk before the King of Scots, as he made his way from one ritual site to another whilst touring the length and breadth of his kingdom, singing his praises and reciting his pedigree [3]. It is not improbable either that they are linked in turn, in archetypal terms at least, with the seven sisters who feature in the ballad of *Cospatrick* which we looked at in full in chapter eight.

At Cawdor, itself the residence of a scion of Clan "Na Cambeulich", the Campbells, there stands in the vault an ancient hawthorn tree said to be over a thousand years old. According to legend, a fifteenth century Thane of Cawdor dreamed that he should fasten a coffer of gold to the back of a donkey and build his new stronghold at the location where the animal first stopped to rest. The story goes that this was the spot where the animal ended up. Could this tree be another sacred thorn like the ones that we have already looked at in connection with Merlin and Thomas of Ercildoune? We shall be looking at another ballad that has definite links with the second of the songs transcribed above, in the meantime it is worth noting that the ballad heroine of *The Royal Forester* can herself be shown to have definite links with the sacred horse goddess previously encountered in the opening chapters of this book; as we shall now see.

In the ancient heroic cycles of Ulster associated with the heroes of the Red Branch and King Conchobar Mac Nessa we find a series of myths associated with the Irish Rhiannon, Macha; herself a human manifestation of the horse goddess much like Leod of Skye's Fairy wife. Amongst her magical attributes she is accredited with being able to run faster than any earthly animal, and, in one of the stories in the Red Branch, Macha, despite being pregnant with twins by Cunniuc mac Agnoman, wins a running race against the King's chariot. This tale in itself parallels certain key elements in the ballad of *The Royal Forester,* in which the Earl of Airlie's daughter is seen to apparently run a foot race with the mounted hero of the ballad. As to the connection of all these ballads with those collected by Scott, amongst the pages of the *Minstrelsy,* we find a ballad which contains certain key lyrical elements which it holds in common with the ballad of *The Royal Forester.* In addition to this, certain aspects of the storyline prove it to have links with the same pagan cult as that centred at the sanctuary of Emain Macha- literally, "The Brooch of Macha"; Navan hill fort in County Armagh.

Before studying the ballad in full the implications of these last facts should be recognized for what they are: The references to the Earls of Airlie, the Royal Forester with several identities who is the son of a blacksmith, in all likelihood one of with magical powers not unlike those attributed to the anti-hero of the first of the ballads examined in this chapter, and Huntly town in what was formerly the old Pictish Mormaership of Moray, show the ballad of *The Royal Forester* to be unquestionably descended from an earlier ballad of undoubted Pictish provenance. Similarly, certain aspects of the above recounted incidents in the "Red Branch Cycles" show them to emanate from the same ancient bardic sources.

After running the race with the King's chariot Macha gives birth to her twins on the spot. The difficulty of the birth is reminiscent in some respects to that of the Arthurian hero Sir Tristrem, whose name in Breton sources shows it to be derived from the Breton words "Dremm" and "Trist", which we saw earlier in corrupted form as "Dylan Draws" in a late Welsh genealogical ms.; meaning literally "Born of Sorrow"; owing to the difficulties surrounding his own birth. Although Macha, being a goddess, does not die as a result of her labours, as she would have done if she were a mere mortal, she curses the warriors gathered at the field of contest for forcing her to compete in the race whilst in a state of pregnancy; and their own descendants are thenceforth afflicted with similar birth pains for nine generations. Given Tristan's own undoubted Pictish descent, these last facts add further weight to this argument; and it is therefore no coincidence that Ulster was the original seat of the Picts of Ireland- the Cruithne of the old Irish chronicles.

I now propose to return to the ballads of Sir Walter's *Minstrelsy*, by drawing the reader's attention to an interesting little song entitled *The Bonny Hynd*, which Scott notes as having been taken from "Mr. Herd's MS., where the following note is prefixed to it: "Copied from the mouth of a milkmaid, 1771, W.L." In the same notes Scott also comments that the ballad "has a high degree of poetical merit".

O May she comes, and May she goes,
Down by yon gardens green;
And there she spied a gallant squire,
As squire had ever been.

And May she comes, and May she goes,
Down by yon hollin tree;
And there she spied a brisk young squire,
And a brisk young squire was he.

"Give me your green manteel, fair maid:
Give me your maidenhead!
Gin ye winna give me your green manteel,
Give me your maidenhead!"

"Perhaps there may be bairns, kind sir;
Perhaps there may be nane;
But if you be a courtier,
You'll tell me soon your name."

"I am nae courtier, fair maid,
But new come frae the sea;
I am nae courtier, fair maid,
But when I court with thee."

"They call me Jack, when I'm abroad;
Sometimes they call me John;
But when I'm in my father's bower,
Jock Randal is my name."

"Ye lee, ye lee, ye bonny lad!
Sae loud's I hear ye lee!

For I'm Lord Randal's ae daughter,
Ha has nae mair nor me."

"Ye lee, ye lee, ye bonny Maid!
Sae loud's I hear ye lee!
For I'm Lord Randal's ae ae son,
Just now come o'er the sea."

She's putten her hand down by her gare,
And out she's ta'en a knife;
And she has put it in her heart's bleed,
And ta'en away her life.

And he has ta'en up his bonny sister,
With the big tear in his e'en;
And he has buried his bonny sister,
Amang the hollins green.

And syne he's hied him o'er the dale,
His father dear to see-
"Sing, Oh! And Oh! For my bonny hynd,
Beneath yon hollin tree!"

"What needs you care for your bonny hynd!
For it you needna care;
Take you the best, gie me the warst,
Since plenty is to spare."

"I carena for your hynds, my lord;
I carena for your fee;
But oh! And oh! For my bonny hynd,
Beneath the hollin tree!"

"O were ye at your sister's bower,
Your sister fair to see,
You'll think nae mair o' your bonny hynd,
Beneath the hollin tree."

Beneath its surface this ballad contains hidden references to the ancient
Scottish system of Tanistry; the origins of which are lost in the mists of time.

Under this system young Pictish aristocrats would be fostered out, to be brought up under the roofs of other, unrelated, members of the nobility. The reason for this was on account of the electoral system of Kingship practised by this ancient people, a system which extended down through the Mormaerships, or Earldoms, of Ancient Pictland, to the lower levels of the nobility as well. The essence of this system was based upon a bond of common trust between the aristocracy themselves and the people who they ruled. Thus, all the King's nobles held their position as a result of their fitness to rule; a fitness to be tried and tested first of all by Druidic initiation; before a number of prospective candidates would be chosen by those over whom they would then govern.

Under the old system a nobleman who had previously been elected to succeed to the lordship of a particular area might be deposed at a later date if his people found themselves unduly oppressed by the sterness of his rule. In such situations another member of his family- a brother, nephew, cousin, possibly even his own son, might be summoned from elsewhere so that he could challenge, and ultimately put to death, the old unwanted ruler. After this, he himself would then succeed as Tanist or Thane in his vanquished relative's stead.

This system was eventually passed on to the Scots at the union of the Pictish and Scottish monarchies under King Kenneth mac Alpin; and it is doubtless as a result of this fact that in the decades leading up to Macbeth's deposition of Duncan we should find the future king's own father being deposed as Mormaer of Moray by one of his own relatives. This relative in turn would find himself being deposed and killed by the Mormaer's own son; who would take as his wife the widow of his own defeated kinsman.

But to get to the point of relevance with regard to this and the ballad previusly transcribed, in view of the fact that the young ballad hero, who has just returned from overseas, and who, like the hero of "The Royal Forester", is called a variety of names - perhaps another subliminal reference to his own possible powers of shapeshifting, is unaware of the existence of his own sister, it seems more than probable that he himself has been fostered out to the family of another nobleman- posssibly in Ireland or Gaul in view of the references to his coming home from overseas, before returning to his native land in full maturity. In view of our definite knowledge of the existence of this ancient system of Tanistry, a system which is itself well documented, it is almost certain that this ballad originally contained references to an unfortunate romantic encounter that occurred as a direct result of this fostering out of the sons of the ruling nobility. It is not beyond the realms of possibility that such occurences were by no means infrequent, and that this is why just such an incident was the subject of this ballad.

In my commentary on *The Royal Forester* I have mentioned the links between that ballad and the old Pictish Kingdom of Moray. Also of relevance to our story is the fact that in verse six of *The Bonny Hynd* we find the ballad hero making remarks as to his own origins identical to those that we have previously seen issue from the lips of the hero of the second of the three ballads that have featured so far in this chapter. It is therefore of great significance then that Lord Randal, or Randolph, the father of the hero of the last given song, should have been created Earl of Moray by his uncle King Robert the Bruce.

The historical Jock or John Randolph, who succeeded his brother as third Earl of Moray of this creation, did not, as the ballad suggests, become the lover of his own sister, Agnes; who was herself to become the wife of Patrick Dunbar, 10th Earl of Dunbar and March. From this marriage came two sons, John Earl of Moray, and George Earl of Dunbar and March; himself the descendant and successor of Thomas of Ercildoune's own patron; not to mention the "Cospatrick" of ballad fame. Perhaps this is one of the reasons why this particular Border ballad should hold definite elements in common with a song that has indisputable connections with the old Pictish Mormaership of Moray. Whatever the true reason, this fact in itself does prove beyond any reasonable doubt that, as has previously been asserted throughout this book, a considerable number of the ballads that Scott and his associates were to incorporate into the pages of the *Minstrelsy* were lineally descended from a corpus of even more ancient ballads, or metrical romances corrupted into ballads, of undoubted Pictish origin.

As for Scott's own comments on the ballad of *The Bonny Hynd*, in the notes prefixed to the version heregiven we find the following: "It was originally the intention of the Editor to have ommitted this ballad, on account of the disagreeable nature of the subject. Upon consideration, however, it seemed a fair sample of a certain class of songs and tales, turning upon incidents the most horrible and unnatural, with which the vulgar in Scotland are greatly delighted, and of which they have current among them in ample store. Such, indeed, are the subjects of composition in most nations, during the early period of society; when the feelings, rude and callous, can only be affected by the strongest stimuli, and where the mind does not, as in a more refined age, recoil disgusted, from the means by which interest has been excited. Hence, incest, parricide- crimes, in fine, the foulest and most enormous, were the early themes of the Grecian muse. Whether that delicacy, which precludes the modern bard from the choice of such impressive and dreadful themes, be favourable to the higher classes of poetic composition, may perhaps be questioned; but there can be little doubt that the more important cause of virtue and morality is advanced by this exclusion. The knowledge that enormities are not without precedent, may promote and even suggest them. Hence the publication of the *Newgate Register* has been prohibited by the wisdom of the legislature, having been found to encourage those very crimes of which it recorded the punishment......"

These comments are important for a number of reasons. First and foremost they attest to the meticulousness and integrity of scholarship applied by Scott in his collection and publication of his beloved Border ballads. Despite his distaste for some of the overtly incestuous elements contained within the lyrics of *The Bonny Hynd,* a distaste doubtless tinged by nineteenth century Scottish Presbyterian sensibilities, Scott has included in his collection a ballad which many contemporary editors of such material would have shied away from. It is perhaps for this reason that Scott was able to obtain the respect of the highly controversial and contrary figure Joseph Ritson; whose help and assistance were to prove invaluable to the Laird of Abbotsford in his authorship of the *Minstrelsy.*

Lockhart, in his biography of Scott, refers to Ritson as a "narrow minded, sour, dogmatical little word catcher" when mentioning the latter's assailing of Bishop Percy of Dromore's "editorial character". As we have already seen, Percy's *Reliques of Ancient English Poetry* was to exert a considerable influence upon Scott; and was one of the principal models upon which he based his own "Border Minstrelsy". It is perhaps surprising then that Ritson, a revolutionary sympathizer and thus a man whose political ideologies were diametrically opposed to those of Scott the monarchist, who had "hated the very name of a Scotsman and was utterly incapable of sympathizing with any of the higher views of his new correspondent" should have been of such invaluable assistance to the editor of the *Minstrelsy.* And yet, to quote Lockhart once again, "the bland courtesy of Scott disarmed even this half-crazy pedant; and he communicated the stores of his really valuable learning in a manner that seems to have greatly surprised all who had hitherto held any intercourse with him on antiquarian topics....." Thus, we are provided with a demonstration of how Sir Walter, in the interests of scholastic integrity, was willing to put all personal differences aside in order to seek out the most ancient and authentic ballad traditions for inclusion in his *Minstrelsy.*

As we have already seen, another of the thoroughly controversial characters who was to assist Scott in this enterprise was the Ettrick Shepherd, James Hogg. As Henderson points out in his preface to his edition of the *Minstrelsy,* "Hogg's contributions have been responsible for much of the controversy over Scott's versions and his methods of editing....." Further elucidation as to the extent of this controversy is in turn provided by the writings of John Buchan; who notes that there are two versions of the story that now follows, Hogg's, which appears in his *Domestic Manners,* and Laidlaw's; which can be found in the *Abbotsford Notanda* appended to the 1871 edition of R. Chambers' *Life of Scott.*

"In the summer of 1802" Buchan writes, "Laidlaw guided Scott by the Loch of the Lowes over the hills to Ettrick, and the latter had his first meeting with Hogg. "Jamie the poeter" was sent for to join the visitors at Ramsaycleuch, and Scott beheld a young man of his own age, burley, brawny, blue-eyed and red-headed, who was in no way abashed by the presence of the Sheriff. They had an evening of conviviality and anecdotage, and the next day Scott and Laidlaw visited Hogg's mother. She proved to be a formidable old woman, who criticized with vigour and point the first volume of the *Minstrelsy* which had just appeared. "There never was ane o' my songs prentit till ye prentit them yoursel', and ye have spoilt them awthegither. They were made for singin' and no' for readin', but ye have broken the charm now an' they'll never be sung mair."

How wrong Mrs. Hogg would be, for, as has previously been noted, many of the songs collected by Scott, or versions of them, have retained their popularity to the present day. As a means of reiterating one of my previously made points as regards the true extent of Scott's great literary achievement in his collation and publication of the *Minstrelsy.* I now propose to take one more quotation from Buchan before going back to the criticisms aimed by the Ettrick Shepherd at the Laird of Abbotsford's editorial and scholastic integrity:

"The *Minstrelsy,* the author of *The Thirty Nine Steps* continues, "is a milestone both in Scott's life and in the story of Scottish letters. Motherwell, who looked upon it with a critical eye, estimated that it gave to the world not less than forty-three pieces never before accessible- among them that marvel of the half-world of dreams, *The Wife of Usher's Well* and some of the best riding ballads like *Johnny Armstrong's Goodnight* and *Jamie Telfer*. Without Scott these things might have survived, but only in shapeless fragments. Moreover, he has given us versions of many others, prepared by one who was himself a poet, and these versions remain today the standard text. Scott was modest about the performance. "I have contrived", he wrote to a friend, "to turn a very slender portion of literary talent to account by a poetical record of the antiquities of the Border." That was his purpose rather than a scholarly edition of different texts, and he therefore not unnaturally included in the volumes modern imitations, based on authentic legends, by himself and Leyden.

"His handling of his material has been often criticized. With Leyden's eye on his, he was more careful with his texts than Bishop Percy had been, and his work passed the scrutiny of the austere Ritson,...." as I myself have pointed out.

Scott's biographer then concludes by noting that ".....Scott was reasonably conscientious, but his primary aim was to achieve a standard text- a literary not a scientific purpose; and he avowedly made up a text out of a variety of copies. Such has been the method of popular editors since literature began. But it seems clear that he never attempted to palm off a piece of his own manufacture as an old ballad, and that, with rare exceptions, he confined his emendations to making sense out of nonsense. Now and then, as in *Jamie Telfer*, where he had no text to work from, he interpolated a good deal, very much to the ballad's advantage, and in *Kinmont Willie,* where he had only a few half-forgotten lines, he produced what is substantially a work of his own. For the rest he was a skilful, and up to his lights, a faithful editor of authentic ancient material."

In his notes to the above quoted from text Buchan also informs his readers of the following, in connection with Scott's compilation of the *Minstrelsy;* and his general methods of working: "The subject has been exhaustively discussed by Mr. T.F. Henderson in his edition of the *Minstrelsy*.......the case aginst Scott's conscientiousness will be found in Colonel Elliot's *Further Essays on Border Ballads* (1910), which is answered- to my mind conclusively- by Andrew Lang's Sir W. Scott and the *Border Minstrelsy* (1910)."

248

Buchan's comments as regards Scott's attempts to produce a standard text for each ballad are certainly true. What he appears to have been doing in this direction is creating a version as close and as true as was humanly possible to the original spirit of the most ancient version of the song with which he happened to be dealing. In certain respects it is defintely true that he sanitized some of the language of the oral versions of the ballads that he edited, but only so that the latter category of songs could be made readily accessible to a literary public unused to the colloquialisms of the Border dialect. This last fact appears to have been at the heart of Mrs. Hogg's criticisms of the *Minstrelsy;* but in view of the fact that all bardic oral literature is a constantly evolving thing, he can certainly be excused the small liberties that he took in this last direction.

Modern folklorists could themselves make similar comments about electric arrangements of some of the traditional ballads recorded in our own century by the likes of "Pentangle" and "Steeleye Span". To compare the folk singing of families such as the Stewarts of Blair to the recorded works of "Fairport Convention" is probably not unlike the comparison that a traditional singer such as Mrs. Hogg would have made between her own musical repertoire and the versions of her ballads included in the *Minstrelsy*. Both are equally valid evolutionary continuations of a far more ancient bardic tradition, a tradition which, as we shall see in a minute, has passed through many evolutionary changes of its own over the course of time.

As to the provenance of Mrs. Hogg's ballads, most notably *Auld Maitland,* about which Scott and Leyden had been suspicious....."; she and her brother had "learned it and many mae frae old Andrew Moor, and he learned it frae auld Baby Mettlin, who was housekeeper to the first laird o' Tushielaw. She was said to have been anither than a gude ane....."

Mrs. Hogg's account of her acquisition of the ancient oral traditions of which she was herself the repository only serves to add further weight to the argument set forth throughout this book: That the ballads, songs and traditions collected by Scott, from the mouths of the Border Peasantry, had filtered down from the bards of old. Doubtless the Laird of Tushielaw's housekeeper had obtained her ballads from the mouths of other serving folk such as herself, whose own predecessors had likewise originally heard them sung by the ancient minstrels who Scott himself had sought to iconize through the medium of his own poetical writings. In a similar way, Mrs. Brown, from whom Scott was to obtain much useful material, as has already been pointed out, first heard the ballads that she herself had set down in the manuscript to which she was to give Scott and others access from "an old maid-servant who had long been in the family". [(4)].

As for Leyden, following his departure for India in 1802, he himself would become one of the countless European visitors to Asia who would succumb to tropical disease. Another of these unfortunates was Captain Joseph Ferguson, another of Sir Adm's brothers, described in a contemporary account as "a modest and promising youth" (5), whose death in India was to be deeply mourned by all those who knew him.

In view of Leyden's great ability as a scholar, his thorough investigation of the Ossianic controversy, and classification of the various Asiatic languages and dialects that he was to encounter during the course of his travels being just two examples of his great achievements in the intellectual fields he was to pursue in addition to the invaluable assistance with which he was to provide Scott, in the latter's editorship of the *Minstrelsy,* it is worth speculating as to what direction Sir Walter's own career would have taken, had his friend returned from the east as he had originally intended. Perhaps he would have finished the *Thomas the Rhymer* fragment previously quoted from. We know that John Leyden provided Scott with a considerable amount of the material that he used in his introductory notes to many of the ballads contained in the *Minstrelsy;* most notably his introduction to the ballad of *The Young Tamlane;* which contains a great deal of valuable information on indiginous fairy traditions. In view of this it is not beyond the realms of possibility that one of the reasons why Scott may have left this fragment unfinished is because he was without his friend Leyden's assistance. We know from the previously quoted from account of Scott at Abbotsford by the American novelist Washington Irving that the idea of writing up some of the traditions relating to Thomas of Ercildoune into a "capital tale" was still very much on Sir Walter's mind as late as 1817, so it is interesting that the Laird of Abbotsford never actually got around to finishing off what he himself had already started long before the publication of his first prose fiction.

But to return to Scott's previously given version of *The Bonny Hynd,* definite proof as to its ancient bardic, and probable Pictish, origins is provided by the constant references throughout its lyrics to the sacred *Hollin Tree.* In the Arthurian metrical romance of *Sir Gawain and the Green Knight,* the hero's adversary is described as follows:

"Whether had he no helme ne hauberghe nauther,
Ne no pysan ne no plate that pented to armes,
Ne no schaft ne no schelde to shuve ne to smyte;
Bot in his one hande he had a holyn bobbe,....."

Robert Graves, in his *White Goddess,* compares the contest between Gawain
and his holly club wielding adversary to a similar duel between Cu Chulainn
and a lake dwelling monster in the Irish sagas. This last fact is of great
significance, in view of the fact that Cu Chulainn is himself closely
associated with the ancient hill-fort of Emain Macha; itself formerly the
stronghold, as we have already seen, of King Conchobor mac Nessa.

In Ulster legend king Conchobor's house is referred to as "The House of the
Red Branch", whilst the warrior elite over whom he himself rules and who
serve as his military entourage are known as "The Heros of the Red Branch"
or "Red Tree" (Craobh Ruadh). Archaeological excavation of the hill fort has
revealed that the original royal residence that once stood there was eventually
superseded by a religious sanctuary of some kind, consisting of several rings
of oak posts with a huge timber in the centre. It has been conjectured that this
central post may well have been the Craobh Ruadh or Red Branch itself, and
in view of this it is perhaps also significant that, amongst Bishop Percy's
Arthurian ballads, we find, in Book Three of the Third Series, an ancient
fragment of an old ballad entitled *The Marriage of Sir Gawaine.* For,
amongst the surviving verses that have come down to us in this particular
version of this ballad, we find the following:

And as he rode over a more
he see a lady where shee sate
betwixt an oke and a greene hollen
She was cladd in red scarlett......

One is here reminded of the metting of the two young lovers in *The Bonny*
Hynde. And, more significant still is the fact that we are here confronted with
another reference to the sacred holly tree is of some significance.

In the Gawain legends the battle between Arthur's champion on the one hand,
who is represented by the oak, and his superhuman adversary on the other,
represented in his turn by the holly, is not only symbolic of the endless cycle
of death and rebirth played out in the cycle of the seasons- summer killing
winter and so forth, but also of the duel between the two tanists over who

should succeed the other. On another level, the tree under which these two rivals may originally have fought in deepest antiquity, when the ancestors of the High Kings of Ireland still ruled in Spain, a location to which they had travelled from Scythia, is the Mediterranean kerm-oak, holm-oak or holly-oak known in the old Cornish language as "Glass-Tann" or "the green sacred tree" [6].

This tree, which shares the same botanical name, ilex, as the holly, is described by Graves as "the evergreen twin of the ordinary oak". He also points out that ".....its classical Greek names of prinos and hysge are also used for holly in modern Greek. It has prickly leaves and nourishes the kerm a scarlet insect not unlike the holly-berry (and once thought to be a berry), from which the ancients made their royal scarlet dye and an aphrodisiac elixir........"

Given the fact that in legend the Picts are said to have reached Britain from Scythia via the same seaborne route as the later Milesian Kings of Ireland in some sources, it is worth asking as to whether or not this is the original "Craobh Ruadh" revered by the heros of the Red Branch Cycles. Perhaps the hero, or anti-hero, of Scott's "Bonny Hynd" had returned from some Mediterranean location with a sapling of this genus amongst his trophies. Just because the tree is alleged to have been unknown in the British Isles previous to the sixteenth century does not mean that our ancestors were unaware of its existence. The skull of a barbary ape found under the ancient hill fort at Tara, coupled with various other British and Irish archaeological finds of undoubted Mediterranean provenance, would appear to indicate definite links between that region and both Britain and Ireland during the Bronze Age. [7]

The hypothesis set out by Graves in *The White Goddess* centres on the presence of a series of hidden ciphers in the Welsh "Hanes Taliesin", the incomprehensible bardic conundrum used to confound the court bards of King Maelgwyn in an earlier chapter, and the Irish *Song of Amergin* (or Amorgin); itself "said to have been chanted by the chief bard of the Milesian invaders as he set his foot on the soil of Ireland....." Both of these ancient compositions, which survive only in late, Christianized, form, contain key elements reminiscent of the shape shifting aspects of several of the ballads that have featured over the course of the last few chapters:

"Primary chief bard am I to Elphin,
And my original country is the region of the Summer Stars;
Idno and Heinin called me Merddin,
At length every king will call me Taliesin....."

Thus run the opening lines of Lady Charlotte Guest's translation of the *Hanes Taliesin*. Elsewhere in the same poem we find the following enigmatic references, couched in the language of the shape shifting initiate:

"I have obtained the muse from the cauldron of Caridwen;
I have been bard of the harp to King Lleon of Lochlin.
I have been on the White Hill, in the court of Cynvelyn,
For a day and a year in stocks and fetters,
I have suffered hunger for the son of the Virgin,
I have been teacher to all intelligences,
I am able to instruct the whole Universe."

Similarly, in the *Song of Amergin,* we are given another set of riddles which are set out in an almost identical fashion. In this case, however, the mention of animals, fish and birds, recalls the animistic deism of the primordial shaman:

"I am an ox of seven fights,
or I am a stag of seven tines,
I am a Griffon on a cliff,
or I am a hawk on a cliff,
I am a tear of the sun,
I am fair among flowers,
I am a boar,
I am a salmon in a pool,
I am a lake on a plain,
I am a hill of poetry,
I am a battle-waging spear,
I am a god who forms fire for a head........"

Like all bardic literature, these poems contain hidden ciphers which are only comprehensible to the initiated. The same is true of many of the ballads recovered by Scott, most notably *The Bonny Hynd*. And, like *The Bonny Hynd*, both the *Hanes Taliesin* and *The Song of Amergin* contain hidden references to the ancient bardic tree alphabets that have featured throughout this text. In view of this it is worth asking yet another question as to whether or not the overtly sexual reference in Scott's version of the ballad is present in the lyrics on account of the aphrodisiac elixir derived from the scarlet kerm that shelters in the branches of the Holm Oak. Or, did the young hero's father conceal his existence from his own daughter deliberately, on account of his knowledge that one day his son might return from afar in order to slay him.

Whatever the truth, the bardic composer of the ballad almost certainly possessed a thorough knowledge of ancient Druidic Tree Alphabets, as is denoted by the fact that this romantic story almost definitely contains hidden references to the ancient Celtic system of Tanistry, as well as direct references to the Tanist's tree- the holly; itself corresponding to the letter "T" or "Tinne" in the Ogham Alphabets of Ireland and Gaelic Scotland. And, as the reader will have gathered, we have Scott's devotion to meticulous scholarship to thank for its inclusion in both the *Minstrelsy* and this interpretative account of the Laird of Abbotsford's own researches into ballads and balladry.

Chapter Twelve

The Battle of the Trees

The alder trees in the first line,
They made their commencement,
Willow and quicken tree,
They were slow in their array.
The plum is a tree
Not beloved of men;
The medlar of a like nature,
Overcoming severe toil.
The bean bearing in its shade
An army of phantoms.
The raspberry makes
Not the best of food.
In shelter live,
The privet and the woodbine,
And the ivy in its season.
Great is the gorse in battle.
The cherry tree had been reproached.
The birch, though very magnanimous,
Was late in arraying himself;
It was not through cowardice,
But on account of his great size........

The pine-tree in the court,
Strong in battle,
By me great exalted
In the presence of kings,
The elm-trees are his subjects.
He turns not aside the measure of a foot,
But strikes right in the middle,
And at the farthest end.
The hazel is the judge,

His berries are the dowry.
The privet is blessed........

Prosperous the beech tree.
The holly was dark green,
He was very courageous:
Defended with spikes on every side,
Wounding the hands.
The long enduring populars
Very much broken in fight.
The plundered fern;
The brooms with their offspring:
The furze not well behaved
Until he was tamed.
The heath was giving consolation,
Comforting the people.
The black cherry tree was pursuing.
The oak tree swiftly moving,
Before him tremble heaven and earth,
Stout door keeper against the foe
Is his name in all lands.
The corn-cockle bound together,
Was given to be burnt.
Others were rejected
On account of the holes made
By great violence
In the field of battle.......

The above given extracts from the great Welsh bardic poem *Cad Goddeu,*
The Battle of the Trees, a title which reminds us at once of the symbolic
advance of the trees of Birnam Wood upon Macbeth's stronghold at
Dunsinane in Shakespeare's play, are illustrative of the importance of ancient
poetical tree lore in Cymric bardic tradition. Similarly, amongst the ballads,
we find constant references, as has already been shown, to the sacred trees of
Britain's long vanished Druidic heritage; a heritage which is itself rooted in
the ancient shamanism of deepest antiquity.

We have already encountered the sacred thorn, the hazel, the apple and the
holly throughout the ballads already examined; not to mention the bramble
and the willow. It should therefore come as no surprise then that amongst the

dozens of ballads that Scott and his colleagues collected we should find many more similar references to the ones already illustrated; a fine case in point being those of *Johnie of Breadislee*, a version of which was itself recorded in recent years by the late Ewan MacColl.

Johnie rose up on a May morning,
called for water to wash his hands-
"Gar loose to me the gude graie dogs
That are bound wi' iron bands."

When Johnie's mother gat word o' that,
Her hands for dule she wrang-
"O Johnie! For my benison,
To the greenwood dinna gang!"

"Eneugh ye hae o' the gude wheat bread,
And eneugh o' the blude red wine:
And, therefore, for nae venison, Johnie,
I pray ye, stir frae hame."

But Johnie's busk't up his gude bend bow,
His arrows, ane by ane;
And he has gane to Durrisdeer
To hunt the dun deer down.

As he came down by Merriemas,
And in by the benty line,
There he has espied a deer lying
Aneath a bush of ling.

Johnie he shot, and the dun deer lap
And he wounded her in the side;
But, atween the water and the brae,
His hounds they laid her pride.

And Johnie has bryttled the deer sae weel,
And he's had out her liver and lungs;
And wi' these he has feasted his bludy hounds,
As if they had been erl's sons.

They eat sae much o' the venison,
And drank sae much o' the blude,
That Johnie and a' his bluidy hounds
Fell asleep as they had been dead.

And by there came a silly auld carle,
An ill death mote he die!
For he's awa to Hislinton,
Where the Seven Foresters did lie.

"What news, what news, ye gray-headed carle,
What news bring ye to me?"
"I bring nae news", said the gray-headed carle,
"Save what these eyes did see.

"As I cam down by Merriemas,
And down amang the scroggs,
The bonniest childe that ever I saw
Lay sleeping amang his dogs.

"The shirt that was upon his back
Was O' the Holland fine;
The doublet which was over that
Was o' the lincome twine.

"The buttons that were on his sleeve
Were O' the goud sae gude;
The gude graie hounds he lay amang,
Their mouths were died wi' blude."

Then out and spak the First Forester,
The heid man ower them a'-
"If this be Johnie o' Breadislee,
Nae nearer will we draw."

But up and spak the Sixth Forester,
(His sister's son was he)
"If this be Johnie o' Breadislee,
We soon shall gar him die!"

The first flight of arrows the Foresters shot,
They wounded him on the knee;
And out and spak the Seventh Forester,
"The next will gar him die".

Johnie's set his back against an aik,
His fute against a stane;
And he has slain the Seven Foresters,
He has slain them a' but ane.

He has broke three ribs in that ane's side,
But and his collar and bane;
He's laid him twa-fald ower his steed,
Bade him carry the tidings hame.

"O is there na a bonnie bird,
Can sing as I can say;
Could flee away to my Mother's bower,
And tell to fetch Johnie away?"

The starling flew to his mother's window stane,
It whistled and it sang;
And ay the ower word o' the tune
Was- "Johnie tarries lang!"

They made a rod o' the hazel bush,
Another o' the slae-thorn tree,
And mony mony were the men
At fetching o'er Johnie.

Then out and spak his auld mother,
And fast her tears did fa'-
"Ye wad nae be warned, my son Johnie,
Frae the hunting to bide awa.

"Aft hae I brought to Breadislee,
The less gear and the mair,
But I ne'er brought to Breadislee,
What grieved my heart sae sair!

"But wae betyde that silly auld carle!
An ill death shall he die!
For the highest tree in Merriemas
Shall be his morning's fee".

Now Johnie's gude bend bow is broke,
And his gude graie dogs are slain;
And his body lies dead in Durrisdeer,
And his hunting it is done......

Again, amongst the verses of this ballad we find yet more references to the now familiar hazel: The inferences in this version of the song are that this Robin Hood like character, himself of Herculean stature, has been brought down as a result of the invocation of the magical forces associated with both it and the blackthorn. Tradition has it that members of the seventh century witch covens of Brewham and Wincanton in Somerset, two more locations in the sacred Vale of Avalon where we earlier encountered the Picts of Picts Hill, used the thorns from this last mentioned genus for sticking into wax images of those they wished to overcome by magic. And, according to Graves, in his *White Goddess,*

"The blackthorn (*bellicum* in Latin) is an unlucky tree; villagers in Galmpton and Dittisham, south Devon, still fear "the black rod" carried as a walking stick by local witches, which has the effect of causing miscarriages. When Major Weir, the Covenanter and self-confessed witch, was burned at Edinburgh in April 1670, a blackthorn staff was burned with him as the chief instrument of his sorceries. Blackthorn is also the traditional timber with which bellicose Irish tinkers fight at fairs (though the Shillelagh, contrary to popular belief, is an oak club), and the words "strife" or "strive", modelled on the old Northern French "estrif" and "estriver", may be the same word "Straif" [1], derived from the Breton; at least no other plausible derivation has been suggested."

As Graves shows, during the course of the above quoted from book, each of the letters in the ancient Druidic Tree Alphabets, referred to over and over again throughout my own text, corresponds to one of the months in the Druidic Calendar: The fact that hazel and sloe, or blackthorn, feature in the same verse in the ballad of *Johny of Breadislee,* provides definite proof of the song's ultimate bardic origins, for sloe, the blackthorn's fruit, ripens in the month traditionally attributed to rulership by the sacred hazel.

260

In another of Scott's ballads, this time a song called *The Broomfield Hill,* we find direct, as opposed to indirect, references to the use of plant lore in the weaving of charms:

There was a knight and a lady bright,
Had a true tryst at the broom;
The ane ga'ed early in the morning,
The other in the afternoon.

And aye she sat in her mother's bower door,
And aye she made her mane,
"O whether should I gang to the Broomfield Hill,
Or should I stay at hame?

"For if I gang to the Broomfield Hill,
My maidenhead is gone;
And if I chance to stay at hame,
My love will call me mansworn."

Up then spake a witch woman,
Ay from the room aboon;
"O, ye may gang to Broomfield Hill,
And yet come maiden hame.

"For, when ye gang to the Broomfield Hill,
Ye'll find your love asleep,
With a silver-belt about his head,
And a broom-cow at his feet.

"Take ye the blossom of the broom,
The blossom it smells sweet,
And strew it at your true love's head,
And likewise at his feet.

"Take ye the rings off your fingers,
Put them on his right hand,
To let him know, when he doth awake,
His love was at his command."

She pu'd the broom flower on Hive-hill,
And strew'd on's white hals bane,
And that was to be wittering true,
That maiden she had gane.

"O where were ye, my milk-white steed,
That I hae coft sae dear,
That wadna watch and waken me,
When there was maiden here?"

"I stamped wi' my foot, master,
And gar'd my bridle ring;
But na kin' thing wald waken ye,
Till she was past and gane."

"And wae betide ye, my gae goss hawk,
That I did love so dear,
That wadna watch and waken me,
When there was maiden here."

"I clapped wi' my wings, master,
And ay my bells I rang,
And aye cry'd, Waken, waken, master,
Before the ladye gang."

"But haste and haste, my gude white steed,
To come the maiden till,
Or a' the birds, of gude green wood,
Of your flesh shall have their fill."

"Ye needna burst your gude white steed,
Wi' racing o'er the howm;
Nae bird flies faster through the wood,
Than she fled through the broom".

In old Gaelic tree alphabets the furze or broom is the letter "Onn", and in Welsh folklore, according to Graves, the flowers of this plant are supposedly "good against witches". The author of The White Goddess also connects this sacred tree letter with the Gaulish goddess Onniona, worshipped in ancient time in sacred ash groves. The plant's flowers are themselves frequented by the first bees of the year, so it is no coincidence that the Sacred Ash Goddess, in whose groves both tree and Onniona were worshipped, should be associated with the month in the Druidic Calendar that ends with the Spring Equinox: a connection further enhanced by the fact that Onniona's name is made up of a compound of the letters for furze or broom, and ash- "Nion".

Similarly, songs with overtly pagan associations, the lyrics of which are bound up, once again, with ancient bardic tree lore, are to be found throughout Percy's *Reliques; The Willow Tree* and *Willow, Willow, Willow* being two fine cases in point. In Scotland we still hear sung that fine and ancient ballad *The Rowan Tree*, which holds certain elements in common with a version of *The Twelve Witches* recorded by "Steeleye Span" on their "Rocket Cottage" L.P. But to return, once again, to the pages of Scott's *Minstrelsy,* one of the most famous ballads collected and published by the Laird of Abbotsford is his *Wife of Usher's Well;* which I mentioned briefly in the last chapter in a quotation from Buchan:

There lived a wife at Usher's Well,
And a wealthy wife was she;
She had three stout and stalwart sons,
And sent them o'er the sea.

They hadna been a week from her,
A week but barely ane,
Whan word came to the carline wife,
That her three sons were gane.

They hadna been a week from her,
A week but barely three,
Whan word came to the carline wife,
That her sons she'd never see.

"I wish the wind may never cease,
Nor fishes in the flood,
Till my three sons come hame to me,
In earthly flesh and blood!"

It fell about the Martinmas,
When nights are long and mirk,
The carline wife's three sons came hame,
And their hats were o' the birk.

It neither grew in syke nor ditch,
Nor yet in ony sheugh;
But at the gates o' Paradise,
That birk grew fair eneugh.

"Blow up the fire, my maidens!
Bring water from the well!
For a' my house shall feast this night,
Since my three sons are well."

And she has made to them a bed,
She's made it large and wide;
And she's ta'en her mantle her about,
Sat down at the bed-side.

Up and crew the red red cock,
And up and crew the grey;
The eldest to the youngest said,
" 'Tis time we were away."

The cock he hadna craw'd but once,
And clapp'd his wings at a',
Whan the youngest to the eldest said,
Brother we must awa."

"The cock doth craw, the day doth daw,
The channerin' worm doth chide;
Gin we be must out o' our place,
A sair pain we maun bide.

"Fare ye weel, my mother dear!
Fareweel to barn and byre!
And fare ye weel, the bonny lass,
That kindles my mother's fire."

Of this ballad, which holds certain elements in common with both *The Grey Cock*, a haunting rendition of which was recently re-released on a Ewan MacColl c.d. compilation entitled *The Real MacColl*, and Sir Walter's *Clerk Saunders*, which likewise appears amongst the pages of the *Minstrelsy*, Robert Graves has the following comments to make:

"In the North Country ballad of *The Wife of Usher's Well*, the dead sons who return to visit their mother, wear birch leaves in their hats. The author remarks that the tree from which they plucked the leaves grew at the entrance of the paradise where their souls were housed, which is what one would expect. Presumably they wore birch as a token that they were not earth bound evil spirits but blessed souls on compassionate leave."

The Ogham letter for Birch, "Beth", is also connected with Brigid, herself a pagan goddess prior to her Christianization as one of the most important saints of Celtic Ireland. It should therefore come as no surprise then that the ballad contains references to fires, sacred to Brigid since pagan times, and a well, which like London's Bridewell under St. Brides Church in Fleet Street, is doubtless another spring sacred to her.

At the beginning of this book I compared the Laird of Abbotsford's authorship of the *Minstrelsy* to Graves's writing of *The White Goddess*. Both books are landmarks in literature on account of their contribution to the preservation, in Scott's case, and resurgence, in Graves's, of the ancient bardic tradition. In his compilation of *The Minstrelsy of the Scottish Border* Scott brought his beloved ballads and the folk traditions of his ancestral Borderlands into the literary mainstream. Previous to this they had languished in the total obscurity of rural oral culture. In a similar way, Graves did exactly the same with the ancient tree lore of Druidism. Before Graves wrote his definitive work on the origins of bardic ciphers it had been a popular misconception that the Ogham Alphabets of Ancient Ireland had been a late Christian invention. Graves and Scott have much in common. Both were novelists who also published non-commercial scholarly works on mythology and folklore. In view of this it could be said that whereas Scott could justly be described as "the last of the True Bards", Graves was quite rightly "the First of the New Bards". His *White Goddess* is still the standard work on what he described as the "historical grammar of poetic myth" and has influenced a whole crop of more modern writers who have been published since; from John Mathews to John Michell.

In view of this it is also thoroughly unsurprising that amongst the pages of Graves we should find references not only to some of the ballads Scott collected, most notably *The Wife of Usher's Well* and *The Young Tamlane*, but also to *True Thomas* and his beloved Fairy Queen. Interestingly enough, Graves compares the legend of Thomas the Rhymer to that of Ogier the Dane and Morgana le Fay. Like Oisin or Ossian, Ogier is said to have spent two hundred years in the "Castle of Avalon". More important than this though, Graves identifies Ogier as being none other than Ogyr Vran; another aspect of the Celtic god Bran; and himself the patron of singers and harpers.

There is evidence to suggest that the Mediaeval tale of "Orfeo and Heurodis", a version of which, as we saw in an earlier chapter, can be found amongst the pages of the celebrated Auchinleck MS from whence Scott obtained the *Sir Tristrem* of Thomas of Ercildoune, is nothing more than a classicized version of a now vanished bardic tract relating to the adventures of Ogyr Vran in the realms of Faery. Owing to certain definite parallels between this series of myths and those associated with Orfeus and Eurydice in Greek mythology, the Celtic cycle has been corrupted into the legend of Heurodis, who is now represented as queen of "Winchester" in the Mediaeval text, and her kidnap by the King of Faery.

A clever, modernized, lyrical rendition of the Mediaeval version of this legend, like the previously referred to ballad of *The Twelve Witches*, was likewise recorded by "Steeleye Span" on their 1976 album "Rocket Cottage":

There was a King lived in the West,
Green the wood so early,
Of all the harpers he was the best,
Where the hart goes yearly.

The King he was a hunting gone,
Green the wood so early,
And left his lady all alone,
Where the hart goes yearly.

The King of Faery with his dart,
Green the wood so early,
Has pierced his lady to the heart,
Where the hart goes yearly.

And he took out his harp to play:
First he played the notes of pain,
All their hearts were weary,
Then he played the Faerie reel,
And all their hearts were cheery.

The King of Faery with his rout,
Green the wood so early,
Has come to hunt him all about,
Where the hart goes yearly.

And he took out his harp to play:
First he played the notes of pain,
All their hearts were weary,
Then he played the Faerie reel,
And all their hearts were cheery.

"Oh what shall I give you for your play?"
Green the wood so early,
"Let me take my lady away."
Where the hart goes yearly.

The Faery King said "Be it so",
Green the wood so early,
"Take her by the hand and go",
Where the hart goes yearly.

And he took out his harp to play
First he played the notes of pain,
All their hearts were weary,
Then he played the Faerie reel,
And all their hearts were cheery....."

The Mediaeval MS. Version of this ballad is quoted extensively by Scott throughout his introduction to the ballad of *The Young Tamlane* amongst the pages of the *Minstrelsy;* which, as we saw in the last chapter, was filled with much valuable source material collected by his friend John Leyden. The Winchester connection in the metrical ms version is an interesting one, for Winchester was the capital of King Alfred's West Saxon Dynasty. In an earlier chapter I noted Alfred's own connections with the Vale of Avalon, as well as the links between the old Saxon dynasty of the Hwiccas, from whom his wife descended, and Bernicia; through the Saxon Kings of Northumbria. Bernicia was originally called "Bryneich" or "Berneich", a fact attested to by the writings of Nennius. The name might well denote that this region was inhabited in Celtic times by the "augurs" or "seers" of Bryn, Bran or Brennus; something which is in itself not altogether impossible in view of the bardic traditions which clearly flourished there from the earliest period; right down to Mediaeval times and the era of classical minstrelsy; when the ballads that Scott and his colleagues were eventually to collect first came into being.

Graves identifies Bran or Ogyr Vran with King Ban of Benwick or Benwyk: "the square enclosure called "Caer Pedryvan" in the poem *Priddeau Annwn;* and it is therefore unsurprising, in view of this last mentioned fact, that King Ban's stronghold is believed to have been located at North Berwick; itself situated on the northernmost tip of old Scottish Bernicia. Just a few miles south west along the same coastline is Dunbar, where the principal stronghold of Thomas of Ercildoune's patrons was itself located; and a few miles south, inland, is Athelstaneford, the name of which was to inspire the creation of another of Scott's principal characters in the novel *Ivanhoe.*

Athelstaneford is within walking distance of Traprain Law, seat of the North British Dynasty from which, as we saw earlier, St. Collen is alleged to have been descended. As was also noted earlier, Collen is also cited in Old Welsh bardic genealogies as being a relative of Matholwch; who likewise appears in the *Mabinogion* in a romance entitled *Branwen daughter of Llyr;* the latter tale being centred around the marriage of Matholwch himself to Bran's sister, Branwen. In the same story we also find references to how Bran's Head, which his comrades cut off after his death and placed in the White Mound upon which the Tower of London was later built by the invading Romans, kept singing and uttering prophecies long after his death in a battle with Matholwch's army. Robert Graves now takes up the story, this time in a reference to Bran's links with the sacred Ogham tree letter "Fearn", or Alder:

"The connection of Bran with the alder....is clearly brought out in the *Romance of Branwen* where the swineherds (oracular priests) of King Matholwch of Ireland see a forest in the sea and cannot guess what it is. Branwen tells them that it is the fleet of Bran the Blessed come to avenge her. The ships are anchored offshore and Bran wades through the shallows and brings his goods and people to land; afterwards he bridges the River

Linon, though it has been protected with a magic charm, by lying down across the river and having hurdles laid over him. In other words, first a jetty, then a bridge are built on alder piles. It was said of Bran, "no house could contain him". The riddle, "What can no house ever contain?" has a simple answer: "The piles upon which it is built." For the earliest European houses were built on alder piles at the edges of lakes. In one sense the "singing head" of Bran was the mummified, oracular head of a sacred king; in another it was the head of the alder tree- namely the topmost branch. Green alder branches make good whistles and, according to my friend Ricardo Sicre y Cerda, the boys of Cerdana in the Pyrenees have a traditional prayer in Catalan:

Berng, Berng, come out of your skin,
And I will make you whistle sweetly.

which is repeated while the bark is tapped with a piece of willow to loosen it from the wood. Berng (or Verng in the allied Majorcan language) is Bran again. The summons is made on behalf of the Goddess of the willow. The use of the willow for tapping, instead of another piece of alder, sugggests that such whistles were used by witches to conjure up destructive winds-especially from the north. But musical pipes with several stops can be made in the same way as the whistles, and the singing head of Bran in this sense will have been an alder pipe. At Harlech, where the head sang for seven years, there is a mill-stream running past the castle rock, a likely place for a sacred alder grove......."

Bran's fleet of ships here reminds us of the forest of Gwyddno Garanhir at Cantref y Gwaelod, and in view of the fact that Bran is accredited, when incarnated in his Ogyr Vran aspect, with being the owner of the Cauldron of Cerridwen, which, when it burst, emptied its contents into the weir of Gwyddno, itself doubtless also constructed of alder, we have a connection here with the Taliesin cycles also. Similarly, there are links with the *Sir Tristrem* cycles too, for in Beroul's version of *The Romance of Tristan* we encounter Ogyr Vran in the guise of Ogrin the hermit; doubtless confirming my previously made assertion that Iseult's uncle, Morholt, who is himself slain by the hero of the romance, is none other than Matholwch in another guise.

Earlier on we saw the link between two ballads, one published by Scott and another by Williams and Lloyd, and the *Tristrem* romances. In view of this it is of further interest that another of the ballads collected by Scott and incorporated into his *Border Minstrelsy* appears to have links not only with the metrical romances of the High Middle Ages, but also with Brittany. Of this ballad, which is itself entitled *Lord Thomas and Fair Annie*, Scott has the following to say in his introductory notes:

"......This ballad is now for the first time published in a perfect state. A fragment, comprehending the 2nd, 4th, 5th and 6th verses, as also the 17th, has appeared in several collections. The present copy is chiefly taken from the recitation of an old woman residing near Kirkhill, in West Lothian, the same from whom were obtained the variations in the tale of *Tamlane* and the fragment of *The Wife of Usher's Well*, which is the next in order.

"The tale is much the same with the Breton romance called *Lay Le Frain* or *The Song of the Ash*. Indeed the Editor is convinced that the farther our researches are extended, the more we shall see ground to believe that the romantic ballads of later times are, for the most part part, abridgements of the ancient metrical romances, narrated in a smoother stanza and more modern language."

Thus, we find Scott confirming once again the interconnectedness of both the ancient bardic and Mediaeval poetic traditions with the ballads, something which has been alluded to over and over again throughout this book. *Lord Thomas and Fair Annie* can be shown to be linked in lyrical and structural terms with a whole host of other ballads like many of the songs that we have already looked at: These include Bishop Percy's *Lord Thomas and Fair Annie, Lord Thomas and Fair Ellinor*, which also appears in this collection, along with *Fair Margaret and Sweet William*, and *Lord Thomas and Fair Eleanor;* a version of which was published by Williams and Lloyd.

This last ballad was collected in 1904 from the singing of one Mrs. Pond, who is noted as being at that time a resident of Shepton Beauchamp, Somerset; itself located just a few miles south of Langport; where we earlier encountered the Dark Age warrior hero Geraint ap Erbin.

More important than this though, as previously seen in Scott's above quoted assertions, the ballad not only has connections with the Breton romances, but also with ancient bardic tree lore; as is evidenced by the title of the romance with which Scott links it. More interesting than this though, a version of *Lord Thomas and Fair Eleanor* existed in the oral folk traditions of East Sussex until comparatively recently; something which will be looked at in Chapter

Twenty Two; at a location where descendants of the celebrated Ussher Family of County Durham, themselves possessed of a possible link with the "Usher's Well" of ballad fame, are known to have had extensive coincidental connections. Thus, we find associations between the Borders and St. Dunstan's stomping grounds of Sussex and the West Country. No coincidence then that an ancient well dedicated to him should lie on what was at one time doubtless the old pilgrimage route between Old Melrose, with its ecclesiastical foundation connected with St. Cuthbert, and Lindisfarne; at the foot of the Eildon Hills and in the shadow of Huntly Bank and the Eildon Tree.

Although there are direct references to the sacred ash in the ballad that appears in the *Minstrelsy*, Mrs. Pond's song contains the following verses, which show it to be tied in not only with the *Tristrem* cycles, but also with two of the ballads set out during the course of a previous chapter:

> *Lord Thomas was buried in the church,*
> *Fair Eleanor in the Choir,*
> *And out of her bosom there grew a red rose,*
> *and out of Lord Thomas a briar.*

> *And it grew 'till it reached the church steeple top,*
> *Where it could grow no higher,*
> *And there it entwined like a true lover's knot*
> *For all true loves to admire.*

Again, there are subliminal Picitish connections, for not only was Tristan of Pictish descent, as has already been seen, but in Scott's ballad Fair Annie is heard to say the following:

> "*The Earl of Wemyss was my father,*
> *The Countess of Wemyss my mother;*
> *And a' the folk about the house,*
> *To me were sister and brother.*"

The Earls of Wemyss are a sept of Clan MacDuff, themselves mentioned in the previous chapter in connection with our shape shifting smith. The name Wemyss derives from the Gaelic "Uamh", meaning "a cave", and in the cliffs beneath the now ruined "MacDuff's Castle at East Wemyss, are the celebrated "Wemyss Caves"; famous for their Pictish markings hewn into the rock face. In pagan times this location was doubtless a religious sanctuary of some importance.

In view of what we have already seen, it is also significant that Scott also remarks in his notes to "Lord Thomas and Fair Annie" that a copy of the *Lay Le Frain*"....is preserved in the invaluable collection (W.4.I) of the Advocates Library", thus showing it to appear in translation in the very same Auchinleck M.S. from which the *Sir Tristrem* and the romance of *Orfeo and Heurodis* were themselves also obtained by the Laird of Abbotsford during the course of his own extensive researches.

Of further interest is the fact that, like the version of *Lord Thomas and Fair Eleanor*, sung by Mrs. Pond at a location on what was at one time the Borderland between the kingdom of the West Saxons and the territory of the Hwiccas, another of the three ballads obtained by Scott from the same old woman at Kirkhill also has West Country connections. This time the links are with the very region in the Western Marches where the Breton ancestors of the Stewart Kings and the Cambro-Saxon predecessors of the Border Laidlaws originally lived prior to their migration north: For, as Wimberley is swift to point out in his *Folklore in the English and Scottish Ballads*, a version of *The Wife of Usher's Well* is also native to Shropshire; and, just like the ballad of *Geordie* which featured in the chapter on "Hughie the Graeme", an Appalachian rendition of the same ballad also exists; and forms part of the repertoire of the celebrated American folk singer Joan Baez; a fact which was previously noted in Chapter 7.

In all probability the original location of Usher's Well was in the vicinity of Ushaw, which overlooks the River Deerness, a tributary of the River Browney, and is located just a few miles west of Durham. A short distance further west still is Esh Winning and Eshwood Hall; as well as the village of Esh with its ancient cross. Close by Ushaw Farm is Hag Wood and Hag House Farm, possibly the original home of the Carline Wife of the ballad. The links with the Borders are given a further twist by the fact that a few miles north is Cheeseburn Grange, the country estate of the English branch of the Riddel or Riddell Family; who have also featured elsewhere in our story. And, in the West Country there may be similar links between the ballad and St. Ishaw's Well in Wales; itself located by Patishaw in Powys.

To the west of Cheeseburn Grange is the southernmost stretch of "The Devil's Causeway", where we had our earlier encounters with the doddering

"False Knight on the Road"; and it is therefore of interest that the warriors of Caer Eidyn galloped this way en route to do battle with the English at Catterick. Catterick in turn is located on the old Roman Road that runs west across the moors to Appleby in Westmorland, past Greta Bridge and Rokeby, which were the setting of one of Scott's most famous narrative poems, as has already been seen, as well as the one time residence of his correspondent Morritt. The old Roman road here passes a series of ancient archaeological sites of Roman and Post-Roman provenance, including an old Roman signal station, like the one atop of the Eildons, itself referred to locally as "The Round Table", and as far as Brougham Castle. Here, another old Roman fort is located next to a large prehistoric earthwork also known as "The Round Table"; a site connected in local legend with King Arthur and his knights of Grail tradition.

Immediately west of Catterick is Richmond, seat of the Breton Earls of Richmond, whose dynastic intermarriage with the Scottish Royal Line has previously been dealt with. In later times the Dukes of Richmond were Tudors, themselves descended from the old North British dynasts of Traprain Law; as well as the bard Llywarch Hen. Perhaps it was through associations such as these that a Breton metrical romance eventually came to be "balladized" in the manner previously outlined by Scott. The Tudors too certainly had French connections of their own: Edmund Duke of Richmond (d.1456), whose son, Henry, was to become King Henry VII of England, was himself the son of a Welsh Knight, Sir Owain Tudor, and Catherine de Valois, daughter of King Charles VI of France and the widow of King Henry V. No coincidence either that legend tells of how King Arthur and his knights lie sleeping in a cavern located between Richmond Castle and the River Swale.

The text of the poem *The Battle of the Trees* is part of the cryptic *Hanes Taliesin*, which has been mentioned elsewhere in this text. According to an obscure Welsh triad, recovered by the great bardic scholar and antiquarian, Iolo Morgannwg, the eighteenth century "Bard of Liberty", this mythic contest was allegedly brought about as a result of one of the "Three Frivolous Causes of Battle in the Island of Britain".

The first of these conflicts referred to in Iolo's triad is our familiar "Cad Goddeau", which, it is said, was caused "about a bitch, a roebuck and a lapwing." Next, we find a reference to the Battle of Arderydd, this time an actual historical engagement which took place in the year 573, and at which, according to the chronicler Nennius, "Merlin went mad". As we shall see shortly, the cause of this battle, which is quite rightly described as one of the events which was to contribute considerably to the eventual conquest of Britain by the Saxons, owing to the severe loss of manpower suffered by the Britons as a direct consequence of their fighting amongst themselves, as a dispute over "a bird's nest". Before going too deeply into the hidden symbolism behind this last reference though, we must now journey back to Sir Walter's beloved Borderland; to the very location where we earlier encountered True Thomas engaged in his tryst with the Queen of the Fairies.

Chapter Thirteen

The Golden Apple and the Queen of the Fairies

O Apple Tree, we wassail thee,
And hope that thou will bear,
For the Lord doth know where we will be,
'till apples another year......

The Carhampton Wassail Song.

In a letter to Adam Ferguson from Edinburgh, dated 12th March 1816, Scott writes to his old schoolfriend of how, at the close of the Napoleonic Wars, he applauds the latter's resolution "to hang up the trumpet in the hall and study war no more.....You must know", Sir Walter then continues, "I have added to Abbotsford a good large farm, on which there is a mansion about the calibre of the "Laird's ain house", or rather larger, commanding a most beautiful prospect of the Eildon Hills and Melrose, or where, as the poet has it-

Soft sleeps the mist on cloven Eildon laid,
And distant Melrose peeps from leafy shade.

".....Now your sisters and you might comfortably inhabit this mansion during the summer, and it would be admirable shooting quarters, near enough to us and others to be quite sociable, and distant enough to be perfectly independent. But it affords us a prospect of laying our old grey pows together, as we used to do our young rattleplates. The house will only cost you paying the window-tax (about 50 shillings), and if you want a paddock for a cow and a horse you shall be handsomely dealt by. I hope you will keep this in your recollection when you think of a summer settlement. The Blucher flying coach sets you down within half-an-hour's walk of the spot. There is an old man in the place whom I will not disturb for a year or so, so we will have enough time to think of it. At all events we will see you at Abbotsford this summer, and I trust you will like Kaeside........"

And so it was that Sir Adam and his sisters came to reside at the house that they and their merry landlord would re-name Huntly burn. The following year, in a letter to John Richardson, the Laird of Abbotsford would write of how, "Certain affairs....have turned out so amazingly profitable as to have enabled me to make considerbale additions to this little property, and to undertake a still further expansion of my wings, which will probably soon flap the Eildon Hills. This has given me many delightful walks and much important and active employment, which is no small object at a period of life when country business suits one better than country sports. Yet think not but what I still course and burn the water; (1) the gun I have resigned to Walter, who is a very successful sportsman, and comes home loaded with grouse, blackcock, and partridges. If I thought it would come safe by the Carlisle coach, I would beg Mrs. R.'s kind acceptance of some game; a black-cock from the Rhymer's Glen would shine in the second course in Fludyer Street.

When you see Tom Campbell, tell him, with my best love, that I have to thank him for making me known to Mr. Washington Irving, who is one of the best and pleasantest acquaintances I have made this many a day. He stayed two or three days with me, and I hope to see him again......"

In Murray's *Romance and Prophecies of Thomas and Erceldoune* the author informs us of how Scott, "with his peculiar enthusiasm, purchased at probably fifty per cent. above its real value", a "wild and picturesque ravine, then called "Dick's Cleuch", located "at the base of the Western Eildon" and identified by him as the original "Huntlee Bankis" of the "True Thomas" legend. In another letter to Richardson, written some three months or so after his previously quoted epistle to Captain Adam Ferguson, he informs his correspondent of how "no sale could be better" than that of *The Tales of my landlord* is "reported to be", before continuing as follows:

"I have enlarged my dominions here not greatly in extent, but infinitely in point of beauty, as my boundary is now a strange secluded ravine full of old thorn trees, hazels, guelder roses, willows and so forth, with a dashing rivulet and certain large stones which in England your cocknies would call rocks. I call it the Rhymer's Glen, as it makes part of the scene where Thomas the Rhymer is said to have met the Queen of the Faires. Vulgarly, it is called Dick's Cleugh- a fico for the phrase....."

In a letter of the same date to yet another of his acquaintances, after writing of how a singer of popular songs has "flattered" him "much by being pleased with Sophia's singing Scotch ballads", Scott tells of how he has "acquired a new glen near the lake", which, he appropriately enough describes as "a quiet, invisible sort of dell where a witch might boil her kettle in happy seclusion among old thorn trees and scathed rocks, in a deep ravine totally out of sight unless you fall into it by accident. My predecessor," he continues, "had a humour of digging for coal in it, which prevented him including it in our first bargain, but being cured of that folly he has bequeathed me two or three lateral excavations which a little coaxing will turn into natural caverns. The last man who wanted work in this parish has been for some time employed in constructing a path up this odd glen. I call it the Rhymer's Glen because it makes part of Huntly Wood where Thomas the Rhymer met the Queen of Fairies. All this is but a sort of trash, but it is what my head is just now most busy about."

In the years that followed Lockhart would come to settle in Scott's "storied" neighbourhood, at a property known as Chiefswood; itself located in another of the tracts of land purchased as a result of the Laird of Abbotsford's literary successes. Amongst the visitors to this idyllic location was Robert Ferguson M.D., and it is to another extract from my ancestor's writings, in which he describes Lockhart's residence at Chiefswood and Sir Adam Ferguson's visits there, that I now propose to draw the reader's attention.

"This romantic little cottage" my ancestor writes, "was placed in a small oval field surrounded by hills, of which the three Eildons were the most remarkable. A burn not three feet broad ran through the little domain; a tree or two studded plateau, which was belted by a beech and other wood, stretching up to Huntly Burn, the residence of Sir A. Ferguson, the Rhymer's Glen, losing itself in the bare downs.....

"On a summer morning, Lockhart was sure to be found in dressing gown and cap, always chosen by his wife with a view to the picturesque, sitting or walking up and down, writing materials and the terrors of a forthcoming "Blackwood" [2] before him, Johnny, his first-born, then a beautiful fair-haired boy, never left his side, urging him to romp, and never in vain. Through the lattice of the bay window "Sophia" was always to be seen, and always ready to relieve the author when the parent was overpowered by the importunities of the child. A dog or two of the "pepper" and "mustard" kind, however, were useful in performing the welcome duty, and undertook to distract the boy not unwillingly by an invitation to scamper. Many a pungent page of sound scholarship and criticism was put forth under these influences.

Illustration 15): Engraving after J.M.W. Turner of J.G. Lockhart's summer residence at Chiefswood in the Borders.

"A little before mid-day a tall, soldier-like figure, with a weather beaten face, emerged from the wood at the bottom of the meadows - a most welcome visitor, Sir A. Ferguson - and then all the work was up, and the fun began, the lattice was thrown open, and a merry ringing laugh within kept up as a chorus to the peals and whouts which were going on outside.

"Abbotsford was then the resting-place of every pilgrim from every part of the world, whose conduct and coversation often afforded the richest treat to both Lockhart and Ferguson. They who know the men need not be told that while no trait of the ridiculous could pass unnoticed, both enjoyed fun far too much to dwell or enlarge upon what could call forth an unkind feeling; indeed, Lockhart never associated with or spoke of those whom he disliked. Everything about him was touched with fun. The children's donkeys were designated by names which made their delinquencies fatal to all gravity, as the stalwart "Dawvid" announced, with the most unconscious seriousness, that "Hannah Moore had broken through the fences, and had been wi' the meenister a' the night."

"At 3 or 4 Sir Walter generally joined the circle, welcomed by a shout from the boy, and the caresses of the doggies which never quitted him. Then came the histories of the past day, and the plans of the morrow, with a thousand tales and illustrations, and a few rebukes to the pungent commentaries of Lockhart.

"Anne and Lady Scott, called in the carriage to take Sophia to dinner or a drive, while Lockhart joined the circle at Abbotsford later."

This unique testament, written by a contemporary of Scott, himself a close relative of the Laird of Abbotsford's most trusted intimates, illustrates how the Author of Waverley used the large revenues generated by his success as a writer not only to purchase the haunts of Thomas of Ercildoune, but to populate them with his own friends and family; in a kind of attempt to create his own private "Garden of Eden". Perhaps his motivation to do this was in some way inspired by the references to the Fairy Garden in the legends relating to the Rhymer's encounters with the Queen of Fair Elfland related in the ballads.

Elsewhere, Lockhart himself paints a very different picture of Ferguson to the one here presented: "I must not omit a circumstance" he writes, "which Scott learned from another source and which he always took pride in relating. In the course of the day when *The Lady of the Lake* first reached Fergusson [3], he was posted with his Company on a point of ground exposed to the enemy's artillery. The men were ordered to lie prostrate on the ground. While they kept that attitude, the Captain kneeling at their head, read aloud the battle of Canto vi., and the listening soldiers only interrupted him by a joyous huzza whenever the shot struck the bank close above them."

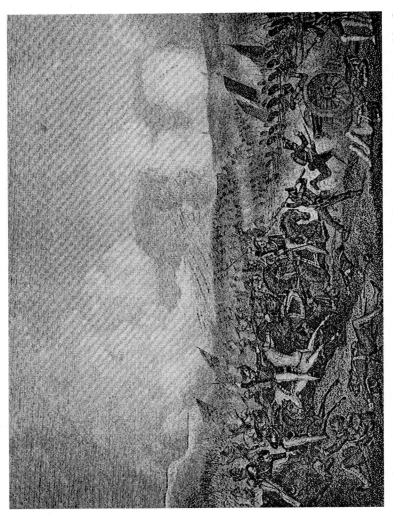

Illustration 9: The Battle of Salamanca, one of the numerous military and naval actions witnessed by Scott's friends and tenants the Fergusons of Huntley Burn; whose real life experiences were to provide much raw material for the Laird of Abbotsford's own novels.

As one would expect, the opening Canto of the poem is filled with much descriptive language reminiscent of much of the Ancient Cymric poetic material dealt with during the course of the previous few chapters:

Boon nature scattered, free and wild,
Each plant or flower, the mountain's child.
Here eglantine embalmed the air,
Hawthorn and hazel migled there;
The primrose pale and violet flower,
Found in each cliff a narrow bower;
Fox-glove and night-shade, side by side,
Emblems of punishment and pride,
Grouped their dark hues with every stain,
The weather-beaten crags retain.
With boughs that quaked at every breath,
Grey birch and aspen wept beneath;
Aloft the ash and warrior oak
Cast anchor in the rifted rock;
And higher yet, the pine tree hung
His shattered trunk, and frequent flung,
Where seemed the cliffs to meet on high,
His bows athwart the narrowed sky.
Highest of all, where white peaks glanced,
Where glistening streamers waved and danced,
The wanderer's eye could barely view
The summer heaven's delicious blue;
So wondrous wild, the whole might seem
The scenery of a fairy dream......

But to return once again to Sir Walter's chosen residence, as well as that of his friends and family, the reader will have noted, not only from the above given quotations from the Laird of Abbotsford's own correspondence, but also the writings of Robert Ferguson M.D., Sir Adam's cousin, as well as my own text, that all of these abodes were located within the immediate vicinity of "Huntlee Bankis", the scene of Thomas of Ercildoune's legendary Fairy encounter. This last point is of particular significance, for it gives us another connection with the group of ballads that we looked at in the chapter entitled "The Song of Amergin"; on account of the fact that the name Huntly has a longstanding association with Clan Gordon; from amongst whom, as we have already seen, Scott's friend Lord Byron was himself descended.

Illustration 16): Sophia Scott, daughter of Sir Walter and the wife of his celebrated biographer, Lockhart. From an original painting by Nicholson currently in the possession of the Laird of Abbotsford's descendants.

Although the present head of Clan Gordon, the Marquess of Huntly, derives his title from Huntly in Aberdeenshire, the Clan originally came from Berwickshire; taking their name from their principal possessions around the parish of Gordon; which lies north east of Earlston on the road to Duns and Berwick-on-Tweed. The name Gordon may derive from the North British or Cymric "Gordin", a "spacious hill"; which in Gaelic translates as a "Goat

Hill" (See James B. Johnstone's *Place Names of Scotland* [4]; thus denoting that the Clan may originally have been of indiginous North British descent.

The compilers of Douglas's *Scottish Peerage* quote a family tradition that one of their ancestors accompanied King Malcolm Canmore on his last raid into Northumberland in 1093, and conjecture that the first members of the Clan to adopt the surname "Gordon" may have been vassals of the Earls of March. The first of these on record is one Richard or Richer Gordon, who appears in charters around 1171, in connection with lands granted by him in the parish of Gordon to the monks of Kelso; who had recently acquired St. Michael's chapel there from the monks of Durham in exchange for the chapel of nearby Earlston.

The connection with Durham is an interesting one, for one of two farm steads located at Lands near Cockfield, just outside of Bishop Auckland, which bear the name of "High" and "Low Gordon" respectively, can be shown to have been occupied continuously as far back as the Middle Ages and beyond. Perhaps there is some kind of ancient North British link between these two sites for which we have no written documentation. The site at Lands is itself a "spacious hill" located several hundred feet above sea level, consisting of pastureland ideal for the grazing of goats; and the fact that it lies within a very short distance of the vast oak forests once owned by the Prince Bishops of Durham is perhaps indicative of some long forgotten connection between the County Palatine, as the old shire of Durham was once referred to, and the Rhymer's ancient residence at Ercildoune.

Between Earlston and Gordon in Berwickshire is Huntlywood, and there is evidence to suggest that both it, and Huntly Bank, where Sir Walter would take up residence and which is itself located just southwest of Earlston, were themselves to influence the naming of Huntly Town in Aberdeenshire; where we earlier encountered the Earl of Airlie's daughter and her Royal Forester, the blacksmith's son. The Gordons first acquired lands in Aberdeenshire in the vicinity of Strathbogie long after they appear on record in the Borders; so the lyrical connections between *The Royal Forester* and *The Bonny Hynd* may well have some association with the Gordons and their landed possessions in both areas. Perhaps travelling minstrels from the Borders visited their seat at Huntly, or perhaps these lyrics travelled south as a result of the Huntly Family's extensive influence in Berwickshire and elsewhere. Whatever the truth, a curious legend is associated with Huntly that seems to tie in with everything that we have looked at so far.

283

Local Aberdeenshire legend associates Huntly with a secret society referred to as "The Horseman's Word". Most of the currently available material on this secret society dates from the 1870s, and tradition asserts that the organization was still active until at least the 1930s; some accounts claiming that it still exists today being referred to in some modern sources (5). "The Horseman's Word", from which this secret society takes its name, is supposed to be a secret word which will give the initiate power over any horse to which it is spoken; and although "The Horseman's Word" has become associated with Witch Cults and Devil Worship in recent times, there is a large amount of evidence to suggest that it was originally rooted in an indiginous pagan cult which may well have become infiltrated, and possibly even taken over, by Satanists with possible Masonic affiliations of their own.

Prospective initiates into "The Horseman's Word" appear to have been initiated blindfold, with their left feet bare and their right hands raised, much like the rolled up trouserlegged rituals of the "Sons of Widow", our meddlesome Masonic brethren from chapter ten. Another aspect of the same ritual involved the newly initiated "Horsemen" being taken into the "Caufhoose" of the barn for a "shake o' Auld Hornie": An aspect of their initiation which involved a goat's cloven hoof being thrust into their hand.

As we saw earlier, the name "Gordon" may derive from the Gaelic for "Goat Hill", and it is therefore possible, and indeed probable, that "The Horseman's Word" was almost certainly originally a pagan cult. The fact that Huntly bank by Melrose is a site almost certainly associated in Pre-Christian times with the Cult of the Sacred Horse- hence the meeting there between Thomas of Ercildoune and the Fairy Queen, is itself perhaps indicative of a close link between the two pagan cults that undoubtedly flourished in Gordon and on Huntly Bank in prehistoric times and the brethren of "The Horseman's Word". Although some might argue that there can be no connection between the rituals practised by the Horsemen themselves and such ancient pagan religious practises as those previously looked at in connection with horse worship elsewhere in my text, it is interesting to note that, in the part of the Horsemen's rituals in which the "shake o' Auld Hornie" was used to initiate new members, the "Goat" was frequently a man dressed in the skins of an animal and wearing a horned mask.

In view of this it is relevant that at Pencoed in South Wales a ritual still takes place once a year in which a man dressed as a horse, referred to locally as "The Mari Llywd", is paraded around outlying farms. Perhaps the Horsemen of "The Horsemen's Word" originally had some link with a similar ritual practise. It is also possible that all that we know of their rituals has been deliberately distorted by an ignorant and intolerant Kirk. Also probable is their infiltration and subversion by Satanists such as Sir Robert Gordon, whose construction of "The Round Square", an overtly Masonic 17th century edifice at Gordonstoun, has its own connections with "Auld Hornie"; who it was built specifically to keep out. In the end, however, Sir Robert was carried off to Hell by Auld Nick, who slung his corpse over his saddle and galloped off to the Underworld with his aristocratic victim; thus providing clues as to how an overtly pagan ritual was in all probability corrupted by a latter day Michael Scott.

The fact that no women were ever admitted into "The Horseman's Word", and that its members were made to take an oath never to reveal any of the society's secrets to anyone who "Wears an apron except a blacksmith or a farrier" (6) shows definite parallels between the activities of the nineteenth century Horsemen and a Border custom dating back to the 16th century. Every year, since that time, the residents of Hawick, centre of the Border woolen industry, have turned out for the annual "Common Riding", a spectacle in which hundreds of local riders gallop around the boundaries of the Burgh to commemorate a victory over English marauders some four hundred years ago.

In recent times participation has been restricted to male members of the community only, following an incident in 1931 in which a Miss Murgatroyd was thrown from her horse and broke her leg; but previous to this the "Common Riding" was open to members of both sexes. In view of this it seems likely that "The Horseman's Word" may well have evolved out of a pagan cult open to both sexes. After all, as I showed in an earlier chapter, the Earl of Airlie's daughter in the ballad of *The Noble Forester* is in all probability a manifestation of the Celtic Horse Goddess of antiquity who marries a blacksmith's son at Huntly Town.

Some three years ago the resignation of the Provost of Hawick, one Tom Hogg, who had previously also chaired the Common Riding Committee, took place as a direct result of a hotly debated controversy over the participation of two women in the 1996 "Common Riding". At the heart of this great controversy, which was to split the entire community, appears to have been the application of what some would most certainly view as a "sexist" policy, with respect to a custom which might well have evolved out of still more ancient rituals of boundary walking; which could well have had Pre-Christian associations with the Fairy Horse Cults that once clearly flourished in the Scottish Borders.

As we have already seen, it was a member of the same Border Clan, James Hogg, who was himself to be of great assistance to Scott in his collection and collation of the Ballads which he was to include in the *Minstrelsy*. Of further relevence is the fact that Hogg's mother, Mrs. Hogg, was to provide Sir Walter with some of his best lyrics; for she herself was a member of the celebrated Laidlaw Clan. As has also been seen, the Laidlaws are not only connected with the town of Ludlow in Shropshire, but also with an individual famed for having concealed horses from the English. Again, this adds further weight to my previously made assertion as regards the possible existence in more ancient times of a pagan cult with rituals not dissimilar to those still pevalent in Wales, in relation to the Mari Llywd, in the vicinity of Earlston and Huntly Bank. This Laidlaw, Ludlow, Mari Llwyd connection provides us with yet more clues with regard to the identity of the original species or genus of tree under which the Rhymer originally uttered his prophecies.

In an earlier chapter I pointed out a possible link with the sacred hazel, a speculation founded as much as anything upon Scott's own references, in his previously quoted from correspondence with Richardson, as regards his acquisition of land around Huntly Bank, to the presence of "thorn trees, hazels, guelder roses, willows, and so forth" in the vicinity of the Rhymer's Glen. In the Ogham Alphabet the letter "L" for Laidlaw, Ludlow and Llywd is "Luis"- the Rowan, Quickbeam or Mountain Ash; a tree which has already been mentioned in brief during the course of a previous chapter.

In view of this, it should therefore come as no surprise that, amongst the pages of *The White Goddess* we should find references to how the ".....quickbeam.....is the tree most widely used in the British Isles as a prophylactic against lightning and witches' charms of all sorts: for example, bewitched horses can be controlled only with a Rowan whip. In ancient Ireland, fires of rowan were kindled by the Druids of opposing armies and incantations spoken over them, summoning spirits to take part in the fight. The berries of the magical rowan in the Irish romance of Fraoth, guarded by a Dragon, had the sustaining virtue of nine meals; they also healed the wounded and added a year to a man's life. In the romance of Diarmuid and Grainne the Rowan Berry, with the apple and the red nut, is described as the food of the gods. "Food of the Gods" suggest that the taboo on eating anything red was an extension of the commoners' taboo on eating scarlet toadstools- for toadstools, according to a Greek proverb which Nero quoted, were "the food of the gods." In ancient Greece, all red foods such as lobster, bacon, red mullet, crayfish, and scarlet berries and fruit were tabooed except at feasts in honour of the dead. (Red was the colour of death in Greece and Britain during the Bronze Age- red ochre has been found in megalithic burials both in the Prescelly Mountains and on Salisbury Plain). The quickbeam is the tree of quickening. Its botanical name Fraxinus, or Pyrus, Aucuparia, conveys its divinatory uses. Another of its names is "the witch" and the witch-wand formerly used for metal divining, was made of rowan. Since it was the tree of quickening it could also be used in a contrary sense. In Danaan Ireland a rowan stake hammered through a corpse immobilized its ghost; and in the Cuchulain saga three hags spitted a dog, Cuchulain's sacred animal, on rowan twigs to procure his death......"

Thus, the sacred Rowan might also be another possible candidate for the "Craobh Ruadh" worshipped by the Ulster Heros of the Red Branch at Emain Macha. The connection with the apple too provides us with yet another link with the legend of *True Thomas,* and the associations outlined above provide us with an explanation for the chorus lines in the previously referred to ballad of *The Twelve Witches;* which run as follows:

> *Rowan Tree, Red Thread,*
> *Hold the Witches all in dread......(7).*

As for the sacred goat, in the opening lines of the previously qoted from *Lay of the Smithy,* Fionn or Finn is heard to make the following announcement:

> *"Fionn Mac Cumhail m'ainm baistidh,*
> *Chan eil agu orom ach sgeula.*
> *Bha mi uair mi uallach ghobhar*
> *Aig Righ Lochlainn a's a' Gheilibhinn......"*

> *"Fionn Mac Cumhaill is my name,*
> *You only know me by reputation.*
> *I herded goats in my time*
> *For the King of Lochlann in Gealbainn......"*

In the Taliesin Cycles Taliesin himself was originally called Gwion, before tasting the legendary Salmon of Knowledge; being chased and eated by

287

Cerridwen; reborn as her child; thrown into the sea; carried to the Weir of Gwyddno Garanhir and fished out by Prince Elphin; who had himself gone there to net fish. As Graves is also swift to point out, "Gwion is the equivalent (gw for f) of Fionn or Finn, the Irish hero of a similar tale....." (and another aspect of the mythical leader of the Fenian heros). "Fionn....was instructed by a Druid of the same name as himself to cook for him a salmon fished from a deep pool of the River Boyne (a Druidic initiation), but forbidden to taste it; but as Fionn turned the fish over in the pan he burned his thumb, which he put into his mouth and so received the gift of inspiration. For the Salmon was a Salmon of Knowledge, that had fed on nuts fallen from the Nine Hazels of Poetic Art......."

As has already been seen, the hazel is just one of a whole host of plants that feature in the poem *Cad Goddeu;* which itself forms part of the celebrated *Hanes Taliesin* or *Taliesin Manuscript.* Elsewhere in the same text, in the section in which "little Gwion answers King Maelgwyn's questions as to who he was and whence he came", he tells of how he "was in the Court of Don before the birth of Gwydion". It is therefore appropriate that, according to legend, "The Battle of the Trees" is said to have been fought between Amathaon and Gwydion, the two sons of Don, and Arawn King of Annwn". (Annwn here is the Welsh equivalent of Hades, the Classical Underworld.)

Amongst the manuscript collections of the eighteenth century Welsh Bard Iolo Morganwg, published collectively by the Welsh Manuscript Society in 1848, are some very interesting references to both Gwydion and Don: In a section on *The Three Irish Invasions* of Cambria, we find a reference to the third Irish invasion of Wales; which is described in Iolo's text as "that of Don or Daronwy, King of Lochlyn, who came to Ireland and conquered it; after which he led 60,000 Irish and Lochlynians to North Wales where they lived for 129 years, when Caswallon Llawhir ap Einion ap Cunedda entered Mona, wrested the country from them and slew Sirigi Wyddel, their ruler, at a place called Llan-y-Gwyddyl in Mona".

Elsewhere we are told of how "Don, king of Lochlyn and Dublin led the Irish to Gwynedd, where they remained for 129 years. Gwydion the son of Don was highly celebrated for his knowledge and sciences. He was the first who.....introduced the knowledge of letters to Ireland and Lochlyn....."

This last reference is of particular interest, for in it we hear of how Gwydion is accredited with having introduced divinatory alphabets into Ireland.

Although, as has already been shown, the Irish evolved their own system independently, a system connected with Ogma, who gave his name to the Ogham Alphabet, some versions of these ancient tree alphabets incorporate a letter "P" into them; something which, as shall be seen below, is slightly out of the ordinary.

In the ancient Irish tongue, spoken in Eriu before the introduction of Christianity, and the adoption of certain linguistic reforms, aimed at incorporating certain Graeco-Hebraic terms into both the spoken and written languages, the letter "P" in Welsh and Pictish is substituted for the letter "Q". Hence, the Cymro-Pictish name for the Picts- "Pretani", becomes "Cruithne" or "Quruithne" in Gaelic. In view of this it is by no means impossible that the "P-Celtic" Ogham Alphabet which Graves reconstructs, by solving the answers to a series of questions or riddles laid out in the *Hanes Taliesin*, was originally a Pictish one; itself associated not only with Gwydion ap Don, or Gwydion the son of Don, but also with the Kings of Lochlin or Lochlyn. For, amongst Taliesin's own previous incarnations, as they are set out in the *Hanes Taliesin,* the master poet claims to have been a "bard of the harp to King Lleon of Lochlin".

In the Scottish Ossianic Tradition, the Kingdom of Lochlyn, or Lochlin, is usually associated with Norway. In reality it may in fact have been the region which would later become the preserve of the Norwegian Kings of Man and the Isles; a dynasty closely associated with the Norse Kingdom of Dublin. What we are told about Gwydion ap Don's line in the Welsh sources would tend to confirm this, for the Iolo M.S. makes mention of both Dublin and Mona- the latter being a name given variously to both Anglesey and the Isle of Man in ancient Welsh bardic sources; and cites both of these locations as being under the control of their dynasty.

Many of the Ossianic Traditions collected and translated during the eighteenth century by James Macpherson are alleged to have been taken from amongst the traditions originally preserved by the Clan Bards to the Clanranalds; the MacDonalds of the Isles. The Chiefs of Clanranald were themselves descended from both Gaels and Norsemen alike- facts which will be dealt with in more detail at a later juncture; and doubtless the original source of the associations made between Lochlyn and the old Norse sub-kingdoms; which had been carved out during the early Middle Ages by marauding Vikings.

Einion Yrth's son, Cadwallon Llawhir, who is credited with expelling the men of Lochlyn from North Wales, is none other than King Maelgwyn's father; which would place the date of the expulsion a generation before the life and birth of Taliesin himself; c.515 A.D. If the assertion that North Wales was dominated by these invaders for some 129 years is also correct, then this would place the date of their original invasion to around 396 or thereabouts. Curiously enough, in another section of the Iolo M.S. we have a direct reference to a member of their dynasty doing battle with Owain Vinddu; who is cited as being a son of "Maxen Wledig". Bona fide historical sources identify Maxen Wledig with the rebel Roman Emperor Magnus Maximus; whose attempt to seize the Empire for himself sadly depleted Britain of valuable soldiers in the late Fourth Century. His defeat and death at the hands of Theodosius is known to have taken place c.388; and old Welsh genealogies identify "Owain Vinddu" as his son Julian. This would tend to suggest that although Iolo's bardic sources are themselves corrupt and fragmentary, there is at least an element of truth in their assertion that some kind of northern invasion from Ireland, Man and the Isles took place during the era in which we are looking at.

Iolo's sources are decidedly vague as regards the exact location to which these invaders were expelled. Some of them were almost certainly driven into Ireland. However, there is another place where many of them might have settled; in view of what we know about Roman governmental practises of the third and fourth centuries. In Gaul, for example, the Frankish tribes who would eventually succeed the Romans as the dominant force in terms of rulership, had originally been settled on the northern frontiers with Germania as "federates" or military auxiliaries. In effect, they were mercenaries who were bound to defend those same frontiers from hostile encroachments in return for land upon which to settle and farm; thus making them an army which had exchanged lands with the Empire it was now defending in return for an obligation to military service.

As we saw in an earlier chapter, place names, old Welsh genealogical documents and fragmentary bardic traditions, would tend to suggest that the eastern frontierlands of the old Welsh Kingdom of Powys, the Cymric province bordering the English Kingdom of Mercia, had, by Cadwallon and Maelgwyn's own time, come to be settled by certain tribes of Gaelic, Goidelic or Irish speaking Picts; the "Gwyddyl Ffichti" of the old genealogies. Could these Picts have also had some sort of connection with the Kings of Lochlyn of the Iolo M.S.?

Nennius dates the arrival of the Saxons in Britain to c.428 A.D., a fact attested to by the Anglo-Saxon Chronicle. By the beginning of the following century the Germanic peoples from the North had made widespread incursions into British mainland territory, from their initial bridgeheads on the Isles of Thanet, Wight & C. Did Cadwallon and his fellow Britons make some sort of deal with a faction of the Pictish heirachy, settling them on their eastern frontier with the Saxons as federates, like the Franks in Gaul; whilst driving other septs from amongst the same clans out of Anglesey and North Wales at the same time?

It is tempting to suppose that this is the case, for Cadwallon's own dynasty can be shown to have intermarried extensively with the old Romano-British nobility; despite their own North British origins. And, in view of this, it is not altogether impossible that they adopted many Roman customs. Such a solution would explain adequately why Gwydion and Don are still looked upon as heros in Old Welsh Bardic Tradition, despite the expulsion of some of their descendants by the dynasties which would later come to dominate Dark Age and Mediaeval Wales; and why the names of the Kings of Lochlyn, who ruled in North Wales prior to their expulsion by Maelgwyn's own father, are identical to many of those that feature in *The Mabinogion:* names like Math and Mathonwy, who are themselves well known in old Welsh legend.

These facts are highly significant with respect to the Border Minstrel Tradition, for, in many ways Taliesin, who confesses to having been "in the court of Don before the birth of Gwydion", as has already been seen a few paragraphs previously, is himself very much the forerunner of Thomas of Ercildoune. Elsewhere in the *Hanes Taliesin* for example we find Merlin and Taliesin engaged in a two-way dialogue, just like our *False Knight on the Road* and the *Wee Boy* he is heard to interrogate in the ballad published by Motherwell:

Taliesin: The Seven sons of Eliffer, seven proven warriors,
  Will not avoid seven spears in their seven battle-sections.

Myrddin: Seven blazing fires, seven opposing armies,
  In every first onset Cynvelyn will be among the seven.

Taliesin: Seven piercing spears, seven rivers full,
  With the blood of chieftains will they swell.

Myrddin: Seven score men of rank lapsed into madness,
   In the forest of Celyddon they perished:
   Since it is I, Myrddin, after Taliesin,
   Whose prophecy will be correct.......

The abovegiven extract from Professor A.O.H. Jarman's translation of *The Dialogue of Myrddin and Taliesin*, which features in *The Black Book of Carmarthen*, ties the confounder of Maelgwyn's bards in with Thomas of Ercildoune; who, in more ways than one, could be said to be his successor; just as he can be said to have succeeded Merlin; who is here depicted in conversation with Taliesin. For, in the prophecy of Berlington, quoted by the Laird of Abbotsford in his introduction to a series of verses printed in the *Minstrelsy*, which specifically relate to the Ancient Prophecies attributed to the Rhymer of Ercildoune, we find the following lines:

Marvellous Merlin, that many men of tells,
And Thomas's sayings, comes all at once.

No coincidence then, in view of the significance of the Sacred Apple in the legend of True Thomas and the Queen of the Fairies, that in another poem, likewise culled from the same source and itself entitled *Afellennau*, or *Apple-trees*, we find the key to Merlin's own connections with North Britain; a connection written about by Sir Walter himself; as we have already seen in an earlier chapter. As one might expect, this last mentioned poem recalls a time when the Apple Tree was still sacred; and is in many ways a forerunner, in poetical terms at least, to the ancient *Wassail* songs still popular in many rural regions of these islands:

Sweet-apple tree with sweet branches
Fruit bearing, of great value, famous belonging to me....
Sweet-apple tree, a tall, green tree,
Fruit-bearing its branches and fair trunk....
Sweet-apple tree, a yellow tree,
Which grows at the end of a hill without tilled land around it.....
Sweet-apple tree which grows beyond Rhun,
I had contended at its foot for the satisfaction of a maiden,
With my shield on my shoulder and my sword on my thigh,
And in the forest of Celyddon I slept alone;
O! Little pig why did'st thou think of sleep?
Listen to the birds, their imploring is heard.....

Sweet-apple tree which grows in a glade,
Its peculiar power hides it from the Lords of Rhydderch;
A crowd by its trunk, a host around it,
It would be a treasure for them, brave men in their ranks.
Now Gwynedd loves me not and does not greet me
-I am hated by Gwasawg, the supporter of Rhydderch-
I have killed her son and her daughter.
Death has taken everyone, why does it not call me?
For after Gwenddolau no lord honours me,
Mirth gives me no delight, no woman visits me;
And in the battle of Arfderydd my torque was of gold,
Though today I am not treasured by the one of the aspect of swans......

A third poem in this same series, likewise from *The Black Book of Carmarthen* and entitled *Oianau* or *Greetings,* also relates to the Battle of Arfderydd; itself a major contributory factor, as has already been noted, to the downfall of the Northern Dynasties which feature throughout the Arthurian sections of my text:

Listen to the call of the sea birds, of great energy.....
A wild man from afar has told me
That Kings with strange connections,
Goidels and Britons and Romans,
Will make adversity and disorder.....
The hair of my head is thin, my cloak is not warm,
The meadows are my barn, my corn is not plenteous.
My summer store does not sustain me.....
My cloak is thin, it is not sufficient for me.
Since the battle of Arfderydd I care not
Were the sky to fall and the sea to overflow.....

In order to understand fully the point of relevance of the Battle of Arfderydd to our own particular story, we must now take a journey back to Galloway. As the reader will doubtless recall, this is the very region where, in the opening chapter of this book, we found Sir Walter's own ancestor, John le Scot, and his companion, Walter the English, journeying into Ettrick Forest from Lancelot Scot's ancestral hall: This place, as has also been seen, was itself formerly located just a short distance from the burial place of Sir Michael Scot; John le Scot's Wizard descendant; and it is therefore appropriate that it is to Galloway that we must travel in order to find definite clues as to the true identity of the individual who may have been responsible for composing the first poetical version of the Tristrem Legends; the enigmatic Thomas of Britain.

Chapter Fourteen

The Lochmaben Harper and the Lady of the Lake

Harp of the North! that mouldering long hast hung
On the witch-elm that shades St. Fillian's spring,
And down the fitful breeze thy numbers flung,
Till envious ivy did around thee cling,
Muffling with verdant ringlet every string-
O minstrel Harp, still must thin accents sleep?
'Mid rustling leaves and fountains murmering,
Still must thy sweeter sounds their silence keep,
Nor bid a warrior smile, nor teach a maid to weep?

"The Lady of the Lake".

Amongst the "Historical Ballads" set out in Scott's *Minstrelsy* is a curious song entitled *The Lochmaben Harper*. Although placed in this last category by Scott, the above set of lyrics consist of a composition not dissimilar, in certain respects, in terms of subject matter at least, to the ballad of *Hughie the Graeme*; in that they are primarily concerned, once again, with the theft of a horse. Unlike the ballad which we looked at in Chapter 7, however, the words to *The Lochmaben Harper* are composed in a somewhat less serious vein to those previously herementioned.

The ballad begins with the arrival, on the English side of the Border, of an old blind harper from Lochmaben town, who rides off with the intent of stealing the Lord Warden of the Marches' own prize stallion. After singing his English audience to sleep in the Lord Warden's hall at "Carlisle Town", the harper's mare, who seems to have been trained up specially for the purpose, escapes from the stables where she has been quartered, with her master's quarry in tow. Whilst she makes her way home to Lochmaben, "the silly blind Harper" is busy bartering a price with the English for the mare that has allegedly been stolen from him by their own lawless countrymen.

295

In Scott's notes to the ballad, he has the following to say as regards the story's origins:

"The only remark which offers itself on the foregoing ballad seems to be that it is the most modern in which the harp, as a Border instrument of music, is found to occur...."

Scott's obsession with the Minstrel's Harp is evidenced throughout his poetry, and, numerous references to what was, for him, a sacred instrument, have already been quoted throughout my text. Perhaps then, this is the reason for its inclusion by the Author of Waverley amongst the previously mentioned category of "Historical Ballads": For, once again, as in the case of *Hughie the Graeme*, no actual historical tradition appears to exist which is substantiative of the story to which it alludes.

As for the region in which this ballad is set, Lochmaben itself is located in Annandale; just a few miles south of the Johnstones' stronghold at Lochwood; and in the middle of a vast ritual landscape associated since time immemorial with the magician Merlin or Meddyn. The name "Lochmaben" is ultimately derived from a connection with the old Welsh pagan god "Maponos" or Mabon, a divine child not unlike the boy Emrys in the legends recounted by Nennius. To the north is Hart Fell, and the remains of the ancient forest of Celyddon or "Calidon". To the south east, along the ancient road to Carlisle, is the Moat of Liddel, site of the Battle of Arfderydd in 573. As we have seen already, this battle, fought over a legendary bird's nest, between various factions of the old North British of Y Gogledd, was one of the greatest military disasters of the Welsh Heroic Age.

On the one side we find the North British Dynasty of York, who have featured already elsewhere in our text. Whilst on the other, pitted against them, is an army led by one "Gwenddolau son of Ceidio", himself a member of another sept of Old King Coel's illustrious clan. The significance of this battle in relation to our own story, however, revolves around the bird's nest over which it was fought. For a few miles further west, along the Dumfrieshire coast, is the castle of Caerlaverock, which in the old North British dialect translates as "The Lark's Nest".

The mediaeval castle of Caerlaverock has, since the thirteenth century, been associated with one of the more senior branches of Clan Maxwell; for centuries the longstanding rivals in the Borders of Clan Johnstone; and themselves of Norwegian descent according to Border tradition. Long before the castle stood in the moat that lies in the shadow of Ward Law, other fortifications stood atop of this ancient hill; eventually bequeathing their name to the later mediaeval structure that was to succeed them; for Ward Law is itself the original site of the "Lark's Nest" of old Welsh legend. In a letter to Ellis dated 14th February 1802, Sir Walter writes as follows:

"I have been silent, but not idle. The transcript of King Arthur is at length finished, being a fragment of about 7000 lines. Let me know how I shall transmit a parcel containing it, with the "Complaynt" and the Border Ballads. I have as yet touched very little on the more remote antiquities of the Border, which, indeed, my songs, all comparatively modern, did not lead me to discuss. Some scattered herbage, however, the elephants may perhaps find. By the way, you will not forget to notice the mountain called Arthur's Seat, which overhangs this city. When I was at school, the tradition ran that King Arthur occupied as his throne a huge rock upon its summit, and that he beheld from thence some naval engagement in the Frith of Forth......"

This letter is important for a variety of reasons: At the beginning of the above quoted extract we have a reference to Scott's transcription of one of the key Arthurian sections of the Auchinleck M.S. in the Advocates Library in Edinburgh; from whence he also transcribed the *Sir Tristrem* of Thomas of Ercildoune. As I made clear in the opening chapters of this book, to find such a piece in the same manuscript as Thomas's *Tristrem* is of some importance. As we also saw, a metrical version of the legend of Sir Owain appears in the same ms.; and it is therefore probable that all three of these pieces had some link with the ancient minstrel traditions of which True Thomas himself was the chief exponent during the middle of the thirteenth century. The next important point made by Scott during the course of this missive is that he has "touched very little on the more remote antiquities of the Border, which, indeed", his songs did not lead him to discuss on account of their comparative modernity.

From an historical point of view this is certainly true. The historical section in the *Border Minstrelsy* only really begins with the era associated with the wars of Bruce and Wallace with the Plantagenets. The one exception to this rule is the ballad of *Kempion,* which is scrutinized in detail, as the reader will have noted, in Chapter One. The principal reason for this is hinted at, once again, in the opening paragraphs to Scott's general introduction to the *Minstrelsy;* in which he informs his readership of the circumstances

297

surrounding the arrival of St. Margaret and her followers in Scotland; after having first dealt with the North British Dark Age history of the same region.

"At a later period", he writes, "the Saxon families who fled from the exterminating sword of the Conqueror, with many of the Normans themselves whom discontent and intestine feuds had driven into exile, began to rise into eminence upon the Scottish Borders. They brought with them arts, both of peace and war, unknown to Scotland; and among their descendants we soon number the most powerful Border Chiefs. Such, during the reign of the last Alexander (1249), were Patrick, Earl of March, and Lord Soulis, renowned in tradition; and such were also the powerful Comyns, who early acquired the principal sway upon the Scottish marches. In the civil wars betwixt Bruce and Baliol all those powerful chieftains espoused the unscuccessful party. They were forfeited and exiled; and upon their ruins was founded the formidable house of Douglas....."

These facts provide us with a definite explanation as to why the historical ballads collected by Scott should date to a period after the rise of de Bruce's dynasty and the Stuart Line that succeeded it. With the fall of these great Border magnates their loyal minstrels doubtless lost their status and drifted into relative obscurity; the only exception being *True Thomas* of Ercildoune. Perhaps the legend, expanded upon by Scott in his own voluminous writings, that towards the end of his life the Rhymer returned to Fairy land, where he still resides much like Arthur and his Knights, sleeping beneath the Eildon Hills, is a specific reference to the end of this poetical Golden Age. [1]. Doubtless, before his departure to wherever it was he went, he dictated the *Sir Tristrem* to a willing scribe, much as the North British bards of the Dark Ages had dictated their own ancient bardic poetical traditions to Christian monks in the preceeding centuries.

As the reader will have noted already, both Merlin and Arthur have featured throughout this book. And, in view of the fact that, as has already been seen during the above quoted letter from Sir Walter to his friend Ellis, King Arthur features in Southern Scottish local tradition, it is perhaps surprising that nowhere amongst the ballads that Sir Walter collected are there any direct references to him. There is evidence to suggest that Scott was hoping to find such a reference or such references during the course of his extensive ballad hunting expeditions in the Borders; and that this is the reason for his slightly disappointed tone in the above letter from which I have previously quoted.

The reasons for this are probably two fold: First and foremost, following the committal to writing of the ancient bardic traditions of the Borders, which had previously been preserved orally by "True Thomas" and his entourage of inferior poets, many of the lesser ballads previously associated with the formal, metrical romance aspect of those self same traditions were either altered to appease new musical fashions and tastes, or else disappeared completely. Secondly, by the time this great committal to writing took place, indiginous North British Culture had been completely and utterly repressed; with only a handful of its folk traditions, such as the one previously referred to by Scott in relation to Arthur's Seat, and the place-names of Lochmaben and Caerlaverock, remaining intact.

Amongst this great corpus of bardic literaure was almost certainly another metrical romance, referred to in brief in Chapter One in relation to the opening cantos of Scott's *Bridal of Triermain*, and entitled *Lancelot of the Laik*. Dating from about 1490-1500 A.D., and therefore about two hundred years or so later than the *Sir Tristrem*, the opening lines of Book One of this metrical romance refer to a time when,

.......the worthi conqueroure
Arthure, wich had of al this worlde the floure
Of cheuelry auerding to his crown,
So pasing war his knychtis in renoune,
Was at Carlill; and hapynnit so that hee
Soiornyt well long in that faire cuntree.....

In view of Scott's previously noted obsession with all things Arthurian, it is therefore thoroughly unsurprising that at the beginning of the metrical romance put into the mouth of Sir Walter's ficitious bard, Lyulph, in *The Bridal of Triermain*, we find the following lines previously quoted at the head of the opening chapter of this work:

King Arthur has ridden from merry Carlisle
When Pentecost was o'er;
He journeyed like errant-knight the while,
And sweetly the summer sun did smile
On mountain, moss and moor......

As has also already been noted in the opening chapter of this book, the fifteenth century Scottish metrical romance of *Lancelot of the Laik* may well have been the original model upon which Scott based his own composition from which I have just quoted. The language in which the "Romans" is written, although predominantly Lowland Scottish in general structure, retains certain elements of Northumbrian dialect, showing it to emanate from the very region where Thomas of Ercildoune was himself wont to reside [2].

In terms of content it is essentially a Scottish re-working of the French romance of *Lancelot du Lac,* which dates from the early thirteenth century in its original form. Unlike the French romance, however, the author of the Scottish version misses out certain important incidents present in the foreign "original", such as the legends relating to Lancelot's birth; his fostering out to the Lady of the Lake, and many other key elements in the French rendition of the story. In fact, the "Romans" of Scottish tradition is primarily concerned with the wars between King Arthur and Galiot; whose name would tend to be indicative of his having some connection with Galloway. This is in fact not inconceivable, in view of the close proximity between Carlisle, where the poem begins, and South West Scotland.

Before going too deeply into the significance of these last mentioned facts though, it is worth noting that, although the French version of the Lancelot legend places this Arthurian knight's birth in the Marches between Brittany and Gaul, in another work, itself entitled the *Queste del Saint Graal,* which also dates from roughly the same period as the French Romance in its present form, Lancelot's ancestors originally came from Scotland:

In the seventh section of the *Queste* [3] Lancelot's father, King Ban, is noted as being a descendant of one "Celydoine", who, the author claims, was "the first Christian king to hold sway over Scotland." In view of this it is worth speculating as to whether or not the "Romans", despite being an apparent re-working of an earlier French original, was in fact a revised indiginous metrical romance, corrected and brought into line with the Anglo-French "Vulgate" editions that came to dominate European literature during the Middle Ages. It is definitely true to say that many Welsh bardic manuscript sources were revised following the publication of Geoffrey of Monmouth's *History of the Kings of Britain* in 1130 A.D. Considering this then, it is therefore not beyond the realms of possibility that some of the Scottish sources were likewise subjected to similar amendments.

Whatever the truth, Lancelot's other ancestors are said to have included one "Jonaan", described as "a good knight and a loyal one, and brave beyond compare". It is therefore tempting to ask, in view of this, as to whether or not "Jonaan" was the original founder of the line of Johnstone; a Border Clan which, as we have already seen, held lands in what was once the old Celtic Principality of Galloway. If this was indeed the case it might conceivably locate Lancelot's original birthplace in Scotland, as opposed to France, in the Marches between North Britain (ie. Rheged or Strathclyde) and Galloway.

Unfortunately, as will now be seen, we are unable to prove the validity of this particular line of speculation one way or the other. "The parish of Johnstone....", as the compilers of Douglas's Peerage are swift to point out, "derived its name....from its having become in Scoto-Saxon times the tun or dwelling of some person who was distinguished by the appelation of John". However, owing to the fact that in 1585 the Maxwells destroyed the Johnstones' ancient family seat at Lochwood Tower by burning it to the ground, only a handful of the most important documents relating to the Clan have survived. Thus, the first of this Clan on record is one Gilbert de Johnstoun, who appears to have flourished about the year 1200.

If it were to be the case that the Johnstones, like the Scotts, were originally of North British stock, and that like Sir Michael the Wizard they had originally possessed a book of some kind recounting their unbroken chain of descent from the likes of Celydoine and King Ban, it might do something to help us locate at least fragments of the old North British bardic tradition, other than those previously referred to elsewhere in my text, amongst the ballads that Scott collected. A possible candidate for such "scattered herbage" which Sir Walter's elephants might quite possibly, even at this late stage, be able to find, is the "ancient ballad of "king Henrie"; which is placed in Henderson's edition of the *Minstrelsy* directly after the ballad of *Prince Robert;* which has appeared elsewhere in the pages of this book.

Of this ballad, a fine modern arrangement of which appears on the "Steeleye Span" album *"Below the Salt"*, Scott has the following comments to make: "The ballad is edited from the ms. of Mrs. Brown......", who, the reader will doubtless remember, furnished Scott with much of the material incorporated into the version of the ancient ballad of *True Thomas* included in his *Border Minstrelsy*; and like it, ".....corrected by a recited fragment...." And so, through the medium of these lyrics, we find ourselves returning once again to the same bardic traditions where we earlier encountered the Rhymer and the Fairy Queen:

Let never a man a-wooing wend,
That lacketh thingis thrie:
A rowth o' gold, an open heart,
And fu' o' courtesey.

And this was seen o' King Henrie,
For he lay burd alane;
And he has ta'en him to a haunted hunt's ha',
Was seven miles frae a toun.

He's chased the dun deer thro' the wood,
And the roe doun by the den,
Till the fattest buck, in a' the herd,
King Henrie he has slain.

He's ta'en him to his hunting ha',
For to make burly cheir;
When loud the wind was heard to sound,
And an earthquake rocked the floor.

And darkness cover'd a' the hall,
Where they sat at their meat;
The gray dogs, youling, left their food,
And crept to Henrie's feet.

And louder howled the rising wind,
And burst the fast'ned door;
And in there came a griesly ghost,
Stood stamping on the floor.

Her head touched the roof-tree of the house;
Her middle ye weel mot span:
Each frightened huntsman fled the ha',
And left the King alone.

Her teeth were a' like tether stakes,
Her nose like club or mell;
And I ken neathing she appeared to be,
But the fiend that wons in hell.

"Sum meat, sum meat, ye King Henrie!
    Sum meat ye gie to me!"
"And what meat's in this house, ladye,
    That ye're na wellcum tee?"
"O ye'se gae kill your berry-brown steed,
    And serve him up to me".

O when he killed his berry-brown steed,
Wow gin his heart was sair!
She eat him a' up, skin and bane,
Left nothing but hide and hair.

"Mair meat, mair meat, ye King Henrie!
    Mair meat ye gie to me!"
"And what meat's in this house. Ladye,
    That ye're na wellcum tee?"
"O ye do slay your gude gray houndes,
    And bring them a' to me."

O when he slew his gude gray houndes,
Wow but his heart was sair!
She's ate them a' up, ane by ane,
Left nothing but hide and hair.

"Mair meat, mair meat, ye King Henrie!
    Mair meat ye gie to me!"
"And what meat's in this house, ladye,
    That I hae left to gie?"
"O ye do fell your gay goss-hawks,
    And bring them a' to me."

O when he felled his gay goss-hawks,
Wow but his heart was sair!
She's ate them a' up, bane by bane,
Left naething but feathers bare.
"Some drink, some drink, ye King Henrie!
    Some drink ye gie to me!"
"And what drink's i' this house, ladye,
    That ye're na wellcum tee?"
"O ye sew up your horse's hide,

And bring in a drink to me."

O he has sewed up the bluidy hide,
And put in a pipe of wine;
She drank it a' up at ae draught,
Left na a drap therein.

"A bed, a bed, ye King Henrie!
    A bed ye make to me!"
"And what's the bed i' this house, ladye,
    That ye're na wellcum tee?"
"O ye maun pu' the green heather,
    And make a bed to me."

O pu'd has he the heather green,
And made to her a bed;
And up he has ta'en his gay mantle,
And o'er it he has spread.

"Now swear, now swear, ye King Henrie,
    To take me for your bride!"
"O God forbid", King Henrie said,
    That e'er the like betide!
That e'er the fiend, that wons in hell,
    Should streak down by my side."

When day was come, and night was gane,
And the sun shone through the ha',
The fairest ladye that e'er was seen,
Lay atween him and the wa'.

"O weel is me!" King Henrie said,
"How lang will this last wi' me?"
And out and spake that ladye fair,
"E'en till the day ye die.
"For I was witched to a ghastly shape,
All by my stepdame's skill,
Till I should meet wi' a courteous knight,
Wad gie me a' my will."

In Sir Walter's notes to his version of this ballad, he informs the reader that the word "tee", for "to", "....is the Buchanshire and Gallovidian pronounciation"; thus indicating that the dialect of the ballad shows it to have emanated from the very region where we earlier encountered our "Silly blind Harper" of Lochmaben fame; not to mention the noble Lancelot of the Table Round. This link with Lancelot provides us with clues as to the true identity of our ballad hero, for north of the Border there never has been a King Henry; the only member of the Scottish Royal Family to have borne such a name being Henry Earl of Huntingdon; who, as we saw in an earlier chapter, was to become husband to Ada de Warenne and ancestor of the Bruce and Baliol claimants to the Scottish throne.

Scott shows certain key elements in the storyline of the ballad to parallel some of those which are to be found in the ancient Icelandic sagas. And, it is therefore possible that the reason for this may have its roots in the Teutonic influences which were to find their way into south west Scotland during the Dark Age Period: place names such as Dumfries- "the Fort of the Frisians", and nearby "Torthorwald" being indicative of the above.

But to return once again to the Arthurian hero Lancelot, the latter's own North British origins may well indicate that the Prince at the centre of the above transcribed ballad was himself of the same stock. For, just as the hero of *The Bonny Hynd* was himself transformed by Mediaeval minstrels into one of Bruce's own kinsmen, so the "King Henrie" mentioned above may well have originally been a North Briton. Circumstantial evidence of this being the case can be found in the Welsh genealogical text *Bonedd y Saint*, to which I referred earlier in connection with the ancestry of St. Collen, in the form of certain enigmatic references to a Welsh Prince known as "Ynyr"or "Ynyr Gwent".

The texts of *Bonedd y Saint,* like most of the old Mediaeval Welsh Bardic genealogies, have suffered from a certain amount of textual corruption over the centuries; largely as a result of the fragmentation of Brythonic Culture in the wake of the Anglo-Saxon and Norse invasions (including the adventure of 1066). And, in the light of the most recent researches in this field, it is now generally accepted that there were likely as not at least two Princes of this name living during the Arthurian Period [4]. In the *Life of St. Beuno,* for example, one of these same characters appears in a storyline which manifests certain not dissimilar "fantasy" elements to those encountered in the above given Border ballad. Although, instead of shapeshifting and physical

305

transformation, as a direct result of enchantment, we have people being brought back to life after their apparent decapitation; a recurring theme in Saints' Lives of the early Middle Ages; to be found everywhere in the Celtic Realms; from Dumbarton to Brittany and beyond.

In view of these facts, it is by no means impossible that the original ballad hero who later came to be transformed into "King Henry", doubtless as a direct result of some later association with Henry Earl of Huntingdon, could have been "Ynyr"- the name "Ynyr" being the Welsh equivalent of the Frankish "Henri". And, if this was the case, it is not impossible that this ballad was originally once part of a cycle of heroic ballads which were perhaps in some way the North British equivalent of the Ossianic ballads of Gaelic tradition.

Whatever, the truth, or lack of it, in the hypothesis set out during the course of the last few paragraphs, the connection between Lancelot of the Lake and Scotland may provide us with clues as to the true identity of the original "Thomas of Britain"; author of the original romance of *Tristan*; upon which Gottfried von Strassburg was to base his own epic of the same title. In the very same genealogical manuscript in which we find the genealogy of St. Collen and the pedigrees of various of Ynyr's kinfolk, we find references to a character who likewise features not only in the *Life of St. Beuno,* where we earlier encountered Ynyr, but also in the *Life of St. Kentigern;* who is himself associated with an ancient churchyard located at Hoddom in Dumfrieshire; in Scott's own time the place of residence of his friend and correspondent Charles Kirkpatrick Sharpe.

According to the old bardic genealogies, a prince named "lewdwn lluydawc o Dinas Eidyn"- Lewdwn llyuydawc of Edinburgh or Caer Eidyn, is cited as being an ancestor of St. Kentigern. The name "Lewdwn" may be a corruption of "Lywd dun" or "Horse Hill"; thus taking us back into the same territory where we earlier encountered the Laidlaws, the Macleods and the sacred "Lara" or "young mare"; not to mention the "Mari lywd" of Welsh folk tradition. In view of the fact that there is also a connection here with "Llew", the Welsh word for "Lion", as well, it is worth conjecturing as to whether or not the Johnstones of Annandale originally adopted their armorial bearings, which are flanked by both a lion and a horse, as a result of some kind of association with, or possible descent from, Lewdwn lluydawc. The fact that he is referred to as coming from the region around Edinburgh, at a time when Lancelot's own dynasty is cited in Arthurian texts as having connections with

North Berwick, which lies just a short distance from the Scottish capital, as well as their supposed ancestral homeland to the west, makes him a possible candidate for the real life Lancelot upon whom the knight of Arthurian romance was himself ultimately modelled. The fact that St. Kentigern is traditionally represented as the son of Ewein ap Urien, the Sir Owain of a poetical romance at the centre of an earlier chapter, would do much to support this idea; especially when it is considered that Kentigern's mother is cited as being a daughter of Lewdwn Lluydawc.

Another obscure Welsh dynast who has likewise featured elsewhere in this book already, and whose family may well have had some sort of connection with the death of Urien of Rheged, is Llawvrodedd varchoc or Llawfrodedd Farchog. In another old Welsh manuscript, which likewise constitutes part of the same ms. collection where we earlier encountered the Picitish Drustanus (5), Llawfrodedd Farchog is made the ancestor of a little known Welsh nobleman from Rhufoniog in Denbighshire; said to have been born around 1070. The genealogy, which, it would appear, is by no means complete, makes this man a descendant of one ".....Greddyff ap Tymyr ap Llawr ap Llawfrodedd Farchog".

And, just as "Ynyr" is the old North British equivalent of the later "Henri", or Henry, so too is "Tymyr" equitable with Thomas in the same Brythonic dialect. In view of this, and in view of the additional fact that his father is cited as being one "Llawr", whose name, like that of Lewdwn lluydawc, may have some connection with the old Gaelic "Lara" or "Lair", thus linking him with the age old emblem of the sacred horse which has featured again and again throughout the pages of this book, it is not beyond the realms of possibility that we have located the individual referred to in Islay legend as "Thomas of Power"; who is himself associated not only with the symbol of the sacred horse, but also with Dumbuck near Dumbarton. As we saw earlier, Llawfrodedd Farchog is connected, not only with the northern British dynasties of the Welsh Heroic Age, but his clan may also have had a hand in the assassination of Urien of Rheged. So, when these last facts are taken into account, it is not altogether impossible that this genealogy refers to a descent from the original "Thomas of Britain"; author of the original Arthurian romance from whence all other variant versions of the "Tristrem" legend are ultimately descended.

Another vital clue which in itself may provide us with some sort of definite indication that "Tymyr" and "Thomas of Britain" are indeed one and the same, appears in another section of the above quoted from genealogy; where, amongst Tymyr's own descendants, we find "Asser ap Gwrgi". The name Gwrgi gives us a definite link with the North British Dynasty of Dark Age York, one of the very clans involved in the Battle of Arfderydd, thus showing that it is by no means impossible that the Mediaeval Welsh warriors whose genealogies are traced in this ancient text were the descendants of men who had originally held lands in the very region where Merlin himself is known to have resided in times past. Similarly, the presence of the name "Asser" might be indicative of these self same individuals being possessed of some sort of definite physical or marital relationship, as far as their ancestors were concerned at least, with King Alfred the Great's biographer; the Welsh monk of the same name.

In effect then, on the face of the above evidence, it is again not unreasonable to conclude, that in view of the fact that Llawfrodedd Farchog's Clan carry names that would appear to connect them with North Britain, Yorkshire, and quite possibly Wessex and the Principality of the Hwiccas, Thomas of Ercildoune himself might have had some sort of dynastic link with this same family. If this is or was the case, it is quite feasible that he was a descendant of Tymyr ap Llawr, and that the *Sir Tristrem* that Sir Walter believed him to have composed may well have been modelled directly on Tymyr's original North British version of the *Tristan* legends.

The Anglo-Norman *Tristan of Thomas,* which was to provide Gottfriend von Strassbourg with the inspiration for his own version of the story, was itself quite defintely the bi-product of the intermingling of Welsh, Breton and other influences in the wake of the Norman Conquest; a coming together of ideas which has been explored over and over again throughout the preceeding chapters in my text. To find the original human source of the Celtic Arthurian elements in this cycle of legends, however, one must get as close to the Dark Ages as is humanly possible; and this is precisely where this genealogy does take us when it identifies an individual named Tymyr or Thomas living just a few generations after Merlin and Arthur.

And so, in the person of Tymyr ap Llawr, we may have located not only the source of the original Tristrem legend, but also the ancestor of Thomas of Ercildoune himself.

But what of Merlin the Magician, whose extensive links with the Border region, where both Scott himself and his hero the Rhymer are likewise

308

known to have resided in the centuries that followed, have been looked at over and over again throughout this book? A little known Welsh genealogy, preserved amongst the pages of Gould and Fisher's *Lives of the British Saints*, traces his ancestry back to Old King Cole through Mar ap Ceneu, ancestor of the chieftains in command of both sides in the much lamented Battle of Arfderydd; at which he himself is said to have gone mad. Perhaps this explains the reason for his sudden loss of sanity, as two septs of his own clan battled it out over a territorial dispute; instead of uniting against a common Saxon foe.

Scott's *Bridal of Triermain* finds Merlin pouring scorn upon the warring factions of the Table Round, following the death of his legendary kinsman Vanoc. Vanoc's own name gives us a link with the town of Vannes on the Breton Coast; itself just a short distance south west of the ancient Forest of Broceliande; where Merlin's own mythical encounter with the enchantress Vivien, immortalized by the nineteenth century poet Alfred Lord Tennyson, is believed to have taken place.

Further north, in the vicinity of Mont St. Michel, a series of Mediaeval traditions connect a site known as "Tomberlaine" with the rape and abduction of the daughter of a local Breton chieftain by a wandering Spanish giant known as "Dinabuc". (6). Perhaps, given the fact that Tristan himself has a close association with Brittany, in particular with the area around the Ile Tristan on the western seaboard, Thomas might also have some distant connection with the Armorican Peninsular as well. If this should turn out to be the case, it may well be that the name of the Spanish giant responsible for this violation may have been corrupted out of "Dumbuck" or "Dun-a-bhuic". And, on the face of this evidence, it is not inconceivable that, just as the Iberian ogre's name has been corrupted out of that of a location, so too could the name of the place where the rape is alleged to have happened have been derived directly from that of an individual. And, as we shall now see, the individual from whose name "Tombelaine" may well have become corrupted, over the course of time, is himself the hero of another of Scott's Border ballads; itself in all probability one of the most famous songs from this region to have come down to modern times. This song, as we shall now see, provides definite clues, once again, to definite Pictish associations with the area around Carterhaugh on the confluence of the Ettrick and Yarrow Valleys; itself just a stone's throw from Sir Walter's beloved "Abbotsford".

309

Chapter Fifteen

The Young Tamlane

O I forbid ye, maidens a,
That wear gowd in your hair,
To come or gae by Carterhaugh;
For young Tamlane is there.

There's nane, that gaes by Carterhaugh,
But maun leave him a wad;
Either gowd rings, or green mantles,
Or else their maidenhead.

Now, gowd rings ye may buy, maidens,
Green mantles ye may spin;
But, gin ye lose your maidenhead,
Ye'll ne'er get that again.

But up then spak her, fair Janet,
The fairest O' a' kin;
"I'll cum and gang to Carterhaugh,
And ask nae leave o' him."

Janet has kilted her green kirtle,
A little aboune her knee;
And she has braided her yellow hair,
A little abune her bree.

And when she cam to Carterhaugh,
She gaed beside the well;
And there she fand his steed standing,
But away was himsell.

She hadna pu'd a red red rose,
A rose but barely three;
Till up and starts a wee wee man,
At Lady Janet's knee.

Says- "Why pu'ye the rose, Janet?
What gars ye break the tree?
Or why come ye to Carterhaugh,
Withouten leave o' me?"

Says- "Carterhaugh it is mine ain;
My daddie gave it me;
I'll come and gang to Carterhaugh,
And ask nae leave o' thee".

He's ta'en her by the milk-white hand,
Amang the leaves sae green;
And what they did I cannot tell-
The green leaves were between.

He's ta'en her by the milk-white hand,
Amang the roses red;
And what they did I cannot say-
She ne'er returned a maid.

When she cam to her father's ha'
She looked pale and wan;
They thought she'd dried some sair sickness,
Or been wi' some leman.

She didna' comb her yellow hair,
Nor make meikle o' her heid;
And ilka thing, that lady took,
Was like to be her deid.

It's four-and-twenty ladies fair
Were playing at the ba';
Janet the wightest of them anes,
Was faintest o' them a'.

Four-and-twenty ladies fair
Were playing at the chess;
And out there came the fair Janet,
As green as any grass.

Out and spak an auld gray-headed knight,
Lay o'er the castle wa'-
"And ever alas! For thee Janet,
But we'll be blamed a'!"

"Now haud your tongue, ye auld gray knight!
And an ill deid may ye die;
Father my bairn on whom I will,
I'll father nane on thee."

Out then spak her father dear,
And he spak meik and mild-
"And ever alas! My sweet Janet,
I fear ye gae with child".

"And, if I be with child, father,
'Twil prove a wondrous birth;
For weel I swear I'm not wi' bairn
To any man on earth.

"If my love were an earthly knight,
As he's an elfin grey,
I wadna gie my ain true love
For nae lord that ye hae".

She princked hersell and prinn'd hersell,
By the ae light of the moon,
And she's away to Carterhaugh,
To speak wi' young Tamlane.

And when she cam to Carterhaugh,
She gaed beside the well;
And there she saw the steed standing,
But away was himsell.

She hadna pu'd a double rose,
A rose but only twae,
When up and started young Tamlane,
Says- "Lady, thou pu's nae mae!

"Why pu' ye the rose, Janet,
Within this garden grene,
And a' to kill the bonny babe,
That we got us between?"

"The truth ye'll tell to me, Tamlane;
A word ye mauna lie;
Gin e'er ye was in haly chapel,
Or sained in Chrisentie."

"The truth I'll tell to thee, Janet,
A word I winna lie;
A knight me got, and a lady me bore,
As well as they did thee."

"Randolph, Earl Murray, was my sire,
Dunbar, Earl March, is thine;
We loved when we were children small,
Which yet you well may mind.

"When I was a boy, just turned of nine,
My Uncle sent for me,
To hunt, and hawk, and ride with him,
And keep him cumpanie.

"There came a wind out of the north
A sharp wind and a snell;
And a dead sleep came over me,
And frae my horse I fell.

"The Queen of Fairies keppit me,
In yon green hill to dwell;
And I'm a fairy, lyth and limb,
Fair ladye, view me well.

"But we that live in Fairy-land,
No sickness know, nor pain;
I quit my body when I will,
And take to it again.

"I quit my body when I please,
Or unto it repair;
We can inhabit, at our ease,
In either earth or air.

"Our shapes and size we can convert,
To either large or small;
An old nut-shell's the same to us,
As is the lofty hall.

"We sleep in rose-buds, soft and sweet,
We revel in the stream;
We wanton lightly on the wind,
Or glide on a sun-beam.

"And all our wants are well supplied,
From every rich man's store,
Who thankless sins the gifts he gets,
And vainly grasps for more.

"Then I would never tire, Janet,
In Elfish land to dwell;
But aye at every seven years,
They pay the teind to hell;
And I am sae fat, and fair of flesh,
I fear 'twill be mysell.

"This night is Hallowe'en, Janet,
The morn is Hallowday;
And gin ye dare your true love win,
Ye hae na time to stay.

"The night it is good Hallowe'en,
When Fairy folk will ride;
And they, that wad their true love win,
At Miles Cross they maun bide."

"But how shall I thee ken, Tamlane?
Or how shall I thee knaw,
Amang so many unearthly knights,
The like I never saw?"

"The first company that passes by,
Say na, and let them gae;
The next company, that passes by,
Say na, and do right sae;
The third company, that passes by,
Then I'll be ane o' thae.

"First let pass the black, Janet,
And syne let pass the brown;
But grip ye to the milk-white steed,
And pu' the rider down.

"For I ride on the milk-white steed,
And aye nearest the town;
Because I was a christened knight,
They gave me that renown.

"My right hand will be gloved, Janet.
My left hand will be bare;
And these the tokens I gie thee,
Nae doubt I will be there.

"They'll turn me in your arms, Janet
An adder and a snake;
But had me fast, let me not pass,
Gin ye wad be my maike.

"They'll turn me in your arms, Janet,
An adder and an ask;
They'll turn me in your arms, Janet,
A bale that burns fast.

"They'll turn me in your arms, Janet,
A red-hot gad o' airn;
But had me fast, let me not pass,
For I'll do you no harm.

"First dip me in a stand o' milk,
And then in a stand o' water;
But had me fast, let me not pass-
I'll be your bairn's father.

"And, next, they'll shape me in your arms,
A tod, but and an eel;
But had me fast, nor let me gang,
As you do love me weel.

"They'll shape me in your arms, Janet,
A dove, but and a swan;
And, last, they'll shape me in your arms,
A mother-naked man:
Cast your green mantle over me-
I'll be myself again."

Gloomy, gloomy, was the night,
And eiry was the way,
As fair Janet in her green mantle,
To Miles Cross she did gae.

The heavens were black, the night was dark,
And dreary was the place;
But Janet stood, with eager wish,
Her lover to embrace.

Betwixt the hours of twelves and one,
A north wind tore the bent;
And straight she heard strange elritch sounds
Upon that wind which went.

About the dead hour o' the night,
She heard the bridles ring;
And Janet was as glad o' that,
As any earthly thing!

Their oaten pipes blew wondrous shrill,
The hemlock small blew clear;
And louder notes from hemlock large,
And bog-reed struck the ear;
But solemn sounds, or sober thoughts,
The Fairies cannot bear.

They sing, inspired with love and joy,
Like sky-larks in the air;
Of solid sense or thought that's grave,
You'll find no traces there.

Fair Janet stood, with mond unmoved,
The dreary heath upon;
And louder, louder, wax'd the sound.
As they came riding on.

Will o' Wisp before them went,
Sent forth a twinkling light;
And soon she saw the Fairy bands
All riding in her sight.

And first gaed by the black black steed,
And then gaed by the brown;
But fast she gript the milk-white steed,
And pu'd the rider down.

She pu'd him frae the milk-white steed,
And loot the bridle fa';
And up there raise an erlish cry-
"He's won amang us a'!"

They shaped him in fair Janet's arms,
An esk, but and an adder;
She held him fast in every shape-
To be her bairn's father.

They shaped him in her arms at last,
A mother-naked man;
She wrapt him in her green mantle,
And sae her true love wan.

Up then spake the Queen o' Fairies,
Out o' a bush o' broom-
"She that has borrowed young Tamlane,
Has gotten a stately groom."

Up then spake the Queen of Fairies,
Out o' a bush of rye-
"She's ta'en awa the bonniest knight
In a' my cumpanie.

"But had I kenn'd, Tamlane", she says,
"A lady wad borrow'd thee-
I wad ta'en out thy twa gray een,
Put in twa een o' tree.

"Had I but kenn'd, Tamlane," she says,
"Before ye came frae hame-
I wad tane out your heart o' flesh,
Put in a heart o' stane.

"Had I but had the wit yestreen,
That I hae coft the day-
I'd paid my kane seven times to hell,
Ere you'd been won away!"

For those readers familiar with the recorded works of 'sixties folk rockers "Fairport Convention", it will be noted that the arrangement of this ballad made famous by them, some three decades or so ago, differs considerably from that collected by Scott. Of this version, the Laird of Abbotsford, in his *Introduction to the Tale of Tamlane* in the *Minstrelsy*, has the following comments to make:

"The present edition is the most perfect which has yet appeared, being prepared from a collation of the printed copies with a very accurate one in Glenriddel's M.S.S., and with several recitals from tradition....."

Elsewhere, in the same essay, he refers to the ballad as "still popular in Ettrick Forest where the scene is laid," whilst adding that it "is certainly of much greater antiquity than its phraseology, gradually modernized as transmitted by tradition, would seem to denote. *The Tale of the Young Tamlane* is mentioned in the *Complaynt of Scotland;* and the air, to which it was chaunted, seems to have been accomodated to a particular dance; for the dance of "Thom of Lynn", another version of "Thomalin", likewise occurs in the same performance. Like every popular subject, it seems to have been frequently parodied; and a burlesque ballad, beginning

Tom o' Linn was a Scotsman born....

is still well known."

The reader will notice that many of the key elements incorporated into the storyline of this mighty ballad have already been encountered amongst the ballads, myths, legends, poetry and song previously encountered during the course of the preceeding chapters. The geographical location to which we are here transported is the very same one to which we were previously taken by the lyrics of *The Wee Wee Man* in the opening chapters of this work. Further on in the text such elements as human sacrifice, as portrayed in *The Well Below the Valley,* shape shifting, as it appears in the Taliesin Cycles, the football game encountered in the ballad of *Little Sir Hugh,* all mixed up with guarded references to what would appear to be fragments of Ancient Celtic Plant Lore, as manifest in the lyrical arrangement, in which magical plants, such as bog-reed and broom, feature as readily as what would likewise seem to be yet more indications of the presence of those Fairy Steeds we have encountered so often in our story, tend to suggest, as in the case of the Ballad of *True Thomas,* that we have here yet another lost remnant of ancient indiginous folklore; certain aspects of which may well be of ultimate Pictish provenance.

Indeed, more than this even, we may, in the person of Tamlane, Tomm o' Linn, Thom of Lynn or Thomalin, as he is variously referred to, be encountering here yet another manifestation of Tymyr ap Llawr, the ancient Cymric nobleman who himself provided the model for Gottfried von Strassbourg's *Thomas of Britain*. As previously noted by Sir Walter himself, the general mythical content and storyline of the ballad appear to indicate a considerably earlier origin than the language in which the presently available transcriptions are composed. The reference to the Fairy Queen speaking "Out o' a bush of rye" in the closing stanzas shows that the earliest date to which the forerunner of the version here re-printed from Scott could have come into being was in the decades immediately after the introduction of rye, originally an Asiatic cereal crop, into Western Europe following the return of the Frankish soldiery from the Crusades.

This fact would appear to substantiate the previously made conjecture that the original ballad hero was of Cymric origin, and this ballad, like so many we have looked at during the course of our exploration of these ancient traditions, was in some way linked to the now largely lost or obscured repertoire of Thomas the Rhymer; and his namesake and predecessor, Thomas of Britain. The ballad itself, in one version at least, is alleged to have associations with Sir Michael Scott's one time residence at Oakwood or Aikwood Tower. Indeed, Scott makes direct reference to this fact in his previously quoted from *Introduction*.

Sir Michael himself, as has already been seen, is known to have possessed extensive connections with the Emperor Frederick II of Hohenstauffen, a Crusading monarch noted for his patronage of Mediaeval Troubadours. And, amongst the many Arthurian epics popular at the Emperor Frederick's court were the compositions of Wolfram von Eschenbach; whose Grail Romance *"Parzival"*, itself based on an earlier, unfinished work, by Chretien de Troyes, was to provide the libretto for Wagner's celebrated opera *"Parsifal"*. In *"Parzival"* we find extensive evidence of a gradual "Asiaticization" of Western Grail Tradition, in that many of the names, locations and characters that appear in it, such as Ipomidon King of Babylon, are clearly of Middle Eastern, as opposed to Celtic origin; as had previously been the norm.

320

Another of Wolfram's characters is the enigmatic Prester John, a legendary priest king whose origins are placed in India by Mediaeval chroniclers and poets. These late literary adaptations may be linked with many of the legends associated with the semi-mythical "Takt-i-Taqdis" or "Throne of Arches", constructed by the Parthian Chosroes II King of Persia as the intended resting place for a supposed portion of the True Cross which he himself had pillaged from Jerusalem. And, in view of this, the name "Tamlane", as it is given in the ballad, may in turn be a corruption, or Asiaticization, of "Tymyr ap Llawr" to "Tamburlaine" or "Timur-i-leng", who was in reality the fourteenth century Turko-Mongol conqueror of Asia. Timur and Prester John appear to have had much in common, aside from the fact that, unlike the mythical Indian Priest King, who was supposed to be Christian, he himself was a follower of the Prophet Mohammed. As has also previously been noted, there may be a connection with a Breton named Tomberlaine; a fact which was hinted at in the closing paragraphs of the preceeding chapter.

Interestingly enough, Scott's own ancestors, the Scotts of Harden, are known to have been the principal occupiers of Aikwood Tower after the 1620s; themselves being descendants of William Scott, second son of Robert Scott of Strickshawes, who had acquired the charters to the lands and barony of Harden in the year 1535. Previous to this, the family who almost certainly constructed the building referred to in a charter of 1541 as "unam honestam masionem cum turre", were that of Maister Michael Scott, a namesake and kinsman of the mediaeval Wizard, hence the probable origin of Sir Michael's legendary association with this particular locality.

Just a stone's throw from Aikwood, itself the newly restored and renovated abode of the Liberal Democrat politician Sir David Steel, is the remains of a Mediaeval motte, of considerably earlier provenance. In the chapter on *The Wee Wee Man* I made reference to how modern ordnance survey maps indicate its apparent geomantic alignment with Carterhaugh, the geographical location of this ballad; as well as the ancient Yarrow Stone; itself another place of importance in Scott's *Minstrelsy,* in that it, in turn, is associated with the ballad of *The Dowie Dens of Yarrow,* an all time classic which could still be heard amongst the folk singing traditions of such travelling families as the Stewarts of Blair right into our own century. It would also appear to be aligned with the remains of an ancient series of prehistoric defensive earthworks, themselves referred to by Scott in his previously quoted from introduction to the *Sir Tristrem,* known as the Catrail; as well as the peak of nearby Mountbenger Law; a prominent landmark in the locality.

Perhaps this Mediaeval earthwork marks the spot where the now vanished stronghold of Sir Michael le Scot once stood. We shall never know for sure. What we can be sure of, however, is that long before Sir Michael took up residence in this particular part of the Borders two other strongholds located within a very short distance of Carterhaugh, one atop of a series of earthworks just north of Torwoodlee Mains, a mansion just northwest of Galashiels, and another, on the eastern bank of Gala Water, above the Dalkeith Road, just a short distance to the north, would appear to attest to a Pictish presence in the region at some point during the Iron Age Period.

The defensive structures which formerly stood on these sites are of a specific type referred to by archaeologists as "Brochs". Like the tower houses of the fifteenth and sixteenth century Border Reivers, these defensive strongholds, built originally by, and for the use and occupation of a warrior aristocracy, predominate in the northernmost reaches of Transmarine Scotland; amongst the ancient Pictish Princedoms so often referred to throughout this text. Perhaps the original occupants of these once mighty strongholds provided the model for the Fairy Folk of later folklore; on account of their undoubted racial, ethnic and religious differences from the indiginous North Britons of the surrounding area.

Perhaps the Fairy Hall to which the ballad singer in *The Wee Wee Man* transports the listener was in reality located at one of these sites. At nearby Edin's Hall in Berwickshire, another ruined Broch came to be associated with the legend of a Giant, so why not a Fairy occupant, or occupants, for either one of these two locations? Could the magical contest between Fair Janet and the Fairy Queen for the hand of the hero of this ballad have its origins in a real dynastic rivalry between an indiginous Iron Age Princess and an invading Pictish heiress from the north?

As has already been seen, the Picts elected Kings and Chieftains from candidates whose eligibility was determined by a system of matrilinear descent. Archaeological evidence from Burghead on the Moray Firth would appear to suggest that they practised human sacrifice on occasion. Could the ballad of *Tamlane* preserve some ancient folk memory of the escape of the intended victim of some such mischief, whose own adventures have likewise been grafted on to later legends associated with Tymyr ap Llawr, Thomas of Britain, and possibly, at some stage during their constant telling and re-telling, Thomas the Rhymer himself?

Whatever the true answers to these questions, we have already looked at a considerable amount of evidence which would suggest a definite link between at least some of the elements that make up the Border Minstrel Tradition, and the long lost myths of the Ancient Picts. Again, in this ballad there are references to the Earl of Moray and the Earl of March; the intermarriage between the respective dynasties of these two individuals having been looked at in the chapters immediately preceeding this one. And, in the chapter on "Cospatrick", itself dedicated to a ballad primarily concerned with the life and times of the ancestor of Thomas the Rhymer's patrons, the Marcher Lords of the High Middle Ages, we noted the presence of recurring references to the daughters of seven kings. Likewise, the reference to the Earl of Moray would hint at a geographical link between this ballad, the landscape in which it is set, and one of the foremost ancient Pictish Kingdoms, albeit a Mediaeval one; an avenue constantly explored throughout the preceeding pages; in particular with respect to the ballad of *The Bonny Hynd*; in which both the Earls of Moray and the Earls of March likewise feature. This in itself almost certainly tends to suggest that not only are these two ballads directly connected, but that they ultimately proceeded out of a single body of bardic literature; itself almost certainly connected with that originally in the possession, or more accurately the oral repertoire, of the Rhymer of Ercildoune himself.

Scott in his turn, as has likewise already been seen, would have been totally unaware of these connections, for reasons outlined again and again throughout this book. The fact that such traditions have been preserved amongst the ballads that he collected and published, whilst he himself had no visible knowledge of their true significance, adds further weight to the validity of my own suppositions as regards his dutiful dedication to meticulous scholarship; something which will now come under further discussion in the chapter that follows.

Chapter Sixteen

Of Robin Hood and Arthur Bold.......

"Sae Bauld Arthur's gane to our King's Court,
His hie chamberlain to be;
But Brown Robin, he has slain a knight,
And to grene-woode he did flee...."
        The Ballad of Rose the Red and White Lilly.

A.N.Wilson, in his introduction to the 1982 Penguin edition of Scott's *Ivanhoe*, with respect to the Laird of Abbotsford's inclusion of Robin Hood and his Merry Men as a key element in the novel's storyline, compares Scott's characterization of the famous outlaw with that of Rob Roy in his novel of the same title."Robin Hood, he says, "is the exact counterpart of Rob Roy, the outlaw fundamentally on the side of justice and an outlawed king; or, in *Waverley*, of Fergus MacIvor, holding court in his mountain fastness. The usurping prince and the wicked barons bear very obvious resemblances to the Scotch view of generations of Whig Governments in London. Thus, in *Ivanhoe*, the key remains Scott's domestic preoccupations with the fate of his own nation. For "Normans" read "English"; for "English", read "Scots"; for "Plantagenet", read "Hanoverian", for the line of Athelstane, that of the exiled Stuarts; for the destruction of the Anglo-Saxon tongue, read that of Gaelic......"

Elsewhere, in the same introduction, Wilson attributes Scott's inclusion of Robin Hood in this novel to the influence of Joseph Ritson's 1795 two volume collection of *Robin Hood ballads;* one of the most comprehensive and exhaustive explorations of the folklore relating to the legacy of Robin of Sherwood ever attempted.

It is within the pages of the *Minstrelsy* however, another work which owes a considerable debt to Ritson's work as a folklorist, that we first encounter references to the celebrated outlaw amongst Scott's voluminous writings.

Amongst the ballads collected, collated and printed by the Laird of Abbotsford from the pages of Mrs. Brown's celebrated M.S. is a little known ballad entitled *Rose the Red and White Lilly*, from which the verse at the head of this chapter was itself quoted. In Scott's somewhat scanty introductory notes to this equally obscure ballad, the Author of *Waverley* conjectures that "the ballad may have originally related to the history of the celebrated Robin Hood, as mention is made of Barnisdale, his favourite abode......"

Bishop Percy, in his own introductory notes to a version of the ballad of *Robin Hood and Guy of Gisborne*, which appears in Volume One of his *Reliques,* makes mention of the Antiquarian William Stukeley's assertions, that the actual historical character upon whom the hero of ballad tradition was based was himself a claimant to the Earldom of Huntingdon; "and that his true name was Robert Fitz-ooth." These ideas of Stukeley's have been pretty much dismissed out of hand, even in the century in which he lived, Percy himself being amongst their foremost critics. However, extensive research into the ancestry of the Family of St. Liz, who were eventually restored to the rights of the Earldom of Huntingdon by the English Crown, has revealed that the name "Fitz-ooth", as it is represented by Stukeley, may well be a corruption of "Fitz-Uhtred".

The Norman appelation "Fitz", like the Scottish "Mac", Welsh "Map" and Irish "Mic", signifies the "son" of a particular individual. And, the Uhtred from whom the St. Liz Family, and their predecessor, with respect to the Rights of the Earldom of Huntingdon and Northumberland, were descended, through Matilda, daughter of Waltheof Earl of Northumberland, Northampton and Huntingdon, by his marriage to Judith, a neice of William the Conqueror, was none other than Uhtred, Prince Bishop of Chester-le-Street; principal ruler of Northumberland between 995 and 1016 A.D. and himself the son-in-law of King Ethelred II of England. (See Appendix 3, Table 2).

Although much of the research relating to the genealogical relationships between Uhtred's later Mediaeval successors has been confused by Dugdale, and others, it is generally accepted that one of his female descendants was married to Robert, fifth son of Richard de Tonbridge; Steward to King Henry I. The son of that union, one Walter fitz Robert, is himself noted as being the father of one Robert Fitz Walter, who is in turn noted as being a "leading rebel against King John and styled "Marshal of the Army of God and Holy Church."

Perhaps this is the individual upon whom the character of Robin Hood in Mediaeval Romance was ultimately based. It is most likely his grave that lies close to Kirklees Priory in Yorkshire. But, as to the origin of many of the Robin Hood legends, in order to find their roots, like the root of origin of many a ballad and Arthurian Tradition, we must go even further back; to the very dawn of myth and history itself.

The reader will have noticed, from the quoted verse from *Rose the Red and White Lilly* at the head of this chapter, that, in the case of this particular ballad, *Brown Robin* is here portrayed alongside another figure, referred to in the sixty or so verses of Mrs. Brown's ballad as *Bauld Arthur*. One is tempted here to jump to the conclusion that, in this ballad at least, the two greatest heros of Mediaeval Folklore, Robin Hood and King Arthur, make their appearance as brothers in this somewhat obscure Border Ballad. The ballad's storyline contains many of the elements common to a great number of those that we have already encountered elsewhere in the text: a cruel stepmother, fated love, the accidental slaying of a lover brought about, ultimately, as a result of the machinations of the villainess in the piece, and so forth. At no point is there any clue as to the true identities of the ballad heros, our two brothers, Robin and Arthur.

In chapter one we looked at the Arthurian connections with what is now modern day Cumbria; with particular reference to the area around Carlisle. In view of this then, it may come as no surprise that Cumbria, like Barnisdale, has its own ancient and longstanding associations with brigandry and outlawry along the lines of that practised by Robin and his band of outlaws in all of the legends associated with Sherwood Forest. Although no actual oral traditions by way of ballads directly related to the Cumbrian outlaws herementioned survived into Scott's time, Percy successfully unearthed a ballad, in the classic *Robin Hood Genre* as explored by Ritson, and categorized as such by James Reed on page 98 of his *Border Ballads*, in which some of these long forgotten heros are referred to by name.

The ballad itself, which is entitled *Adam Bell, Clym of the Clough and William of Cloudesley*, appears in Volume 2 of Percy's *Reliques*, where it is noted that the three individuals of the title "were three noted outlaws, whose skill in archery rendered them formerly as famous in the North of England, as Robin Hood and his fellows were in the Midland Counties. Their place of residence" he then adds, "was in the Forest of Englewood, not far from Carlisle......"

As the reader will already have seen, in chapter five, Englewood or Inglewood was one of the locations which may have had some kind of association with "Wat the English", the supposed brother of the founder of Clan Scot, who, like Scott's own direct male line ancestor, is described as being descended from amongst the ancient indiginous tribal inhabitants of what were later to become the Borders; collectively referred to in Roman sources as "the Brigantes". The fact that many of these self same tribespeople may have retreated into the forests to escape the oppression of the Roman Yoke, much as the rebellious Saxons were to in Robin Hood's time, living an existence not dissimilar to that indulged in by the Merry Men of Sherwood, may have given rise to the modern word "Brigand", or outlaw, in the contemporary English language. And, given that such outlawry may well have existed in King Arthur's own time, provides us with a clue as to how both Arthur and Robin came to feature in the same ballad as contemporaries.

Arthur himself is represented in all Mediaeval Arthurian Tradition as being the son of Utherpendragon - Uther being the latter's forename, whilst Pendragon refers to his title: The self same epithet that Maelgwn of Gwynedd was later to adopt upon succeeding Arthur as principal war leader of the Cymru- that of "Chief Dragon" or "High King" of all Britain. Hence, in the Book of Gildas, he is referred to as "insularis Draco". Arthur too would doubtless have held the same title, and the reason why he is never referred to in Mediaeval texts, such as Geoffrey of Monmouth, as "Arthurpendragon", may well have originally been to distinguish him from his father, as "Uther", like the Breton "Withur" is merely another rendition of the name Arthur; much as "Koel" or "Coyl" are variant spellings of Old King Coel's own name.

We have now unearthed a vital clue as to the identities of the two heros of the Brown M.S. ballad. The reason for this is because some of the Mediaeval accounts of Uther's own life that have come down to us refer to him as being the brother of a far earlier Dark Age hero, who, in reality, lived at least one, possibly two, generations before Uther himself, and whose name is Ambrosius Aurelianus. In fact, Ambrosius Aurelianus was in all probability the Grandfather of Uther, if the Breton sources are to be believed, and in reality Uther's own brother may well have been the hero of another old Welsh folk tale whose name was not Ambrosius Aurelianus, but Ambrosius Merlin.

It is at this point that the picture starts to get a little clearer, especially when it is realized that the original mythological archetype, who provided the model for Robin Hood of the ballads, was not some half-Norman, half-Northumbrian warrior aristocrat who rebelled against the Mediaeval tyranny of John Plantagenet, but the Saxon "Rof Breoht Woden"; whose name, literally translated means "Bright Strength of Woden"; and who is in turn identified by Robert Graves, in chapter twenty-two of his *White Goddess*, with Merddyn or Merddin Wyllt; "Merlin of the Wildwood"; himself an inhabitant of the very region where Scott's own ancestors were to flee, in the company of their Inglewood or Englewood kinsman, in the years immediately after the arrival of the marauding Vikings off the western coasts of North Britain. And this, in all probability, is how Arthur, or Uther, came to feature, along with a Saxon personification of Merlin, in a Robin Hood ballad from the Scottish Borders. For, it is by no means impossible that the inhabitants of Englewood may well have been descended, as has already been conjectured, in part at least, from ancient Cymric stock; and to have taken at least some of their legends into the forest with them when they were forced to retreat from the piratical incursions of plunderers from abroad during the Dark Age and Pre-Norman Periods. And that this ballad was a fragmentary survival of those self same traditions.

In view of the clear antiquity of much of the material contained in Mrs. Brown's quite remarkable manuscript collection, it is also worth noting that, in the notes to the ballad inserted directly after *Rose the Red and White Lilly* in Scott's *Border Minstrelsy*, a piece entitled *Fause Foodrage*, with particular reference to a line that occurs in it, in verse 31, and which runs as follows:

The boy stared wild like a gray goss-hawk,

the Author of Waverley observes that the above given "expression....strongly resembles that in *Hardyknute.....*" (itself published in 1719 by Sir Gilbert Elliot, the Lord Justice Clerk of Scotland, and Lord Advocate Duncan Forbes of Culloden):

Norse e'en like gray goss-hawk stared wild.

"A circumstance which led the Editor (ie. Scott himself) to make the strictest enquiry into the authenticity of the song. But every doubt was removed by the evidence of a lady of high rank, who not only recollected the ballad, as having amused her infancy, but could repeat many of the verses.......The Editor is therefore compelled to believe that the author of *Hardyknute* copied the old ballad; if the coincidence be not altogether accidental....."

Thus, once again, in spite of what Scott's latter day critics would have us believe, we are presented with direct evidence of the Laird of Abbotsford's meticulous dedication to scholarship. This in itself proves beyond question that the fragments of Ancient Arthurian, Northumbrian, and indeed Picitish tradition which survived in the late Mediaeval and Jacobean ballad and romance traditions that he and his colleagues collected, were indeed genuine survivals from a far off era, and not the elaborate inventions of a mischevious Border Peasantry. Such hidden references to Arthur and Merlin, who is here portrayed in his Saxon manifestation, provide incontrovertible proof of this; as Scott himself possessed insufficient knowledge to ascertain such facts for himself and the readership that he was writing for.

We shall now move on to the next stage in our journey, where we shall look still further on the effects of the demise of Pictish and Gaelic Culture on the traditions of indiginous myth, ballad and oral history. First stop along the way, as we near our final destination, is the ancient town of Dunfermline; sometime royal centre of the Anglo-Scottish Kings.

Chapter Seventeen

The King Sits in Dunfermline Town.......

The King sits in Dunfermline town,
Drinking the blude-red wine;
"O whare will I get a skeely skipper,
To sail this new ship of mine?"

The Ballad of Sir Patrick Spens.

As has previously been noted, at the very opening of our story, Scott himself was to organize the ballads that were to become edited into the *Minstrelsy* into the three separate categories of "Historical Ballads", "Romantic Ballads" and "Imitations of the Ancient Ballad". In view of this, it is perhaps surprising, that the very first ballad to appear in the section of his work under the heading of "Historical Ballads", that of "Sir Patrick Spens", is centred upon a story which has no historical basis to support any of the incidents recounted in it whatsoever.

Scott, it seems, would appear to have been aware of this fact, for, in his introductory notes to the version of the ballad which he himself was to edit and publish, he makes the following comment, when speaking of the voyage and shipwreck recounted in the ballad's storyline: "I find no traces of the disaster in Scottish history; but when we consider the meagre materials whence Scottish history is drawn, this is no conclusive argument against the truth of the tradition...."; thus referring to the ballad being a possible fiction; whilst at the same time justifying its inclusion in the section of the *Minstrelsy* here referred to. But the real hint as to why the Laird of Abbotsford, whose meticulous attention to scholarship has been conclusively proven throughout the preceeding pages, should want to include these lyrics in a section devoted to actual historical ballads as such, is itself contained in the opening paragraphs of his own previously quoted from introductory notes:

"One edition of the present ballad is well known, having appeared in the *Reliques of Ancient Poetry,* and having been inserted in almost every subsequent collection of Scottish songs. But it seems to have occurred to the editor that a more complete copy of the song might be procured. That with which the public is now presented is taken from two MS. Copies, collated with several verses recited by the Editor's friend, Robert Hamilton, Esq., advocate......."

The influence of Percy's *Reliques* upon the young Scott has already been explored in depth at an earlier juncture. In view of what we have already observed in relation to this it is safe to conjecture that by publishing a more complete edition of *Sir Patrick Spens*, in the opening pages of the *Minstrelsy,* Scott was clearly intending to demonstrate a certain degree of innovativeness in a field of scholarship into which others, such as Percy, had already made substantial inroads. It is also possible, that by paying lip service to Percy, Scott wished to avoid the scathing ciriticism that Macpherson, the publisher of *Ossian,* had encountered when his translations were brought to the attention of the intellectual elite of London; people like Dr. Johnson; of whose literary circle Bishop Percy of Dromore was himself a member. The *Ossian* controversy was in itself of special interest to Scott, owing to the fact that both Professor Ferguson, himself a Gaelic speaking Highlander, and Hugh Blair, were themselves instrumental in bringing Macpherson's text into publication.

In the notes to Percy's version of the ballad, which is placed in Book One, directly before his *Robin Hood and Guy of Gisborne,* we find an editorial comment which echoes those of Scott, in relation to the previously explored ballad of *Rose the Red and White Lilly* which we looked at in the preceeding chapter. With respect to some of the phraseology used in the last verse of *Sir Patrick Spens*, or *Spence,* as it appears in the *Reliques,* Percy himself has the following to say:

"An ingenious friend thinks the Author of Hardyknute has borrowed several expressions and sentiments from the foregoing, and other old Scottish songs in his collection......"

In this way Scott was to place himself firmly out of reach of English critics anxious to demean or debase the Scottish traditions he was to collect. Macpherson had doubtless suffered as a direct result of the intellectual rivalries which had existed between the literary circles of London, and those of Edinburgh, during the Enlightenment Period. Edinburgh, the "Athens of the North", and the home of David Hume and Adam Smith, was, together with Paris, one of the two unrivalled intellectual capitals of Europe; leaving the London of the time a sad third in terms of scientific and literary distinction. Indeed, many of the foremost intellects of the English Capital, men such as Dr. Hunter, the noted surgeon, Allan Ramsay, the Court painter and a distinguished man of letters, and of course Johnson's friend and biograher, James Boswell, were themselves Scots; with far more in common with the likes of Professor Ferguson and Dugald Stewart than the English intellectuals with whom they sat at table.

As for the ballad, the reference to "Dunfermline town" in the first verse is perhaps illustrative of the demise of Gaelic and Pictish Culture, along with the complete eclipse of the Celtic Church by that of Rome, which took place with the Anglo-Norman Ascendancy of the High Middle Ages; which, as we have already seen, began in earnest with the arrival of St. Margaret in Scotland. Dunfermline was to be the site of the great church she founded, intended primarily as a Scottish rival to the Abbey at Westminster; constructed by her own Saxon forbears. Following her marriage to Malcolm Canmore, and the latter's suppression, with English help, of the old electoral system of monarchy in Scotland, rebellion after rebellion would have to be repressed in the old Celtic Princedom of Moray; itself a stronghold of the followers of Macbeth and the rival MacWilliam claimants to the Scottish throne; themselves descended from Malcolm's own previous marriage to a daughter of the Jarl of Orkney.

Amongst the foreign mercenaries drafted in to suppress these rebellions was, as has previously been noted, the Flemish Freskin of Moravia, whose numerous descendants were to include, as if by some ironic coincidence, the heiress of the old Earldom of Sutherland; whose husband, George Granville Leveson-Gower, Marquis of Stafford; was himself to succeed as first Duke of Sutherland in 1833. The Duke is renowned in Scottish history for being the principal architect of the Highland Clearances; an additional factor which, in later times, was to erode further the prevelance of Gaelic Culture in the Highlands.

Freskin himself is accredited with having married an heiress of the old Picto-Moravian Royal Dynasty, thus legitimizing, in some respects, his claim to the lands to which he was to be granted rights by his Anglo-Scottish masters. And, it is due to a similar series of dynastic interconnections that we owe the gradual evolution of the ballad traditions that Scott himself was to recover; and indeed their ultimate survival into the current era.

Now, as we fast approach the closing chapters of our story, we shall look afresh at some of the foreign influences to have cross-fertilized those indiginous to Scotland; and their relevance to the survival of the "Ossianic" and other related traditions.

Chapter Eighteen

The Lord of the Isles

"Nor deem", said stout Dunvegan's knight,
"That thou shalt brave alone the fight!
By Saints of isle and mainland both,
By Woden wild, (my grandsire's oath),
Let Rome and England do their worst,
Howe'er attained or accursed.
If Bruce shall e'er find friends again,
Once more to brave a battle-plain,
If Douglas couch again his lance,
Or Randolph dare another chance,
Old Torquil will not be to lack
With twice a thousand at his back-
Nay, chafe not at my bearing bold,
Good Abbot! For thou know'st of old,
Torquil's rude thought and stubborn will
Smack of the wild Norwegian still......."
            "The Lord of the Isles", Canto II, vv. xxvii.

W.F. Skene, the noted nineteenth century scholar whose many works were to include *Chronicles of the Picts, Chronicles of the Scots, and other Early Memorials of Scottish History* (publ. Edinburgh, 1867, H.M. Register House), in a quotation from a Cotton M.S. in the British Museum Collection, referred to as *The Northern Annals,* throws light upon the state of affairs in what is now Southern Scotland towards the end of the Dark Age Period:

> "870: The Tower of Alclyde was destroyed.
> 944: Strathclyde was ravaged by the Saxons.
> 974: Dunwallawn King of Strathclyde went on Pilgrimage to
> Rome........"

The somewhat sketchy data, and the decidedly erratic method of compilation, in this, the only surviving historical North British primary source from the end of the Dark Ages, is illustrative of the final collapse of North British Culture in Southern Scotland; and what is now Northern England. Henceforth, what little was to survive did so in the oral traditions of the bards and minstrels, thus indicating the fashion by which the ancient traditions of "Y Gogledd" were to become inter-connected with those of the Southern Picts and at least some of their Northumbrian counterparts.

By the opening decade of the Second Millennium A.D., the Norwegian Jarls of Orkney, by now already intermarried with the Scottish Royal House, had established themselves as overlords of all the Scottish and Irish islands; including even the Isle of Man. Sigurd the Stout, described by Johannes Brondsted as "mightiest of the Orkney Earls" in his highly acclaimed treatise on *The Vikings* (publ. Penguin, 1965), and himself ancestor of the Norwegian Kings of Man, from whom Sir Walter's Chief of Dunvegan on Skye, who features in the above quoted passage from one of the Laird of Abbotsford's best known poetical compositions, was himself to descend, is likewise noted for his erection of elaborate stone crosses which "display a significant mixture of motifs, and traditions- Norwegian and Celtic, pagan and Christian...."

This intermarriage of different cultural styles would appear to parallel exactly the kind of interaction, between Saxon and Briton, Norseman and Gael, which was already well under way in Scotland; and which would ultimately influence the manner in which the folklore and traditions that Scott and his contemporaries would come to collect in the centuries that followed would eventually evolve. The legacy of the Atlantic Empire that Sigurd and his kinsmen were to found along the northern and western seaboards of Scotland would eventually give rise to the Lordship of the Isles; a title held for centuries by the MacDonalds of Clanranald; who were themselves amongst the principal benefactors of the bardic custodians of the Ossianic Traditions later collected by Macpherson.

The most renowned ancestor of the MacDonalds of Clanranald was the semi-legendary Somerled Lord of the Isles, who met his end whilst marauding up the Clyde near Renfrew in the year 1164; at the head of some 160 galleys of warriors. According to Celtic tradition, Somerled was the son of Gillebrede mac Gilladomnan, sixth in descent from Godfrey MacFergus, described in Irish sources as "Toshach of the Isles". His Father is alleged to have been descended from the old Scottish Princes of Argyll, themselves in certain definite respects a rival Royal House to that of King Malcolm, who ruled a semi-autonomous kingdom of their own. Other sources propose a Norse origin for him, but in all probability he was of both Norse and Gaelic descent; being married into the bargain to a scion of the old Moravian Princely Line; herself a probable descendant of Macbeth.

Whatever his ultimate genealogical origins in the direct male line, this great warrior and adventurer, a constant thorn in the side of King Malcolm IV, against whom he was engaged in repeated rebellions, passed on a cultural inheritance of dual ethnicity which was to result in the preservation of a unique branch of the Ossianic Tradition which might otherwise have died out altogether. Indeed, it was some six centuries or so after he himself had flourished, that Niel Macvuirich, last of the old Hereditary Bards of the MacDonalds of Clanranald, whose ancestors had held the post for some several generations, finally died; in the year 1726. A sworn statement by Neil's son, Lachlan Macvuirich, reproduced in James Browne Fullarton's four volume work on *The Highland Clans* (publ. Glasgow, 1838), attests to some eighteen generations of hereditary bards in the direct male line before the death of his Father; an institution which at least in part owed its very existence, survival, and indeed probable inception, to Somerled.

On the eastern seaboard of what had formerly constituted the old North British confederation of the Post-Roman Era, and what had become Deira and Bernicia, the two Saxon kingdoms which were to give rise to that of Northumbria, the Vikings were to become no less influential; with the setting up of their own independent colonies at York; and in a vast tract of land located between the North Bank of the Thames in the South East, Chester in the West, and encompassing much of Mercia, Deira and all of East Anglia; known to historians as "Danelaw". Indeed, the "Hardyknute" of ballad poetry was himself of Norse origin; and in reality the half brother of King Edward the Confessor; St. Margaret of Scotland's Great-Uncle.

These great Nordic incursions were to result in the marginalization of the once semi-autonomous Pictish, English and North British Princedoms that had preceeded the arrival of the Norsemen on British soil. And, as they disappeared beneath the onslaught of the Viking Hosts, the ancient bardic traditions, which had once been succoured by these previously culturally distinct ethnic groups, gradually became intertwined with one another as a result of widespread migration, inter-marriage and cross fertilization; the

336

ultimate legacy of which was the perpetuation of the fragmentary remains of the ancient traditions which were to come to adorn the ballads that the Laird of Abbotsford himself collected, amongst the eighteenth and nineteenth century descendants of these ancient peoples.

As has already been seen, certain Norse elements are known to have been incorporated into the storyline structure of some of the Border Ballads collected by Scott; most notably that of *King Henrie;* the original of which, the editor of the *Minstrelsy* informs us, in his introductory notes to the above, is directly derived from the Old Icelandic Sagas; a fact attested to by the writings of Torfaeus; from which he himself quotes. But, a more important influence upon the evolution of Border Culture generally were the repeated rebellions against Malcolm Canmore's Dynasty far to the north, in Moray; a location with which not only Somerled could claim a very close association, but which may well also have spawned the lineage from whence one of the most celebrated Reivers of the Golden Age of Border Balladry was himself ultimately sprung; that individual being none other than the legendary Outlaw Murray; who, like Johnnie Armstrong, was one of the greatest heros of Border legend; whose exploits were recounted in the songs of generations of Border Minstrels. And, it is to the tower of this self same Border Reiver that we shall now travel, as we approach the final leg of our quest.

Chapter Nineteen

The Sang of the Outlaw Murray

Ettricke Foreste is a feir foreste,
In it grows manie a semelie trie;
There's hart and hynd, and dae and rae,
And of a' wilde beastes grete plentie.

There's a feir castelle, bigged wi' lyme and stane;
O! gin it stands not pleasauntlie!
In the forefront o' that castelle feir,
Twa unicorns are bra' to see;
There's the picture of a knight, and a ladye bright,
And the grene hollin abune their brie.

There an Outlaw keepis five hundred men;
He keepis a royalle cumpanie!
His merryemen are a' in ae liverye clad,
O' the Linkhome grene sae gaye to see;
He and his ladye in purple clad,
O! gin they lived not royallie!

Word is gane to our nobil King,
In Edinburgh, where that he lay,
That there was an Outlaw in Ettricke Foreste,
Counted him nought, nor a' his courtrie gay.

"I make a vowe", then the gude King said,
"Unto the man that deir bought me,
"I'se either be King of Ettricke Foreste,
Or King of Scotlande that Outlaw sall be!"
Then spak the lord, hight Hamilton,
And to the nobil King said he,

"My sovereign prince, sum counsell take,
First at your nobilis, syne at me.

"I redd ye, send yon braw Outlaw till,
And see gif your man cum will he:
Desyre him cum and be your man,
And hald of you yon Foreste frie.

"Gif he refuses to do that,
We'll conquess baith his landis and he!
Or else, we'll throw his castell down,
And make a widowe o' his gay ladye."

The King then call'd a gentleman,
James Boyd (the Earl of Arran his brother was he),
When James he cam before the King,
He knelit before him on his kne.

"Wellcum James Boyd!" said our nobil King;
"A message ye maun gang for me;
Ye maun hye to Ettricke Foreste,
To yon Outlaw, where bydeth he:

"Ask him of whom he haldis his landis,
Or man, wha may his master be,
And desyre him cum, and be my man,
And hald of me yon Foreste frie.

"To Edinburgh to cum and gang,
His safe warrant I sall gie;
And gif he refuses to do that,
We'll conquess baith his landis and he.

"Thou may'st vow I'll cast his castell down,
And make a widowe o' his gay ladye;
I'll hang his merryemen, payr by payr,
In ony frith where I may them see."

James Boyd tuik his leave o' the nobil King,
To Ettricke Foreste feir cam he;
Down Birkendale Brae when that he cam,
He saw the feir Foreste wi' his e'e.

Beith dae and rae, and hart and hinde,
And of a' wilde beasties great plentie;
He heard the bows that bauldly ring,
And arrows whidderan' hym near bi.

Of that feir castell he got a sight;
The like he neir saw wi' his e'e!
On the fore front o' that castell feir,
Twa unicorns were gaye to see;
The picture of a knight, and ladye bright,
And the grene hollin abune their brie.

Thereat he spyed five hundred men,
Shuting with bows on Newark Lee;
They were a' in ae livery clad,
O' the Linkome grene sae gaye to see.

His men were a' clad in the grene,
The knight was armed capapie,
With a bended bow, on a milk-white steed;
And I wot they ranked right bonilie.

Therby Boyd kend he was master man,
And serv'd him in his ain degre.
"Got mot thee save, brave Outlaw Murray!
That ladye, and all thy chyvalrie!"
"Marry, thou's wellcum, gentleman,
Some King's messenger thou seemis to be."

"The King of Scotlande sent me here,
And, gude Outlaw, I am sent to thee;
I wad wot of whom ye hald your landis,
Or man, wha may thy master be?"

"Thir landis are MINE!" the Outlaw said;
"I ken nae King in Christentie;
Frae Soudron I this Foreste wan,
Whan the King nor his knights were not to see."

"He desyres you'l cum to Edinburgh,
And hauld of him this Foreste frie;
And gif ye refuse to do this,
He'l conquess baith thy landis and thee.
He hath vow'd to cast thy castell down,
And mak a widowe o' thy gaye ladye;

"He'll hang thy merryemen, payr by payr,
In ony frith where he may them finde."
"Aye, by my troth!" the Outlaw said,
"Than wald I thinke me far behinde.

"Ere the King my feir countrie get,
This land that's nativest to me!
Many o' his nobilis sall be cauld,
Their ladyes sall be right wearie."

Then spak his ladye, feir of face,
She sayd, "Without consent of me,
That an Outlaw suld cum befor a King;
I am right rad of treasonrie.
Bid him be gude to his lordis at hame,
For Edinburgh my lord sall nevir see."

James Boyd tuik his leave o' the Outlaw kene,
To Edinburgh boun is he;
When James he cam befor the King,
He knelit lowlie on his kne.

"Wellcum, James Boyd!" seyd our nobil King;
"What Foreste is Ettricke Forest Frie?"
"Ettricke Foreste is the feirest foreste
That evir man saw wi' his e'e.

"There's the dae, the rae, the hart, the hynde,
And of a' wild beasties grete plentie;
There's a pretty castell of lyme and stane,
O gif it stands not pleasauntlie!

"Ther's in the forefront o' that castell,
Twa unicorns, sae bra' to see;
There's the picture of a knight, and a ladye bright,
Wi' the grene hollin abune their brie.

"There the Outlaw keepis five hundred men,
He keepis a royalle cumpanie!
His merryemen in ae livery clad,
O' the Linkome grene sae gaye to see.
He and his ladye in purple clad;
O' gin they live not royallie!

"He says, yon Foreste is his awin;
He wan it frae the Southronie;
Sae as he wan it, sae will he keep it,
Contrair all kingis in Christentie."

"Gar warn me Perthshire, and Angus baith;
Fife up and down, and the Louthians three,
And graith my horse!" said our nobil King.
"For to Ettricke Foreste hie will I me."

Then word is gane the Outlaw till,
In Ettricke Foreste, where dwelleth he,
Then the King was cuming to his cuntrie,
To conquess baith his landis and he.

"I mak a vow", the Outlaw said,
"I make a vow, and that trulie,
Were there but three men to tak my pairt,
Yon King's cuming full deir suld be!"

Then messengers he called forth,
And bade them hie them speedilye-
"Ane of ye gae to Halliday,
The laird of the Corehead is he.

"He certain is my sister's son;
Bid him cum quick and succour me!
The King cums on for Ettricke Foreste,
And landless men, we a' will be."

"What news? What news?" said Halliday,
"Man, frae thy master unto me?"
"Not as ye wad; seeking your aide;
The King's his mortal enemie."

"Aye, by troth!" said Halliday,
even for that it repenteth me;
For gif he lose feir Ettricke Foreste,
He'll take feir Moffatdale frae me.

"I'L meet him wi' five hundred men,
And surely mair, if mae may be;
And before he gets the Foreste feir,
We a' will die on Newark Lee!"

The Outlaw called a messenger,
And bid him hie him speedilye,
To Andrew Murray of Cockpool-
"That man's a deir cousin to me;
Desyre him cum, and mak me ayd,
With a' the power that he may be."

"It stands me hard", Andrew Murray said,
"Judge gif it stands na hard wi' me;
To enter against a King wi' crown,
And set my landis in jeopardie!
Yet, if I cum not on the day,
Surely at night he sall me see."

To Sir James Murray of Traquair,
A message cam right speedilye-
"What news? What news?" James Murray said,
"Man, frae thy master unto me?"

"What neids I tell? For well ye ken,
The King's his mortal enemie;
And now he's coming to Ettricke Foreste,
And landless men ye a' will be."

"And by my trothe" James Murray said,
"Wi' that Outlaw will I live and die;
The King has gifted my landis lang syne-
It cannot be nae worse wi' me."

The King was cuming thro' Caddon Ford,
And full five thousand men was he;
Thy saw the derke Foreste them before,
They thought it awesome for to see.

Then spak the lord, hight Hamilton,
And to the nobil King said he,
"My sovereign liege, sum coucil tak,
First at your nobilis, syne at me.

"Desyre him mete thee at Permanscore,
And bring four in his cumpanie;
Five erles sall gang yoursell befor,
Gude cause that you suld honour'd be.

"And gif he refuses to do that,
We'll conquess baith his landis and he;
There sall nevir a Murray, aftir him,
Hald land in Ettricke Foreste frie."

Then spak the kene Laird of Bucksleuth,
A stalworthe man, and sterne was he-
"For a King to gang an Outlaw till,
Is beneath his state and his dignitie.

"The man that wons yon Foreste intill,
He lives by reif and felonie!
Wherefore, brayed on, my sovereign liege!
Wi' fire and sword we'll follow thee;
Or gif, your courtrie lords fa' back,
Our Borderers sall the onset gie."

Then out and spak the nobil King,
And round hin cast a wilie e'e-
"Now had thy tongue Sir Walter Scott,
Nor speak of reif nor felonie:
For had everye honeste man his awin kye,
A right puir clan thy name wad be!"

The King than calle'd a gentleman,
Royal banner-bearer there was he;
James Hoppringle of Torsonse, by name;
He cam and knelit upon his kne.

"Wellcum James Pringle of Torsonse!
A message ye maun gang for me;
Ye maun gae to yon Outlaw Murray,
Surely where bauldly bideth he.

"Bid him mete me at Permanscore,
And bring four in his cumpanie;
Five erles sall cum wi' mysel,
Gude reason I suld honour'd be.

"And, gif he refuses to do that,
Bid him luke for nae gude o' me!
There sall nevir a Murray, after him,
Have land in Ettricke Foreste frie."

James came before the Outlaw kene,
And serv'd him in his ain degre-
"Wellcum, James Pringle of Torsonse!
What message frae the King to me?"

"He bids ye mete him at Permanscore,
And bring four in your cumpanie;
Five erles sall gang himsell befor,
Nair mair in number will he be.

"And, gif you refuse to do that,
(I freely here upgive wi' thee)
He'll cast yon bonny castle down,
And make a widowe o' that gaye ladye.

"He'll loose yon bluidhound Borderers,
Wi' fire and sword to follow thee;
There will nevir a Murray, after thysell,
Have land in Ettricke Foreste frie ."

"It stands me hard," the Outlaw said;
"Judge gif it stands na hard wi' me!
Wha reck not losing of mysell,
But a' my offspring after me.

"My merryemen's lives, my widowe's teirs-
There lies the pang that pinches me!
When I am straught in bludie eard,
Yon castell will be right dreirie.

"Auld Halliday, Young Halliday,
Ye sall be twa to gang wi' me;
Andrew Murray, and James Murray,
We'll be nae mae in cumpanie."

When that they cam before the King,
They fell before him on their kne-
"Grant mercie, mercie, nobil King!
E'en for his sake that dyed on trie."

"Sicken like mercie sall ye have;
On gallows ye sall hangit be!"
"Over God's forbode," quoth the Outlaw then,
"I hope your grace will bettir be!
Else, ere you come to Edinburgh port,
I trow thin guarded sall ye be:

"Thir landis of Ettricke Foreste feir ,
I wan them from the enemie;
Like as I wan them, sae will I keep them,
Contrair a' kingis in Christentie."

All the noblis the King about,
Said pitie it were to see him die-
"Yet graunt me mercie, sovereign prince!
Extend your favour unto me!

"I'll give thee the keys of my castell,
Wi' the blessing o' my gaye ladye,
Gin thou'lt make me Sherife of this Foreste,
And a' my offspring after me."

"Wilt thou give me the keys of thy castell,
Wi' the blessing of thy gaye ladye?
I'se make thee sheriffe of Ettricke Foreste,
Surely while upward grows the trie;
If you be not traitour to the King,
Forfaulted sall thou nevir be."

"But Prince, what sall cum o' my men?
When I gae back, traitour they'll ca' me.
I had rather lose my life and land,
Ere my merryemen rebuked me."

"Will your merryemen amend their lives?
And a' their pardons I grant thee-
Now, name thy landis where'er they lie,
And here I RENDER them to thee."

"Fair Philiphaugh is mine by right,
And Lewinshope still mine shall be;
Newark, Foulshiells, and Tinnies baith,
My bow and arrow purchased me.

"And I have native steads to me,
The Newark Lee and Hangingshaw;
I have mony steads in the Foreste shaw,
But them by name I dinna knaw."

The keys o' the castell he gave the King,
Wi' the blessing o' his feir ladye;
He was made sheriffe of Ettricke Foreste,
Surely while upward grows the trie;
And if he was na traitour to the King,
Forfaulted he suld nevir be.

Wha ever heard, in ony times,
Sicken an Outlaw in his degre,
Sic favour get before a King,
As did the OUTLAWE MURRAY of the Foreste Frie?"

"This ballad", writes Scott, in his introductory notes to the lyrics of this heroic "sang", once a key element in the "chaunt" of many a Border peasant, "appears to have been composed about the reign of James V".This assertion is certainly substantiated, in some degree at least, by historical fact, in that the Boyds of Arran were noted members of that King's Grandfather's "royalle cumpanie"; Thomas Boyd, Earl of Arran, having married Mary Stuart; sister of King James III; who took as her second husband James Lord Hamilton; himself in all probability the "lord, hight Hamilton" of the ballad.

The ballad itself, according to Scott, "commemorates a transaction supposed to have taken place betwixt a Scottish monarch and an ancestor of the ancient family of Murray of Philiphaugh....." Elsewhere the Laird of Abbotsford adds that "It is certain that, during the civil wars betwixt Bruce and Baliol, the family of Philiphaugh existed and was powerful; for their ancestor, Archibald de Moravia, subscribes the oath of fealty to Edward I, A.D. 1296.

It is therefore not unlikely that, residing in a wild and frontier country they may have, at one period or other during these commotions, refused allegiance to the feeble monarch of the day, and thus extorted from him some grant of territory or jurisdiction....."

The ballad itself portrays in every respect the state of lawlessnes prevalent in the Borders during the Fifteenth and Sixteenth Centuries, when Border Reivers ".....arrayed in the most warlike manner...." in "jak of plaite" and "steill bonnetts", were wont to plunder their own side of the Border as readily as that of their country's foe; a situation summed up admirably in chapter one of Reed's *Border Ballads:*

For, as Reed himself is swift to point out, "These were Borderers before they were either Scots or English; their allegiance was first to the family, the Surname, not to the Crown; they would marry, or steal, or kill among their own countrymen as well as across the Border. "They are a people", wrote a harassed official in 1583 "that will be Scottishe when they will, and Englishe at their pleasure...."

And this, in certain definite respects, is the thrust of the poetical storyline here presented. Archibald, founder of the Murrays of Philiphaugh, is styled in the ancient charters as "Archibald de Moravia", a fact which would tend to suggest that his ancestors originally came from amongst the peoples of the Pictish north. As we have already seen, the House of Buccleuch, like the Johnstones of Annandale, were in all probability of Cymric or old North British stock; just as Clan Inglis may have descended from one "Wat the English"; whilst the forefathers of the Maxwells originally sailed in raiding parties from beyond the northern seas.

These facts, as well as explaining the reason for the lawlessness of the Borders, where refugees from every conceivable part of Scotland, as well as further afield, places such as Ludlow in Shropshire, supposed ancestral homeland of the Laidlaws of "Ettricke Foreste", itself the geographical location where the events here described are supposed to have taken place, carved out lands and territories for themselves on the fringes of both societies, also do much to explain as to why so many diverse cultural elements, English, Scottish, Pictish, Gaelic and Norse, ultimately crept into the substance of so many of the ballads extant in the Borders at the time of Scott's researches.

The fact that they are present also does much to substantiate, as has already been observed, the authenticity of the material that he himself collected.

The illiterate Border peasants, who had preserved these traditions, orally, for generation after generation, had no knowledge of history as we understand it. The Latin texts that refer to the ancient painted peoples of the north were beyond their comprehension. Instead, they portrayed these ancient ethnically and racially diverse invaders, who had vanished as mysteriously as they had appeared, together with their now abandoned Iron Age Brochs, the Fairy Halls of the Ballads, whether driven out or, as is more probable, assimilated into the population as a result of intermarriage between the real life equivalents of the "Young Tamlane", as the Elves and the Fairies of folklore.

The lists of names in both parties here portrayed in the *Sang of the Outlaw Murray,* Boyd and Hamilton being notable in the Royal camp, whilst those of Murray and Halliday are most prominent amongst the freebooters who live "by reif and felonie", place the song in a context not so very far away from the Dark Age poetry examined in the first chapter; where the names of heros and their clans are an integral part of the recitation. This fact does much to explain how Surtees, a friend of Ritson, to whose work Scott himself owed many a debt in the compilation of the *Minstrelsy,* and a noted genealogist, so easily deceived the Laird of Abbotsford with his references to "Hughie of Hawdon, and Will of the Wa'....." in his self composed *Death of Featherstonehaugh.*

The union of the two kingdoms, in accordance with the ancient prophecy relating to Merlin's Grave, marked the end of the Reiver Golden Age, a fact referred to amongst the lyrics of Satchells's poetical *History* of Scott's own *Sirename*:

> It's most clear, a freebooter doth live in hazard's train;
> A freebooter's a cavalier that ventures life for gain:
> But since King James the Sixth to England went,
> There has been no cause of grief;
> And he that hath transgress'd since then,
> Is no FREEBOOTER, but a THIEF.

Ironically, unlike the Reivers, whose lifestyle was to slowly die out in the wake of the accession of the Stuarts to the English throne, the principal instrument that was to result in the death of Border Minstrelsy in its purest sense, was to be as much responsible for its preservation as it was for its ultimate destruction. In the next stage on the road towards my text's conclusion we shall look at the impact of this technological innovation in more detail, as well as its impact on wider society; something which was to lead to its instrumentality in taking the Border Ballads of the Great Reiver Golden Age, such as the one we have just looked at, to a far wider audience than the scattered rural communities in which they were ultimately nurtured.

Illustration 6): Nineteenth century engraving of the Arrest of the Duke of Buccleuch and Monmouth after the Battle of Sedgemoor in 1685.

Chapter Twenty

The Lay of the Last Minstrel

On Philiphaugh a fray began,
At Hairhead wood it ended;
The Scots out o'er the Graemes they ran,
Sae merrily they bended......

"The Battle of Philiphaugh".

The last six sets of lyrics, chronologically speaking, in the volume of the *Minstrelsy* dealing specifically with ballads of an historical category, are devoted, in their entirety, to the wars and strifes of the seventeenth century in Scotland; an era epitomized in the novels of the Laird of Abbotsford by such acknowledged classics as *Old Mortality*. Perhaps the most prominent of the family names that feature in the deeds of which these verses tell are the Graemes, or Grahams; who, as has been noted in chapter seven, are a family, like the Murrays, with both Highland Scots and Border Reiver associations.

The two figures who feature most prominently in this section of the *Minstrelsy,* which begins with *Lesley's March,* a ballad associated with those stalwart Calvinists who fought in the Civil Wars upon the English Parliamentary side, are James Graham, Marquis of Montrose, whose great defeat at the Battle of Philiphaugh is immortalized in the ballad of the same title, as well as in another of Scott's ballads entitled *The Gallant Grahams,* and Graham of Claverhouse, "Bloody Clavers", who has likewise featured elsewhere in our story.

The defeat of the staunchly Presbyterian Cameronian Sect, who themselves play an active, although somewhat cameo, role, at times, in some of Scott's most intriguing novels, *Guy Mannering* being a particular case in point, is celebrated in *The Battle of the Pentland Hills;* where the "gallant Grahams" of the first verse are not the Highland Clan or Border Surname, but the elite troops of horse raised by "Bonnie Dundee" for dealing with these dissenters. An interesting "supernatural" element in these ballads is made mention of in Scott's introductory notes to *The Battle of Loudon-Hill,* where, the author refers to how the Presbyterian preachers, "Mssrs. Kid, King, Cameron, Peden", and others "boasted of prophetic powers, and were often warned of the approach of the soldiers..." involved in their persecution, ".....by supernatural impulse....." Captain John Crichton, on the other hand, who is counted by the Laird of Abbotsford as being among their pursuers, "....dreamed dreams and saw visions (chiefly, indeed, after having drunk hard), in which the lurking holes of the rebels were discovered to his imagination....."

The last of the songs contained in Scott's volume of historical ballads is *The Battle of Bothwell Bridge,* which concerns itself with the defeat of the Cameronians inflicted upon them by James Duke of Buccleuch and Monmouth, the King's illegitimate son; who, as we saw in chapter one features not only in Scott's *Lay of the Last Minstrel,* together with his wife, Anne, but also in Scott's own correspondence relating to one of his own ancestor's staunch adherence to the Stuart Cause. Again, the historical circumstances recounted in this ballad are in some ways quite ironic, for in the years that followed the Duke himself would become a rebel; upon the accession to the throne of his uncle; King James II.

So now, we have come full circle. Having begun our story with Sir Walter's fictional *Last Minstrel,* we find ourselves returning here to the self same era where we last encountered him. For, strange as it may seem, it was not the collapse of a now vanished, or marginalized, civilization that led to the demise of Minstrelsy in the Borders; as had been the case with regard to the death of Bardism in Wales and the Scottish Highlands, but the technological developments which had ultimately led to the rise of the staunch brand of Protestantism that the Duke himself was so closely involved in suppressing.

This long drawn out process had begun with William Caxton, whose own printed production of Sir Thomas Mallory's *Le Morte d'Arthur,* in 1485, was to coincide with the rise to power of Henry Duke of Richmond in Yorkshire; himself a descendant of those very same heros immortalized by the likes of Aneirin, Llywarch and Taliesin; who had ascended the throne after the defeat of Richard Crookback at the Battle of Bosworth Field; thus founding the Tudor Dynasty; and who would ultimately sire, on an heiress of Plantagenet blood, the daughter whose marriage to a Scottish King would result in the

Union of Kingdoms set out in ancient prophecy. Caxton's *Morte d'Arthur* was to break the monopoly, previously possessed by the Bards, Minstrels and Troubadours of the Dark and High Middle Ages, with respect to the Arthurian Traditons. Henceforth, any man able to read could gain access to these ancient traditions without the intercession of a wandering Minstrel and his lute or harp; much as modern recording and video technology has given music and film to the masses.

In the following century translations of the Bible into the tongues of the dissenters would break the monopoly of direct access to spiritual truth previously held by the Roman Catholic Church; or at least by those who read Latin. And, as a direct result of the forment of ideas which were to bring about the gradual demise of the old established order during the Thirty Years War in Europe, and the Civil Wars in England and Scotland, with which these last mentioned ballads were principally concerned, a dramatic new invention, the portable printing press, was not only to assist in the dissemination of radical ideas, in particular those of the English Levellers, who were agitating for Parliamentary and Social Reform in the wake of the King's defeat and the rise of the Commonwealth at the end of the 1640s, but in the wholesale production, and distribution, of the self same printed ballads, or broadsides, which were to exert such a formative influence upon the young Sir Walter Scott; who was to collect and bind an abundance of these curiosities; much like modern schoolboys compile albums of exotic postage stamps and first day covers in our own century.

These developments were to undermine further still the position in society of the Minstrel; and result in the gradual disappearance of the traditions that had for so many centuries been principally nurtured by those of his caste. Within a few decades of the execution of Monmouth however, and the banishment of his Catholic Uncle James to the Continent of Europe, the first of the bardic revivals in the Borders would begin; albeit from humble beginnings and from a totally unexpected quarter.

Chapter Twenty One

The Flowers of the Forest

O Young Lochinvar is come out of the west,
Through all the wide Border his steed was the best;
And save his good broadsword he weapons had none.
He rode all unarme'd, and he rode all alone,
So faithful in love, and so dauntless in war,
There never was knight like the young Lochinvar......

Marmion, Canto V. vv. xii.

These lines utilized by the contemporary novelist, Alan Massie, to invoke and epitomize Scott's poetical composition at its best in part of his scripted dialogue for the 1997 B.B.C. television documentary *The Wizard of the North*, are taken from one of Sir Walter's best known Border poems; itself centred upon the disastrous Battle of Flodden in 1513. Before the day was done the flower of Scottish chivalry had fallen; along with their sovereign, King James IV.

This particular section of the poem, like another segment we looked at earlier, in connection with the forgeries of Surtees of Mainsforth, is, once again, taken from the lines of one of the many ballads Scott was to collect for the editing and publication of the *Minstrelsy*. In the first edition of the work it was to appear under the title *The Laird of Laminton*, whilst in later impressions the name "Katherine Janfarie" is substituted. The ballad is concerned with an affray that took place at the wedding feast of the lady who gave her name to the second of its heregiven titles; but in historical terms, it is significant, in that Alexander Gordon of Lochinvar, who is the principal figure, both in the ballad, which is, unlike Surtees's forgery, an acknowledged original, and this section of Scott's poem, was himself amongst those to fall on the Scottish side at Flodden; along with his lamented monarch.

The importance of the battle, to Scott, his fellow countrymen and to Borderers in general can never be underestimated. And, it is perhaps for this reason that, in the Henderson edition of Scott's *Minstrelsy*, at the end of the second section, devoted principally to Romantic Ballads, amongst which *Katherine Janfarie* is perhaps amongst the more notable, in that it revolves around real incident, rather than romantic fiction or mythology, we find a modern composition, *in imitation of the Ancient Ballad*, by Scott's friend and collaborator John Leyden; itself entitled *An Ode on Visiting Flodden*.

Elsewhere, in the same section, we find another ballad, itself at least in part of modern composition, the lyrics of which are given in full below:

I've heard them lilting, at the ewe milking,
* Lasses a' lilting before dawn of day;*
But now they are moaning, on ilka green loaning;
* The flowers of the forest are a' wede awae.*

At bughts, in the morning, nae blithe lads are scorning;
* Lasses are lonely, and dowie, and wae;*
Nae daffling, nae gabbing, but sighing and sabbing;
* Ilk ane lifts her leglin, and hies her awae.*

In har'st, at the shearing, no youths now are jearing;
* Bandsters are runkled, and lyart or grey;*
At fair, or at preaching, nae wooing, nae fleeching;
* The flowers of the forest are a' wede awae.*

At e'en in the gloaming, nae younkers are roaming
* 'Bout stacks, with the lasses at bogle to play;*
But ilk maid sits dreary, lamenting her deary-
* The flowers of the forest are wedded awae.*

Dool and wae for the order, that sent our lads to the border!
* The English, for ance, by guile wan the day;*
The flowers of the forest, that fought aye the foremost,
* The prime of our land, are cauld in the clay.*

We'll hear nae mair lilting, at the ewe milking;
Women and bairns are heartless and wae:
Sighing and moaning, on ilka green loaning-
The flowers of the forest are a' wede awae.

As readers who are familiar with the historical background of this ballad will be aware, the Flowers of the Forest of both title and lyric are symbolic of those who fell on Flodden Field; much as the poppy has come to symbolize those who perished in Flanders Fields by their hundreds of thousands in the opening decades of our own century. In his introductory notes to the version of *The Flowers of the Forest* here reproduced, the lyrics of which are considerably different to the much updated version recorded by "Fairport Convention" at the height of their popularity, the Laird of Abbotsford has the following comments to make:

"The following well-known and beautiful stanzas, were composed, many years ago, by a lady of family in Roxburghshire. The manner of the ancient minstrels is so happily imitated that it required the most positive evidence to convince the Editor that the song was of modern date. Such evidence, however, he has been able to procure; having been favoured, through the kind intervention of Dr. Somerville (well known in the literary world as the historian of King William etc.) with the.........authentic copy of *The Flowers of the Forest.*

The "lady of family", to whom the Laird of Abbotsford here refers, was none other than Jean Elliot; daughter of the famous laywer who had been instrumental in the publication of *Hardyknute*; and whose brother was a moderately famous poet and songwriter:

"One day, according to tradition....", recounts Henry Grey Graham in his *Scottish Men of Letters in the Eighteenth Century,* "Jean Elliot was riding in the family coach with her brother Gilbert. They spoke of the battle of Flodden whose memories clung to their country-side- for that historic tragedy had burned itself on the national mind. Her brother wagered her a pair of gloves or set of ribbons that she could not compose a ballad on Flodden Field. She was then about thirty, and had shown no turn for ballad-making, but she accepted the challenge. One or two lines only remained of the ancient ballad on the battle, though the famous air lingered on the ears of the people bereft of its words. Jean Elliot wrote her version, and her brother when he read it saw that he had lost his wager, and Scotland had gained a ballad which would never die. Copied out by family pens, recopied by those who saw or heard it, it went on its way to popularity. Gradually, it found its way into every drawing-room, and was played at every concert, though who the writer was no one could tell. With stately reserve or maidenly modesty Miss Jean Elliot kept her secret, and her family gave no sign, and never did she exert her lyrical genius in any such effort again. Hopeless uncertainty exists as to the dates and priority of the rival sets of *The Flowers of the Forest*; yet her song must have been written after that of Mrs. Cockburn, if it be true, as Dr. Somerville told Sir Walter Scott, that the song was written while he was staying at Minto House, for it was in 1767 he became minister of the parish, and lived with the Elliots as tutor. A far finer work than its rival, Jean Elliot's ballad reaches near to perfection....."

Curiously, the Mrs. Cockburn here referred to, was, like Scott's Mother, a Rutherford by descent, being the daughter of Rutherford of Fairnalie. Scott, in his introduction to her version of the ballad, which is likewise transcribed in the *Minstrelsy,* makes mention of the fact that he himself knew her well; an interesting anecdote when we consider that it was she who was perhaps to influence in some way the composition of the ballad which was to rekindle the dying embers of Minstrelsy in the Borders; and ultimately exert a not inconsiderable influence of its own upon the scholarly revivers of the tradition; who, as has already been seen, were to include, besides Scott and Leyden, the likes of Ritson and Kirkpatrick-Sharpe.

The key here as to why *The Flowers of the Forest* is so significant is rooted in the fact that the Border Minstrel Tradition, like its Welsh and Gaelic counterparts, is rooted in the singing traditions of the local people. We have already heard Scott give his opinion on the significance of Scottish folk song, in the transcription of his conversations with Washington Irving, quoted in whole and in part throughout several preceeding chapters. And, this fact in itself does much to explain as to why the two greatest figures in Scottish literature, Robert Burns and Sir Walter Scott, should have devoted so much of their time to studying it. Indeed, in an essay penned by Scott under the title *Imitations of the Ancient Ballad,* and dated April 1830, the Laird of Abbotsford has the following to say about Burns:

"The poet, perhaps, most capable, by verses, lines, even single words, to relieve and heighten the character of ancient poetry was the Scottish bard Robert Burns. We are not here speaking of the avowed lyrical poems of his own composition, which he communicated to Mr. George Thomson, but the manner in which he recomposed and repaired the old songs and fragments for the collection of Johnson and others, when, if his memory supplied the theme or general subject of the song, such as existed in Scottish lore, his genius contributed that part which was to give life and immortality to the whole......"

As for the legacy of what Scott set about doing, in his compilation of the *Minstrelsy*, we will now complete our journey across the Border Landscape, and through the books and dusty manuscripts at the heart of its most ancient traditions, as we take a walk along St. Cuthbert's Way; in the footsteps of the Rhymer himself.

Chapter Twenty Two

A Ploughman's Life

"We will play by the Cross, we will play by the Bow
We will drink at St. Dunstan's Well;
We'll slide doon the scaurs on the green Weirhill,
And list to the Abbey Bell....."

"Here's Tae Melrose!"

Modern day visitors to the town of Melrose, which lies along the recently re-created "St. Cuthbert's Way", a rambling route from Holy Island to Melrose Abbey aimed at modern tourists, linking up with the celebrated Pennine Way, will find a well established tourist industry; centred on Sir Walter's novels, Melrose Abbey and the archaeological remains over which Scott himself once rambled; in the company of Washington Irving. Frequenters of the tea rooms and public houses that are scattered throughout the town will find no modern equivalents of Mrs. Hogg or Will O'Phawhope however. The days when ballads were the principal source of entertainment during the long winter nights, and conversation with the fairies in the morning mist commonplace are long gone.

In an age of sattelite tv and cd-rom, global communications and their derivatives have banished those dark evenings of storytelling by the fireside into undeserved obscurity.

In spite of this, in a place that one would least expect, a hidden musical legacy of what Scott and his contemporaries set out to collect, and indeed preserve, lies gently awaiting discovery. Curiously, young Robert Ferguson, whose writings were quoted from in the opening chapters of this book, produced three strapping sons, one of whom married the daughter of Maxwell of Ardwell; themselves a scion of the mighty Maxwells of Caerlaverock, whose Clan and name have featured throughout this story.

361

The Ardwell branch of the Maxwells, natives of the western coastal fringes of the Border region, were in turn related, through marriage with the Bunburys, to that celebrated nineteenth century soldier Field Marshal Earl Roberts; known affectionately to his men as "General Bobs".

Amongst the Earl's numerous friends and acquaintances was the poet, author and journalist Rudyard Kipling. And, it was as a direct result of "Uncle Bobs's" longstanding association with the author of *Kim* and *The Jungle Book* that Robert Ferguson's three young grandsons would visit the village of Rottingdean in Sussex on their arrival from a colonial childhood in India; where the rigours of a turn-of-the-century public school education awaited them.

The eldest, Robert Ferguson M.D.'s namesake, would grow up to feature in one of Kipling's most celebrated historical works, his *Irish Guards in the Great War*; described as "His Forgotten Masterpiece" on the cover of the recently re-issued and updated edition. But, unbeknown to any of them, a hidden connection between their own ancestor's circle of friends and associates lay amongst the tombstones of the church at Rottingdean; and echoed across the fields where the morning larks sang.

Part of the churchyard where Kipling was to make his home in the final years of the last century is known to the locals as "Coppers' Corner". This obscure patch of ground, between the Sussex Downs and the sea, is not some refuge for truant Bobbies absconding from a day's duty. No indeed, it derives its name from the fact that one of the local farming families, the Coppers of Rottingdean, have had so many of their ancestors buried in this particular part of the churchyard that it is impossible to tell just how many of them still lie there.

For at least two centuries into the bargain, this family, the earliest of whom appears in the Parish Registry in the year 1593, have been noted folksingers in the locality. And, strange as it may seem, amongst the many songs contained in this Family's repertoire is an ancient Sussex ballad entitled, appropriately, *The Shepherd of the Downs*.

A shepherd of the Downs, being weary of his port
Retired to the hills where he used to resort.
In want of refreshment he laid himself down,
He wanted no riches, or wealth from the Crown.

362

He drank of the cold brook, he ate of the tree,
Himself he did enjoy from all sorrow was free,
He valued no girl be she ever so fair,
No pride nor ambition he valued no care.

As he was a-walking one evening so clear
A heavenly sweet voice sounded soft in his ear.
He stood like a post not one step could he move,
He knew not what hailed him but thought it was love.

He beheld a young damsel a fair modest bride
She had something amiss and disguised in her face.
Disguised in her face she unto him did say,
How now, Master Shepherd, how came you this way?

The shepherd he replied and modestly said,
I never was surprised before at a maid.
When first you beheld me from sorrow I was free,
But now you have stolen my poor heart from me.

He took her by the hand and thus he did say
We will get married pretty Betsy today.
So to church they did go and were married we hear,
And now he'll enjoy Pretty Betsy his dear.

Earlier in this book reference has been made at one juncture or another to the poet Allan Ramsay; himself a noted collector, editor, and in some cases a corrupter, of ballads. Amongst the songs from the *Minstrelsy* which feature in Ramsay's own voluminous writings is a version of *Annan Water;* to which reference is made in the latter's *Tea Table Miscellany*. And, amongst the pages of that same book, is another song which bears at least some resemblance, in terms of its lyrical content, as well as the general thrust of its storyline, to the song transcribed above. Entitled *The Shepherd Adonis*, the ballad, in spite of its Scottish provenance, belongs to a class of lyric whose origins lie rooted in the Shepherd's Songs of Elizabethan England; some of which were traditional in origin, dating in part from the Fourteenth and Fifteenth Centuries, whilst others, composed by gentlemen, such as Christopher Marlowe and Nicholas Breton, were written in imitation of the above. An excellent collection of the songs that fall into the latter category was published in 1912 at the Chiswick Press; with a foreword and notes by

Adelaide Gosset; amongst them being fine examples by Sir Henry Wotton
and the two composers mentioned above.

The Shepherd Adonis
Being wearied with sport,
He for a retirement,
To the woods did resort.
He threw by his club,
And he laid himself down;
He envied no monarch,
Nor wish'd for a crown.

He drank of the burn,
And he ate frae the tree,
Himself he enjoyed,
And frae trouble was free.
He wish'd for no nymph,
Tho' never so fair;
Had nae love for ambition,
And therefore no care.

But as he lay thus
In an e'vning sae clear,
A heavenly sweet voice
Sounded saft in his ear;
Which came frae a shady
Green neighbouring grove,
Where bonny Aminta
Sat singing of love.

He wander'd that way,
And found wha was there;
He was quite confounded
To see her sae fair:
He stood like a statue,
Not a foot could he move,
Nor knew he what griev'd him,
But he fear'd it was love.

The nymph she beheld him
With a kind modest grace:
Seeing something that pleased her
Appear in his face,
With blushing a little
She to him did say,
"Oh, Shepherd! What want ye,
How came you this way?"

His spirits reviving,
He to her replied,
"I was ne'er sae surpris'd
At the sight of a maid:
Until I beheld thee
From love I was free;
But now I'm ta'en captive,
My fairest, by thee."

Amongst those who had taken an active role, on the English side, at the bloody Battle of Flodden, some eighty years before the first appearance of the Copper Family in the Parish Records at Rottingdean, was Lord Dacre; whose family were hereditary Wardens of the English West March during much of the Tudor Period. Possessing numerous Cumbrian connections, the Dacre Family, when acting in their role as March Wardens on the north western fringes of the English Kingdom were to centre many of their activities in the area around Carlisle. Coincidentally, however, they were also to acquire lands in the south as a result of their extensive services to the English Crown; Hurstmonceux Castle in Sussex being their principal residence in the southern shires.

Centuries ago, at the time when the Coppers first appear on record, Sussex was a major centre for the iron and metal working industries which assisted Britain's early mercantile expansion, and the creation of the naval forces which were to come to dominate the globe in the centuries to follow. Although Sussex possessed an abundance of iron ore at one time, one commodity which, like Cornish tin, would have to have been imported, was copper. And, the principal copper producing region in the British Isles, during the Middle Ages at least, was Cumbria.

Did the ancestors of the singing Copper family originally travel, in the company of the much prized copper ore required in the manufacture of brass, from the far distant reaches of Cumbria in the north? A noted ancestor of theirs was nicknamed "Brasser" by the local Rottingdean Worthies. Or, is there some other explanation for the apparent link between these two songs? Perhaps their ancestors had some connection with the Dacres and followed them here as part of their entourage, never to return. Curiously enough, Allan Ramsay is not the only Scottish poet and songwriter to have come into contact with material closely related to the Rottingdean songs here described.

Between Rottingdean and the Sussex port of Newhaven lies a blot on the landscape known as Peacehaven, knocked up out of asbestos by unscrupulous land grabbers during the years immediately after the Great Depression and the Second World War; on land originally set aside for Australian Ex-Servicemen; who had served the Empire in World War One. Little trace now remains of the green fields where young boys, such as Bob Copper, the most senior member of the present three generations of Coppers who still inhabit the area where their ancestors once worked the land, would catch larks in nets for the tables of the seafront hotels in Brighton in the early years of the twentieth century.

The land on which the town now stands originally belonged to one Charles Neville, himself a northerner born at Darlington in 1881, the grandson of Sir Thomas Ussher, who had accompanied Napoleon on his exile to Elba. This strange connection between Peacehaven and the northern homeland of both Surtees and Ritson, two noted individuals to whom Scott himself was considerably indebted, in one way or another, is made stranger still by the fact that one of the songs often sung by these young lads, out in search of a few extra bob, features in a re-working of tradition by Scotland's most celebrated poet, Robert Burns; who, as we have already seen, was greatly admired by the Laird of Abbotsford.

Entitled, appropriately, *The Ploughman's Life,* in view of the vast number of references to ploughing, ploughmen and ploughshares contained in the Copper Tradition, which includes *Seasons or Ploughshare* and *The Brisk Young Ploughboy,* to name but two, it bears more than a passing resemblance to the Copper's *Lark in the Morning.* The lyrics now given below appeared on page eight of Andrew Laing's *Poems and Songs of Robert Burns,* published by Methuen & Co. in 1896; and are believed to date from the years 1773-1779; or thereabouts.

366

As I was a-wand'ring ae morning in spring,
I heard a young ploughman sae sweetly to sing;
And as he was singin', thir words he did say,-
"There's nae life like the ploughman's in the month o' sweet May.

The lav'rock in the morning she'll rise frae her nest,
And mount i' the air with the dew on her breast,
And wi' the merry ploughman she'll whistle and sing,
And at night she'll return to her nest back again".

Laing, in his notes to the above lyrics, has the following to say about them: "Possibly this is a scrap from tradition, which Burns may have written down, with no idea of claiming it for his own". Whatever the origins of the first verse, which are quite probably Burns's words composed to the tune of the English ballad, which appears in many versions besides that peculiar to Rottingdean and which, in every English version, is always entitled *The Lark in the Morning,* the chorus of at least one set of this ancient Sussex song is identical to the second of the two verses printed here; apart from the obvious fact that the Scottish "lav'rock", as it appears in the Burns, is substituted for the original English "lark" of the title.

"The lark in the morning she arises from her nest
And she ascends all in the air with the dew upon her breast,
And with the pretty ploughboy she'll whistle and she'll sing,
And at night she'll return to her own nest again".

During the last century the only buildings along the South Coast Road between Newhaven and Rottingdean were the Customs Cottages at Portobello which housed the Excise Men engaged in fighting the illicit trade in contraband wine and spirits; and another set of similar buildings at nearby Saltdean. Burns worked for a time as a Customs Officer, albeit at a later period in his life than that from which these lyrics supposedly date, and doubtless came into contact with many a seafaring man from both sides of the Border during the course of his work and extensive travels in Scotland. Could some roving Jack Tar have sung him a version of this song one night over a dram of illegal brandy or rum? We shall never know for sure. What is certain, however, is that the Copper Tradition is itself not without its seaborne influences, in spite of the agrarian character of the Family who preserve it; as the following verse from another of their songs, entitled *Warlike Seamen,* admirably demonstrates:

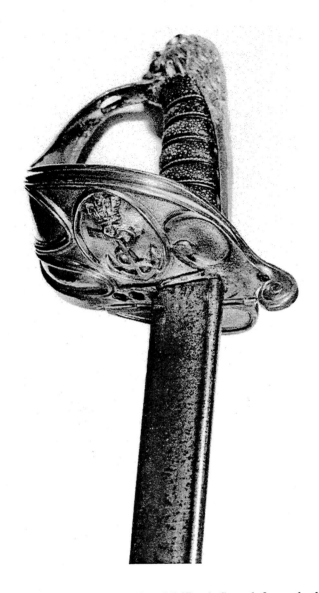

Illustration 13): "1827" type Naval Officer's Sword, formerly the property of Captain J.M. Ferguson R.N., Scott's "Honest Tar".
(Photo: Zoe Bridger).

Come all you warlike seamen that to the seas belong,
I'll tell you of a fight my boys on board the Nottingham.
It was of an Irish Captain- his name was Somerville,
With courage bold, did he control, he played his part so well.....

Appropriately, the hero of this piece is himself of the same surname as one of
Sir Walter's previously mentioned assistants in his researches into the
Border Minstrel Tradition. And, in view of the fact that the storyline of the
ballad is concerned with the capture of a French ship by a smaller British one
during the Napoleonic Wars, it is perhaps also of interest that Scott's *Honest
Tar,* whose Father was to introduce the Laird of Abbotsford to Burns on the
only occasion that the two of them ever met, features in O'Byrne's *Dictionary
of Naval Biography* in connection with a series of similar incidents in which
he himself played a more than passing role.

Curiously, the events here described have a strange and unexpected
connection of their own with Peacehaven, the town where the Singing
Coppers now reside. According to O'Byrne's *Dictionary of Naval Biography,*
on the 20th of October 1806, the young Lieutenant John Macpherson
Ferguson took up post aboard the Redwing Sloop, stationed in the Straights
of Gibraltar. Just two days previously, on October 18th of the same year,
according to the *Dictionary of National Biography*, Captain Thomas Ussher
(1779-1848), the self-same Thomas Ussher who would later become
Grandfather to Charles Neville, Peacehaven's founder, had been newly
promoted to the rank of Commander, and appointed captain of the very same
vessel "in which he", Captain Ussher, "was chiefly employed in protecting
the trade against the Spanish gunboats and privateers near Gibraltar. On this
service he was repeatedly engaged with the gunboats or armed vessels, often
against a great numerical superiority, and especially on 7 May 1808, near
Cape Trafalgar, when he fell in with seven armed vessels conveying twelve
coasters. Of the nineteen, three only escaped, eight of the others being sunk
and eight taken; the loss of men to the enemy killed, drowned and prisoners
was returned as 240."

With regard to the Honest Tar's role in this, and several other similar actions,
O'Byrne's informs us that "Mr. Ferguson, who continued in that vessel for a
period of 20 months as her First-Lieutenant, bore a conspicuous part in a
number of very dashing exploits. On 20th April, 1807, he ably supported
Capt. Ussher in a spirited engagement with a division of Spanish gun-boats
and several batteries near Cabritta Point; and, on 7 Sept. following, he

commanded the boats and displayed much gallantry in an attempt made to destroy several vessels, under a most galling fire from the town of Calassel. The day after the latter event he obtained the highest praise of his Captain for his bravery in boarding a polacre ship whose yard-arms nearly touched the castle of Benidorme, and for his conduct throughout a stiff action which terminated, in the destruction, near Jovosa, of three privateers, mounting altogether 20 guns. On 7 May, 1808, he further contributed, by his unsurpassingly cool and determined conduct, to the utter defeat of seven armed vessels, carrying in the aggregate 22 guns and 271 men, of whom 240 were killed, drowned, or taken prisoners; subsequently to which he again commanded the boats at the capture and destruction, on 1 June, of a mistico and two feluccas in the Bay of Bolonia, where he also landed with Captain Ussher, stormed a battery and blew up the magazine......"

As to whether or not Captain Ussher or Lieutenant Ferguson ever heard the Copper Family's *Warlike Seamen* sung aboard ship, or snug in port, we shall never know. But it must have been a popular song amongst the sea dogs of the time, for its lyrics are full of dramatic sea fighting incident which could only really be accurately recounted by one who was actually there, as the following lines from the fifth verse show:

The first broadside we gave to them which made them for to wonder,
Their main mast and their rigging came a-rattling down like thunder,
We drove them from their quarter, they could no longer stay,
Our guns did roar, we made so sure, we showed them British play!

But what of the links between the Copper Tradition and that of the Rhymer? Well, curiously enough, amongst the ballads extant in the village during the early years of this century was a song which had developed out of the Mediaeval Minstrel Tradition which we ourselves encountered at an earlier juncture in our story. The song itself is entitled *Lord Thomas and Fair Eleanor,* and was originally in the repertoire of one of the local shepherds, by the name of Steve Barrow. The ballad is a version of *Lord Thomas and Fair Annie*, which is inserted in the *Minstrelsy* directly between the Arthurian *Kempion* and the supernatural *Wife of Usher's Well;* which, as has already been noted at an earlier juncture in this book, may have a subliminal connection with the family of Sir Thomas Ussher mentioned above.

Curiously enough, during the Middle Ages, the Earls of Warenne and Surrey held lands in Sussex in the neighbourhood of Lewes castle, itself just a few miles inland from the seaside village of Rottingdean. As has already been seen, one of their descendants married into the Scottish Royal House, and was thus ancestress not only of the Lines of de Brus and Stuart, but may also have been connected with the real life rebel upon whom the ballad character of Robin Hood was ultimately based (See Appendix 3, Tables 1 & 2). For, Ada de Warenne's husband was a supposed half brother of one of the St. Liz Family, who was himself to succeed as Abbot of Melrose in the middle of the Twelfth Century; and was therefore connected with a supposed wife of one the de Tonbridge Family who were to become ancestors of the aristocratic insurgent who lies under the stone at Kirklees Priory where the Mediaeval outlaw supposedly rests.

As was also hinted at with the quotation from a famous Melrosian song at the head of this chapter, St. Dunstan, himself with inumerable links with both Glastonbury and Sussex, likewise has a well dedicated to him close to the ancient Abbey ruins; a fact also touched on briefly during the course of an earlier chapter. More significant still is the fact that a monastic foundation at Old Melrose, where the original Abbey once stood, was presided over by St. Cuthbert, with whom the Border town has numerous connections, and who was himself a contemporary of St. Wilfred; the man accredited with the stamping out of paganism in Sussex. Like the latter saint, Cuthbert was educated at Lindisfarne, the most important religious centre in the old Earldom of Northumbria; the ruling family of which could also claim connections with the de Warennes at the height of the Middle Ages. These facts do more to explain the reasons why, in some versions at least of the *Tristrem* legend immortalized by the Rhymer of Ercildoune, there are references to such obvious Sussex locations as Arundel; a fact looked at once again during an earlier stage in our story.

But whatever the true origin of these clear and provable associations between the folk singing of Rottingdean and that of Scotland, in particular that of the Borders, the one reason why the Copper Family Tradition survives intact, whereas the Border Minstrelsy collected by Scott some two centuries ago has been scattered to the four winds, is that the rural community that preserved it remained tied to the land right into our own century. And, despite the destruction of the Downland environment by overdevelopment of housing, the Family at the centre of this tradition has remained largely undispersed.

There are no wool mills on the Sussex Downs as there are along the Tweed; and as a result the village of Rottingdean and its environs lay undisturbed in agrarian obscurity until the manifestation of Peacehaven and Saltdean less than eighty years ago.

As for Scott, he himself succeeded as regards what he set out to do. He realized that times were changing and the destruction of the communities that had preserved the traditions that he wrote down for posterity was imminent. And, before the industrialization process set in, he was there with his pen, writing everything down for posterity. Now, thanks to him, Leyden, and their associates, this material can be accessed through major libraries across the country. And, thanks to the likes of Ewan MacColl in our own century, many of the ballads that they collected can still be heard today.

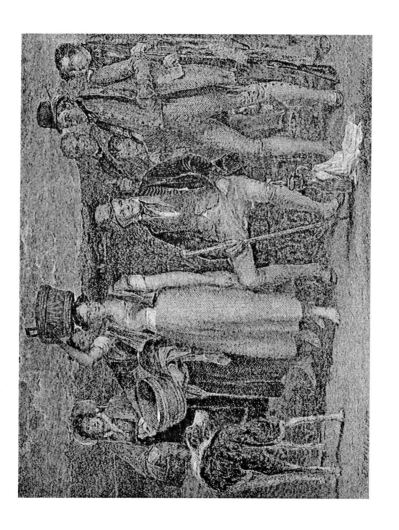

Illustration 14): Victorian engavring of Wilkie's "Abbotsford Family". For notes, see illustration no. 8.

Appendix 1

Surtees and Hogg: Key to A Literary Controversy?

Robert Surtees's forgeries of Border ballads, supposedly culled from popular traditions prevalent in his native County Durham, provide the key, in many respects, to those anxious to criticize the Laird of Abbotsford's scholastic integrity. As is shown in Chapter Eleven of this book, however, Scott's main contemporary critic was James Hogg; the celebrated Ettrick Shepherd.

In view of these facts, it is perhaps interesting that Hogg himself may provide one of the keys to the motivations that were to result in these Durham forgeries. Professor Eric Birley, in his 1972 introduction to the E.P. Publishing re-issue of the four volume 1816-1840 edition of Surtees's *History and Antiquities of the County Palatine of Durham*, writes extensively of the latter's acquaintance with Hogg; quoting Raine's 1852 footnotes to his account of the pair's first meeting in Edinburgh in the year 1819:

"The atmosphere was sultry, of itself enough to make Mr. Surtees, at any time, uncomfortable, and Hogg would walk arm in arm with him upon the hot flags in Prince's Street. This custom Surtees always abominated most heartily, but he submitted, for a while, in patience. He soon, however, withdrew to write letters......"

Upon perusal of Chapter Eleven, and Buchan's account of Hogg's summing up of his opinion of Scott's editorship of the *Minstrelsy,* the reader may be forgiven for concluding that, at times, Hogg's criticisms, are pompous to say the least. Hogg's mercilessness as far as Scott was concerned is even more unforgivable when it is considered that he himself never managed to unmask the forgery committed by Surtees; thus making it equally forgivable for Scott not to have done so.

In Hogg's case there may have been ulterior motives. Scott's blind spot as far as his friend was concerned has been dealt with at length, but Hogg's motivation appears to have been purely financial. Taylor and Raine's accounts of the relationship attest to Hogg having been given money by Surtees; as a means of assisting him in his poetical writings; a fact which was to lead Hogg to write, in a letter to Surtees dated 18th March 1807, of how he was "not a little proud of the approbation" Surtees had been "pleased to bestow upon a mountain bard...."; whilst simultaneously adding that the latter had sent him "that which is still more beneficial to the generality of poets, especially one of..." his own "rank of life".

In view of this, it is by no means impossible that Surtees concealed the extent and nature of his forgeries, so that future generations might judge the Ettrick Shepherd's assessments of Scott whilst at the same time considering Hogg's apparent silence with respect to his own contributions to the *Minstrelsy*. This is in itself a subject which may well generate yet more speculation by future generations of writers as the passage of time continues.

Appendix 2

A Note on the Metrical Manuscript Sources Relating to the Ballad of Thomas of Ercildoune

In the "note and appendix" to his version of the Ancient Ballad of Thomas the Rhymer, Scott presents his readers with the text of "an old and unfortunately imperfect" copy of a manuscript original of "Thomas the Rhymer's intrigue with the Queen of Faery". Elsewhere in the same text the Laird of Abbotsford adds that "There is a copy of this poem in the museum in the cathedral of Lincoln, another in the collection in Peterborough, but unfortunately they are all in an imperfect state, Mr. Jamieson, in his curious collection of *Scottish Ballads and Songs,* has an entire copy of this ancient poem, with all the collations....."

The poem itself, which consists of a metrical rendition of the tale which is at the centre of Chapter Three of this work, is in turn a manifestation of direct proof that yet another of the key ballads collected by Scott had evolved out of the metrical minstrel traditions of the High Middle Ages. Scott's version of the text, which begins as follows:

> *In a lande as I was lent,*
> *In the gryking of the day,*
> *Ay alone as I went,*
> *In Huntlie bankys me for to play;......*

is taken from the Cotton ms. Vitellius E. X. In the British Museum Collection. The manuscript, which is described by Murray as "A paper volume in folio, in very bad condition..." is roughly datable to the middle of the fifteenth century by the latter's reckoning. (See Murray's *Romance and Prophecies*, p.lviii et seq.)

Appenòix 3: Table 1: Kings of Scotland from Malcolm I to Robert the Bruce:

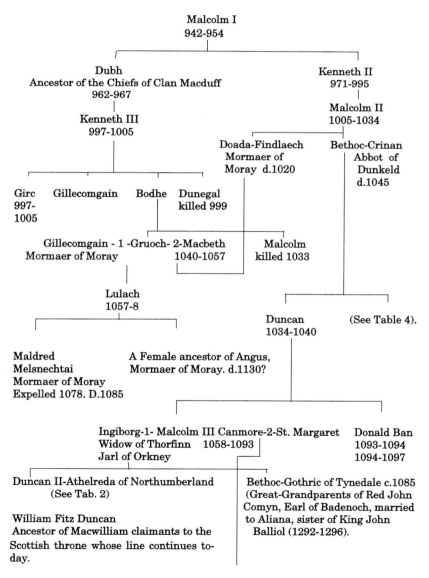

Malcolm I
942-954

Dubh
Ancestor of the Chiefs of Clan Macduff
962-967

Kenneth III
997-1005

Kenneth II
971-995

Malcolm II
1005-1034

Doada-Findlaech
Mormaer of
Moray d.1020

Bethoc-Crinan
Abbot of
Dunkeld
d.1045

Girc   Gillecomgain   Bodhe   Dunegal
997-   killed 999
1005

Gillecomgain - 1 -Gruoch- 2-Macbeth
Mormaer of Moray   1040-1057

Malcolm
killed 1033

Lulach
1057-8

Duncan   (See Table 4).
1034-1040

Maldred
Melsnechtai
Mormaer of Moray
Expelled 1078. D.1085

A Female ancestor of Angus,
Mormaer of Moray. d.1130?

Ingiborg-1- Malcolm III Canmore-2-St. Margaret
Widow of Thorfinn   1058-1093
Jarl of Orkney

Donald Ban
1093-1094
1094-1097

Duncan II-Athelreda of Northumberland
(See Tab. 2)

William Fitz Duncan
Ancestor of Macwilliam claimants to the
Scottish throne whose line continues to-
day.

Bethoc-Gothric of Tynedale c.1085
(Great-Grandparents of Red John
Comyn, Earl of Badenoch, married
to Aliana, sister of King John
Balliol (1292-1296).

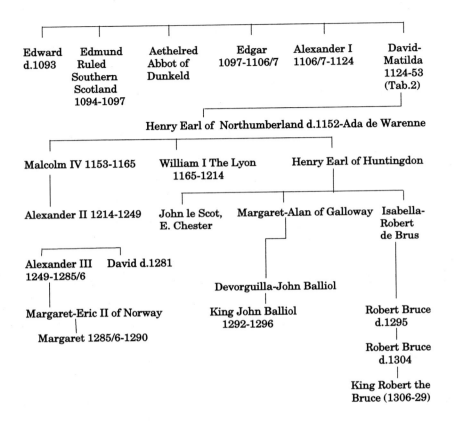

Edward
d.1093

Edmund
Ruled
Southern
Scotland
1094-1097

Aethelred
Abbot of
Dunkeld

Edgar
1097-1106/7

Alexander I
1106/7-1124

David-
Matilda
1124-53
(Tab.2)

Henry Earl of Northumberland d.1152-Ada de Warenne

Malcolm IV 1153-1165

William I The Lyon
1165-1214

Henry Earl of Huntingdon

Alexander II 1214-1249

John le Scot,
E. Chester

Margaret-Alan of Galloway

Isabella-
Robert
de Brus

Alexander III   David d.1281
1249-1285/6

Margaret-Eric II of Norway

Margaret 1285/6-1290

Devorguilla-John Balliol

King John Balliol
1292-1296

Robert Bruce
d.1295

Robert Bruce
d.1304

King Robert the
Bruce (1306-29)

Appendix 3: Table 2: The Saxon Earls of Northumberland:

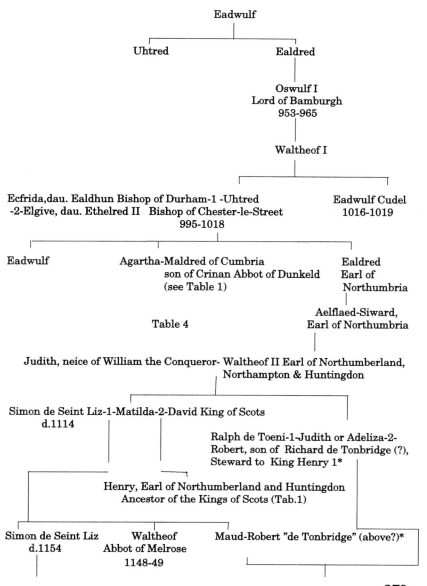

Eadwulf

Uhtred   Ealdred

Oswulf I
Lord of Bamburgh
953-965

Waltheof I

Ecfrida,dau. Ealdhun Bishop of Durham-1 -Uhtred   Eadwulf Cudel
-2-Elgive, dau. Ethelred II   Bishop of Chester-le-Street   1016-1019
995-1018

Eadwulf   Agartha-Maldred of Cumbria   Ealdred
son of Crinan Abbot of Dunkeld   Earl of
(see Table 1)   Northumbria

Aelflaed-Siward,
Table 4   Earl of Northumbria

Judith, neice of William the Conqueror- Waltheof II Earl of Northumberland,
Northampton & Huntingdon

Simon de Seint Liz-1-Matilda-2-David King of Scots
d.1114

Ralph de Toeni-1-Judith or Adeliza-2-
Robert, son of Richard de Tonbridge (?),
Steward to King Henry 1*

Henry, Earl of Northumberland and Huntingdon
Ancestor of the Kings of Scots (Tab.1)

Simon de Seint Liz   Waltheof   Maud-Robert "de Tonbridge" (above?)*
d.1154   Abbot of Melrose
1148-49

379

| | Walter fitz Robert |
| | | |

St. Liz Earls of Northampton   Robert fitz Walter, "Marshal of
& Huntingdon**   the Army of God and Holy Church",
                                 and the real life model for Robin
                                 Hood?

*Confusion due to Dugdale's errors.

**The St. Liz Family were restored to the rights of the Earldom of Huntingdon, to which the Kings of Scots had succeeded during the reign of Henry II; following William King of Scots' support of Prince Henry's rebellion. (P.120 Burke's Ext. Peerages).

Appendix 3: Table 3: The de Toenis and their Connections (after Hewins and Others):

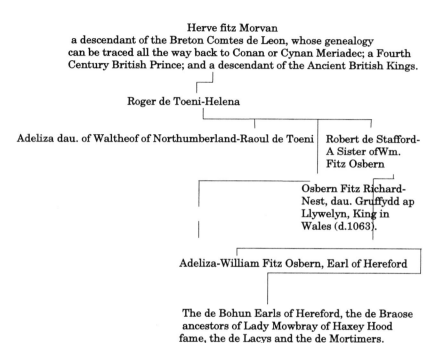

Herve fitz Morvan
a descendant of the Breton Comtes de Leon, whose genealogy
can be traced all the way back to Conan or Cynan Meriadec; a Fourth
Century British Prince; and a descendant of the Ancient British Kings.

Roger de Toeni-Helena

Adeliza dau. of Waltheof of Northumberland-Raoul de Toeni | Robert de Stafford-
A Sister ofWm.
Fitz Osbern

Osbern Fitz Richard-
Nest, dau. Gruffydd ap
Llywelyn, King in
Wales (d.1063).

Adeliza-William Fitz Osbern, Earl of Hereford

The de Bohun Earls of Hereford, the de Braose
ancestors of Lady Mowbray of Haxey Hood
fame, the de Lacys and the de Mortimers.

Appendix 3: Table 4: The Legacy of Wessex in the North:

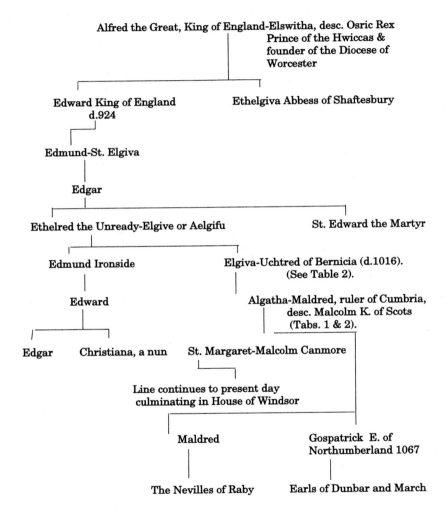

Alfred the Great, King of England-Elswitha, desc. Osric Rex
Prince of the Hwiccas &
founder of the Diocese of
Worcester

Edward King of England
d.924

Ethelgiva Abbess of Shaftesbury

Edmund-St. Elgiva

Edgar

Ethelred the Unready-Elgive or Aelgifu

St. Edward the Martyr

Edmund Ironside

Elgiva-Uchtred of Bernicia (d.1016).
(See Table 2).

Edward

Algatha-Maldred, ruler of Cumbria,
desc. Malcolm K. of Scots
(Tabs. 1 & 2).

Edgar   Christiana, a nun   St. Margaret-Malcolm Canmore

Line continues to present day
culminating in House of Windsor

Maldred

Gospatrick E. of
Northumberland 1067

The Nevilles of Raby

Earls of Dunbar and March

Appenðíx 3: Table 5: The Merciαn Ancestry of ðe Bohun, ðe Braose, ðe Mortimer αnð the Griffiths of Garn: *

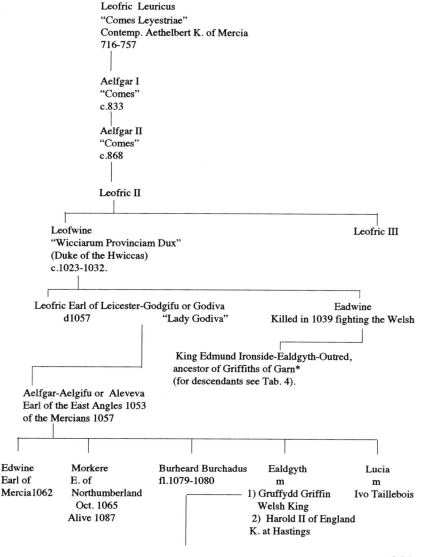

Leofric Leuricus
"Comes Leyestriae"
Contemp. Aethelbert K. of Mercia
716-757

Aelfgar I
"Comes"
c.833

Aelfgar II
"Comes"
c.868

Leofric II

Leofwine
"Wicciarum Provinciam Dux"
(Duke of the Hwiccas)
c.1023-1032.

Leofric III

Leofric Earl of Leicester-Godgifu or Godiva
d1057   "Lady Godiva"

Eadwine
Killed in 1039 fighting the Welsh

King Edmund Ironside-Ealdgyth-Outred,
ancestor of Griffiths of Garn*
(for descendants see Tab. 4).

Aelfgar-Aelgifu or Aleveva
Earl of the East Angles 1053
of the Mercians 1057

Edwine	Morkere	Burheard Burchadus	Ealdgyth	Lucia
Earl of	E. of	fl.1079-1080	m	m
Mercia1062	Northumberland		1) Gruffydd Griffin	Ivo Taillebois
	Oct. 1065		Welsh King	
	Alive 1087		2) Harold II of England	
			K. at Hastings	

383

Nest
m
Bernard de Neufmarche

Houses of de Bohun, de Braose and de Mortimer
(See Table 4).

*See Chapter 4.

Appendix 4

Glossary of Old Scottish and Northumbrian Terms

a' : all
ablins: perhaps
aboon (aboun, abune) : above
abread: abroad
ackward: backward
ae: a, one, sole
aff: off
afore: before
aft: oft
agen: again
ahint: behind
aiblins: perhaps
aik: oak
ain (awn, awin): own
aince: once
air: court (eyre)
airn: iron
aith: oath
alake: alack
alane: alone
alterchange: exchange
amang: among
an: if, although
ance: once
ane: one
aneath: beneath, under
anent: over against
anes (anis): once
anither: another
ankers: anchors
anow: enough

arblest: crossbow
armis: arms
ask: newt
aspin: aspen
asteer (asteir): astir
atween: between
aught: possess
auld: old
awa': away
awin (awn, ain): own
ayd: aid
ay(e): always, ever, yes
ayont: beyond

ba: ball
back: mount
bair: bored
bairn(ie): child
baith: both
baken: baked
bale: evil
bale: faggot
band: bound, bond
bandsters: binders of sheaves
bane: bone
bangisters: victors, the prevailing party
barken'd: tanned
barmkin: barbican, outmost fortification
basnet: helmet

385

bassen'd: white-faced
batts: beating
bauld(ly): bold(ly)
beet: aid
begoud: began
beild: shelter
belang: belong
belive: by and by, immediately
banachadee: blessing of God
beneith: beneath
benison: blessing
bent: bent-grass
benty: covered with bent-grass
beseen: provided
bespak(e): spoke
bet: better
betyde: befall
bickering: pelting
bide: dwell (abide), stay, endure
bigg: build
bigged (bigget): built
bigging: building
bigly: pleasant
billie: brother, comrade
binna: be not
birks: birches
birled: plied
birst: burst
blae: blue
blan: drew breath
blaw: blow
blawn: blown
blee: bloom
bleed (bleid, blude, bluid, blode): blood
blink: glance, glitter
bluidhound: bloodhound
bluidy: bloody
bodie: body
bogle: goblin

bonile(bonnily): prettily
bonny: pretty, beautiful
boud: must
boun: bound
bour: bower
boustouslie: boisterously
bout: bolt
bouted: sifted (of flour)
brae: hillside, declivity
brag: boast
braid(er): broad(er)
braid letter: royal warrant
brak: break or broke
braken: bracken-fern
brand: sword
branking: prancing
branks: halter
brash: sickness
braw: beautiful (brave)
brayd: press
brecham; horse-collar
brechans: bracken-fern
bree: brow
breist: breast
bricht: bright
brie: brow
brieks (breeks): trousers
brig(g): bridge
brither: brother
broach: clasp (brooch)
brock: badger
brokit: spotted
broo: broth
broomcow: brush of broom
broun: brown
browheid: forehead
bryttled: cut up (of a deer)
bucht: sheep- or cattle-fold
bug: built
b(o)ughts: see bucht

bunch: punch, a blow
burd: maiden
burd alane: quite alone
burn: brook
bursten; burst
busket; dressed
bussing: covering
but and ben: into the kitchen and into the parlour
by: besides
bydeth: dwelleth
byre: cow-house

ca': call
ca': drive (as "ca' a nail"- drive home a nail)
ca's: calves
cam: came
canna: cannot
capapie: head to foot (cap-a-pied)
carknet: necklace
carle: man
carline: old woman
carped: sang (minstrel fashion)
cauf: calf
caugers: carriers
caukers: hind parts of horse-shoes, sharpened and turned down
cauld: cold
causeways: streets, pavements
channerin': grumbling
chapp'd: knocked
cheir: cheer
childe: youth
Christentie: Christendom
claes: clothes
claith: cloth
clam(b): climbed clark: clerk
claw: scratch
clead: clothe

cleiding: clothing
cleugh: a narrow valley
cloathes: clothes
clogged: burdened
closeheads: entrance to a "close", ie. to a tenement of houses.
coats: petticoats
coft: bought
cog: wooden milking-pail
coll'd: cut
conquess: conquer
contrair: contrary to, opposed to
convey: escort
convoy'd: escorted
corbie: raven, crow
cosh: quiet
coulter: plough-share
courtrie: courtiers
cout (cowt): colt
couthie: pleasant
c o w l s : n i g h t c a p s (c o w l s o f Kilmarnock = weavers of Kilmarnock)
crack: talk
craig: crag
craig: neck, throat
craw: crow
craw'd: crowed
craw'n: crowed
crew: crowed
cronach: dirge (coronach0
croon: hum a song
croun: crown
crouse(ly): conceited(ly)
cum: come
curche: coif
cutted: cut
dae: do
dae; doe
daffin: joking

dang: knocked, defeated
dar: dare
darna: dare not
daunton: frighten
daur: dare
daw(ing): dawning
dead-wounded: mortally wounded
dee: die
dee: do
deid: death (dead)
deil: devil
deir: dear, deer
derfe: cruel
derke: dark
dern: obscure, secret
didna: did not
dight: clad
dight: prepared
dight: wipe
dight: defeat
ding: knock
dinna: do not
dints: blows
disna: does not
dole: terrible
donot: silly slut
doo: dove
dool: sorrow
dought: could
douk: dive (duck)
doun: down
dour: determined, hard to move
douse: sedate (douce)
dow (doo): dove
dow(na): can(not)
dowie: drear
drap: drop
dree (drie): suffer, endure
dreid: dread
dreim(it): dreame(ed)

drierie: dreary
drifts: flocks
drivand: driving
drumly: discoloured, cloudy, turbid
drunkily: drunkenly
dub: pool
dune: done
dure: door
dwalt: dwelt
dyke: a wall (of stone or of turf)

eard: earth
e'e: eye
een: eyes
e'en: even, to put into comparison
e'en: evening
eery (eerie, eiry): weird, uncanny, awesome
eldern: elderly
el(d)ritch: ghastly, unearthly
elshin: shoemaker's awl
eneuch, eneugh: Enough
ensenzie: ensign
erlish: ghastly, unearthly (eldritch)
erne: eagle
esk (ask): newt
evermair: evermore

fa': fall, befall
fae: foe
fae (fay): faith
faem: foam
fa'en: fallen
fail: turf
fain(e): eager
falla: fellow
fand: found
fang: grasp, catch
fashes: troubles
fauld: sheepfold

fause: false
fear'd: afraid
fecht: fight
fee: wages, recompense
feid: feud
feir: Fair
fell: hillside
fell: hide, skin
fell: Knock down
fend: support, defence
feres: companions
ferly (ferlie): wonder
fewes: fellows
fie (fey): doomed, predestined
fireflaught: flash of lightning
flain: arrow
flang: flung
flatter'd: fluttered
flee: fly
fleeching: coaxing, fluttering
flesher: butcher
fley'd: frightened
flinders: splinters
flour: flower
flyting: scolding
forbye: beside(s)
foredoor: front door
forfaulted: forfeited
forfoughten (forfochen): wearied
out, weary
forletting: abandoning
fou: full
fra(e): from
frie: free
frith: a wood, a clearing in a wood
frush: brittle, flimsy
fu': full
fule: fool
fure: went, fared
furs: furrows

fute: foot
fyne: fine

gabbin': chatting, gossiping
gad: goad
gae: go
gae; gave
gaed: went
ga'en: going
gane: gone
gane: suffice
gang: go
ganging: going
gangna: go not
gar: cause, compel
gat: got, begot
gate: road
gaun: going
gear (geir): goods (merchant-geir =
merchandise): spoils
geck: scoffed
genzie: engine of war
gie: give
gif: if
gillyflowers: clove-carnations,
wallflowers
gilt: gold, gilded
gin: if
girds: hoops
glassen: made of glass
gled: hawk, kite
gleed: a fiery ember
gleuves: gloves
gloaming: twilight
glour: stare
glowr'd: stared
gotten: got
goud (gowd): gold
goud: began
gowden: golden

gowk: cuckoo, fool
graith: harness, accoutrements
gramarye: magic
grat: wept
gravat: scarf (cravat)
green (grien): long for
greet: weep
grewhound: greyhound
grids: hoops
grie (gree): prize
griesly: fearsome
grippit: arrested
grit: great
gronde: ground
gryming: sprinkling
gude(ly): good(ly)
gudeman: husband
gudemother: mother-in-law
guesten'd: been a guest
gullies: large knives
gurly: stormy, boisterous

ha' : hall
had: hold
hadna: had not
hae: have
haftet: handled
*haggis-bag:*sheep's stomach containing the ingredients of a haggis
haik: keep in suspense
hail: whole
hala mischy doch: I can take a drink
halden: hold
half-fou: eighth part of a peck
hals (hause): neck
hame: home
hang: hung
happ'd: covered
happers: hoppers (of a mill)

harneist: harnessed, accoutred
har'st: harvest
hasna: has not
haud: hold
hauld: stronghold
hause-bane: neck-bone, collar-bone
head: behead
heid: head, chief
heir: here
hende: young man
hente: hoisted, laid hold of
her: their
herry: harry, plunder
he's: he will
het: hot
heugh: hollow
heugh: cliff
hicht: height
hided; hid
hie: high, haughty
hight: named
hirsels: flocks
hoigh: an ejaculation of sorry or pain
hollin: holly
honde: hand
hooly: cautiously
hoot awa'; an ejaculation of derision
hough: thigh (shin of a cow)
houlet: owl
hover'd: paused
how(e): hollow
howm: holm (river-meadow)
hoysed: hoisted
hunder: hundred
hye: high

ilk(a): each, every
ingle: fireside
inglenook: chimney corner

intill (intull): in, into
I'se: I shall
isna: is not
ither: other
it's be: it will be

jaw: dash, splash
Jeddart: Jedburgh
jimp: slender, neat

kaim: comb
kale: colewort
kane: rent-in-kind
keekit (keeked): peeped
kell: shroud
kemp: champion
ken: know
kend(t): knew
kenna: know not
keppit: caught
kern: foot-soldier (Irish or Highland): rogue, vagabond
kevils: lots
kilted: turned back, tucked up
kinmen: rabbits
kirns: churns
kirtle: mantle
kist: chest
kittle: difficult
knapscap: steel head-piece
knave: boy
knaw: know
kneepan: kneecap
know: hillock
knowes: knolls, hillocks
ky(e): cattle

laddie: boy
lade: load
laigh: low

laiming: laming
laird: landlord
lair'd: bogged
laith: loath
lance: leap
lane: lone
lang: long
lang or: long before
lang syne: long ago
lap: leaped, sprang
latten: allowed
lave: the rest
lav'rock: lark
law: a conical hill
lawing: reckoning (tavern bill)
Lawland: Lowland
lay: lea
layne: hide
leafu': lawful
leal (leil): faithful, loyal, loyalty
lear: learning
lee: lie
leeching: physicianship
leeze: expression of great pleasure
leglin: milking-pail
leman: light-of-love, lover
leugh: laughed
leven: a lawn
levin: lightning
libbards: leopards (emblem of England)
lien: lain
lift: sky
lightly: make light of
lilting: singing cheerfully
limber: supple
limmer: rascal
Lincome: Lincoln
ling: heath
linkin': riding briskly

linn: waterfall, pool
lirk: hollow
lither: lazy
loan(ing): lane
lookit: looked
loon (loun, lown): fellow, rogue
loot: allowed, let
loup: leap
louped: leaped
loupen: leaped
lourd: rather
louted: bowed
low(e): flame
luke: look
lurdane: lazy fellow
luve: love
lyart: grizzled (of hair)
lykewake: watch kept over a dead body
lyth: joint

ma(e): more
mail(l): rent, a levy
mair: more
maist: most
mak: make
make (maik): equal (match)
malisoun: curse
mane: moan
manhead: fortitude
manteel: mantle
march: border
marrow: equal, partner, spouse
mault: malt
maun: must
maunna: must not
maw: mow
may: maiden
mear: mare
meik: meek

mell: mallet
mergh: marrow
merle: blackbird
mese: soothe
meikle: great, much
minnie: mother
mirk: dark (pit-mirk = pitch dark)
monie: money
Moninday: Monday
mony: many
moodiehill: molehill (mowdiehill)
morn: to-morrow
moss: boggy moor
mote: might
moul: earth (mould0
mowse: joke
muckle: big
muir: moor
mysell: myself
mystery: trade

na(e): no, not
naething: nothing
nagie: pony
naigs: horses (nags)
nane: none
neids: needs
neir: near
ne'er: never
neist: next
neuk: corner (nook)
nevir: never
nicher (nicker): whinny (neigh)
nie: neigh
nogs: notches
nogs: stakes
nor: than
nourice: nurse
nowt: cattle
o': of

o'erword (owerword): refrain, watchword, slogan
ohon!: alas!
ony: any
or: ere (lang or : long ere)
o's: of his
oure (ower): over
ousen (owsen): oxen
outher: other
outspeckle: laughing-stock

pa': a slight movement
pallion(e)s: tents (panlions)
pang'd: crammed
papinjay: parrot
pat: put
paughty: haughty
pawky: shrewd
peck: a large quantity
pick: pitch
pickle: a little of
piggin': pot with two ears
pike: pick
pit: pitch
pith: spirit, substance
plat: pleated, interwove
plea: dispute
pleas: pleads
pleugh: plough
plooky: pimpled
plummet: pommel of a sword
poin'd: distrained; attached by legal distress (poinded)
popinjay: parrot
port: gate
pow: head
pricking: riding
propine: usually gift, but in the ballad of *Lady Anne*, the power of giving or bestowing

p(o)u'd: pulled
puir: poor
puirly: poorly, softly
putten; put
pyne: grief
pyot; magpie

quair; choir
quey: heifer
quick: alive
quire: choir
quo': quoth

rad: afraid
rade (raid): rode
rae: roe
rair: roar
raise: rose
ramp: headstrong
rane roch: rough chatter
ransha(c)kle: ransack
rapes: ropes
raw: row
rax: reach, ie. "stretched out to"
raxed: stretched
'ray: order
reasun: reason
red: clear up
redd: advise
rede: council
reid: red
reif: robbery
reiver: robber
rerd: hubbub
rewd: rude
reyn: rein
rig: ridge, a section of field
rigging: ridge of roof
right: used adverbially = very (right puir = very poor)

rin: run
roose: praise
roudes (rudas): haggard
routing; bellowing
rowe(s): roll(s)
rowfooted: rough shod
rowing: rolling
rowth: abundance (routh)
rue: regret
rug: slice
ruke: rook
runkled: wrinkled
ryme: satirize

sabbing: sobbing
sackless: blameless
sae; so
saft(ly): soft(ly), light(ly)
saften'd: softened
sain'd; hallowed
sair: sore
sall: shall
sang: song
sark: shirt
saughel (saugh): willow
saul: soul
saut: salt
saw: sow
sax: six
sayne: said
scale (skail): disperse
scelp'd (skelped): slapped
scoup: fly
screech: shriek
scroggs: stunted trees
scug: expiate or shelter
seamaw (seamew): seagull
selcouth: wondrous
sel(l): self- usually in compounds,
eg. *hersell:* herself

selle: saddle
sen: sent
sestow: see'st thou
seyd: said
shanna: shall not
sharp'd: sharpened
shaw: show
shaw(s): woods
shearing: reaping
shee: shoe
sheen: shining
sheugh: ditch, hollow
shoon: shoes
shot: assessment
shot-window: bow-window
sic(k): such
siccan: such a
sicht: sighed
sicken: such a
sicker(lie): sure(ly)
siller: money (silver)
simmer: summer
sinsyne: since that time
skaith('d): harm(ed)
skeely: skilful
skeigh: shy
skelp: slap
skimmering: shimmering
skrei(c)h: peep of the day
slae: sloe
slee: sly
slogan: war-cry
sloken: slake
sma': small
smit: clashing noise (smiting)
smoor'd: smothered
snaw: snow
sneer: snort
snell: keen (of a wind)

snood: ribbon for confining the hair, worn by maidens
sooth (suith): south
soudron: southron, southerner (Englishman, as distinguished from Scotsman)
souter: shoemaker
south: truth (sooth)
spaebook: book of spells or prophecies
spait: flood
spak: spoke
spauld: shoulder
speer (speir): ask
speik: speak
speir: Spear
sprattle: scramble
spule (spaul): shoulder
spunkie: mettlesome
sta': stall
sta': stole
stalward: stalwart
stalworth(y)e: valiant
stane: stone
steads: farm buildings, settlements
stear (steer): stir
steek: stitch
steek: shut
stell'd: placed, posted
stern: star
stey: steep
stint(ed): ceease(d)
stoor: wild
stour(e): stern, rough
stour: strife
stown (stoun): stolen
strack: struck
strae: straw
strang: strong
straught: straight

streak: lie
streamers: Northern Lights
streeked (streikit): stroked
streekit: laid out (of a corpse)
striped: thrust
stroken (struken): struck
stude: stood
st(o)un: pang
sture(stour): stern
sturt: disturbance
stythe: place
s(o)uld: should
sune: soon
swakked: wielded
swapped: exchanged
sware: swore
swat: sweated
swoom'd: swam
syde: hanging low down
syke: a marshy, hollow, depth
syne: then, thereafter

ta'en: taken
tak: take
tane: the one
targats: tassels
taul: the one
tauld: told
tee: to
teind: tithe
teirs: tears
tetherstakes: spikes for fixing a tether in the ground
tett: lock of hair or wool
thae: these
thair: their
than: then
theek: thatch
thies: thighs
thir: those

tho: then
thole: endure
thrall: captivity
thraw: throw, twist
thretty: thirty
thrie: three
thristlecock: thrush
throw: through
till: to
tint: lost
tirl: cause to vibrate and so to call attention
tod: fox
toom: empty
tother (tither): the other
toun: town (used frequently of a farm)
tours: towers
tows: ropes
traivelling: travail, childbirth
trattels: prattles
trayne: train
treasonrie: treachery
trew: trust
trew: true
trie: lance-shaft (tree)
trig: neat
trone: scaffold
trouth (trowth): truth
trow: feel sure, believe
tryst: a meeting, or meeting-place, assignation
tuik: took
tul: to
twa(e): two
twafald: twofold, double
twain: part
twal: twelve
twalt: twelfth
twasome: couple

twine(d): separate(d)
tykes: dogs
tyne (tine): lose
tyning: losing
tyres: bands for the hair

ugsome: ugly
unkensome: unknown
unwordily: unworthily
upgive: surrender
urchin: hedgehog

vera: very

wa': wall
wace: wax
wa(l)d: would
wad: wager, pledge
wadded at: wagered on
wadna: would not
wadst: wouldst
wae: sad
wae: woe
wains: waggons
wake: watch over the dead before burial
wale: choose
waled: chosen
wallowing: roaring, bellowing
waly: exclamation of grief
wame: belly, womb
wan: won
wane: number of people
wanna: won not
wap: wrap
wapp'd: twisted, wrapped
war: were
ware: squander
wark: work
warld: world

warrand: warrant
warse: worse
warwolf: werewolf
wat: knew
wat: wet, wetted
water: a river
waur: worse
wear: guard
wede: vanished
wee: little
wee(l): well
weel-fa(u)r'd: handsome, well-favoured
weet: wet, rain
weetless (wyteless): blameless
weil(heid): eddy(head)
weir: war
weird(wierd): fate, transformation
wha(e): who
whang: long lace, thong
wha(u)r: where
whase: whose
whaten: what kind of
wheit: wheat
whew: whistle
whidderan: whistling
whiles: occasionally
whilk: which
whingers: daggers, swords
wi': with
wicker: a pliant sapling or twig
wight: stout (man), brave
wil: wild
wimplin': rippling
win to: arrive at
win up: rise up, ascend
winna: will not
wis: believe
wist(na): knew (not0
wite (wyte): blame
withouten: without

wittering: knowledge, hint
Wodensday: Wednesday
wons: resides
wood: mad
wordie: worthy
wot: know
wow: an exclamation of grief
woxe: waxed
wrang: wrong
wrang: wrung
wrote: written
wud: mad

yate (yett): gate
yeir: year
ye'se: you shall
yestreen: last night (yester eve)
ynome: taken
youlin': howling
younkers: youths
yoursell: yourself
yowe: ewe

Díscographíc Notes

Since the advent of recorded sound a vast number of collections have been produced in which songs referred to in the text, or at least versions of them, have featured. Recent releases on compact disc include a number of very good compilations produced and distributed by the "Past Times" chain of gift shops. Amongst these are *The Traditional Songs of England,* on which the Williams and Lloyd version of the ballad of *Geordie* appears, and *The Fairy Dance* which contains excellent versions of *The Twa Magicians* and *Tam Lin.* Both of these collections incorporate excellent, informative and well researched sleeve notes into their art work.

On the Robert Burns front, one of the most up to date and comprehensive collections currently available is Ian Bruce's *Complete Songs of Robert Burns,* presently out on the Linn label. Amongst the numerous guest musicians who accompany Bruce as backing on this, and others in the same series of albums are the likes of John Martin, Bill Jackson and Catriona Macdonald. At the opposite end of the same spectrum is *Robert Burns Scottish Airs* in 18th Century Classical arrangements by Leopold Kozeluh produced by Campion Records, Cheshire, in 1993.

Other recent releases on cd compilation include the vast and highly comprehensive Ewan MacColl collection *The Real MacColl,* widely available in high street record shops and containing a very fine version of *Johnny O' Breadislee,* one of the best *Outlaw Ballads* contained in the *Minstrelsy.* This collection, likewise, comes complete with very fine sleeve notes.

Amongst the rarer and more difficult to come by recordings from the *Golden Age of Electric Folk,* the late 'sixties and early 'seventies, are Fairport Convention's *Full House* and *Leige and Leaf.* Although another large cd compilation entitled *The History of Fairport Convention* has been widely available for quite some time, from the point of view of Border Ballads, many of their finest arrangements of *Minstrelsy* classics such as *Tam Lin, The Flowers of the Forest* and *Sir Patrick Spens* were sadly ommitted from the latter collection. Two other classic albums from the same era, recorded by *Fairport* contemporaries *Pentangle,* are the 1968 album *Pentangle* and *Basket of Light.* Amongst the numerous songs referred to in this book which were recorded by Bert Jansch and his fellow minstrels at this time were *A Lyke Wake Dirge* and *The Bramble Briar*.

Folk rockers "Steeleye Span", have, as will be noted in the text, likewise presented several excellent versions of the Scott ballads referred to in this book, most notably, their almost "Heavy Metal" re-working of the Ballad of *True Thomas;* which appeared on their classic 'seventies album *Now We Are Six*. Their version of *The Twa Corbies* is made mention of in my introduction to this work, and another of the classic ballads that features in my text is the immortal *Wife of Usher's Well,* recently re-released on cd by "Beat Goes on Records" under license from Chrysalis.

The recordings listed here are intended to provide the reader with a basic guide to what has become a vast and varied legacy of the traditions that Scott, Ritson and others attempted to preserve for future generations. The fact that many of these ballads have been modernized in certain definite respects, paticularly by the more electric and studio oriented musicians here referred to, only goes on to ensure that these traditions will continue to be appreciated into the decades to follow; and will thus survive into the New Millennium.

Notes to Chapters

Introduction:

Note 1: Anne, Duchess of Buccleuch and Monmouth, had, as will be seen shortly, featured in Scott's *Lay of the Last Minstrel* which had been published the previous year. Similarly, Invernahyle's encounter with Colonel Charles Whitefoord on the field of Preston Pans eventually "supplied the groundwork of the chivalrous contest between Edward Waverley and Colonel Talbot in the forty-seventh and following chapters of *Waverley*. (See Scott's revised preface to the 1829 edition of that novel).

As for Surtees, he will play an important role in our story. For, as will be noted in Chapter 1, he is perhaps the most controversial character connected with Scott's researches into Border Traditions. For, although he was to provide Scott with much useful anecdotal information of an historical nature, as the above quoted extract from one of Scott's letters to him shows, he also succeeded in palming the Laird of Abbotsford off with some forged ballads of his own; most notably *The Death of Featherstonehaugh*, which, as we shall see in the first chapter, was to be used by Scott for some of his own poetical composition. Appendix One gives a full appraisal of Surtees's relationship with both Scott, and another member of his circle, James Hogg, the celebrated "Ettrick Shepherd"; with respect to the Border Minstrel Tradition.

Chapter One:

Note 1: *See Burke's Landed Gentry,* 1898 edition, *MacGregor of Glengyle,* pp. 1025-1026.

Chapter Two:

Note 1: At the time when Captain Adam Ferguson wrote the above quoted from letter to Sir Walter from St. Heliers in the Channel Islands, his Father, Professor Ferguson, was himself resident at Hallyards, in the neighbourhood of Peebles; together with Sir Adam's three sisters. In the immediate vicinity of their then residence, close to nearby Woodhouse, is the cottage of David Ritchie, Scott's Black Dwarf.

It was from Hallyards that Sir Adam and Sir Walter set out in 1797, on their fateful journey to the Lake District, during the course of which Scott was first to encounter Margaret Charpentier; the young lady who would eventually become his wife. It was also during the course of a childhood visit to Edinburgh and Hallyards, in 1806/7, that, in addition to sitting to the artist Henry, later Sir Henry, Raeburn, the young Robert Ferguson M.D. would first find himself being introduced to Walter Scott; an introduction that was to change completely the course of his life.

Note 2: In Scott's "Conclusion" to his novel *The Surgeon's Daughter,* the first in his celebrated *Chronicles of the Canongate* series, written in the first person of his fictitious narrator Croftangry, Colonel Ferguson features in the guise of the narrator's "excellent friend and neighbour, Colonel MacErries, one of the best fellows who ever trode a Highland Moor, or dived into an Indian jungle....."

The name MacErries, or MacKerras, belongs to the Sept or branch of the Clan associated with Fergusson of Kilkerran, themselves attributed in some accounts with being the ultimate ancestors of the Dunfallandy Fergussons; from whom the Colonel and his brothers possessed provable descent.

Chapter 3:
Note 1: See Scott's entry in *Chambers' Dictionary of Eminent Scotsmen,* Vol. 3. p.232.
Note 2: See Robert Graves in Chapter 14 of *The White Goddess*, p.253.
Note 3: The original Mediaeval sources out of which this ballad evolved are focussed on in Appendix Two.

Chapter 4:
Note 1: It is not beyond the realms of possibility that "Brydine" was the individual who inspired Scott's creation of the Lowland Lairds of Bredwardine in his novel *Waverley*; in view of his own ancestor's connections with this individual; not to mention his Great Grandfather's previously mentioned Jacobite affiliations. In Scott's first novel these fictitious Lairds are numbered amongst the Pretender's Lowland supporters.
Note 2: See Professor Child's *English and Scottish Popular Ballads*, publ. In 3 Vols. by Folklore Press, 1957.
Note 3: Who but a Druidic dodman would be building a road to the top of Bennachie in the first place?
Note 4: See the Revd. Roderick Macleod of Macleod's *The Macleods: Their History and Traditions*. A short history of their Clan, history, folklore, tales etc. Clan Macleod Soc. Edinburgh, 1929.

Note 5: See also "Note 1" in the notes to the Introduction.

Note 6: See John O'Meara's translation, publ. Penguin, 1982. pp.109-110.

Chapter 5:

Note 1: See E. O. Gordon's *Prehistoric London,* p.32.

Note 2: See Graves's *White Goddess,* pp.25-26.

Note 3: Thomas of Ercildoune features in the novel *Castle Dangerous.* In addition to this, in *The Bride of Lammermoor,* we find Scott composing his own prophetic rhyme after the fashion of Thomas; and using it as a key element in the plot:

> *When the last Laird of Ravenswood to Ravenswood shall ride,*
> *And woo a dead maiden to be his bride,*
> *He shall stable his steed in the Kelpie's Flow,*
> *And his name shall be lost for evermore....*

This last quoted verse is a reworking in certain respects of various lines from the Border Ballad *Annan Water;* which features in the *Minstrelsy.* The ballad is of particular significance, for it links Scott to both Burns and Allan Ramsay the poet; in that the verses given by Scott are "the original words of the tune of *Allan Water,* by which name the song is mentioned in Ramsay's *Tea Table Miscellany* (see Scott's own introductory notes to that ballad, as they appear in the *Minstrelsy.)* A version of this ballad was re-worked by the Bohemian composer Leopold Kozeluh (1747-1818) for the Edinburgh folklorist and publisher George Thomson, in1798. This composition formed part of "A Select Collection of Original Scottish Airs for the Voice, to each of which are added Introductory and Concluding Symphonies and Accompanyments for the Piano Forte and Violin by Kozeluh, with select and characteristic verses......the greater number of those written for this work by Burns."

Amongst the same collection is a version of yet another of the ballads published by Sir Walter in the *Minstrelsy,* itself entitled *Lochroyan.* Burns's version of the same song, published under the title *Lord Gregory*, has recently been recorded in the Kozeluh arrangement by the tenor James Griffett on Campion Records cd.

Chapter 6:

Note 1: See T.W. Rolleston, *Myths and Legends of the Celtic Race,* pp.187-188.

Note 2: For an account of Owen mac Duracht's slaying of the sons of Usna, see ibid. p.201.

Note 3: See Graves, p.28.

Note 4: See Mary Caine in her *Glastonbury Zodiac: Key to the Mysteries of Britain*, Ch. 15, p.140.

Note 5: *The Genealogie of the Saint Claires of Rosslyn* by Father Augustin Hay (Prior of St. Pieremont, including the Chartulory of Rosslyn). Thos. G. Stevenson, Edinburgh, 1835.

Note 6: The fact that a seventh century Pictish lordship is alleged to have existed just a few miles north of the principal region from which Scott was to collect a huge proportion of his ballads only serves to confirm the assertions made throughout our story so far, that the ballads which he recovered contain the fragmentary remains of the lost literary traditions of the Ancient Picts; something which we will hear more of in the succeeding chapters.

Chapter 7:

Note 1: See Tom Scott (ed)., *The Penguin Book of Scottish Verse*, p.239.

Chapter 8:

Note 1: See Lockhart's *Life* in 4 vols. Publ. Macmillan, 1900, Vol. i) p.290.

Chapter 9:

Note 1: Curiously, another strange anecdote connects Macbeth with Sir Walter's beloved ancestral Borderland, in that just a short distance south of Professor Ferguson's residence at Hallyards and the Black Dwarf's Cottage nearby is an ancient hill fort referred to in local tradition as "Macbeth's Castle".

Note 2: All of the genealogical relationships outlined in this and the following chapters are fully tabulated in Appendix 3.

Note 3: See McIan's *Clans of the Scottish Highlands*, p.44.

Chapter 10:

Note 1: See Monica Margaret Maxwell-Scott, *The Making of Abbotsford* and *Incidents in Scottish History*; (publ. Adam & Charles Black; London, 1897); from which the above extract is taken.

Note 2: Baigent and Leigh *The Temple and the Lodge* p.163.

Chapter 11:

Note 1: Francis Collinson,*The Traditional and National Music of Scotland,* (Routledge and Keegan Paul, 1978), pp.40-41.

Note 2: Boack's *Middlesex Antiquities* quoted in M.Caine's *The Kingston Zodiac,* publ. Kingston p.12/13.

Note 3: Baigent and Leigh pp.44-45.

Note 4: See Murray's *Romance and Prophecies of Thomas the Rhymer*, liiii, note 1.

Note 5: *The Records of the Clan and Name of Fergusson, Ferguson and Fergus* ed. By James Ferguson and John Menzies Fergusson, David Douglas, Edinburgh, 1895 pp.166-167.

Note 6: See Graves in his *White Goddess,* pp.179-181.

Note 7: See Peter Harbison's *Pre-Christian Ireland from the First Settlers to the Early Celts*, Guild Publ. 1989.

Chapter 12:

Note 1: "Straif" here is the old Gaelic word for the blackthorn species.

Chapter 13:

Note 1: An old Border expression for "spearing the salmon by night".

Note 2: The Blackwood Magazine.

Note 3: See Chapter 2 of this work relating to Sir Walter's correspondence with Captain Ferguson whilst the latter was on active service in the Peninsular War.

Note 4: Quoted under the *Gordon Marquess of Huntly* entry in Douglas's *Scottish Peerage.*

Note 5: See *Folklore, Myths and Legends of Britain*; Reader's Digest Publications, 1979.

Note 6: Ibid pp.462-463.

Note 7: This theory, that the original Eildon Tree was in fact a Rowan, is given further credence when we refer back to Washington Irving's account of his visit to Abbotsford; previously quoted in the opening chapters. In it, the celebrated American novelist refers to the Rhymer's Glen being full of "mountain ash" trees; Mountain Ash being a popular name for Rowan.

Chapter 14:

Note 1: These legends are at the centre of Scott's own composition in the *Minstrelsy* dedicated to his great idol and previously referred to in a quotation from Lockhart in an earlier chapter.

Note 2: See *Lancelot of the Laik,* A Scottish Metrical Romance with an introduction, notes and glossarial index, by W.W.Skeat, publ. *Early English Text Society* by the Oxford University Press pp.xv-xvii.

Note 3:*The Quest for the Holy Grail* trans. P. Matarasso, publ. Penguin. pp.152-153.

Note 4: See *Early Welsh Genealogical Tracts* by Professor P.C. Bartrum, publ. University of Wales Press, 1966.

Note 5: Ibid. pp.118-119.

Note 6: See Deike Rich and Ean Begg's *On the Trail of Merlin*, the Aquarian Press, 1991, p.161.

Notes to Illustrations

Illustration 1): "The Laird of Abbotsford as Border Minstrel.": Raeburn's 1808 portrait of Scott, originally executed for Scott's publisher, Constable, and now in the possession of the Duke of Buccleuch, shows the Author of Waverley, sketchbook in hand, faithful dog at his feet, and in the romantic setting of the Border landscape. In the background is Hermitage Castle, referred to in old documents as "the Strength of Liddesdale". Amongst its numerous occupants was James Hepburn, Earl of Bothwell, whose many visitors at "Th' Armitage" were to include his lover Mary Queen of Scots; herself most noted for crossing fifty miles of rough country to visit the Earl whilst he lay wounded after a famous confrontation with an Elliot Reiver. The portrait pays homage to a famous visit of Scott's to Hermitage in the company of one of the Shortreed Family, during the course of which he made one of his sketches of the castle, "from the side of Earnton Fell", standing "all the time he took it to his knees in snow".

Illustration 2): "Scott's image of the Border Minstrel": The last of Scott's published novels, "Castle Dangerous", transports the reader back in time to the Middle Ages; where, in one of Scott's own favourite Border settings, the prophecies and poetry of Thomas of Ercildoune are skillfully interwoven into the novel's storyline.

Illustration 3): "The Merry Knight": Scott's lifelong friend Captain, later Sir Adam Ferguson, sometime Keeper of the Scottish Regalia and Secretary to the Duke of Buccleuch, was himself a major contributor to many of Scott's adventure stories; particularly with respect to real life descriptions of actual fighting incident which were to enable Scott to use the personal experiences of others to furnish his novels with an additional edge of authenticity. A noted collector of old Scottish anecdotes, Ferguson's singing and storytelling were often a central feature of social gatherings at Sir Walter's dinner table or beside his fireside.

Illustration 4): J.B. Lane's engraving, after Sir Henry Raeburn, of Professor Adam Ferguson, 1723-1816: A principal figure in the world of the Scottish Enlightenment, the historian, moral philosopher and man of letters Adam Ferguson was himself intimately acquainted with the likes of David Hume and Adam Smith, as well as being on friendly terms with such noted French intellectuals as Voltaire; whom he visited at Ferney whilst engaged in a tour of Europe between 1774 and 1776. It was as a result of Ferguson's prominence in Edinburgh intellectual circles that the young Sir Walter Scott was able to attend a literary gathering at Ferguson's house at which Robert Burns was the central attraction.

Illustration 5): Zeitter's engraving of the famous Nasmyth portrait of Robert Burns: Alexander Nasmyth(1758-1840), described by David and Francesca Irwin in their "Scottish Artists at Home and Abroad" (Faber and Faber 1975) as "a Janus figure in the development of landscape painting in Scotland", was originally schooled as a portraitist in the studio of Allan Ramsay; where he succeeded David Martin as one of the painter's principal assistants. In certain respects his portraitist's pallette resembles that of Ramsay Richard Reinagle, son of another employee of Ramsay's studio. In terms of landscape his paintings, like much Scottish art of the time, owes a considerable degree to the influence of French and Italian art.

Illustration 6): Nineteenth century engraving of the Arrest of the Duke of Buccleuch and Monmouth after the Battle of Sedgemoor: An important historical figure in terms of Scott's own personal iconography, the Duke of Monmouth and Buccleuch, whose wife, Anne, is noted for having interceded on behalf of Scott's own Great-Grandfather on account of the latter's involvement in "Dundee's Wars" and the '15 Rebellion, thus saving him from possible execution, is amongst the many real life characters whose lives were to influence both the novels and poetical writings of Scotland's most celebrated penman. His connections with the Border ballads of the seventeenth century are outlined in full in Chapter Twenty One.

Illustration 7): Contemporary engraving, by Finden, of Abbotsford Hall: Originally a modest farm house known as "Clarty Hole", the much enlarged property seen here, and constructed by Scott in the Scottish Baronial Style, in all its Regency Glory, acquired its name as a result of its situation on land originally belonging to the old Abbey of Melrose before the Reformation. For an interesting nineteenth century account of the Author of Waverley's construction of this palatial dwelling, refer to Mary Monica Maxwell-Scott's essay "The Making of Abbotsford", published as part of a collection of short tracts on "incidents in Scottish history" by Adam and Charles Black, London, 1897.

Illustration 8): Worthington's 1827 engraving of Wilkie's genre painting of Scott and his family in the garb of "South Country Peasants.": Wilkie's portrayal of Scott and his family, in the company of various retainers and Sir Adam Ferguson, pictured here on the right of the group, in the guise of "a country wag somewhat addicted to poaching", to quote directly from a letter of Scott's dated 7th March 1827, owes much to the Laird of Abbotsford's obsession with the folksinging and storytelling of the Border Peasantry. In the middle-distance, behind Scott's own right shoulder lies Abbotsford Hall; with the three peaks of the Eildon Hills towering above it.

Illustration 9): The Battle of Salamanca: Amongst the numerous engagements witnessed by Sir Adam in the company of the "Rough sons of the Fighting 3rd Division", as a Captain in the 101st Foot, was the celebrated Battle of Salamanca; fought on 22nd July 1812. In this spirited nineteenth century engraving we see the 5th Inniskilling Dragoon Guards annihilating the 66th French Infantry of the Line; an incident which was to result in them relieving the French regiment of their drum major's mace. Ever since this memorable battle both nations have been arguing about the trophy's possible return to France; a matter which has led to much interesting political banter emanating from both sides of the Channel.

Illustration 10): Branxholme Castle, Co. Roxburgh: Originally the property of Inglis of Branxholm, the castle of Branxholm was exchanged, together with the lands of Branshaw, Whitlaw, Whitrigs, Goldilands, Todishaw, Todholes & C. by Sir Walter Scott of Buccleuch, in 1446, for his estates of Murdieston.

Illustration 11): Goldieland Tower, Roxburghshire: The Tower of Goldieland or "Gaudilands" features in one of Scott's favourite historical ballads, "Jamie Telfer of the Fair Dodhead", which concerns itself with a cattle raid conducted by the Captain of Bewcastle into Teviotdale, on the Scottish side of the Border. In some versions of the ballad it is the Elliots who are portrayed as the heros of the piece; whilst in the rendition given by Scott his own Clan take the lead in dealing with the depredations of the English Reivers. In the Scott ballad his own ancestor, Scott of Harden, is made mention of in the very verse where this isolated and ancient ruin is itself referred to.

Illustration 12): Dore's "Castle of Astolat": A key feature of Arthurian and early Welsh literature, where, in the *"Mabinogion"*, they feature in connection with the legends associated with the Princess Elen, daughter of Old King Coel, the ancient trackways of Britiain were in later times to fire the imagination of poets such as Alfred Lord Tennyson; whose own "Elaine" was to influence this spirited nineteenth century drawing by Gustav Dore. Hidden references to this ancient and half forgotten landscape can be found in the Ancient Ballad of Thomas the Rhymer.

Illustration 13): "1827" type Naval Officer's Sword: Like his brother, Captain John Macpherson Ferguson R.N. was on active service throughout the Napoleonic Wars; serving aboard the Victory, at the Battle of Copenhagen, and aboard the Redwing Sloop in the Straights of Gibraltar. For a fuller account of his exploits see Chapter 22.

Illustration 14): Victorian engraving of Wilkie's "Abbotsford Family". For notes, see illustration no. 8.

Illustration 15): Engraving after J.M.W. Turner of J.G. Lockhart's summer residence at Chiefswood in the Borders.

Illustration 16): Sophia Scott, daughter of Sir Walter and the wife of his celebrated biographer, Lockhart. From an original painting by Nicholson currently in the possession of the Laird of Abbotsford's descendants.

Bibliography

Adam, Frank *The Clans, Septs and Regiments of the Scottish Highlands* (Revised by Sir Thomas Innes of Learney), Johnstone and Bacon 1970.

Alcock, Leslie *Arthur's Britain,*Allen Lane, 1971.

Anderson, Marjorie O. *Kings and Kingship in Early Scotland,* Scottish Academic Press, Edinburgh and London, 1980.

Anglo-Saxon Genealogies Extracted from the Proceedings of the British Academy, Vol. 39, 1953.

Ashe, Geoffrey *King Arthur's Avalon: The Story of Glastonbury,* Collins, 1957 (ed). *The Quest for Arthur's Britain*, Pall Mall Press, 1968.

Ashley, Maurice *The Life and Times of William I,* Weidenfeld and Nicholson, 1973.

Asser (ed. Simon Keynes and Michael Lapbridge)*The Life of King Alfred the Great,* Penguin, 1983.

Baigent, Michael and Leigh, Richard *The Temple and the Lodge,* Corgi 1990.

Balfour, Sir James Lord Lyon King of Arms, (ed.) *The Scots Peerage,* founded on Wood's edition of *Sir Robert Douglas's Peerage of Scotland,* David Douglas, Edinburgh, 1910.

Baring-Gould, The Revd. Sabine & Fisher *Lives of the British Saints,* Hon. Soc. Of Cymrodorion, London, 1907.

Bartrum, P.C.*Early Welsh Genealogical Tracts,*Univ.Wales Press, Cardiff, 1966.

Bede (trans.Leo Sherley-Price) *A History of the English Church and People,* Penguin, 1984.

Begg, Ean & Rich Deike *On the Trail of Merlin,* Aquarian, 1991.

Bellenden, John (trans.)*The History and Chronicles of Scotland by Hector Boece,* W. Harrison, Edinburgh, 1822.

Benjamin, R *The Seed of Avalon,* Zodiac House, Glastonbury, 1986.

Biden, W.D. *A New History of Kingston-Upon-Thames,* Wm.Lindsey, Kingston, 1852.

Beroul, (trans. Alan S. Frederick) *The Romance of Tristan,* Penguin, 1982.

Betham, Revd. William *Genealogical Tables of the Sovereigns of the World,* 1795.

Book of Saints, The - A Dictionary of the Servants of God Canonized by the Catholic Church. Compiled by the Benedictine Monks of St. Augustine's Abbey, Ramsgate.

Branston, Brian *The Lost Gods of England,* Thames and Hudson, 1984.

Briard, Jacques *The Bronze Age in Barbarian Europe,* Routledge & Kegan Paul, 1979.

Burke's *Extinct and Dormant Baronetcies,* Scott, Webster and Geary, London, 1838 *Family Index,* Burke's Peerage, London, 1976. *A Genealogical and Heraldic History of the Commoners of Gt. Br. & Ire,* 1833-35. *A Gen.&Her.Hist.of the Landed Gentry*(1882 & '98 edns.)*Landed Gentry,* 68th Edition, Vol. 1, 1965, Vol. 2, 1967, Vol. 3, 1972.*Burke's Peerage and Baronetage,* 105th Edn. Bur. Prg. Lon. Ltd. 1978 *A General History of the Dormant, Abeyant, Forfeited and Extinct Peerages of the British Empire* by Sir Bernard Burke, London, Harrison, Pall Mall, 1883, (6 Vols.)

Burns,Robert(ed.Laing),*PoemsandSongs,*Methuen,1895.(ed. Carol McGuirk),*Selected Poems,* Penguin 1993.

Burrow, J.A.*Sir Gawain and the Green Knight,* Penguin, 1972.

Byrne, F. J. *Irish Kings and High Kings,* Batsford, 1973.

Byron, Lord *The Works of...,* Wordsworth Poetry Library, 1994.

Caesar *The Conquest of Gaul,* Penguin, 1984.

Caine, Mary *The Glastonbury Zodiac, Key to the Mysteries of Britain,* Kingston, 1985. *The Kingston Zodiac,* Kingston, 1984, new edition published 2001.

Campbell, J.F.*Popular Tales of the West Highlands, Orally Collected, with a trans.,* 4 Vols. Alexander Gardner, Paisley and London, 1892.

Chadwick, Nora *The Celts*, Pelican 1970.

Chambers, E.K. *Arthur of Britain*, Sidgewick and Jackson, 1964.

Chambers, James *The Norman Kings*, Weidenfeld and Nicholson, 1981.

Child, Francis James *The English and Scottish Popular Ballads*, (3 Vols)., Folklore Press, New York, 1957.

Chretien de Troyes *Arthurian Romances*, Dent, 1914.

Clancy, Joseph P. *The Earliest Welsh Poetry*, Clarendon Press, Oxford, 1970.

Clemoes, Peter *Anglo-Saxon England*, (Vol.2), Cambridge, 1973.

Collinson, Francis *The Traditional and National Music of Scotland*, Routledge and Kegan Paul, 1978.

Corley, Corin (trans.) *Lancelot of the Lake*, Oxford, 1989.

Dames, Michael *The Avebury Cycle*, Thames and Hudson, 1977.

Davies, R.H.L. *The Normans and Their Myth*, Thames and Hudson, 1976.

Dickinson, W. *Croft Scotland from the Earliest Times to 1603* (3rd Edition, revisd. & ed. Archibald Duncan), Oxford, 1977.

Dictionary of Welsh Biography, A, Hon. Society of Cymmrodorion, London 1959.

Donovan, John O' (Ed). *The Annals of the Kingdom of Ireland by the Fours Masters: From the earliest period to the year 1616*, publ. Hedges & Smith, Dublin, 1851.

Douglas, David C.*William the Conqueror*, Eyre & Spottiswoode, 1964.*The Norman Achievement*, Eyre and Spottiswoode, 1969.*The Norman Fate*, Eyre Methuen, 1976.

Duckett, Eleanor Shipley *Alfred the Great*, University of Chicago Press, 1956.

Dunbar, Sir Archibald *Scottish Kings: A Revised Chronology of Scottish History, 1005-1625*, Edinburgh, 1899.*Duncomb's History & Antiquities of Herefordshire*, Hereford, 1812.

Dyer, James *The Penguin Guide to Prehistoric England and Wales*, Penguin, 1981.

Finberg, H.P.R.*The Formation of England:550-1042*, Hart-Davies McGibbon, 1974.

Folklore, Myths & Legends of the British Isles, Readers Digest, 1977.*Gantz, Jeffrey (trans.) The Mabinogion*, Penguin, 1976. *Early Irish Myths and Sagas*, Penguin, 1981.

Garmonsway, G. N. *The Anglo-Saxon Chronicle*, Dent, 1953.

Gerald of Wales (trans. O'Meara, John) *The History and Topography of Ireland*, Penguin, 1988.

Gibbs & Doubleday (ed.) *The Complete Peerage of England, Scotland, Ireland, Gt. Br. & U.K., Extant, Extinct and Dormant*, Alan Sutton, 1982.

Gildas (ed. John Morris) *The Ruin of Britain and Other Documents*, Phillimore, 1978.

Gordon, E.O. *Prehistoric London, Its Mounds and Circles*, Covenant, London, 1932.

Gottfried von Strassbourg (trans. A.T. Hatto.) *Tristan* with *The Tristan of Thomas*, Penguin, 1982.

Graham, Henry Grey *Scottish Men of Letters in the Eighteenth Century*, Adam and Charles Black, London, 1901.

Grant, F. *The Clan Macleod*, Johnstone and Bacon, 1953.

Graves, Robert *The White Goddess*, Faber, 1986.

Harbison, Peter *Pre-Christian Ireland from the First Settlers to the Early Celts*, Guild Publ. 1989.

Harvey, John (comp.) *English Mediaeval Architects*, A Biographical Dict. down to 1550, B.T. Batsford, London, 1954. *The Plantagenets*, Fontana, 1981.

Hawks, Patrick, and Hodges, Flavia *A Dictionary of British Surnames*, Oxford, 1988.

Hay, Richard Augustin *Genealogies of the Saint-Claires of Rosslyn*, Thos. G. Stevenson, Edinburgh, 1835.

Hewins, W.A.S. *The Royal Saints of Britain*, privately publ. at the Chiswick Press, 1929.

Hill Elder, Isabel *Celt, Druid and Culdee*, Covenant Press, 1973.

Hodgkin, R. H. *A History of the Anglo-Saxons*, Oxford, 1935.

Hogg, A.H.A. *A Guide to the Hill Forts of Britain*, Paladin, 1975.

Home, John Douglas, *A Tragedy*, John Bell, London, 1791.

Howarth, David *1066: The Year of the Conquest*, Collins, 1977.

Husband, M.F.A. *A Dictionary of the Waverley Novels*, George Routledge, London, 1910.

Innes, Sir Thomas of Leary *The Tartans of the Clans and Families of Scotland*, Johnstone and Bacon, Edinburgh, 1964.

Irving, Washington *Abbotsford and Newstead Abbey*, Henry G. Bohn, London, 1850.

Jackson, Kenneth (ed.) *The Gododdin*, Edinburgh Univ. Paperbacks, 1969.

A Celtic Miscellany, Penguin, 1982.

Jackson, Robert *Dark Age Britain*, Stephens, 1984.

Johnson, James *The Scots Musical Museum in Six Vols.*, Edinburgh, 1787-1803.

Johnstone, J.*Ogham, Koelbren and Runic*, (2 Vols.) Inner Keltia Publications, 1986. (ed.) *The Pictish Shaman*, I.K.P. 1985.

Jones, Francis F. *The Princes and Principality of Wales*, Cardiff, 1963.

Jones, Gwyn (ed.) *The Oxford Book of Welsh Verse in English*, Oxford, 1983.

Keltie, John *A History of the Scottish Highlands*, Edinburgh, 1875.

Lewis, Lionel Smithett *St. Joseph of Arimathea at Glastonbury*, James Clarke, 1932.

Lloyd, Sir John Edward *A History of Wales*, (Vols. 1 & 2), Longmans, 1954.

Lockhart, J.G.*The Life of Robert Burns*, George Bell, London, 1882.*The Life of Sir Walter Scott*, (5 Vols.) Macmillan & Co. 1900.

Loomis, R.S. *Wales and Arthurian Legend*, Cardiff, 1956.

MacColl, Ewan *Folk Songs and Ballads of Scotland*, Oak, 1965. *Journeyman*, Sidgewick and Jackson, 1990.

McIan, R.R. and Logan, James *The Clans of the Scottish Highlands*, Webb and Bower, 1980.

Mackie, J.D. *A History of Scotland*, Penguin, 1984.

MacLean, Fitzroy *A Concise History of Scotland*, Thames and Hudson, 1970.

McLynn, Frank *The Jacobites*, Routledge and Kegan Paul, London, 1985.

MacLeod, Revd. R.C. of Macleod *The Macleods of Dunvegan*, Clan Macleod Soc. Edinburgh, 1927.*The Macleods: Their History and Traditions*, Clan Mac. Soc. 1929.

Mac NioCaill, Gearoid *Ireland before the Vikings*, Gill & Macmillan, Dublin, 1972.

Macpherson, James *The Poems of Ossian*, (2 Vols.), Strahan, London, 1784.

Malory Sir Thomas *Le Morte d'Arthur*, 2 Vols. Penguin, 1986.

Maltwood, K.E.*The Enchantments of Britain*, James Clarke & Co. Cambridge, 1982.*Glastonbury's Temple of the Stars*, Jas. Clarke, 1982.

Marsh, Henry *Dark Age Britain*, David and Charles, 1970.

Marshall, Rosalind K. *Bonnie Prince Charlie*, H.M.S.O. 1988.

Matarasso, Pauline (trans.) *Le Queste de Saint Graal (The Quest for the Holy Grail)* Penguin. 1984.

Matthews, John *The Grail, Quest for the Eternal*, Thames and Hudson, 1981.

Maxwell-Scott, Mary Monica *The Making of Abbotsford*, Adam and Charles Black, 1897.

Maxwell-Scott, P. and Maj.-Gen. Sir Walter Bart. *A Guide to Abbotsford*, Abbotsford Publications.

Michell, John *The View Over Atlantis*, Garnstone Press, 1972.

Miller, Hugh *Scenes and Legends of the North of Scotland*, Johnstone & Hunter, London, 1850.

Milner, Revd. W.M.H. *The Royal House of Britain, An Enduring Dynasty*, Covenant Publishing, Buckingham Gate, London.

Moncrieffe, Sir Ian of that Ilk *The Highland Clans*, Barrie and Jenkins, 1982.

Monmouth, Geoffrey of (trans. Lewis Thorpe) *A History of the Kings of Britain*, Penguin, 1966.

Morgan, Morien O.*The Mabin of the Mabinogion*, Research Into Lost Knowledge Organization, London, 1984.

Morganwg (Iolo) *The Iolo M.S.*, Welsh mss. Society, 1848.*The Triads of Britain*, originally published as *The Third Series of Triads* in the *Myvyrian Archaiology of Wales*, 1801, trans. V. Probert, 1823 and repr. Wildwood House, 1977, with notes and glossary by Malcolm Smith.

Morris, Christopher *The Tudors*, Fontana, 1982.

Morris, John *The Age of Arthur: A History of the British Isles from 350-650*, Weidenfeld and Nicholson, 1973.

Murray, James A.*The Romance and Prophecies of Thomas of Erceldoune*, N. Trubner, Ludgate Hill, 1875.

Nennius (ed. John Morris)*British History and the Welsh Annals*, Phillimore, 1980.

Newark, Tim *Celtic Warriors*, Guild Publishing, London, 1986.

Nicholson, Ranald *Scotland in the Later Middle Ages*, Edinburgh, 1974.

Oakley, Isabel Cooper *Masonry and Mediaeval Mysticism*, Theosophical Publishing House, 1977.

O'Hart, John *Irish Pedigrees*, (2 Vols) (repr. 1892 edn.) Genealogical Publ. Co. Baltimore, 1989.

Pennar, Meirion (trans.) *Taliesin Poems*, Llanerch, 1988.

Pegram, Jean *Bruce Castle. From Manor to Museum*, Hornsey Historical Society.

Percy, Thomas *Reliques of Ancient English Poetry*, John Templeman, London, 1839.

Piggot, Stuart *The Druids*, Penguin 1981.

Platts, Beryl *The Setons of Parbroath*, Procter Press, London, 1989.

Prestwick, Michael *The Three Edwards: War and State in England, 1272-1377*, Weidenfeld and Nicholson, 1980.

Powell, T.G.E. *The Celts*, Thames and Hudson, 1983.

Reaney, P.H. *A Dictionary of British Surnames*, Routledge and Kegan Paul, 1978.*The Origin of English Surnames*, R.K.P. 1967.

Richmond, Ian *Roman Britain*, Penguin, 1955.

Ritchie, Anna *The Picts*, H.M.S.O. 1991.*Scotland B.C.* H.M.S.O. 1992.

Rolleston, T.W. *Myths and Legends of the Celtic Race*, Harrap & Co. 1911.

Salway, Peter *Roman Britain*, Clarendon Press, Oxford, 1981.

Saint Clair, Louis Anatole de *Histoire Genealogique de la Famille de Saint Clair et ses alliances France-Ecosse*, Paris, 1905.

Savage, Anne (ed.) *The Anglo-Saxon Chronicles*, Papermac, 1984.

Saul, Nigel (ed.) *The Age of Chivalry*, Collins and Brown, 1992.

Sawyer, P.H. & Wood, I.N. (ed.), *Early Mediaeval Kingship*, Leeds, 1977.

Scoffham, Stephen *The Romans in East Kent*, Albion Printers, Maidstone.

Scott, Tom (ed.) *The Penguin Book of Scottish Verse*, Penguin, 1970.

Scott, Captain Walter of Satchells *A True History of....The Right Hon. Name of Scott*, George Caw, Hawick, 1786.

Scott, Sir Walter *A Minstrelsy of the Scottish Border* (ed. Henderson), Harrap, 1931.*Poetical Works* , (ed. Alexander Leighton), Nimmo, Edinburgh, 1865.*Guy Mannering*, Nimmo, Hay & Mitchell, Edin.*Old Mortality*, Collins Clear-type Press edn. *Castle Dangerous*, Dryburgh re-issue edn. *Waverley* (ed. Andrew Hook), Penguin, 1985.*Ivanhoe* (ed. A.N. Wilson), Penguin, 1986. *Rob Roy*, Dent, 1991.*Familiar Letters of.....* (2 Vols.) David Douglas, Edn. 1895. *Journal*, (2 Vols.) David Douglas, Edn. 1891. *Some Unpublished Letters of.....* (ed. Symington) Basil Blackwell, Oxford, 1932.

Scottish Clans and Their Tartans, The, Wordsworth Editions, 1992.

Seton, G. *A History of the Family of Seton*, (2Vols.) 1896.

Shapiro, Max S. and Hendricks, Rhoda A. *A Dictionary of Mythologies*, Granada, 1981.

Skeat, W.W. (trans).*Lancelot of the Laik: A Scottish Metrical Romance* (about 1490-1500), re-ed. from a ms. in the Cambridge University Library, Oxford, 1965.

414

Skene, W.F. *The Four Ancient Books of Wales*, Edinburgh, 1868.*Celtic Scotland*, (3 Vols.), Edinburgh, 1886-90 *Arthur & the Britons in Wales & Scotland*, (ed. Bryce) Llanerch, 1988.

Smart, T.C. *A History of the Scottish People*, Collins, 1969.

Squire, Charles *Celtic Myth & Legend, Poetry & Romance*, Newcastle 1975.

Stell, David *Ballads and Music of the Early Seventeenth Century*, Stuart Press, Bristol, 1994.

Tacitus *The Agricola and the Germania*, Penguin, 1970.

Tolstoy, Nikolai *The Quest for Merlin*, Hamish Hamilton, 1985.

Thompson, K. *100 Great Scottish Songs with Words and Music*,Waltons, Dublin, 1986.

Vaughan-Williams, Ralph and Lloyd, A.L. (eds.) *The Penguin Book of English Folk Songs*, Penguin, 1975.

Wace and Layamon *Arthurian Chronicles*, Dent. 1914.

Waddell, L.A.*The Phoenician Origin of the Britons, Scots, and Anglo-Saxons*, Luzac and Co. 1931.

Wade-Evans, A. W. *Vitae Sanctae et Genealogiae*, Cardiff, 1944.

Wainwright, A.*Old Roads of Eastern Lakeland*, Engraved, Printed and Published by the Westmoreland Gazette, Kendal, 1985.

Watkins, Alfred *The Ley Hunter's Manual: A Guide to Early Tracks*, Turnstone Press, 1983 *The Old Straight Track*, Abacus, 1980.

Wheatley, Henry B. *London Past and Present*, John Murray, Albemarle St., 1891.

Williams, John *Barddas, or A Collection of Doctrines illustrative of the Bardo Druidic System of the Isle of Britain*, Abergavenny Soc. for the Publication of Ancient Welsh mss. 1862.

Williamson, Robin *The Craneskin Bag*, Canongate, 1995.

Wilson, A.N. *The Laird of Abbotsford*, Oxford, 1989.

Wilson, David *The Anglo-Saxons*, Thames and Hudson, 1960.

Wimberley, Lowry Charles *Folklore in the English and Scottish Ballads*, Dover Publ. New York, 1965.

Wood, Michael *In Search of the Dark Ages*, B.B.C. 1981.

Woodruff, Douglas *The Life and Times of Alfred the Great*, Weidenfeld and Nicholson, 1974.

Wright, Thomas *A History of Ireland* (3 Vols.) John Tallis Publ.

Zink, David D. *The Ancient Stones Speak*, Paddington Press, 1979.

A selection of other titles published by Capall Bann

Crowning Disasters by Yeoman Warder Geoffrey Abbott

As a member of the Queen's Bodyguard of the Yeoman of the Guard Extraordinary (Beefeater) Geoffrey Abbott is well qualified to write books on strange happenings at regal events. The topics covered in this fascinating book range from the hilarious to the unlikely and in some cases quite macabre. Contents include: SLIP-UPS AT THE CEREMONY things that went wrong at coronations, both English and foreign; OMENS AND AUGURIES when disasters occurred during a monarch's reign, the "I told you so' brigade was quick to identify omens which foretold them; FEASTS AND AFFRAYS coronation banquets which frequently ended in chaos, riots and looting; table manners of the day; royal menus; FINERY, FASHIONS AND FRIPPERY coronation robes and their ultimate fate - sold; given to Mme Tussaud's; used in plays; SLEAZE FOR SYCOPHANTS perks for parasites, favours for flatterers, titles for toadies; PALACE PASTIMES flirting and wooing, masques and mistresses, dice-playing, jesters, and other right royal entertainments; ROYAL ODDITIES regal pretenders and their fate; the English queen tried for witchcraft; coronation medals; duties of the Yeomen of the Guard; attempted assassinations; Napoleon Bonaparte once a London Special Constable! APPENDICES - Royal letters ISBN 186163 1324 £10.95

Regalia, Robbers and Royal Corpses by Yeoman Warder Geoffrey Abbott

Anyone with even the vaguest interest in tradition will be fascinated, amused and in some cases shocked by the incredible facts disclosed here. Contents include: GEMS AND THEIR JOURNEYS the magical world of coronation jewels, the peacock throne, Koh-i-Nur, Star of Africa, Moon of the Mountains; their origins and travels; owners tortured to hand them over; diamond dust used as poison. "STOP THIEF!" stories behind famous jewel thefts; the missing Irish regalia; Colonel Blood and the Crown Jewels; the gem found in the stomach of the slain messenger who had swallowed it when attacked; this nation's treasures stolen by Westminster monks. CORPSES, COFFINS AND CONTENTS when royal coffins were opened centuries later, some contained no heads, others too many; crowns and jewels had been stolen. Why did Elizabeth I's corpse explode? Who stole Richard II's jawbone? Eastern tombs plundered : the craft of mummification. ISBN 186361 1367

Ogham and Coelbren - Keys to the Celtic Mysteries by Nigel Pennick

This book explores the "Wattles and Branches" of the Celtic tree alphabets and the tree-lore of the British Isles. It is a wide-ranging explanation of, and commentary on, Celtic tree traditions, covering the Oghams of Ireland and the Bardic alphabets of Wales. These symbolic systems encapsulate the ancestral spiritual traditions of the British Isles; their teachings express the Druidic world-view and ways of thought that contemporary education has forgotten. Ogham and Coelbren contains the variants of the Irish Ogham tree "alphabet" - its colours, trees, birds and symbols, cryptic codes and hidden inner meanings that encapsulate a creative energy available to-day. The Welsh Bardic system is also detailed, with rare illustrations from scarce texts. A comprehensive appendix details the meanings, correspondences and cosmology that Ogham and Coelbren contain. ISBN 1 86163 102 2 £10.95

The Legend of Robin Hood by Richard Rutherford-Moore

"A must-read for Robin Hood freaks, like your editor!" The Cauldron

Robin Hood is known throughout the world, but who was he, where did he come from and how and where did he and his followers live? Over the years, the Legend of Robin Hood has lost nothing in the telling. Indeed, it is with the telling that the legend originated; many have since placed Robin Hood under the microscope and tried to document, explain and justify him, but as the Sheriff found out, he is a very elusive character! From the far ages and mists of antiquity he grew; some of the very first printed works in England were of him and his exploits, already well-known in stories and songs. What has come down to us is a memory, embellished by fantasies and facts woven into today's story of the dispossessed nobleman or stout yeoman, seeking revenge and fair play from an unjust system, righting Wrongs and doing Right, struggling against adversity and oppression, finally winning through and finding love and freedom - and immortality. The truth about a real man may never now be known, but the legend is there for all to see. The shadowy figure of Robin Hood himself stands smiling impartially today against a background of individuals and groups who rival for his favour, lay claims to his birth, life and death; and see him - amongst other things - as a medieval knight, a bloodthirsty thief or a magical wood-elf. Richard Rutherford-Moore brings his skills to bear on this enduring legend, bringing us not just solidly researched facts, but a real feel for the life and times of the most legendary bowman of all time. ISBN 1 86163 069 7   £9.95

Caer Sidhe vol 1- The Celtic Night Sky by Michael Bayley

"well illustrated...in depth..very interesting and informative" Stone Temple *"a must"* (Touchstone)
The Celtic tribes of ancient Europe saw nearly the same night sky as we do, except that it was clearer. The constellations were the same, but they were interpreted in a different way, with different names and interpretations. Caer Sidhe explores the Celtic night sky maps, the constellations of the zodiac and the moving stars, the associated deities and legends, uses of deneholes (as used by Merlin to view the stars) and much, much more fascinating information. Profusely illustrated with maps and drawings. ISBN 1 86163 014X   £10.95

Caer Sidhe vol II - Hanes Gwyddionaeth Crefydd - History Science and Religion   by Michael Bayley

A spellbinding book of discovery. Looking firstly at the stars, those watchers above that men call angels. There are tales that geometry, mathematics and astronomy flowered earlier and in a purer form in the British Isles before the classical period in Greece and Rome. The Druids or their predecessors certainly brought astronomy into the daylight hours and the sacred apple, cultivated in the Hesperades, still survives in the English shires of the 20th century. Contents include: Stars and Angels; Meteorites, annual meteor showers and the Cog Almanac; Druids, Deneholes and Astronomy; The Applewell, the Meaning of Numbers, Related Pagan Ballads. The science of this second volume in the *Caer Sidhe* series helps to explain and underwrite the theories and interpretations of volume one. ISBN 186163 0204   £10.95

Sacred Dorset - On the Path of the Dragon   by Peter Knight

"Archaeological sits happily alongside information obtained by dowsers...an interesting read. There's something in it for everyone...it really is a must" Fatea *"comprehensive guide...Most impressive, obviously an ideal guide for planning a day out...a relaxed but informative read"* Daily Echo Dorset *"richly illustrated...a comprehensive guide"* Prediction
Peter Knight guides the reader through Dorset's spiritual heritage, from prehistory to Celtic, Roman and Christian times. Using examples from Dorset and elsewhere we are taken on a tour of the sacred landscape, folklore, ancient sites and sacred symbology. The book encompasses: The folklore of ancient sites, Prehistoric Pagan and Christian symbology, Discerning the Earth Goddess landscape, The astronomy of local ancient sites, Perceiving sacred Trees and Nature, New Dorset ley lines and the shamanic link, Sacred wells and springs, Awaken the dragon within - towards new perceptions ISBN 186163 058 1   £12.95

Constable's Cottages John Constable

John Constable takes us on a journey of discovery into the architectural and social structures of cottage living. Here are the cruel realities of a past rural Britain and the natural opportunities that our rush itno 'progress' left behind. Not the beaten track of sentimental nostalgia, but an insight into the fabric and devlopment of cottages and the real lives they sheltered. Cottage building is explained clearly, leaving the reader with a coherent understanding of the developments in cottage architecture and the diversity of natuarl building materials. Our cottage ancestors were the most important factor in the formation of the British heritage of ideas, attitudes and aspirations. As life is breathed into these old homes, and the society which surrounded them, it can be seen that thew workaday majority never did live in a cottage idyll. To allow ourselves to be beguiled by the fantasy of some past golden age can only foster a false perception of society and the trends which shape our future. The affects of the past on the present day families are rationally examined, encouraging individual expectations anda gentler pace. The author's meticulous research has enabled him to rebuild improtant cottages as they were in their heyday. The use of traditional materials and methods ensure that these structures are faithful to the originals in all but size. Set among the trees of a small, living countryside, they provide unique photographs of a lost Britain. We travel from deep in the past through to the present day, to arrive with a real understanding of the significance of Britain's cottage heritage. ISBN 186163 1782

Subterranean Kingdom by Nigel Pennick

Cave dwellings, catacombs, earth houses, rock-cut temples, tombs, hermitages, tunnels and mines - these are just a few of the fascinating and mysterious subterranean structures that are uncovered and described in this unique history. Nigel Pennick traces the history and use of subterranea and explores the myths and legends that they have inspired. This panoramic survey includes the legend of the vast tunnel system beneath the Andes, the majestic and awesome Oracle of the Dead at Baiae, the Hellfire Club of Sir Francis Dashwood, the secret underground city of Ivan the Terrible and a concise guide to British subterranea. ISBN 186163 073 5

The Mythology of the Mermaid and Her Kin by Marc Potts

Explores the origin of Mermaids and Mermen. Sea deities, especially those depicted as being fish-tailed are explored, as is the mythology of woman's association with water. The folklore of mermaids is related, especially from Britain and Northern Europe, with relevant examples from other parts of the world. Other topics related include: the mermaid's image in bestiaries, the mermaid and the Christian church, carvings and heraldry, recorded sightings and captures, the seal/siren explanation, mermaid hoaxes and the mermaids' image today.The text is illustrated by Marc's superb paintings - for an example see the superb covers of 'The Wildwood King' and ISBN 186163 0395   £10.95

Free detailed catalogue

Titles can be ordered direct from Capall Bann, post free in the UK (cheque or PO with order) or from good bookshops.
Do contact us for details on the latest releases at: Capall Bann Publishing, Freshfields, Chieveley, Berks, RG20 8TF.
Website: www.capallbann.co.uk email : capallbann1@virginbiz.com